Ligeti, Kurtág, and Hungarian Music during the Cold War

Drawing on key elements from musical thought in inter-war Hungary, this book provides a new perspective on the nation's musical heritage both inside and outside Hungary's borders during the Cold War. Although Ligeti became part of the Western avant-garde after he left Hungary in 1956, archival sources illuminate his ongoing contact with Hungarian musicians, and their shifting perspective on his work. Kurtág's music was more obviously involved with Hungarian traditions, was entangled with the Soviet occupation, and was a contributing part of the city's diverse musical culture. However, from the mid-1960s onwards, critics identified his music as an artistic and moral 'truth' distinct from the broader musical life of Budapest: it was an idealised symbol of life beyond the everyday in Hungary. Grounding her interpretations of works in these complex political circumstances, Beckles Willson is nonetheless sympathetic to arguments by Ligeti, Kurtág, and Budapest music critics that their music might have a life beyond nationalist and Cold War ideology.

RACHEL BECKLES WILLSON is Reader in the Music Department at Royal Holloway, University of London. She is the author of *György Kurtág's 'The Sayings of Péter Bornemisza' op. 7* (2004) and she has many articles published in journals including *Contemporary Music Review*, *Slavonica*, *Music and Letters*, and *Central Europe*.

Music in the 20th Century

GENERAL EDITOR Arnold Whittall

This series offers a wide perspective on music and musical life in the twentieth century. Books included range from historical and biographical studies concentrating particularly on the context and circumstances in which composers were writing, to analytical and critical studies concerned with the nature of musical language and questions of compositional process. The importance given to context will also be reflected in studies dealing with, for example, the patronage, publishing, and promotion of new music, and in accounts of the musical life of particular countries.

Other titles in the series

James Pritchett
The music of John Cage

Joseph Straus
The music of Ruth Crawford Seeger

Kyle Gann
The music of Conlon Nancarrow

Jonathan Cross
The Stravinsky legacy

Michael Nyman
Experimental music: Cage and beyond

Jennifer Doctor
The BBC and ultra-modern music, 1922–1936

Robert Adlington
The music of Harrison Birtwistle

Keith Potter
Four musical minimalists: La Monte Young, Terry Riley, Steve Reich, Philip Glass

Carlo Caballero
Fauré and French musical aesthetics

Peter Burt
The music of Toru Takemitsu

David Clarke
The music and thought of Michael Tippett: modern times and metaphysics

M. J. Grant
Serial music, serial aesthetics: compositional theory in post-war Europe

Philip Rupprecht
Britten's musical language

Mark Carroll
Music and ideology in Cold War Europe

Adrian Thomas
Polish music since Szymanowski

J. P. E. Harper-Scott
Edward Elgar, modernist

Yayoi Uno Everett
The music of Louis Andriessen

Ethan Haimo
Schoenberg's transformation of musical language

Rachel Beckles Willson
Ligeti, Kurtág, and Hungarian Music during the Cold War

Ligeti, Kurtág, and Hungarian Music during the Cold War

Rachel Beckles Willson

CAMBRIDGE UNIVERSITY PRESS
Cambridge, New York, Melbourne, Madrid, Cape Town, Singapore, São Paulo

Cambridge University Press
The Edinburgh Building, Cambridge CB2 8RU, UK

Published in the United States of America by Cambridge University Press, New York

www.cambridge.org
Information on this title: www.cambridge.org/9780521827331

© Rachel Beckles Willson 2007

This publication is in copyright. Subject to statutory exception
and to the provisions of relevant collective licensing agreements,
no reproduction of any part may take place without
the written permission of Cambridge University Press.

First published 2007

Printed in the United Kingdom at the University Press, Cambridge

A catalogue record for this publication is available from the British Library

ISBN 978-0-521-82733-1 hardback

Cambridge University Press has no responsibility for the persistence or
accuracy of URLs for external or third-party internet websites referred to
in this publication, and does not guarantee that any content on such
websites is, or will remain, accurate or appropriate.

*For Tony, Robina, Mark and Rob.
And with warm memories of Naomi, who even learned some Hungarian.*

I am even jealous of their language, which contains nothing human, whose sound calls forth another world – forceful and harsh as a prayer, comparable to a roar, to a plea, its enunciation perpetuating the very accents of hell. Even if I know only its swear words, it gives me endless pleasure; I cannot listen to enough of it – it enchants me and petrifies me – I am astounded by all the beauty and the horror its words contain, words as sweet as nectar and as bitter as cyanide, so perfectly appropriate for the expression of death throes. It is in Hungarian one must expire, or refuse death altogether.

Émile Cioran: *History and Utopia* (1960)

Imagine a garden maze, a maze in which mirrors conceal the hedges, giving the illusion of open space and free movement but also distorting wildly, as in a fairground hall of mirrors. At one corner you look impossibly tall, thin, and pale, like the poet Petőfi; at the next, absurdly squat. First you confidently step forward – and hit a mirror. Then you nervously edge around an open space. But sometimes you can walk straight through a mirror (or hedge), only to find yourself in another alley. Here you meet the administrator of the maze, himself lost in it.
This is Hungary . . .
The maze has its own language. I call it the Hungarian Periphrastic. It is a language of diabolical circumlocution, of convoluted allegory and serpentine metaphor, all guarded by a crack regiment of sub-Germanic abstract compound-nouns. Nothing is said directly. Everyone is taken from behind. A spade is never a spade. A crime is never a crime . . . It is the intellectual version of an attitude that prevails in the whole society: that of getting around the system rather than confronting it, of finding loopholes and niches rather than making demands of the state; and the premise of this attitude is . . . the essential permanence and immutability of the system . . .
The hedges move daily.

Timothy Garton Ash
('A Hungarian Lesson', 1985)

Contents

List of music examples   page xi
Acknowledgements   xiii
Note on the text   xvi

Introduction   1

PART I

1 **After 1920: on land, language and music**   13

2 **After 1945: a new empire forms**   26
   Institutional transformations   27
   Discourses about music: an overview   31
      1945–1948 ♦ After 1949
   Specific discourses and their musics   42
      Music for children ♦ Music for worship ♦ Instrumental music (Music without language?) ♦ Formalism
   Silences   59
      Public silence ♦ Private silence (music and language reconsidered)

PART II

3 **After 1956: the parting of ways**   77
   Hungarian contexts   78
      Budapest ♦ Kurtág, at home ♦ Ligeti, escaped
   Juxtapositions   92
      Language as music ♦ Language in music ♦ Music as 'language' (Darkness and Light)
   Hungarian contexts revisited   115
      Ligeti as longing ♦ Kurtág as object of longing

4 **After 1968: Budapest, Kurtág, and events**   127
   Politics and culture in Budapest   127
   Kurtág's presence   137
      Music and Passion ♦ Interlude: *Games*, or passing the message on ♦ Music and teaching, music and seeking

5 **After 'The West': Ligeti looks back**   163
   Ligeti as émigré   164

Hungary abroad?   169
 Language in music: home? ♦ Language as music ♦ Light and dark
Ligeti in Hungary   187

6 After Budapest: out of Hungary?   194
Budapest, dissolution, and the end of the Cold War   194
Kurtág's Voices   199
 Russian intimations ♦ Central European truths ♦ Hungarian ideals
 ♦ Voices from elsewhere?

Epilogue: On 'Hungary', and (our) longing for Moscow   226
Bluebeard and *Three Sisters*   228
Longing and myth   230
Coming home   233

Personalia   234
Bibliography   244
Index   273

Music examples

2.1   Ligeti, 'A Merchant Came with Giant Birds', from *Three Weöres Songs*, close   70
2.2   Ligeti, *Night*, bb. 39–44   73
3.1   Kurtág, String Quartet op. 1, movement 1, bb. 1–5   93
3.2   Kurtág, analytical note to Ligeti's sound blocks   94
3.3   Kurtág, Eight Piano Pieces op. 3, movement 1, extract   95
3.4   Kurtág, 'Spring', movement 1 from *The Sayings of Péter Bornemisza*, close   102
3.5   Kurtág, Wind Quintet op. 2, movement 1   108
3.6   Kurtág, Eight Duos op. 5, movement 7   109
3.7   Kurtág, 'Sin', movement 1 from *The Sayings of Péter Bornemisza*, close   110
3.8   Kurtág, 'Death', movement 7 from *The Sayings of Péter Bornemisza*, bb. 1–4   111
3.9   Kurtág, 'Death', movement 3 from *The Sayings of Péter Bornemisza*   112
3.10 Pascal Decroupet and Inge Kovács, analysis of Ligeti's *Atmosphères*   113
3.11 Kurtág, String Quartet op. 1, movement 1, close   115
3.12 Ligeti, String Quartet no. 2, close   116
4.1   Kurtág, 'In memoriam F. M. Dostoevsky' (*Four Songs to Poems by János Pilinszky* op. 11)   142
4.2   Kurtág, *Splinters* op. 6c, movement 2   146
4.3   Kurtág, *Splinters* op. 6c, movement 4, opening   147
4.4   Kurtág, 'Key to Signs Used', from *Games*   150
4.5   Kurtág, 'Let's Be Silly', from *Games* Volume I   151
4.6   Kurtág, 'Objet trouvé (2)', from *Games* Volume I   152
4.7   Kurtág, Prelude and Waltz in C, from *Games* Volume I   154
4.8   Kurtág, 'Antiphony in f-sharp', from *Games* Volume II   156
4.9   Kurtág, 'So that We Never Get out of Practice', from *S. K. Remembrance Noise* op. 12   158
4.10 Kurtág, 'Two Lines from "Tapes"', from *S. K. Remembrance Noise* op. 12   159
4.11 Kurtág, 'The Sadness of the Bare Copula', from *S. K. Remembrance Noise* op. 12   160
4.12 Kurtág, *Hommage à Mihály András. 12 Microludes for String Quartet* op. 13, movement 1   161

5.1 Analysis of Ligeti, *Drei Hölderlin Fantasien* no. 1, bb. 1–13   171
5.2 Kodály *Evening Song*, bb. 1–18   174
5.3 Ligeti, *Hungarian Studies* no. 2, bb. 1–8   175
5.4 Ligeti, 'Fém' (Metal), from *Piano Études*, extract   179
5.5 Bocet 'dupā soṭ' (Lament for husband)   180
5.6 Bartók, String Quartet no. 6, movement 4, bb. 1–6   186
6.1 Kurtág, 'Rimma Dalos: O Love, the Edifier!', *Omaggio a Luigi Nono* op. 16, close   203
6.2 Kurtág, 'Hommage-message to Pierre Boulez', *Kafka Fragments* op. 24, opening   213
6.3 Kurtág, 'I Am Dirty Milena', *Kafka Fragments* op. 24, close   214
6.4 Kurtág, 'The Water Thickens', *Attila József Fragments* op. 20   216
6.5 Kurtág, 'Song, Lean Out of My Lips', *Attila József Fragments* op. 20   217
6.6 Kurtág, 'Mercy, Mother', *Attila József Fragments* op. 20   218
6.7 Kurtág, 'The Sweet Breeze Purls Along', *Attila József Fragments* op. 20   219
6.8 Kurtág, 'There'll Be Tender Meat', *Attila József Fragments* op. 20   220
6.9 Kurtág, *. . . quasi una fantasia . . .* op. 27 no. 1, movement 1, close   223
6.10 Ligeti, Piano Concerto, movement 2, close   224

Acknowledgements

I began gathering materials for this book in 1999, and the long intervening period has placed me in debt to a large number of people. At the Paul Sacher Foundation I received much help from Felix Meyer and Ulrich Mosch, as well as unstinting technical support from Evelyn Diendorf, Christina Dreier, Carlos Chanfón and Matthias Kassel. At the Hungarian Music Council Ágnes Páldy welcomed and aided my research process, I was also well supported by staff at the Hungarian National Archive, at Artpool, the National Philharmonia concert agency, as well as many libraries in Budapest, including the Hungarian Music Information Centre (special thanks to Eszter Vida). Márta Papp, at Hungarian Radio, was exceptionally generous with her time. The staff at Boosey and Hawkes in London have kindly opened their cabinet of archived concert reviews to me on more than one occasion.

Sabbatical leave funded by the University of Bristol, along with Parallel Leave funded by the Arts and Humanities Research Board, underwrote my major archival searches in Budapest in 2002 and 2003. A British Academy Small Research Grant enabled me to research at the Paul Sacher Foundation in 2003 and 2004, as well as pay for research assistance from Vera Kusz, István G. Németh and Lóránt Péteri, who filled some gaps in my archival searches. An award from *Music & Letters* contributed to final reproduction costs and musical typesetting (for which thanks to Christopher Brown).

I should like to express gratitude to a number of individuals in Budapest whose conversations have been of special guidance. Mária Feuer, Eszter Lázár, Tibor Tallián and Bálint András Varga each had a story to tell about the media in the 1970s and 1980s. László Vidovszky, Zoltán Jeney, László Sáry and András Wilheim offered valuable insights into the New Music Studio and its controversies; László Tihanyi provided recollections of concert life in the 1980s. János Breuer, Adrienne Csengery, János Demény, László Dobszay, Péter Eötvös, István Láng, András Székely and András Szőllősy each offered personal perspectives. I was immensely privileged to work with Kurtág during my studies at the Liszt Academy between 1992 and 1995, and I am grateful for both the contact I have had with him subsequently and the generosity with which he has responded to my queries.

Invitations to interdisciplinary conferences organised in 2001, 2003 and 2004 by György Péteri (as part of the Program on East European Cultures & Societies at the Norwegian University of Science and Technology) were of considerable value and inspiration as I mapped out the broader intellectual background for the research. Conferences on which I collaborated with Adrian Thomas at Cardiff University and the University of Bristol in 2001 (Socialist Realism in Central European Music: 1945–1955) and 2002 (The Modernisms of the 1960s in Czechoslovakia, Hungary and Poland) also contributed substantially as the project evolved.

In bringing the book to its final form, I've had great support from colleagues and friends who have read all or part of the manuscript in earlier versions. Here I should mention Andrea Bohlman, Anna Dalos, Péter Halász, Barry Millington, Ferenc Rados, Jim Samson, Florian Scheding and Richard Steinitz in particular, as well as my ever-supportive editor Arnold Whittall. Peter Sherwood's checking my Hungarian translations was also of tremendous assistance, but was really only the final touch to eight years of regular input to and encouragement of my work on Hungary, for which I am extremely grateful. I also thank other Hungarianist friends Lynn Hooker, Michael Kunkel, David Schneider, Claudio Veress, Alan E. Williams and Tim Wilkinson for their interest and frequent help. And without the involvement of Béla Simon, of course, the book would have been scarcely imaginable.

I presented material from Chapters 2 and 3 in a paper entitled 'Dr Faustus and the demonisation of dodecaphony in Hungary 1947–1963' at the American Musicological Society Annual Conference 2004. My paper 'Reconstructing Ligeti', presented at the conference of the Répertoire International de Littérature Musicale ('Music's Intellectual History: Founders, Followers & Fads', New York, 2005) included material appearing here in Chapter 3. The Epilogue is published in a somewhat different form in 'Sehnsucht als Mythos? Zur musikalischen Dramaturgie in den Drei Schwestern', trans. Elke Hockings, in Hans-Klaus Jungheinrich (ed.) *Identitäten: Der Komponist und Dirigent Peter Eötvös*. Mainz: Schott 2005, pp. 17–26.

I acknowledge the permission given by publishers for the reproductions of musical extracts as follows:

Works by Kurtág

Eight Piano Pieces op. 3 © Copyright 1965 by Zeneműkiadó Vállalat, Budapest, with rights with Universal Edition A. G., Vienna for all countries other than Hungary, the Czech Republic, Slovakia, Poland, Bulgaria, Romania, Albania, and the former Soviet Union.

Four Songs op. 11 © Copyright 1979 by Editio Musica, Budapest, for Hungary, Albania, Bulgaria, the Czech Republic, Slovakia, China, the former Yugoslavia, Poland, Romania and the former Soviet Union. © Copyright 1979 for all other countries by Universal Edition A. G., Vienna.

Acknowledgements xv

The Sayings of Peter Bornemisza op. 7 © 1973 by Editio Musica, Budapest for Hungary, Bulgaria, the Czech Republic, Slovakia, Poland, Romania and the former Soviet Union. © 1973 by Universal Edition A. G., Vienna for all other countries. German text © 1973 by Universal Edition A. G., Vienna. English text © 1973 by Editio Musica, Budapest. String Quartet op. 1, Wind Quintet op. 2, Eight Duos op. 5, *Splinters* op. 6c, *Games S. K. Remembrance Noise* op. 12, *Hommage á Mihály András 12 Microludes for String Quartet* op. 13, *Omaggio á Luigi Nono* op. 16, *Attila József Fragments* op. 20, *Kafka Fragments* op. 24, *. . . quasi una fantasia . . .* op. 27 no. 1 © Copyright Editio Musica, Budapest. Reproduced by kind permission.

Works by Kodály

Evening Song © Editio Musica, Budapest. Reproduced by kind permission.

Works by Ligeti

String Quartet no. 2 © 1971
Éjszaka © 1973
Magyar Etűdök © 1983
Piano Concerto © 1986.
'Fém' [Metal] No. 8 from Etudes, Book II © 1998
Három Weöres Dal © 2004
All copyright Schott Musik International GmbH & Co. KG, Mainz. Reproduced by permission. All rights reserved.

I also thank the Paul Sacher Foundation for permission to quote from letters housed in the collections of György Kurtág, Ligeti, and Sándor Veress. Copyright remains with the authors of these letters, and I have gained permission to make citations wherever possible.

Finally, I thank Mr János Vasilescu for permission to reproduce Lili Ország's 'Sárga holdportré, Holdak, Holdfej, Hold és föld' [Yellow Moon Portrait: moons, moon head, moon and earth] (1957) on the dust jacket.

Note on the text

The text refers to a large number of critics and composers whose names will be unfamiliar to most readers. On their first appearance I have attempted to make their significance clear, but I have also provided a 'Personalia' at the back of the book that fills out additional biographical data, including professional genealogies and affiliations.

Archives are abbreviated in footnotes as follows:
MOL   Magyar Országos Levéltár (Hungarian National Archive)
MZT   Magyar Zenei Tanács (Hungarian Music Council)
PSF   Paul Sacher Foundation

Documents housed at the MOL and MZT are listed individually and numbered in the 'Archives' section of the Bibliography, and are referenced in the footnotes as 'MOL document 1', 'MOL document 2', and so forth.

Collections within the Paul Sacher Foundation:
GKC   György Kurtág Collection
GLC   György Ligeti Collection
SVC   Sándor Veress Collection

I have presented the titles of Hungarian musical works initially in Hungarian (with an English translation), and thereafter in English only. I have provided translations of journal titles appearing only once in the text itself; but more significant and/or regularly appearing journals and newspapers remain in Hungarian. These are the following:

A Zene	Music
Élet és Irodalom	Life and Literature
Filharmónia műsorfüzet	Programme Booklet of the Philharmonia Concert Agency
Magyar Kórus	Hungarian Chorus
Magyar Nemzet	Hungarian Nation
Magyar Zene	Hungarian Music
Magyar Zenei Szemle	Hungarian Musical Review
Népszabadság	People's Freedom
Nyugat	West
Pesti Napló	[Buda]Pest Diary

Note on the text

Szabad Nép	Free Folk
Színház	Theatre
Új Zenei Szemle	New Musical Review
Zenei Szemle	Musical Review

Introduction

Danilo Kiš fled Serbia for Hungary in 1942, learning at the tender age of seven that Hungarians were the most hospitable, industrious, religious, valiant, loyal people of all, that the Hungarian plain was the most beautiful vista in the world, and that the Hungarian language was the most ravishing in the world ('all others pale in shame beside it'). He would also discover that Hungary protected Europe from Turkish barbarians, that its history was thus the most bloody and heroic in the world, that Hungarian rulers were the most noble and civilised ever, and yet that these unimpeachable heroes had frequently been betrayed by evil foreign powers.[1] These last myths, alas, may now seem fatefully self-perpetuating. Indeed Hungary's twentieth century might be represented as a domino-like chain of disasters, each typical of the country's fate since its 1526 defeat by the Turks, yet in sum transcending all past crises. Hungary in the twentieth century was oppressed by Austria under the Habsburgs, stripped of its most cherished territories after the First World War, and taken over by German fascists during the Second World War. Then, tragically, it was absorbed into the Soviet bloc in 1949 to become a pawn in the Cold War.

Viewed in a broader perspective, a more balanced view of power relations between Hungary and its neighbours emerges rather rapidly. Contextualising the country in the post-Habsburg lands shifts attention from the country's unique and tragic fate to a more realistic portrayal of regional strife. (Had Kiš fled Hungary to Serbia, he would have heard in Serbia the mirror image of the myths he absorbed in Hungary.) Reading Hungary as a satellite of the Soviet Union is a comparable move and currently a very enticing one for musicology, as recent scholarship has potently analysed the way the cultural Cold War shaped musical thought and practice.[2] Indeed the three elements in my title can be slotted neatly into this frame: Hungary experienced the Soviet attempt to force music into slick communist propaganda;

---

[1] 'The Gingerbread Heart, or Nationalism', trans. Ralph Manheim and Michael Henry Heim in Kiš 1996: 15–34, at 24–5.

[2] Following on from related projects in the visual arts, the research of Amy C. Beal, Mark Carroll and Richard Taruskin in particular has positioned modernist music and music criticism of the West within political ideologies hitherto ignored; meanwhile, the research of Peter Schmelz and Danielle Fosler-Lussier is testimony to the value of examining the intersections between political currents and musical practices in the former Soviet bloc. Beal 2000 and 2003; Carroll 2003; Taruskin 2005: 1–174; Fosler-Lussier 2001; Schmelz 2005.

the Iron Curtain ensured, moreover, that György Kurtág's celebrated status was invisible in the West; it also led György Ligeti to cut himself off from the East. In Hungary we have a model for communist homogenisation, and in Kurtág and Ligeti we have prisms through which to examine the musical and ideological East–West divide.

In fact, however, focusing on a nation complicates the polarised global picture considerably and, I suggest, usefully. Sundering the world of music along a single axis runs the risk both of essentialising musical narratives into the bombastic rivalry of superpowers, and of erasing national and regional complexities. It is instructive, for example, to observe that although writers and composers in Cold War Budapest adopted Soviet rhetoric, they nonetheless conceptualised music in ways that were bound up with long-established aspirations particular to Hungarian musical thought. Additionally, as decades of the Cold War passed, writers came to identify a leading compositional figure for their national musical life, Kurtág, who thus became an ennobled musical presence – a 'genius' for Budapest, but not for the East generally. In time Ligeti, a long-absent compatriot, re-entered national discussions, reaffirming what should really be obvious: when he became a player in the post-war avant-garde in the West, he was not only a dissident from the East, but an émigré from a particular national sphere. Émigré, genius, and nationalist discourse: these are three facets of a culture that was involved in, but not saturated by, the Cold War. Even while wary of Hungarian nationalist mythology, then, we would lose much by subsuming the country entirely into the Soviet bloc.

The main part of this book, consequently, is informed by the Cold War but consists of three nationally defined explorations. Broadest of these is an analysis of ways in which music and competing ideas about it evolved in Budapest during the period. In order to give this some historical depth, I initially set the scene in the inter-war years. Indeed several key concerns in the Cold War period are rooted in that time.[3] Thus in Chapter 1, 'After 1920', I map the era with the central power of Dohnányi, the rise of Kodály, the choral movement, the departure of Bartók and, crucially, the way the centrality of the national language in political and cultural debate could impact on musical development. My outline of this particular phenomenon is indebted to Otto Dann's theorisation of the 'invention' of national languages, in which vernaculars evolve into written languages, and can then be administered and

---

[3] As Tony Judt observes, the roots of the Cold War extend at least as far back as the end of the First World War and the subsequent series of communist experiments in Europe. Judt 2005: 103. Hungary's communist government of 1919 was the first to be established after that of Russia, but lasted only 133 days. The ensuing regime ('White Terror' replacing 'Red Terror') could play on fears of communist resurgences to justify its intolerance of dissent.

Introduction

policed as 'state languages'.[4] As will become clear, there was an attempt to implement an analogous process in the sphere of music. The first sections of Chapters 2, 3, 4 and 6 illuminate the prime ways in which the Soviet Union's occupation effected change and reaction, how new compositional ideas were subsumed into or rejected by ingrained habits, and how shifts in global and regional political situations can be linked to musical activities and arguments.

I narrate these sections of the book in order to provide a frame against which the others (Ligeti and Kurtág) create friction. This seems a necessary step to establish a provisional basis for grasping the period, for this is clearly lacking at the moment.[5] Rather than attempting a comprehensive history, however, I offer a critical starting-point, namely a construction of what writers and musicians in Budapest expansively termed 'the Hungarian music life' (*a magyar zenei élet*), and an exploration of its relationship with institutions and events.

The aim of providing a much more specific narrative too – the meteoric rise of Kurtág – is both to reveal a highly characteristic facet of Hungarian culture more broadly, and to offer a particular insight into art under communism. Hungarian constructions of Kodály and Bartók have frequently had recourse to messianic rhetoric, and the tendency is equally evident in the reception of writers and painters: Kurtág's rise is thus representative of a pervasive trend in Hungarian thought in the twentieth century.[6] The construction of Kurtág, however, was also a product of the society that had evolved under the Soviet regime. As I discuss in Chapters 3, 4 and 6, 'Kurtág' as figure of discourse was initially a product of oppositional desire, for he was understood as resistance to the occupation. Increasingly, he was constructed as an otherworldly individual, pure, and beyond the reach of language, and yet he was also increasingly involved with mainstream organisations, and became engaged in a symbiotic relationship with official institutions and their narratives.[7]

---

[4] 'The Invention of National Languages' in Blanning and Schulze 2006. I am grateful to Professor Dann for sharing his paper with me prior to publication.

[5] Kroó's book from 1975 surveying Hungarian compositional development over the preceding thirty years is the most recent study. See Kroó 1980 for the German version.

[6] Recent publications bear this out. See, for instance, Hadas 1987, a sociological analysis of the Kodály phenomenon. Peter Laki's 'The Gallows and the Altar: Poetic Criticism and Critical Poetry about Bartók in Hungary' (Laki 1995: 79–100) reveals multiple examples of the devotional spirit of 'following' Bartók. Éva Forgács addresses the critical construction of the 'national genius' in the sphere of visual arts in Hungary in Forgács 2003. András Schiff's account of the 'guru system' in Hungarian performance pedagogy is also suggestive: see Schiff 2003: 40.

[7] In the context of a Cold War study the Kurtág phenomenon gives pause for thought, for there is a distinct contradiction between communism and romantic individualist ideology. Might such romanticised constructions of artistic 'geniuses' have been part of other communist societies? I suspect that translations of the communist cult of the individual into the artistic sphere deserve

To use Ligeti as a third story in a study of Hungarian music may seem a forced move. Whether one subscribes to the rupture or the continuity narrative of his development over the 1956 watershed, there is little doubt that the music he wrote subsequently was a response to developments in Western Europe, rather than in Hungary.[8] And yet from another perspective, positioning him alongside discussions about contemporary Hungary is long overdue for, as I demonstrate in Chapter 3 below, his severance from Budapest was by no means complete. During the first three years after his departure he corresponded regularly with compatriots (both outside and inside the country). Then in the late 1960s he began what proved to be an exceptionally extensive project of public reminiscence and self-construction, and I discuss this printed material in Chapter 5. Once it is combined with the (very different) ways in which he was discussed in Budapest, we have a rich textual basis through which to examine Ligeti as Hungarian émigré.

My main sources for constructing these narratives are Hungarian music periodicals and cultural journals from 1920 to 1989, complemented by newspapers and books from the same period. During the early years of communism (1949–56) the single music periodical in Budapest, *Új Zenei Szemle* (New Music Review), was the party organ, and consequently it represented the party line alone. New journals founded in 1958 (*Muzsika*) and 1960 (*Magyar Zene* – Hungarian Music), however, reveal that the party came to take a less monolithic position at that stage: the journals included some cautious coverage of artistic developments in the West. During the 1970s *Muzsika* began to shift in tone by providing a channel for arguments about central institutional change: this style became more prominent in the 1980s. In addressing these sources I have benefited from recent work on nineteenth-century criticism, not only drawing from research into the social construction of musical meaning and value (as in DeNora's work on Beethoven), but also more recent explorations of how music affords – and may cater to – particular modes of appreciation (as in Gooley's work on Liszt).[9]

---

more attention than they have yet received. The term 'genius' was not used of Kurtág until 1982 (see Kroó 1982b, and also Tibor Tallián's remarks in Tallián and Ujházy 1987: 47), indeed it would have jarred with official printed vocabulary prior to that. Nonetheless there are many links to be made with the romantic genius construct, and my own understanding of this benefited from Tia DeNora's groundbreaking sociological study of Beethoven in Vienna. See DeNora 1995.

[8] The key works in debates about Ligeti's relation to his Hungarian past are Dibelius 1994; Friedemann Sallis '1950 – Un tournant décisif pour György Ligeti?' in Albèra (ed.) 1995: 14–27; Sallis 1996, and Pierre Michel's 'Die Sechs Bagatellen für Bläserquintett von György Ligeti und ihre musikalische Substanz im Vergleich mit Musica ricercata und seinen Werken der folgenden Perioden' in Fricke, Frobenius, Konrad and Schmitt (eds.) 1999: 155–61.

[9] DeNora 1995; Gooley 2004.

I have also drawn on less readily available sources to thicken out the picture that published texts provide. Minutes from meetings of the Hungarian Musicians' Union (housed at the Hungarian National Archive and the Hungarian Music Council) offer traces of the practical enactment of music policy between 1949 and 1956 in less than predictable ways. Sketches in the György Kurtág Collection and letters in the György Ligeti and Sándor Veress Collections of the Paul Sacher Foundation in Basel have also provided material through which to move beyond the well-established narratives about Ligeti and Kurtág. Whenever possible I have also interviewed musicians and writers in Budapest, and reference these where drawing on them directly.

While I base much of the book on sociological observations and discourse analysis, aiming to construct the social fabrics that shaped music and the ways in which it was experienced, I am nonetheless concerned to reconstruct some of the intractable ways in which this music could have been experienced too. Despite current scholarly suspicion of the aesthetic sphere, if we are seriously interested in understanding music as a part of history, it is not sufficient to point out its political context, mediated political suggestiveness, or ready-textualised political messages alone. Rather, it seems important to parallel those projects with an attempt to find dimensions of it that are resistant to that.

To this end, I have additionally drawn attention to the way music by both Kurtág and Ligeti is not only very multivalent (and thus difficult to pin down with specific political readings), but also resistant to the conceptual in general as if in a *deliberately* engineered strategy. Needing a broad concept to characterise this feature, I draw on 'presence', thanks partly to a recent essay by Hans Ulrich Gumbrecht. Gumbrecht's theorisation reaches back to Aristotle and draws on a range of writers including Heidegger, Karl Heinz Bohrer, Jean-Luc Nancy and Gianni Vattimo in order to challenge the current dominance of metaphysical hermeneutics in cultural criticism.[10] His primary argument is that we should consider vacillating between historical interpretation and presence 'moments'. We should, he argues, embrace – not evade – the fact that we can be overwhelmed by certain experiences in ways that momentarily prevent us from conceptualising and historicising them.

The point of Gumbrecht's argument for me is not only that it reminds us of the unpredictable and unstable effects of musical events in the past, but also that it can be harnessed to problematise what may seem highly persuasive musical readings. As is entirely obvious, but often tacitly avoided, listening

---

[10] Gumbrecht 2004.

to music may impact substantially on our construction of its history: there is an implicit reciprocity between reading texts, listening and writing. I am particularly resistant to the implications of the claim by Taruskin in the context of Shostakovich's Symphony no. 5 that if one rejects a certain type of narrative about the work, one is also 'rejecting the music outright'.[11] Do we wish to graft meanings onto music permanently? Is it even possible? I suggest that – fortunately – it is not and, especially in the explicitly political field of 'Cold War Studies', it may be important not to harden up our interpretations too resolutely. Thus, and as a deliberately provocative step, at certain moments in Chapter 3 I supply an alternative and more speculative historical suggestion by invoking what I term the 'presence' suggested by Ligeti's music. In Chapter 4 I use 'presence' to explore (and complicate) the dynamics of Kurtág's composing and reception in Budapest.

Rather than the writing of Gumbrecht, however, it is Jean-Luc Nancy's philosophy of presence that I draw on directly. Nancy has used presence to theorise qualities of experience that are essentially uncapturable, events that are (always already) over. His most salient example is Birth, for the happening of birth also contains its ending; but Death is another key 'presence moment', for it is 'always already past'.[12] Nancy reflects on these moments as means through which to approach art's evocation of transient and affecting happenings, thereby drawing us away from textual explication of artworks towards the continuing recollection that artworks themselves can intrude on us as illusive (and always past) events. Using laughter (and problems of 'representing' it) as exemplary, he says:

> Laughter always bursts – and loses itself in peals. As soon as it bursts out, it is lost to all appropriation, to all presentation. This loss is neither funny nor sad; it is not serious, and it is not a joke. We always *make* too much of laughter, we overload it with meaning or nonsense, we take it to the point of tears or to the revelation of nothingness . . . Let's not make too much of it. If possible, let's let it present – lose – itself.[13]

It seems to me that this description of laughter is something to keep in mind when addressing certain music – even when historicising that music. Of course, our experience is mediated by our social conditions (as is that of past listeners). But music nonetheless can make an inexplicable impression. It can make skin creep, eyes prick, cause shivering, excitement, laughter, or embarrassment. And it is over: it will not be heard in exactly the same way again.

---

[11] Taruskin 1997: 519.   [12] 'Identity and Trembling' in Nancy 1993: 9–36, at 13.
[13] 'Laughter, Presence' in Nancy 1993: 368–92, at 368.

Nancy's discussion of presence is sufficiently broad to offer a space through which to create friction between quite disparate musical experiences. One can hardly claim similarity between the music of Ligeti and Kurtág, and yet they seem to me to invite us to engage with two sides of the same coin. Ligeti's music is often heard as a highly physical presence. As noted in analytical literature, it often seems to 'become present' by delineating an 'emergence' (rather than a clearly established beginning) and a 'dissolution' (rather than a conclusive ending). The music opens with a very quiet, extended note that expands progressively in dynamic and is joined by other notes; it closes in a reversal of the process: *Lontano* (1967) is perhaps the archetype for this 'emergence–dissolution' model. To take one example from the many attempts to grasp this music's quality of 'presentification', I quote Britta Sweers on a section within *Lontano*:

> When the micropolyphony evolves into a homophonic surface, the constitution of the sound shifts from indistinctness to an increasing presence and clarity until it seems to stand there right in front of the listener.[14]

Volumina (1961–2, rev. 1966) for organ may serve as an even better illustration. It seems almost symbolic that its title coincides with Hans-Georg Gadamer's word for the non-conceptual dimension of poetry: 'volume'.[15] The listener experiences this 'volume' not just as something 'right in front', but as pressing from all around, especially if that listener is in a church, where the organ is frequently invisible. The term 'sound mass' is particularly apposite not just because of its evocation of indistinct density, but because 'mass' also suggests that sound develops weight, pushing into the body of the listener. Something seems to 'arrive', heavily, and then sweep away from us and back to us in various different guises and capacities for fifteen minutes.

Kurtág's musical presence, on the other hand, is primarily a highly spiritualised mode of performance and interpretation. Indeed a historical and romantic notion of presence may explain aspects of his music that are otherwise baffling. The first piece in his collection of piano miniatures, '12 Microludes' (part of *Játékok* (Games) Volume II, 1973–8), consists of a middle C (a breve), followed by a chord of the same C and its neighbouring B and D (a crotchet, with a staccato marking and a horizontal line above it), followed by a pause mark. Beneath the C, there is also a crescendo

---

[14] Britta Sweers, 'Raum und Zeit' in Engelbrecht, Max and Sweers 1997: 67–88, at 78. The reference is to a section beginning in bar 41. 'Presence' is translated from 'Präsenz', 'constitution of sound, from 'Klanggebilde'.
[15] Referred to in Gumbrecht 2005: 64–5 and 107. Gumbrecht quotes from Hans-Georg Gadamer's *Hermeneutik, Ästhetik, Praktische Philosophie*, ed. Carsten Dutt (Heidelberg 2000), 63.

marking, which, approximately two thirds of the way into the C, is replaced by a decrescendo. In other words, the pianist holding the already struck note is requested to make it expand in volume, before allowing it to decay. As Halász puts it,

> The dynamic stipulation is not a technical instruction, but a demand that the performer who has an adequate strength of concentration should conjure up the illusion intellectually.[16]

Halász goes on to quote Kurtág's own words about his first 'Microlude' to demonstrate that his thinking is basic to the Western classical tradition, for it hinges on 'opening', 'closing', 'tension' and 'release'. Halász argues that Kurtág's music weaves that tradition further because, although its sonorities are novel, they evoke 'traditional musical communication'. Indeed the conundrum of the 'Microlude' and the remarks of Kurtág – but also the claims of Halász – bespeak, even construct, that tradition. The construction involves music's ostensible power to mysteriously effect sensations and elevate the spirit, combined with the wager that this power lies beyond the materiality of the notes on the page that are but codes for something intractable, 'beyond'. This is the 'Real Presence' of George Steiner.[17]

These presences oppose Ligeti and Kurtág diametrically: one is an illusion of physicality, while the other is an attempt to canonise, a romanticisation of music's immateriality. Yet Speers' and Halász's commentaries share something: they are engaged with the 'event' character of music, they have an explicit concern with the emergence and dissolution of the sounding reality, its 'presence – loss'. Both make explicit the sonorous intransigence that is music, the sonorous intransigence that emerges within a world of concepts, can be grasped with new concepts and yet – importantly – does not contain any concepts of its own, and may affect us in ways that we find hard to conceptualise. They provide enticing ways of taking musical sounds seriously.

Taking sounds quite this seriously may seem to rub history up the wrong way. In part, though, I do it here as a component of historical narrative. The move should help us lend a sympathetic ear to Ligeti's fiery insistence that while music reflects its social environment and can be made into a tool, on another plane, and *additionally*, it is 'of a region which lies elsewhere'.[18] One cannot entirely detach this resoluteness from the years Ligeti spent in a regime where music's alleged 'meanings' and political programmes were discussed with so much dogma and so little sophistication. To that extent

---

[16] Halász 1995: 172.   [17] 'Real Presences', in Steiner 1996: 20–39.   [18] Ligeti 1978a: 22.

his striving for the 'elsewhere' is rooted in Hungarian history. An admission of music's intransigence also opens us up more generously to the aestheticist critical discourses of Budapest I discuss in Chapters 4 and 6. By examining the ways in which music's 'elsewhere' was constructed, we can understand how desirable it was for some to believe in its remoteness; moreover, even while claims about being moved 'beyond words' by music are a function of ideology, they may not be *purely rhetorical*.[19] Language mediates listeners' senses and offers us a cipher for their time and place; but those listeners opened themselves up to being moved and touched by music.

Ultimately, though, I seek to confront the (usually tacitly buried) fact that no matter how hard we desire to imagine a past world of ideologically mediated listening, we are embedded in our own. I do want to 'make sense' – to borrow Bernard Williams' terms – of the musical traces of the past by placing them in a historical narrative.[20] Yet I also accept the thought that my placings are provisional, something that the illusiveness of musical presence – paradoxically – can make particularly tangible.

In my Epilogue I take another, equally sceptical, glance at my histories, reflecting back from a rather more distanced and detached perspective. All these arguments have their own ephemerality: I let them 'present – lose' themselves here.

---

[19] In making this statement I am not judging the ideology of the past, but drawing on the neutrality with which Geertzian anthropology reads ideology as an operative system that structures meaning and – by extension – mediates feelings, understandings, and behaviour. See Geertz 1973.
[20] Williams 2003: 233–70.

PART I

1 After 1920: on land, language and music

Let fortune bless, let fortune curse, hence you shall not roam![1]

Everything changed in 1920. Hungarians found themselves distributed among various successor states of the dissolved Monarchy, and the Hungarian state, moreover, had shrunk. Its new borders enclosed only one third of its former landmass, so that some twelve million residents were left outside. Additionally, and for many nationalists tragically, the land most cherished as a putative site of national origin, Transylvania, had become a part of Romania.[2] The sense of injustice was overwhelming. Thus the government's foreign policy came to focus entirely on a campaign for territorial return. But everything would change in 1941 too. After two decades of irredentism, still hell-bent on re-acquiring lands and peoples, Hungary pinned its hopes on Hitler and joined Germany to attack the Soviet Union.[3]

It causes something of a jolt to move from a snapshot of such portentous events to the sound of music. And yet musical discourses bear traces of these happenings in ways that can serve to introduce the main themes of this chapter. Three years on from the loss of territories, for example, a concert programming Bartók's *Dance Suite*, Dohnányi's *Festival Overture* and Kodály's *Psalm 55* was regarded by a leading critic as both consolation and remedy. Aladár Tóth wrote in response to Kodály's *Psalm* that 'everybody felt that some kind of sublime miracle had occurred, that something rose up in us that compensated for our entire loss: the Lord was resurrected within us whom the plaint of the Hungarian poet had conjured among us, to comfort us all'.[4] A month later he published an extended article portraying Kodály

---

[1] Extract from Mihály Vörösmarty, *Szózat* (Appeal) trans. Watson Kirkconnell, modified by Rachel Beckles Willson. Dávidházi *et al.* (eds.) 1997: 75–8.
[2] The figures for Hungarian population loss are contested, and vary depending whether territorial space, ethnicity or language is used as a basis for categorisation. The former Kingdom of Hungary had a population of *c.* twenty million people, whereas post-1920 Hungary had only seven million.
[3] While ostensibly balancing relations between Germany and England, Hungary won back a portion of Slovakia in November 1938 and in March 1939, the army marched on and took a further area (Ruthenia). The desire for neutrality then became incompatible with the longing for territorial recovery. Thanks to a complex set of shifts involving not only Hitler but also Stalin, in August 1940 Hungary won back a large part of Transylvania. By November of that year the country had abandoned neutrality, which then enabled it to grasp a further region, this time part of Croatia, in April 1941. It made its first military attack in the battles of the Second World War when it joined the German invasion of the Soviet Union in June that year. Romsics 1999: 197–204.
[4] Reproduced in Bónis 1992a: 206. This article provides a discussion of the context of this concert and extracts of the fifteen reviews pertaining to *Psalm 55*.

as a messenger emerging as if from a mystical tempest. Kodály was a genius who had recognised the divine in the peasant and had elevated the essence of Hungarian nature into an art form.[5] Once renamed the 'Hungarian Psalm', *Psalmus Hungaricus* became synonymous with the hope of national resurrection.

Seventeen years later in 1940 there was a comparably significant concert, namely Bartók's last performance before abandoning Europe for the USA. Critic Sándor Jemnitz described Bartók with reference to his 'crystalline purity of artistic and human character', while other commentators used metaphors of motion to grasp his musical and moral integrity.[6] Bartók, argued one, hovered like a predatory bird, always observing creative paths that were becoming dead-ends from high above. On exhausting the possibilities of neoclassicism, for instance, Bartók 'soared beyond' to greater things, and similarly left romantic nationalism, impressionism, and expressionist experimentation behind him.[7] Patently, Bartók was 'soaring beyond' not only these musical styles, but precisely the mess in which parts of Europe – including Hungary – found itself. That is, against the imperative of the popular song *Szózat* (Appeal), 'hence you shall not roam!', he was making the supremely ethical step of doing precisely that.

If these two conceptualisations of musical genius are suggestive of Hungarian music's uncomfortable connection with the homeland, it is crucial nevertheless to trace one more. This takes us to the heart of Budapest itself where, in the interwar years, the leading musician was unquestionably Ernő Dohnányi. Not only was he prominent as a virtuoso pianist – famous for marathon programming and phenomenally vast repertory – but from 1919 until 1944 he held the powerful position of chief conductor of the Philharmonic Orchestra. He was the leading musical icon for the conservative government of the time, thus there was simply no significant area of Budapest's musical life in which he was not involved.[8]

Considering Aladár Tóth's passionate advocacy of Bartók's progressiveness (of which more below), we might read irony into his remark about Dohnányi that 'nobody understands Brahms more deeply'.[9] Even if we do

---

[5] Reprinted in Breuer 1978 (ed.): 214–26, at 214–18. First published in *Nyugat* (West).
[6] Sándor Jemnitz, quoted in Schneider 2001: 188. His review appeared in *Népszava* (People's Word).
[7] Bence Szabolcsi, 'A hatvanéves Bartók Béla' [Béla Bartók at sixty], first published in *Nyugat*. See Breuer 1978 (ed.) 468–72, at 468, 470 and 471. Dénes Tóth suggested that Bartók did not even 'singe his wings on the flames of expressionism'. Tóth 1941.
[8] By 1928 he was head of both composition and piano faculties at the Liszt Academy. Reflecting on his colossal contribution to Budapest musical life, Tóth proposed that his artistry was the *ne plus ultra* of performers. 'Under his fingers,' he wrote of his piano playing, 'it is as if the instrument speaks of its own accord'. 'Dohnányi (mint zongoraművész)' (1919) [Dohnányi (as pianist)] in Breuer (ed.) 1978: 154–9, at 154; and 'Dohnányi és Bartók kétzongorás hangversenye' (1936) [Dohnányi's and Bartók's two-piano concert] in Bónis (ed.) 1968: 184–5, at 184.
[9] 'Filharmonikus hangverseny' [Philharmonic concert] in Bónis (ed.) 1968: 176–7, at 176.

not, we can take the hint that Dohnányi's preferences lay in the traditional frameworks within which he worked, and we recognise his distinctiveness from both Bartók and Kodály. Dohnányi's compositions catered to the prevailing tastes among audiences of the day, primarily through romantic patriotism. *Festival Overture*, for instance, drew on the national anthem, the *Appeal*, and a popular irredentist song projecting Hungary's 'resurrection'. When he incorporated other new music into his programmes, Dohnányi emphasised tonal voices from outside the country – Respighi's in particular – and programmed Kodály, the popular works of Bartók, and other Hungarians less consistently.[10]

The period between 1920 and 1940, then, would probably be best conceived as a competition between the centralised, institutionalised music of Budapest represented by Dohnányi, and a range of more marginal groups and individuals. I use this structure to set out the main developments of the period in what follows now.

During the 1920s there were two avant-garde movements that attempted to challenge the Dohnányian mainstream. Most important was the new Hungarian music, setting itself against Dohnányi's type of patriotism and growing from Bartók and Kodály's view that art music drawing on urban popular song and music performed by gypsies – that of Ferenc Erkel and Liszt for instance – could no longer be understood as the musical embodiment of Hungary. In the service of their new ideals, one particular group of writers generated a new vocabulary of national musical virtues. On the one hand, they attributed particular goodness to peasant music, for it guaranteed Hungarian art music 'nature' and 'humanity'. On the other, and in a circular formation around the music of Kodály, they outlined a nationalist conception of classicism.[11] The two merged alchemically in the work of the most prolific commentator on new music, Antal Molnár. As he expressed it, thanks to the mystically inspired formal genius of Bartók and Kodály, 'virgin' Hungarian folksong (untouched by 'Western culture') could become a fresh kernel for Europe.[12] Bartók and Kodály's classicism was the correct response to the contemporary need for social solidarity and cosmic unity:

---

[10] The positions taken on Dohnányi's representation of Bartók tend to be polarised between Dohnányi commentators who claim that he did so much (Vázsonyi 1971: 106) and Bartók commentators who claim that he neglected Bartók. For an attempt to provide a fair overview of Dohnányi's promotion of modernist music in general, based on the analysis of archival data, see 'Az elnökkarnagy: Dohnányi Filharmonikusai és a kortárs zene' [The chief conductor: Dohnányi's Philharmonic players and contemporary music], in Breuer 2002: 134–47.

[11] The circularity of the defining process – as initiated by musicologist Bence Szabolcsi – is discussed in Wilheim 2001: 4. Szabolcsi, Tóth, Antal Molnár (the original violist of the Waldbauer-Kerpely String Quartet), who were the primary mythmakers, were all private students of Kodály.

[12] Molnár 1925: 152–4.

according to Molnár these two composers were 'writing the first bible for the new faith'.[13] Kodály employed equally religious rhetoric in his battle with the conservative mainstream press. His students, he argued, strove to fight Hungarian music's colonisation and encourage it to stand alone, but they were like Jews returning from Babylon to a ruined Jerusalem. Even while they rebuilt the walls, hostile enemies tormented them unceasingly.[14]

The other challenge to Dohnányi was more eclectic. Composer Ferenc Szabó (1902–69) and composer pianists Pál Kadosa (1903–83) and István Szelényi (1904–72) formed their own promotional enterprises at the end of the 1920s. All three had been taught by Kodály at some time, but none of them followed his compositional style. Kadosa's music was angular and rugged to a fault, its primary model the most chromatic work of Bartók; that of Szabó was more melodic, occasionally also indebted to the chromatic writing from nearby Vienna. Their 'Modern Hungarian Musicians' put on four events between 1927 and 1928, 'Independent New Artists' staged two in 1928, and the composers were also involved in the cultural (and legal) offshoot of the (otherwise illegal) communist party, 'New Land', which had a role to play too.[15] Each of these projects attempted to present a range of modernist music from both Hungary and outside, and was promoted by musicologist Ottó Gombosi – who was editor of a new journal, *Crescendo* (modelled on Vienna's *Musikblätter des Anbruchs*) – and Sándor Jemnitz (who was not only a critic, but also a composer). Like Aladár Tóth, these writers were critical of Dohnányi's programming, scorning his gestures towards the new as inadequate or feeble.[16]

Although the primary challenge to Dohnányi, the new Hungarian music, was initially conceptualised in opposition to the romantic Austro-German tradition, its justification evolved as it developed new rivals. In this area, and although he was by no means a prominent public figure, the role of Bartók should not be overlooked. By 1919 his progressiveness had tangible rivals in the form of Stravinsky and Schoenberg and, as if elbowing a space for himself in the new situation, Bartók openly criticised Stravinsky, the

---

[13] Molnár 1925: 210 and 267. Kodály himself argued that Hungarian folk music had its own classicism. See Dalos 2002a: 192.
[14] The students included Jenő Ádám, Lajos Bárdos, Géza Frid, György Kerényi, Mátyás Seiber, Tibor Serly and István Szelényi. See 'Thirteen Young Hungarian Composers' in Bónis (ed.) 1974: 70–4.
[15] The background to New Land is described in Breuer 1985b.
[16] Gombosi explained the Budapest audience's distaste for *Jonny spielt auf!* with its ignorance of Schreker, Schoenberg, Berg, Milhaud, Stravinsky and modern Italian composers. See Gombosi 1928: 3. In another issue he criticised the Philharmonic for its sidelining of Debussy (see *Crescendo* I/9 (April 1927), 21–2); elsewhere he harangued it for not programming modern Hungarian works, for not rehearsing modern works properly, for not inviting Hungarian artists living abroad, and for not reaching out to audiences. See Gombosi 1927. Jemnitz was often critical of Dohnányi's actual conducting. See Lampert (ed.) 1973.

popular composer he had previously held in great esteem, for the 'impersonal' and 'objective' quality of his music. Bartók's own compositions, he claimed, remained 'natural', and essentially 'human'.[17] Such antimonies could be rapidly adopted by critics to describe other modernist developments from abroad, and those of Vienna in particular. Schoenberg's music was the emblematic counter-example of the new humane music of the future, because it rejected folk music; Schoenberg's insistence on 'inner truth' clashed with the hopes of a new society, because his individualism precluded collectivity, argued Tóth.[18] These claims gathered weight during the 1920s as Bartók's music came to place more emphasis on classical forms and tonal balance, moving away from the intense chromaticism represented by his Three Studies op. 18, Improvisations on Hungarian Peasant Songs op. 20, Sonatas for Violin nos. 1 and 2, and, of course, *The Miraculous Mandarin*.

Bartók's discursive intervention and compositional development can hardly have helped the other groups competing to be heard. Indeed the events organised by Szabó and others were met with minimal critical interest, and were reviewed consistently only in *Crescendo*. Jemnitz, as apologist, attempted to persuade readers to listen favourably to new music from Vienna: Schoenberg's songs were 'beautiful', Berg's works were 'intense' and Webern's purgation to the ultimate was 'visionary'. Szelényi made pleas for an art that would transcend race and religion.[19] But these views could barely compete with the prevailing rhetoric of dismissal, especially because the most prominent writers who were interested in musical novelty were constructing such a powerful vision of the forward-looking community music of Hungary. Programme notes by Molnár for performances of works by Schoenberg, Berg and Webern described them all as 'outdated'.[20] Musicologist Bence Szabolcsi echoed Molnár when reviewing the concert: Schoenberg was a composer with his eyes fixed on the German

---

[17] Schneider (trans.) 1995: 232. See Schneider 1995 for an analysis of Bartók's shifting position in relation to Stravinsky. Breuer's 'A magyarországi Stravinsky-kultusz nyomában' [On the trail of the Stravinsky cult in Hungary] provides a list of Stravinsky performances between 1911 and 1940. See Breuer 1978a: 305–23.

[18] See Tóth, 'A Francia zene új iránya és Darius Milhaud' [The new direction of French music and Darius Milhaud], first published in *Nyugat* (June 1921), reprinted in Breuer 1978: 163–5, at 164. See also Schneider 1996 and 2001 for a discussion of Bartók's reception in the period in the context of Hungarian nationalism. Bónis suggests that Tóth was biased against Stravinsky, Strauss, Hindemith, Ravel and Schoenberg, a bias that is usually explained by the need to campaign on behalf of Bartók and Kodály who felt sidelined by Dohnányi at the Philharmonic. See 'A szerkesztő utószava' [The editor's afterword] in Bónis 1968 (ed.): 624–5.

[19] Jemnitz 1927a: 16–17. Szelényi 1927 and 1928.

[20] Schoenberg's *Das Buch der hängenden Garten* op. 15, Berg's Four Pieces for clarinet and piano op. 5, Webern's Four Pieces for violin and piano op. 7 and Three Short Pieces for cello and piano op. 11. This concert, put on by 'New Land', is discussed in Breuer (1985a) and (1985b). Programme notes by Molnár reproduced in Demény (ed.) 1989: 570.

past, while Webern's pieces were 'more appropriate for the test tubes of the aesthetician's musical laboratory than the concert platform'. This evocative notion would secure 'speculative', 'scientific' music its position in a nether land distant from the 'natural', experiential one of Hungary.[21] Indeed the 1930s witnessed a near obliteration of this briefly flowering branch of the avant-garde.

Any conceptualisation of the 1930s, of course, must initially recognise the altered political circumstances, the heightened concern about Hungary's close relations with Germany, and the horrifying unfolding of legislation there. That done, however, it should also reflect the fact that all three leading composers of Hungary – and many of the less prominent ones too – were initially both well supported, and increasingly successful. Dohnányi's centralised institutional authority simply grew, for example: in 1931 he became the Music Director of Hungarian Radio, and in 1934, Director of the Liszt Academy. He held the three most powerful musical positions in the city, while his romantic and lightly entertaining compositions continued to reflect the conservative mainstream taste.

After 1934 Bartók benefited from a new government policy that led to support for ethnographic research. For the first time, there was official agreement that 'Hungarianness' could be found in peasant music and consequently, he was at last granted his long-desired research position at the Hungarian Academy of Sciences.[22] Already in 1930, he had made a turn towards larger-scale, monumental 'community' music that would characterise the decade more broadly, in his *Cantata profana*. This he followed with a series of choral works: Four Hungarian Folksongs for mixed choir, Székely Folksongs for male choir, *From Olden Times* for male choir and Twenty-seven Choruses for women's and children's choir.[23]

Meanwhile, and most significantly, the groups of composers that Kodály had supported and encouraged for some time were becoming officially established. Striving to actualise Kodály's ambitions, and exploiting the openings offered by the increasingly heated religious nationalism of the government, these groups began to reconstruct the country's musical repertories and practices by purging them of their putative foreign colonisers and dependents. Hitherto 'crushed' by German melody, Kodály had argued, music should be written that would finally instil people with a sense of their own

---

[21] Sz. B. 1927. When Kadosa programmed Schoenberg's Three Piano Pieces op. 11 in 1930, the composer's 'laboratory test-tubes' were invoked by a critic referring to his more recent music. F. L. 1930. Molnár's 1937 book on new music referred repeatedly to Schoenberg's music as mere 'laboratory work', and 'experiments'. Molnár 1937.
[22] See Schneider 1996: 38–9 and Schneider 2001: 187 for discussions about the renewed impulses towards ethnographic research and Magyarization in the cultural sphere following 1934.
[23] See Vikárius 2004 for a thoughtful survey of Bartók's contribution to choral repertoire.

music and its own natural prosody.[24] We can trace this occurring in two distinct areas.

One was new repertory for children that was intended to lead 'great masses' (as Kodály referred to the young populace) to music.[25] Kodály regularly articulated the belief that children should not study music by learning instruments, but by singing the Catholic and Protestant choral repertories of Italy, France, Germany and England and – crucially – by encountering their own tradition by singing Hungarian folk song. 1934 saw the launch of a nationwide choral movement under the banner of 'Singing Youth' (*Éneklő Ifjúság*); later it would develop a journal of the same name. The Hungarian Scouts' Song Book too had a nationalist makeover in 1935.[26]

The other strand was explicitly religious. Two of Kodály's pupils, Lajos Bárdos and Gyula Kertész, founded the publishing house *Magyar Kórus* which had a periodical of the same name from 1933.[27] Kertész and yet one other Kodály pupil, György Kerényi, founded a further periodical, *Énekszó* (Chorusing) in the same year. These composers wrote Hungarian chant, masses and other Catholic music for all occasions and published them in collected editions such as *Magyar Cantuale* and *Harmónia Sacra*. Their express aim was to provide choirs with a repertoire unbesmirched by German characteristics.[28]

These various publication projects contributed to a widespread process of national musical canonisation. Drawing on French and Italian Renaissance models, the new repertoire was conceived as a Hungarian Renaissance, in which the incorporation of ancient indigenous texts and melodies into canonical genres would generate a flowering of the country's musical culture. Kodály contributed not only with eleven volumes of Hungarian folk songs and ballads transcribed for voice and piano, *Magyar népzene* (Hungarian Folk Music), but with concert pieces too. His *Dances of Galánta*, *Peacock Variations* and another national historic sacred work, the *Buda Castle Te Deum*, were similarly dedicated to laying down a national corpus for the country's edification. As we have seen, Bartók too contributed with a range

---

[24] 'A magyar népdal művészi jelentősége' [The artistic significance of the Hungarian folksong] (1929) in Bónis (ed.) 1982 (Volume I): 33–5, at 35.

[25] 'Children's Choirs' in Bónis (ed.) 1974: 119–27, at 123. His pupil Lajos Bárdos edited the first publication of folk songs for the young in 1929, for which Kodály wrote a Preface. Ivasivka 1997: 39. Kodály's Preface is reprinted in Bónis (ed.) 1982 (Volume I): 46–7.

[26] An exhaustive account of Singing Youth's activities up to 1944 (including its prehistory from 1925) is available in Szabó 1983 and 1984a. Bárdos added Hungarian folk songs to the Scouts' Song Book. Ivasivka 1997: 41.

[27] Bárdos was music director of the Hungarian Catholic Musicians, the Association of Hungarian Choral Societies and in 1938, the National Cecilia Union; he also led Hungary's Cecilia Choir 1925 to 1942 and conducted the Palestrina Choir 1929–33. Nagy 1997: 27.

[28] Tardy 1997: 139.

of choral works, while one of his piano pupils (also a student of Kodály), Sándor Veress (1907–92), was particularly active in this field.[29] In 1936 Veress wrote 15 Children's Choral Pieces and a *Transylvanian Cantata*, a five-voice *a cappella* suite that set folk songs from Bartók's, Béla Vikár's and his own ethnographic collections.[30]

Two somewhat peripheral composers were also able to continue working productively for some time. Although neither László Lajtha (1892–1963) nor Kadosa was programmed by Dohnányi, and neither was engaged with new nationalist projects, each had good contacts abroad. Kadosa's *Lehrstück, Irren ist Staatlich* (1931) indicates his interest in progressive, engaged theatre in Germany, while Lajtha was associated with France's modernist concert series *Le Triton* from its foundation in 1932; each composer had a publisher outside Hungary.[31] As the political situation worsened, however, they were to be increasingly cut off from their international contacts. Additionally, many intellectuals had moved out. Ottó Gombosi left in 1929, for instance, and Ferenc Szabó in 1931. Kadosa stayed, struggling to present new music in the 'New Hungarian Music Society' (UMZE) concerts in a fundamentally unsupportive climate; Jemnitz, similarly, was alone in promoting international new music in the press.[32]

After the middle of the decade, writing about Bartók and Kodály altered markedly in tone, reflecting the change in both the musical styles and the political positions of the two composers. In a general sense, and as hinted above, Bartók's works had come to fulfil the idea of an inimitably Hungarian classicism, this affording Molnár the opportunity to propose in 1937 that Bartók was laying foundations for the great classicism of the future. Distinct from Schoenberg's disastrous 'laboratory experiments', this synthesised the depths of humanity with mystical, cosmic and revolutionary vision. Molnár

---

[29] For an outline of critical responses to Veress' first concerts in 1931–3, see János Demény 'Életmű-vázlat' [Oeuvre sketch] in Berlász, Demény and Terényi (eds.) 1982: 12–57 at 16–18.

[30] For an account of this interesting work see Ziegler 1986.

[31] Alongside his three ballets and two symphonies, Lajtha also wrote for choir (setting French poetry, not Hungarian folk songs); meanwhile he was active as a choral conductor in the Calvinist Church of Budapest. Kadosa's main influence continued to be Bartók, but he embarked on a series of concertos and also – as did Jemnitz – wrote for workers' choirs.

[32] On the evidence of reviews published in the *Pesti Napló* and the *Népszava*, UMZE put on at least fourteen concerts between 1932 and 1938. Kadosa made a point of programming Schoenberg, Berg, Stravinsky, Weill, Cowell, Ives and Varèse among others on his own solo programmes. Breuer 2002: 165–71. Jemnitz reviewed two books about Alban Berg in 1938 and provided news about Schoenberg's latest compositions and performances; he even advertised a conducting course to be given by Scherchen focusing on Schoenberg, Hindemith and Stravinsky. Jemnitz also published almost daily concert reviews, and thus covered performances of Honegger in 1942 and 1943 and also occasional concerts of new Hungarian compositions by composers such as Veress and Szervánszky. He also drew attention to the 'Italian music of today' series at the Italian Cultural Centre in the spring of 1941, which included works by Pizzetti, Casella, Petrassi and Dallapiccola. This series was a musical sign of Hungary's joining the Tripartite pact between Germany, Italy and Japan in the previous year.

identified Bartók as 'the artistic conscience of the time', arguing that his music had a portentously metaphysical power: it evoked the spirit of 'a new type of person'.[33] The significance of these claims was that they were made at the expense of Kodály, whose newest works offered less for Molnár to celebrate in such terms.

But Kodály's energy had by no means diminished: it had simply shifted into the broader community and into a more political sphere. Not only had he become an instrumental member of the practising music world through his education movement, but he was also engaged with a discussion of pointed national interest, Hungary's language. This was not a new discussion, for a Herderian regard for language as a tool for self-definition had been established with independence movements in the mid-nineteenth century. In its early days this was essentially a battle between those asserting Hungarian's linguistic kin in Ugrian tongues against those claiming that its origins were Turkish.[34] But this kinship debate peaked in intensity at the turn of the century, whereas the inter-war discussions were dedicated to a different project, namely establishing Hungary's linguistic uniqueness. This project was also committed to cultivation and preservation.

In 1931, for example, the Hungarian Academy of Sciences established a new department for language cultivation and launched a new periodical, *Magyarosan* (Hungarianly). The subject-matter of this publication was vocabulary, grammar, dialects and pronunciation, and while the basic tension between language preservation and renewal was much discussed, the overwhelming attitude was that the Hungarian language needed more of the former than the latter. Regular 'weeding' was recommended (poet and novelist Dezső Kosztolányi conceived language as organic nature in 1933) and the perceived deterioration of language was understood as a consequence of the encroachment of foreign bodies. Articles in *Magyarosan* and contemporary periodicals such as *Nyelvőr* (Language Guard) and *Magyar Nyelv* (Hungarian Language) positioned the Hungarian speaker and writer in a position of tremendous responsibility. Anyone who

---

[33] Molnár 1937a: 22 and 39. His remarks about Schoenberg's scientific 'desert' were repetitive and explicit. Kodály had a strong position in the book, but was cast in the shade by Molnár's effusions about Bartók.

[34] More extreme proposals claimed 'ancestors' in languages from Chinese, to Hebrew, to Sumerian; one writer asserted that six thousand words of the Bible were Hungarian; another, that both the Hungarian language and the Hungarian people were actually all but identical to ancient Greek language and people. These arguments are summarised in Pusztay 1977: 17–24; for an English-language account of more recent debates see also Sherwood 1996. The evident debt to Herder is not incidental: Herder's *Ideen zur Philosophie der Geschichte der Menscheit* of 1790 had included a suggestion that as Hungarians were so outnumbered by Germans, Slavs and Wallachians in the area, within a few centuries their language would probably die out. Preserving the language was a matter of preserving the people: see Géfin 1997 for some discussion of Hungarians' 'quasi-existential angst' as expressed in and about literature.

committed errors in the mother tongue was nothing other than a national traitor.[35]

By the latter part of the decade Kodály himself had become a prominent figure in the movement. His 1937 lecture on language cultivation at his *alma mater*, the Eötvös College of the Budapest University, became a reference point for linguists in subsequent years.[36] It argued specifically that foreign languages (whether spoken by Hungarians or foreigners) were harming pronunciation of the mother tongue, and that the damage was going unchecked because so many Hungarians spoke badly and taught badly.[37]

Before leaping to denounce Kodály's linguistic chauvinism and intolerance, it is worth situating his claims within an essentially defensive expression of resistance to greater national powers. As Etienne Balibar has argued, for smaller and weaker nations – and after 1920 Hungary was certainly one of those – nationalism is a form of self-defence.[38] The country was still smarting from the territorial loss of 1920, and Hungarians in Transylvania were being forced to speak Romanian where, consequently, the Hungarian mother tongue was understood as under attack.[39] Such defensive nationalism, however, slips all too easily into xenophobic mythologising. Kodály's claims are emblematically purgative, attempting to eradicate anomalies and weaknesses from a fictionally purist national ideal. They become particularly problematic once read alongside the policies of the university at which Kodály delivered his lecture, policies that discriminated against Jewish students through the *numerus clausus*.

Exclusionary ideas became more pernicious and were also expressed more widely as the political situation in Europe worsened.[40] The only means found to challenge the proto-fascist government once the war broke out

---

[35] 'A tudomány nyelve' (1933) [The language of science], in Kosztolányi 1977: 30–5. He was himself a member of the Language Cultivation Council. For an example of the discourse on 'traitors' see Nagy 1938.

[36] Lőrincze 1982. The university (now the Eötvös Lóránd University) was Royal Hungarian Pázmány Péter University.

[37] 'A magyar kiejtés romlásáról' [About the deterioration of Hungarian pronunciation] (1937), in Bónis (ed.) 1982 (Volume II): 289–99. See 292.

[38] Balibar 1992.

[39] Nagy 1937 is just one example of writing engaged with the Hungarian/Romanian language problem. This is a review of a book entitled 'In defence of our mother tongue' in which the main point articulated is the need to protect the language from the Romanian. Klobucka (1997: 131) argues that the desire of peripheral nations to join the centre 'has often authorized and encouraged xenophobic resentment not merely toward the European core . . . but also, more disturbingly, toward other cultural and ethnic minorities sharing the living space and the epistemological predicament of the periphery'.

[40] One writer argued that ninety per cent of the Hungarian vocabulary was Anglo-Saxon; another that Hungarian was affiliated to Japanese; a further group claimed that the Hungarian language and the Hungarian people themselves were the oldest layer of the German language and people. Pusztay 1977: 28–30. Research into Hungary's language was by no means the only field of spurious research into Hungarian origins, of course.

was – paradoxically – a highly ostentatious nationalism. Even traditionally opposed factions – liberals, leftists and illegally operating communists – united to organise demonstrations celebrating historical moments of national heroism. Such gatherings were broken up by the police, moreover, and crackdowns against the communist groupings – with which younger composers such as András Mihály (1917–93) and Endre Szervánszky (1911–77) were involved – led to arrests, torture and even executions.[41]

When Hungary joined Germany in the war in 1941, Jewish Laws were enforced at the Liszt Academy so that several professors had to leave; one sign of Dohnányi's own resistance was his consequent resignation from the position of Director.[42] A National Hungarian Israeli Cultural Association (OMIKE) offered some support to Jewish musicians such as Kadosa in the form of orchestral work, concerts and teaching at the Goldmark Music School.[43] (Kadosa lost his position as Secretary General of the New Hungarian Musical Association and was forced to leave the Fodor Music School where he had taught for fifteen years in 1943.) But these opportunities ended in 1944, the year in which Dohnányi disbanded the Philharmonic Orchestra. As we know, Bartók's form of resistance was leaving the country altogether.

Kodály, on the other hand, had subsumed the rhetoric of language cultivation into his pedagogical projects, and was arguing for music's value as a means of national preservation. He claimed that the 'Ur-granite' of the Hungarian spirit was nothing other than the nation's language and music, and that it was therefore imperative to cultivate what he termed the 'musical mother tongue'.[44] This new concept encompassed the main characteristics

---

[41] For an overview of Hungary's uncoordinated and terrorised resistance, see Romsics 1999: 208–11. There is to date no published research on Kodály's role in these activities, although Trumpener implicitly constructs Kodály as a hero (set against Bartók), 'working in the resistance'. Trumpener 2000: 413. According to Hadas 1987: 485 (footnote 8), in 1938 he signed a petition against racial laws, and in 1936 wrote an oppositional choral work for the Munkásdalos Szövetség (Union of Singing Workers). As Hadas argues, however, his activities never challenged the inter-war spirit directly, only its musical habits (473). The current state of research suggests he made no outspoken political statements or actions during the war either, remaining essentially in the 'cultural' sphere; given that his wife at the time was Jewish, he had particular reason to keep quiet.

[42] For a brief analysis of Dohnányi's controversial wartime activities, see Walker 2002: 127–34.

[43] János Breuer, 'Kadosa Pál az új magyar zene-egyesületben' [Pál Kadosa in the New Hungarian Music Society], in Breuer 2002: 165–71. See also Breuer 1978c: 86–8 and 115–17 for further recollections by Kadosa of his life during the war. Aladár Tóth had fled to Sweden to protect his Jewish wife Annie Fischer; other composers and writers mentioned above and to be discussed below, including Ottó Gombosi, Géza Frid, Ödön Pártos, Tibor Serly and János Weissman, had already fled.

[44] 'Magyarság a zenében' [Hungarianness in Music] (1939) in Bónis (ed.) 1982 (Volume II): 235–60, at 259. 'Juliánusz nyomában. Előszó a IV. füzethez' [In the footsteps of Juliánusz. Preface to the fourth edition] (1942), in Bónis (ed.) 1982 (Volume II): 69–70. See also 'Music in the Kindergarten' (1941, 1957) in Bónis (ed.) 1974, 127–51, especially 160. The musical 'mother tongue' concept appears here and there throughout his essays of the late 1930s and 1940s. Tóth

of Hungarian folk music, but also drew on the Hungarian language. The Hungarian musical mother tongue was pentatonic and structured in fourth relationships (unlike the triadic and fifth-based relationships characteristic of classical and romantic music), and adhered to Hungarian prosody's shunning of the iambus.

Kodály's mother tongue, moreover, was no mere theoretical tool. In 1940 he described his earlier folk-song publications as 'doves' sent out from a Noah's Ark (doves that in the 1930s had found 'olive branches' in the form of schoolchildren), and during the war he continued to release 'doves' in the form of his pedagogical collections, *Bicinia Hungarica*.[45] Inspired by unaccompanied two-part songs of Renaissance Germany, these pieces were modelled on Curwen's Tonic Sol-Fa system but also drew on the most vital characteristics of the national 'musical mother tongue', namely its Hungarian prosodic rhythms and its pentatony. In pentatony, Kodály claimed in the Preface, lay an important source of the strength that would feed the 'Hungarian of the future, the more Hungarian Hungarian'. If used as pedagogical material for children, he argued, truly Hungarian music would be implanted in their subconscious.[46] Because music was like a mother tongue, he explained, children should hear only their own music until the age of ten. Their Hungarian essence would thenceforth be 'natural' and instinctive.[47]

Kodály and his 'doves' served the irredentist and fascist currents of the regime rather less well than other contemporary songbooks. They did receive some governmental recognition: the Education Council supported a string of publications by the Kodály circle, and commissioned his 'Song Book for Elementary Schools' in 1942; the Minister for Religion and Education described Kodály as 'one of the greatest educators of Hungary' on his sixtieth

---

had described Kodály's process of composition as an absorption of peasant music to the extent that it became his 'musical mother tongue' as early as 1920. I have not attempted to check whether it is the very first published reference. In *Béla Bartók and Turn-Of-The-Century Budapest* Frigyesi refers in passing to Bartók's comments about his own 'musical mother tongue', but she draws on his essays from the 1930s, something which suggests that it did indeed grow up primarily in the inter-war period. It is likely, given his literary training, that it stemmed originally from Kodály.

[45] 'Noé Bárkája. Bevezető a Liszt Ferenc Társaság Folklore-Matinéján' [Noah's Ark. Introduction at the Folklore matinee of the Franz Liszt Society.] (1940), Bónis (ed.) 1982 (Volume I): 81–2. In this brief lecture, Kodály drew on the Noah's Ark allegory directly to illuminate his work from the preceding decade, and the music the audience was about to hear.

[46] 'Juliánusz nyomában. Előszó a IV. füzethez' (1942) in Bónis (ed.) 1982 (Volume I): 69–70 at 70. 'Nyilatkozat a "Fiatalok" című lapban' [Statement in the magazine entitled "Young people"] (1941) in Bónis (ed.) 1982 (Volume I): 90–1, at 90.

[47] Kodály drew on popular belief that people needed a single mother tongue and that multi-lingual people lacked something fundamental: just as if they heard more languages too young they would never learn to speak their own properly, children needed protection from foreign musics until they had absorbed pentatony, he said. 'Music in Kindergarten' in Bónis (ed.) 1974: 130; also 'Hungarian Music Education', *ibid.*, 153.

birthday. Yet his publications were not sufficiently widely disseminated to gain functional power at this stage.[48]

Their time, however, would come later. After 1945 Kodály would emerge as the sole musical figurehead in Budapest, and, for some people his essentialised ideas of the nation's music would have retained an ethical integument that much else had lost. Dohnányi left in 1944 just ahead of the Eastern front, his name cast in dark shadow not only by his move to Austria, but by reports of a collusion with Hungarian fascists. He was briefly on the list of war criminals. Bartók, as we know, had been spirited away: although he was upheld as an ideal, he was singularly absent from the city. Only Kodály would remain on the case. Fortune cursed, once again, but, loyal to the *Appeal*, thence he did not roam.

[48] Hadas 1987: 473, 485.

2   After 1945: a new empire forms

[The Russian soldier] will, of course, carry off the pigs, the wheat, the oil, the coal and the machines; there was no doubt about that. (At the time I didn't expect he would take people away too.) But what does he want besides the pigs, wheat and oil? Does he want my "soul" and thus my personality too?[1]

'I asked him [the Hungarian communist poet recently returned from Moscow] whether it was possible for a person to remain silent in the Soviet Union. In the long run, silence is also one of the rights of freedom wherever freedom exists. He looked at me distrustfully and answered warily. In the Soviet Union no need for silence exists, he said, and, besides, the reason *why* someone is silent is not vitally important, only what he is silent *about*. To the question of whether he believed in the possibility of humanizing the revolution, he replied that this is not the task of the revolution, that the greatest transitional phase of humanization can be found in the consolidated revolution itself which, like the ocean, continually decontaminates itself, no matter what is thrown into it.'[2]

For a nation that had been concerned about its future 'resurrection' for twenty-five years, the loss of material goods might have seemed a small price to pay for the Red Army rescue in 1944. Yet the realisation that the increasingly invasive army presence could threaten another dimension of life – the nation's very spirit – was for writer Sándor Márai a great deal more disquieting. It suggested that fate would once again take its most terrible course, and that the small country would sacrifice its voice to the commands of a greater power.

From the other side of the ideological divide, the metaphor of a 'decontaminating' ocean, however, evokes a small nation being cleansed by great waves of strength and promise. For those sailing on the oceanic wave from Moscow, moreover, there were chances of employment and power: this was the case for composer Ferenc Szabó. Those who had been kept on the edge of society by the anti-Jewish laws and had barely managed to stay alive during the war would find better chances of integration: Kadosa was one such case, musicologist Bence Szabolcsi was one more – but the list could go on at great length and would include newcomers to Budapest such as Ligeti and Kurtág. For these people, the winter of 1945 represented a moment in

---

[1] Márai 1996: 35.   [2] Márai 1996: 233.

which Hungary, it seemed, might become a place that they could build in their own image.

Institutional transformations

Sándor Márai expressed anxieties that were probably widespread and were certainly congruent with the position of Kodály and his acolytes before and during the war. The urgency of the national renewal project after the war, however, made Kodály open to collaboration with the left-wing parties such as the Social Democrats. The Communists, moreover, were quick to use his music (along with Soviet mass songs) for their political rallies, as if legitimating their endeavours with the ultimate symbol of the musical nation.[3]

The alliance was an odd one, for there was little that Kodály, Social Democrats and Communists had to share at core. A common periphery, however – rhetorical claims about social equality and democracy – was clearly a convenient veil for their divergences. Kodály even claimed to see hope in the social group he had hitherto despised, the workers in Budapest. In the first issue of the periodical *Éneklő Munkás* (Singing Worker) he conceived a union of peasants and workers in a collective that would transform Hungarian music culture through its united choral singing. This was an apparent about-turn from his earlier dichotomised vision of urban versus rural peoples. His aims nonetheless remained equally purist, for he intended the choirs to unite seamlessly to produce a uniquely and authentically Hungarian singing style.[4] Kodály's reconstruction was a matter of picking up the pieces and putting them back on their original track again – while drawing on any newly forthcoming sources of help.

One practical offshoot of these ideas was a plan for an East European Folk Music Institute that was proposed by Bence Szabolcsi with Kodály as president. It was to focus primarily on building connections with lands outside Hungary's post-1920 borders where Hungarian folk song could be collected. But challenges to the plan emerged from two other researchers, most notably from Lajtha who, from his vantage point on the International

---

[3] Tokaji 1983: 53–68 attempts to identify the song repertoire favoured by Communists and Social Democrats in these years. Hadas 1987: 474 refers to the Communist Party's appropriation of Kodály. The Communists had been illegal before and during the war, whereas the Social Democrat party had had a small (and declining) membership in the same period. It won a small place in parliament in 1945, but in 1948 it would be forced to merge with the Communist Party to form the Hungarian Workers' Party.

[4] 'The National Importance of the Workers' Chorus', in Bónis (ed.) 1974: 156–9. See also Frigyes Juhász, 'Vázlat 30 év magyar kórusirodalmáról' [Sketch of Thirty Years of Hungarian Choral Music] in Nagy 1975: 149–73, at 162–3.) *Singing Worker* was the organ of the Social Democrat party. (See previous note.)

Folk Music Council in London, cautioned that it was out of line with ethnographic research concepts and practices elsewhere. The political left disputed the very concept of 'Eastern Europe' and the plan did not get beyond the various (shifting) committee structures that were presented with it.[5]

In a modest way, the Hungarian Musicians' Free Association (Magyar Zeneművészek Szabad Szervezete), founded in February 1945, was more successful. The obstacles it faced were less political than practical: tortured progress among the war ruins can be sensed from the fact that its periodical, *Zenei Szemle* (Musical Review), emerged only in 1947. Moreover, a report on the foregoing two years' Association activities published in the first issue reveals that its initial reputation as a distributor of rations had been hard to transcend. Nonetheless this report viewed three prongs of the Association's activities with optimism: networking opportunities for composers, concert organisation for performers, and support for pedagogical endeavours. The premises of the Association offered a small concert hall in which members could organise lectures or concerts.[6] If such events were low-key and on a small scale, nonetheless new orchestras were being formed in tandem, so that an active, if not particularly diverse or challenging concert life came into being.

Although Bartók died just months after the war ended, he was to become a powerful symbol of national renewal. Most visibly, he was embraced and celebrated as never before at a Bartók Festival in 1948. The Bartók Seminars led by musicologist Bence Szabolcsi, however, were of a more sustained impact, for they became a focal point for young composers from 1946 onwards. Ligeti enthusiastically reported in *Melos* that they were the very core of the Liszt Academy: Szabolcsi's knowledge of Hungarian music was unparalleled, new Hungarian music was unimaginable without his presence, Szabolcsi was none other than 'the crystallisation centre' of 'the new Hungarian school'.[7]

Whereas these initial post-war enterprises developed under a coalition government – albeit one with forceful direction from the Soviet Union – they started to collapse as the government was purged and streamlined. Most denominational schools were brought under state control in 1948, and the same thing happened to the colleges and to the Hungarian Academy of Sciences in 1949 (Kodály was removed from the Presidium). The Catholic church's most vociferous campaigner against communism, Cardinal Mindszenty, was arrested in 1948, Calvinist and Lutheran Bishops succumbed to pressure and took an oath of loyalty to the new communist Hungarian

---

[5] Péteri 2000: 161–3.   [6] Fenyő 1947: 62–3.
[7] Ligeti 1950a: 47–8. It is worth noting that Szabolcsi's influence in these years extended well beyond the Academy: some of his meetings were held at the Cserépfalvi publishing house too, at which not just composers, but also musicologists and teachers were present.

People's Republic and constitution in 1950, and, after Archbishop Grősz was imprisoned in 1951, Catholic prelates did the same.[8]

As if a chain of dominoes, religious and nationalist organisations folded one after another and were replaced by communist institutions on the Soviet model. Lajos Bárdos could conduct the Budapesti Kórus only until 1947. *Magyar Kórus*, which had published sacred as well as non-sacred choral repertoire, and had been an advertising organ for events of the Saint Cecilia movement, folded directly before its twentieth-anniversary issue would have been published in June 1950.[9] As the most active disseminator of sacred music, Bárdos was targeted with threatening criticism: one writer in the new journal *Éneklő Nép* (Singing People) proclaimed, 'we must take care to eradicate men such as Lajos Bárdos as soon as possible'.[10] Kodály fared little better. His authority in the years immediately following the war having soared, he was suddenly undermined by criticism from the new government. His liturgical works were indicted as 'insincere' and he was chastised for attempting to rescue Catholic choirs that were by then termed 'cover organisations for the political reactionaries'.[11]

The Musicians' Free Association was another casualty, disbanded and replaced by the Soviet-style Hungarian Musicians' Union (Magyar Zeneművészek Szövétsége) in 1949. This organisation became the central body for activities such as commissioning, concert programming and festival planning. All active musicians had to become members and a number of new committees became responsible for the various areas of musical life. The most important events for composers were the Union's extended festivals of new music ('Hungarian Music Weeks'), the programmes of which were constructed through panel auditions and critical discussions.

In this new context in 1950, the communist Ministry for People's Education raised the idea of an East European Folk Music Institute, and the unpredictability of the political environment is evident from the personnel shifts that occurred even at the planning stage. Kodály and Szabolcsi, now 'reactionary bourgeois', unprincipled class enemies, were beyond consideration. Kodály protégé Pál Járdányi was in the plan initially, proposed as director of what would be called the 'Institute for Advanced Studies'. He did not last long, however, being rapidly replaced by the younger communist János Maróthy. Yet Maróthy was also replaced, so that composer and musicologist András Szőllősy led the Institute from 1950 to 1952 – the very same musicologist who had just been removed from his position at the Liszt

---

[8] Romsics 1999: 257–9 and 281–3. Hungary's religious communities suffered less than those in other Soviet satellites: although their outreach activities were curtailed, they were able to conduct services throughout the regime. I discuss this further in Chapters 3 and 4.
[9] Papp 1997: 111. [10] Katanics 1997: 123. [11] Péteri 2003 (I): 13. Fosler-Lussier 1999: 327.

Academy for his 'reactionary' behaviour. Meanwhile, Szabolcsi's position as head of the musicology department of the Musicians' Union came under review.[12]

Music had been driven into a situation paralleled in all areas of the arts. The fortunes of writers, for instance, reflected something very similar. After the war several literary journals had been formed that were the focal point for groups of independent modernist writers such as Sándor Weöres (1914–89) and János Pilinszky (1921–81). *Újhold* (New Moon), for instance, was westward-looking in its orientation (deriving inspiration from the famous *Nyugat* (West) from earlier in the century). Regarded by the new communist powers as 'bourgeois', 'decadent' or worse, however, such publications were banned from 1949, and much Western literature – Mauriac, Proust and Joyce, for instance – was withdrawn from circulation. Hungarian literature from the past was bowdlerised, as was music: Bartók's middle-period works were banned.[13]

While all this indicates that Hungarian music was set to become a pawn in the Cold War battle, fundamental changes were about to take place. At the level of government, there had been a systematic replacement of 'home-grown' communists for Moscow-trained communists, a process emblematised by the show trial and hanging of László Rajk (former interior minister). Similar favouritism in the music world ensured that Ferenc Szabó, recently returned from Moscow, was appointed President of the Hungarian Musicians' Union. However, the music world's 'trial' of home-grown communists, a public victimization of composers András Mihály and Endre Székely (1912–92), functioned at least partly as a cover operation for a personnel change that was highly paradoxical. The regime had had to confront a major obstacle to its streamlining, namely that Kodály and Szabolcsi were such revered members of the professional music community that denying them functional roles was going to create more problems than their banishments would solve. Not only were they exceptionally capable players on the musical scene, but they were held in great admiration by communists and non-communists alike.[14]

Consequently, rather than losing his post at the Association to Maróthy, Szabolcsi was promoted to being its President in 1950. When a musicological council was established at the Hungarian Academy of Sciences, it came under the direction of Szabolcsi and Kodály. Similarly, other 'enemies' were invited to conduct research into folk music, which promoted precisely that continuity with the inter-war era that had seemed so undesirable some

---

[12] Péteri 2000: 164–7 and Péteri 2003 (I): 13–15.
[13] Fosler-Lussier 1999 is a detailed analysis of this process. For a summary, see Fosler-Lussier 2001.
[14] Péteri 2003 (I): 15–17.

months earlier.[15] All this rendered the musical life very different indeed from other artistic and academic communities in Hungary. Despite the military occupation, Szabolcsi and Kodály assumed positions of such authority that they could work in relative autonomy.

Discourses about music: an overview

A notion of 'relative autonomy' might seem to underplay the power imbalance that shaped the positions of Kodály and Szabolcsi, for although they had institutional authority in the world of music, their lives were overseen by an oppressive regime. As I shall attempt to demonstrate below, nonetheless, their professional losses were less substantial than one might imagine. The most important characteristic of their discourse was a sustained fudging of reality: to borrow a term from political scientist George Schöpflin, they were engaged in a network of 'mutual deception and self-deception'. A single example will serve to illustrate this.[16]

One new choral society (called, ironically, the 'Béla Bartók Union') was parasitic on the two main choral societies that Kodály pupils had purged of German influences in the inter-war period. Rather than continuing to propagate the essentialised notion of Hungarian folk song, however, it focused on a peculiarly Soviet genre, the mass song. Its affiliated publication, originally to be called *Éneklő Magyarok* (Singing Hungarians) but later appearing as *Éneklő Nép* (Singing People), contributed to the colossal dissemination of mass songs, also broadcast by Hungarian Radio. Kodály, meanwhile, publicly identified his own goals with those of Soviet Russia. He even spread his earlier distaste for German petty-bourgeois music to the whole German race: the Soviet Union, he claimed in 1951, not only posed no threat to Hungary's national existence but could also support the country's fight against 'the Germans'.[17] He produced such statements in the same year that he renewed his dedication to Hungary's ancient musical traditions and insisted that mass songs be written *only* on the country's '1500-year-old' folk songs.[18]

It is in such emblematically contradictory statements that the discursive complexities of the Soviet occupation emerge. There is an obvious irony that while a notion of language – and a musical mother tongue – had been so essentialised and preserved, the discursive use of language proper could be so usefully malleable. Language could, after all, suggest loyalty and apparently support the surrounding realities; it could also make assertions that were entirely at odds with those realities. (Whether or not it subverted them in

---

[15] Péteri 2003 (I): 20.   [16] Schöpflin 2000: 158, 165.
[17] 'A Békéről' [About Peace] (1951) in Bónis (ed.) 1982 (I): 223–4, at 224.
[18] 'Ősi hagyomay – mai zeneélet' [Ancient Tradition – Musical Life Today] (1951) in Bónis (ed.) 1982 (I): 225–45, at 236.

practice is another matter altogether.) Most importantly, while in a rather different way from that envisaged in the inter-war period, language could continue to be a site for (claims to) national self-preservation. In order to grasp that self-preservation, however, it is first of all instructive to revisit quite how the 'self' was defined before it found itself under threat.

1945–1948

Immediately following the war, discourses developed through somewhat competitive attempts to rebuild the idea of Hungarian music. The rhetoric of Járdányi, writing in a Budapest daily in 1947, was highly essentialised on the Kodály model: folk song, he claimed, embodied 'the purity and depth of Hungarianness' and – contradictorily – could provide the route to the country's new democracy.[19] The myth of a pure Hungarian peasantry had, however, worn thin with many people: Kodály's portrayal of the country as a rural idyll in his opera *The Ballad of Panna Czinka* of 1948 was a disaster with the public and withdrawn after two performances.[20] Notwithstanding the authority of Kodály, the warm reception provided for orchestral works such as Ferenc Farkas' *Musica pentatonica* and Endre Szervánszky's *Serenade* indicates that composers who worked less blatantly with national symbols were better in tune with the mood of the moment. Such works, moreover, could be understood as building not on Kodály alone, but also on Bartók.

That said, the two heritages were rarely so clearly separated out, because the historical tendency of constructing Hungarian music as a totality in opposition to modern Germanic music remained strong. A notional 'Bartók and Kodály school' served as a reference point for Szabolcsi, for instance, in his review of concert works by Ferenc Farkas (1905–2005), Szabó, Szervánszky and Veress in 1948. This music was generically and stylistically much indebted to Bartók, and, fleshing out the implications of the school's moral high ground, Szabolcsi drew on ideas familiar from inter-war Bartók reception: none of these composers were mere experimenters, none of them wrote 'test-tube music', he said.[21] But the primary characteristic he identified in the compositions was their social activism. 'From the moment of their conceptions', he wrote, 'they seek the path to the visible and invisible community of which they desire to be the expressions'. Szabolcsi's 'school' was essentially Bartókian music, heard through Kodály-ian morality.

---

[19] '"Népzene – Műzene"' ['Folk Music – Art Music'] (1947) in Berlász (ed.) 2000: 364–5, at 365. See also 'Zene a Magyar társadalomban' [Music in Hungarian Society], 339–42, at 342 and 'Bartók, Kodály, és a zöld tányérsapka' [Bartók, Kodály and the Green Flat Cap] (1945): 349–50, at 350. He claimed that Hungary was 'the cultural centre of Europe'.
[20] Extracts of reviews are reproduced in Boros 1979: 14–17.   [21] Szabolcsi 1948: 444.

As we have observed, even in the initial post-war years Szabolcsi occupied an influential position. He was not only active as concert reviewer and music historian, but through his Bartók Seminars was also a 'crystallization centre' for composers. The Seminars were a practical enactment of his search for a socially responsible music practice, a 'Hungarian school'. According to participants' descriptions they encouraged composers to build a musical future with reference to Mozart, Bartók, 'folk music, mass dissemination, [and] classical purity'.[22] They promoted a very particular image of Bartók, one that was highly selective and that had its roots in the war years or earlier.

It was actually extremely prevalent by this time. A narrative was in place according to which his middle-period works were of absolutely secondary interest, because they were merely 'transitional'. Szabolcsi's description of Bartók's 'soaring' stylistic transcendence in 1941 already had contained the central idea, but the first explicit statement appeared in 1942, when István Szelényi proposed that Bartók overcame his 'lonely', 'individualist' phase by writing democratic, community works such as the *Dance Suite* and the *Divertimento*.[23] Thereafter Molnár went as far as speaking for the composer (by then deceased) in order both to flesh this out and to construct an apologia. Bartók, he claimed, came to dislike his violin and piano sonatas, because of their linguistic and formal problems: as Molnár put it, 'at the end of his life Bartók realized his earlier "error" and turned back to real music!'[24]

Molnár's judgements had an unmistakable political and social resonance that is patently in line with Szabolcsi's 'school'. *The Miraculous Mandarin* was the 'experiment', wrote Molnár, not of a true artist but of a 'linguistic courier'. Such a work failed to be cleansed by suffering and purgation, and was stuck in pure dissonance and psychology.[25] Fortunately, argued Molnár, Bartók finally saw the light and moved forward, and thus he overtook Schoenberg. Whereas Schoenberg's represented a denial of the past, Bartók re-evaluated,

---

[22] The consequence had been a widespread production of 'magyaros' divertimentos, serenades and other *verbunkos*-inspired pieces. Maróthy 1975: 502. According to Frigyes Juhász, Maróthy himself was at the centre of these meetings. See Juhász 'Vázlat 30 év magyar kórusirodalmáról' [Sketch of 30 years of Hungarian Choral Music] in Nagy 1975: 149–73, at 151. See also Tallián 1980: 403. The seminars also contributed to pedagogy and audience development (this latter in particular following Szabolcsi's own interests). Szabolcsi published a repertoire guide for audiences, and made substantial commentaries on the function of the Municipal Orchestra in this audience-building programme. Extensive quotations from these are reproduced in Kroó 1994 (II): 516–20.
[23] Szabolcsi 1941 (see Chapter 1 for a further reference). Szelényi 1942a: 72. Of the *Dance Suite*, Szelényi proclaimed 'there is no more democratic work'.
[24] Molnár 1947: 120–1, 130. Molnár was not a communist – unlike Szervánszky, Mihály, and others who seemed to have shared this view – which suggests that the position was shared across political divisions. Fosler-Lussier writes of the Hungarian reception of Bartók's *Concerto for Orchestra* in 1947 (and drawing on reviews by leftist writers): 'most embraced the work as a harbinger of progress towards socialist, folk-oriented music'. Fosler-Lussier 2001: 209.
[25] Molnár 1947: 95.

recombined and rebuilt it. Where Schoenberg's polyphony disintegrated, that of Bartók's later works was synthesised into classical forms. When in the final stages of his development, Bartók's classical work process emerged most perfectly and he used a language that brought new life, Schoenberg worked only with a stillborn one.[26]

It is intriguing to reflect on this position in the light of the imminent cultural Cold War. As has been much discussed, in the West, Leibowitz's and Adorno's texts from this period contributed to a celebration of musical 'autonomy' that was understood as a moral absolute, and was set against music with an obvious human appeal that was regarded as ethically compromised. In Hungary, a specifically oppositional perception had developed historically and still prevailed; predictably, Leibowitz's notorious attack on Bartók's own putative moral 'compromise' in 1949 simply deepened commitments to Bartók's ostensible social humanism. It also, consequently, caused the stakes of Schoenberg and Webern to fall even lower.[27]

In fact the national 'self' that would need preserving in the face of the Soviet threat was not only deeply indebted to earlier Hungarian thought, but would actually have a great deal in common with the sorts of dogmas that the Soviet Union would seek to promulgate. This was far from invisible at the time. In 1948, the Soviet Communist Party issued a decree that castigated selected Soviet composers for their neglect of audiences and their overemphasis on technical experiment and atonality. Kodály would remark privately on the overlap between his views and those of its writer Andrei Zhdanov, noting that he himself had been saying the same thing for thirty years.[28]

After 1949

Printed discourse

Zhdanov's decree would, nevertheless, cause consternation, because for countries being subsumed into the Soviet bloc it heralded an era of artistic and linguistic hijacking: notorious Soviet buzzwords such as 'socialist realism' and 'formalism' entered national vocabularies by force. Although,

---

[26] Molnár 1947: 24, 69, 121–2. The music of Schoenberg and Webern – escalating in importance for composers in some musical centres in Western Europe – could thus have little or no significance. It represented precisely the darkness and suffering that the nation needed to overcome. When Járdányi reviewed Berg's Violin Concerto at the Bartók Festival in 1948, he diagnosed it as an abortive attempt to transpose the mystique of death into the living world. He found it to be unnatural and inhuman. Járdányi and Jemnitz 1948: 441. Jemnitz's positive review appeared in the same journal (*Zenei Szemle*), but his sympathies were not supported in print by anyone.

[27] The relevant texts are Leibowitz 1947, Adorno 1948 and a range of Hungarian responses including Mihály 1950.

[28] There is no date attached to this private note. Published in Vargyas (ed.) 1989: 164.

therefore, many Hungarians agreed with some principles in Zhdanov's resolution, they were obliged to make considerable changes to their practices, and adjustments to their rhetoric. Some such adjustments involved exchanging old symbols for new, but writers nonetheless adhered to their habitual structures and patterns of thought: Kodály ceased to speak admiringly of English choral pedagogy and referred to that of the Soviet Union instead, for instance; and Szabolcsi abandoned his use of 'God' as an ideal category in music, substituting it with 'revolution'.[29] Other changes – those involving the national heritage – were more peculiarly manipulative. But they were not wholesale transformations or ruptures.

A key example is offered by a defensive paper written by composer András Mihály, in which he examined the alleged 'Western' aspects of Hungarians' use of folk music but strove to retain Bartók as their prime model.[30] Part of his strategy was to construct a monstrous 'other' against which to set Bartók, and appropriately enough, he drew on a work of fiction to help him do so, namely Thomas Mann's *Doctor Faustus*. This novel portrays a German composer during the Second World War who attempts to renounce the human dimension of music through constructing an entirely mathematical system of composing, who meanwhile contracts venereal disease, loses his sanity, and makes a pact with the devil. Inspired by Nietzsche and Schoenberg and also influenced by Adorno, even while fictional, the book was a profound critique of German intellectual thought and barbaric racial politics.[31]

The novel was especially appropriable for Mihály's task because Hungarian philosopher Georg Lukács had published an article about it in which he constructed Leverkühn, Mann's antihero, as representative not just of Germany but of the entire imperialist world.[32] Mihály thus constructed Bartók as a composer who had understood the dangers represented by imperialist composers – symbolised by Leverkühn – and had avoided them. He quoted Lukács to make his political justification absolutely clear. Lukács himself had politicised his interpretation explicitly, writing:

> By a remarkable coincidence (if coincidence it be) I had just finished reading *Doctor Faustus* when the Central Committee of the Communist Party of the Soviet Union published its decree on modern music. In Thomas Mann's novel this decree finds its fullest intellectual and artistic confirmation, particularly in those parts which so brilliantly describe modern music as such. For *Doctor Faustus* encompasses the whole of modern art, its problems of style (down to their most technical) and its human and social foundations.[33]

---

[29] Hadas 1987: 479 makes the case for Kodály's exchange; for that of Szabolcsi, see Péteri 2003 (I): 27–43.
[30] Mihály 1949. [31] I discuss the novel's Hungarian reception in Beckles Willson 2003: 136–38.
[32] Lukács 1964: 47–97 at 63. Also Beddow 1994: 102. [33] Lukács 1964: 71–2.

Mihály argued that Bartók's difference from Leverkühn was precisely his resistance to the allure of formalist techniques that were 'speculative', divorced from human society, and that led to devilish Faustian temptation and fascism. As Mihály put it, the 'wine of hell' by which Leverkühn had been intoxicated was no poetic turn, but a grave reality, and Bartók having transcended these realities he was a crucial model for the future. 'No questions should be reopened that Bartók closed', he argued, 'nothing should be viewed as unresolved, which he himself resolved'.[34] Of course this New Bartók was not really so very new at all, but once clothed in Lukácsian rhetoric he emerged in a somewhat refracted light.

Another key debate in the Soviet Union entered Hungary with rather more ironic consequences, and this focused on the nature of language. Until 1950, Stalin's slogan 'national in form, socialist in content' had allowed cultural activities to develop in the national languages of individual Soviet republics or satellites. Stalin had been a supporter of the theories of Nikolai Y. Marr, according to which languages would eventually merge into a single language as part of communist evolution, because they were part of society's superstructure. In 1950, however, he published an extensive interview in *Pravda* that attributed new depth to language. Unlike culture, which 'changes in content with every new period in the development of society', he argued, language 'remains basically the same through a number of periods, equally serving both the new culture and the old'.[35]

As was required at such times, appropriate political action was taken so that his new statements could be seen as triggering responsive Hungarian discussions of language and also of music. Yet Stalin's pronouncements largely heightened an already familiar set of arguments about language cultivation: they simply shifted the power to those who believed in preservation. Indeed, Kodály noted appreciatively that the 'sober mind' of Stalin had clarified that there were indeed characteristics of language that were immutable even during social change, and his confidence would lead him to engage critically with linguist Lajos Lőrincze within the preface for Lőrincze's collected essays in 1953. Whereas Lőrincze regarded linguistic evolution as inevitable, and the preservation of 'dying' words, phrases or pronunciations as an impossible task, Kodály insisted that one could, and should, strive to preserve patterns of language that were threatened.[36] Kodály's belief that music was essentially of the same quality as language (and thus, in the new Stalinist linguistics,

---

[34] Mihály 1949: 6, 9.   [35] Stalin 1976: 20.
[36] 'Előszó' [Preface] in Lőrincze 1953: 5–8, at 7. Lőrincze himself is critical of Kodály's attempts to preserve qualities of language; the fact that he discusses these attempts in academic publications, however, is testimony to the respect in which Kodály's views were held.

no longer part of the cultural superstructure) meant that he could feel supported by Stalin in his argument that certain melodies remained unchanged over 1500 years.[37]

For Szabolcsi, moreover, Stalin's pronouncement was valuable in encapsulating a notion of language's 'classlessness'. Stalin argued that language was 'created for the satisfaction of the needs not of one particular class, but of the entire society, of all the classes of the society': national language, thus, could be understood as entirely democratic.[38] 'History shows', wrote Stalin, 'that national languages are not class-, but *common languages*, common to all the members of each nation and constituting the single language of that nation.'[39] This provided Szabolcsi with a rhetorical strategy with which to preserve his increasingly disputed research techniques and justify why it was valuable to identify folk-music elements in the music of Bach.[40] Inserting one of Stalin's concepts into his methodological toolkit, Szabolcsi proposed that there was a musical version of the 'common language', namely 'the link between folk music and art music'.[41] Research into this newly defined 'musical common language' – the quest, that is, for folk music in art music – could thus be understood as both a route towards its national content, and the democratisation of art music.

Spoken discourse
Although the discourses presented above were a continuous part of Hungarian musical life, they developed in tandem with an entirely new forum, namely discussions in panel auditions at the Musicians' Union. These events offered opportunities for putatively democratic discussion and shared practice, but were also set up as a means of censoring certain sorts of music, controlling what would be heard in public concerts. Minutes taken of such meetings survive in part and – as is the case for all such texts – provide only partial traces of what sort of atmosphere prevailed on any one occasion. Nonetheless in what follows I use these minutes as entry points into a discursive space that was more exploratory than published texts could be. In many ways it had to be, for all composers were engaged in it, and that included young composers for whom self-construction, rather than

---

[37] 'Ősi hagyomány – mai zeneélet' [Ancient Tradition – Today's Music Life] (1951), in Bónis (ed.) 1982 (I): 225–45, at 228. One Soviet writer published in the *Új Zenei Szemle* (New Musical Review) offered a functionalist rationale for preserving the national musical tongue. Although formalists deny it, she wrote, there is an 'order' of 'national intonation', and it 'helps to bring people together'. Uritskaya 1951: 6 and 7.
[38] Stalin 1976: 5.   [39] Stalin 1976: 11. My italics.
[40] Wilheim 1999: 1102 discusses the political nature of Szabolcsi's Bach research. Péteri 2003 (I): 34 points out that it had already emerged before the 1949 shift.
[41] Szabolcsi 1951a: 5.

self-preservation, was the primary task. And yet inevitably the self-construction was also self-censorship.

To frame the space, it is initially helpful to grasp its standard patterns, for some meetings seem to have bordered on the ritualistic. They were organised formally into speeches, responses, and – when community decisions were to be made – voting. One example may suggest a particularly recurrent formula. The day after the death of Stalin, a panel met to adjudicate (among other works) Ligeti's *Hortobágy* for female choir and his didactic *Inaktelki nóták* (*Tunes from Inaktelke*). The chair of the meeting, Kadosa, made a sombre reference to the previous day's event. According to the minutes, he was emotionally moved as he recalled the 'blow' they had all suffered. Thereafter he affirmed the Union's renewed determination to continue, and announced that its very own mourning ceremony would take place on the next day. Only one speaker echoed Kadosa's regret: Hugó Kelen pronounced that the Union expressed its deepest sympathy, was fully aware of the gravity of the blow, and remained prepared for every task ahead.[42] Their responses to the situation are closely related: they balance bad with good, they follow up their sorrow with hope, and they affirm that the *community* (the Union) has fortitude to proceed further.

Composers adopted similar rhetorical patterns when making statements about works submitted for consideration. The technique was to embrace the community, workshop ethos of the ritualistic judging ceremony itself by praising potential in the material offered, while identifying work that had yet to be done. Exemplary in these respects were the contributions of Ligeti, who seems to have been an outstandingly polished and adroit rhetorician when speaking up for and defending friends' works. When Kálmán Halász offered a sketch for a symphony in December 1953 that came under dismissive criticism, Ligeti argued that it was of a complexity that required several hearings before it could be understood. He then described the material contained within the work as exceptionally rich and original. Finally, he framed his acknowledgement that it needed some reworking in the form of a claim for its musical quality: it was so significant that it warranted expansion into a multi-movement work.[43] His speech had three components: it provided a reason why one listener had not liked the music, argued for its value in terms that could be fleshed out were there to be an opportunity, and guided the discussion of the piece towards an area that the panel might address to help the composer.

An element of theatre could emerge when the discussion became a vehicle for animosities entirely irrelevant to the subject at hand. This was the

[42] MOL document 1.   [43] MOL document 2.

case at the meeting where listeners pronounced on Ligeti's *Tunes from Inaktelke*. Ostensible mourners of Stalin, Kelen and Kadosa, were detractors, and Mihály joined them. Two others, Enyedi and Járdányi, sat on the fence, offering anodyne, but typically balanced responses of both support and criticism. Yet the nature of Kelen's main criticism, the way he expanded on it when it proved provocative, and the way the other speakers, in particular Szervánszky, oriented themselves to it, shifted the discussion into comedy mode. Kelen's complaint was the inappropriateness of the 'male' text for female voices. 'After all', he said, 'women don't smoke pipes.'

Szervánszky interrupted Kelen's first speech to ask him not to confuse realism with naturalism. Attempting to justify his complaint further, Kelen then asserted that the whole mood of the piece was 'manly'; Szervánszky, in response, argued that love serenades were often performed with traditional roles exchanged. Enyedi supported Kelen, remarking that the whole scenario of the text, with its swineherds and young men, was indeed manly, but he felt that a mixed choir was able to pull it off. He then led the discussion away from the gender question by criticising its musical qualities; Mihály responded analogously, and at the request of Ligeti, they all listened to the piece again. Yet Kelen apparently used the time while the piece was being played to build a more theoretical justification for his reservations. Once Ligeti had finished, and invoking Bartók, Kelen claimed that when peasants sang folk songs, the songs reflected the reality of the singer; thus using women to sing a man's song weakened its rustic, manly intonation and character. Szervánszky stepped back into direct confrontation with Kelen, claiming expansively that Hungarian poetry was 'the manliest in the world' and that the same was true of its folk music. This did not mean, he said, that it couldn't be arranged for women. Kadosa, while critical of the piece from other perspectives, felt that women were capable of presenting manly content. Járdányi sat on the fence once more, advising that in villages, folksong texts were interchangeable between men and women, but that a more authentic impression might be created if male voices sang the explicitly manly sections of text. The fact that the piece was published and performed in the Second Hungarian Music Week later in the year demonstrates that the discussion was to have no impact on the fate of the piece. Yet it provided a punchbag for two panel members, and formed a channel through which ongoing concerns with realism and folklore could be aired.

The relationship between the theatrical listening meetings and the final fate of works was rarely so efficient or transparent as the 'democratic' community process set itself up to be. A number of different committees operated at different hierarchical levels, and final programming might involve omitting a work that had once been voted in. Many of the committee voting procedures would only spin out a programming decision rather than actually effect one. Thus the Minutes are rarely useful in charting a work's progress towards – or away from – the public stage. A particularly mysterious case is offered by Ligeti's *Romanian Concerto*, which was commissioned by the Soldiers' Orchestra, and about which two sets of minutes survive from 1951. Those taken at the meeting when it was first considered for the First Hungarian Music Week indicate that fourteen people voted for it out of a total of seventeen present, although comments made were vaguely critical or non-committal.[44] A further set of minutes reveals that at another meeting two weeks later, the work was rejected, but these minutes provide no trace of any reasons for the rejection, unless it was the result of an uncertainty about quite what the First Hungarian Music Week's agenda should be:

> Szervánszky considered that it was the sort of work that should be performed.
> Kadosa: it offers interesting colours, but its development is primitive in places. The final movement is the most successful, although it is somewhat on the borders of notational possibilities.
> Ferencsik thought there should not be Romanian folk songs in a Hungarian Music Week.
> Járdányi disagreed, because Bartók also wrote Romanian folk-song transcriptions. Moreover, within this particular work there were serious qualities. Possibly the third and fourth movements could be performed.[45]

Despite not making it onto the prestigious platform for which it was evaluated on this occasion, however, according to the composition catalogue that Ligeti maintained at the time, the Soldiers' Orchestra premièred it on the radio on 1 April 1952. This source suggests that it had an ongoing popularity, as it was performed three more times that year, three times in 1953, three times in 1954 and twice in 1955; according to this source it was also published by the state publisher, Zeneműkiadó, in 1954.[46]

Yet such gaps between language, meaning and events do not suggest that the meetings had the sole function of vacuously 'performing' a communist musical community. The meanings of rituals are always in flux, and there are frequently opportunities for putting them to use. It should not, then, be

---

[44] MZT document 1.   [45] MZT document 2.
[46] Steinitz 2003: 50 states that it was not broadcast, but as I have suggested above, Ligeti's composition catalogue (PSS: GLC) is a persuasive source arguing entirely otherwise. Given that a comprehensive search for reviews of these concerts has yielded nothing at all, it is likely that many of the performances noted down by Ligeti in those years were low-key events, not comparable with the platform of a Hungarian Music Week. There again, in this period the press commentary is a rather approximate measure of the concert's significance, because not even all 'prestigious' music events were covered in the press. The score publication may not have occurred, but the publisher had the fair copy ready to prepare it for publication, because it attempted to do so in the 1970s. See letters from László Sarlós; and László Eősze and László Kalmár (all with the renamed state publisher Editio Musica), 8 February and 15 October 1973 respectively. PSF, GLC.

surprising to realise that Ligeti could use the occasion of an audition to reflect on his music and might even benefit both from the chance of listening to the work and from having a forum for discussing it with musician colleagues. If the atmosphere was tense and even threatening in some sessions, the content of many of the speeches reveals a serious engagement with the music. Presumably there were meetings at which allies, rather than foes, were on the committee. Ligeti was his own sternest critic on the occasion that his *Romanian Concerto* was first accepted:

> Ligeti: On hearing it his own opinion of the work is not positive. He tried to listen to it objectively and found it heterogeneous. The harmonic world of the passagework in the last movement is entirely different from that of the ostinato section. He agrees completely with Járdányi's view. [That the passagework section of the final movement should be cut.] Of course he can't say just now what he will cut and what he will do with it, because if he leaves out the introductory section of the final movement, which is heard again later on too, then there is a danger that the four movements of the work will each be in a different style. Just now he feels that the piece will sound as if each movement was written by a different composer.[47]

It is of course possible that Ligeti was assuming a self-critical persona that was expected, and that it had little or nothing to do with what he had learned. Yet it does seem that this occasion was the first time he heard his piece, and his comments remain pertinent today. Moreover, there are other sets of minutes that indicate something similar. When Ligeti submitted his *Dialogo* and *Capriccio*, not only Kelen, but also cellist Vera Dénes and Kurtág, both presumably allies of Ligeti, engaged critically with the pieces.[48] Dénes, who had performed them, spoke after some exchanges between six others, complaining that although she liked the pieces and would play them in concert, their difficulty was out of proportion to their duration. Kurtág liked the second piece very much but found the difficulty of the first piece problematic and detrimental to the cello sound. He made several suggestions about what alterations should be made. Ligeti then made a well-crafted concluding statement in which he said he accepted the criticisms made by Dénes and Kurtág. It is not clear whether or not he did make alterations in the light of their suggestions, but it is perfectly possible that they were sensible ones, that he did, and that the meeting had performed a useful function for him. In other words, Ligeti – just as many others – was practising a self-censorship that he had integrated into his working practice.

---

[47] MZT document 1. This rather limited text is all that the Minutes offer of the discussion about the *Romanian Concerto*.
[48] MOL document 3.

Specific discourses and their musics

This account having framed some of the ways in which we could grasp the transition to communism on a general level, in the four sections that follow I examine some more detailed cases. These give a somewhat more nuanced view of the discourses of self-preservation. In each section I follow through the developments in a particular sphere, travelling carefully over the 1949 watershed to note its effects, and I give some emphasis to the ways in which we can position the work of Ligeti and Kurtág within the shifting environment.

Music for children

Directly after the war support for Kodály's wartime education project expanded considerably and so, unrivalled in authority, the celebrated pedagogue could project an unshakable confidence in the future. When lecturing in the USA in 1946 he emphasised that it was crucial for the country's regeneration that children feel that 'music belongs to everyone and is available to everyone', and simultaneously revealed his hope in a new model for the country. In the Soviet Union, he asserted, there was respect for art and artists, and for the rights of small nations too.[49] This Russian embrace was essentially opportunistic, for his interest remained focused on precisely the nationalistic repertory and ideology that he had promulgated in the preceding years: as he explained to an interviewer in 1949, there was no point in writing music for children unless they could recognise their own 'essence' when they heard it. People felt most 'at home' with folk songs, he claimed.[50]

In fact, even if Kodály was the most authoritative musical figure after 1945, he was not the sole leader of, or model for, pedagogical movements. The musicians on the political left shared some of his ideals (they constructed the child and the peasant as contiguous ideal categories – the profundity of one (the peasant) was to be instilled in the innocent other (the child)); but they took Bartók, not Kodály, as the ideal model. Most prominently, piano pedagogue Erna Czövek edited a new journal called *Zene-pedagógia* (Music Pedagogy) from 1947 onwards and issued a piano tutor in 1948, *Útmutatás a zongora Ábécé tanításhoz* (Directions for Teaching the Piano ABC). Her publications shared their anti-mechanism and anti-intellectualism with Kodály: each campaigned against technical exercises

---

[49] 'The Role of the Folksong in Russian and Hungarian Music' (1946) in Bónis (ed.) 1974: 34–9. See 37.

[50] This remark was made in an interview in which he was asked about the mass popularity of his own *Pioneers' March*. 'A magyar zenei élet jövője' [The Future of Hungarian Musical Life] (1949) in Bónis (ed.) 1982 (Volume I): 215–16, at 216.

and each elevated the importance of folk song. Czövek also put forward the ideas familiar from Kodály about the 'language' of music: children were to learn Hungarian folk song before other music, so that they had their own musical mother tongue.[51] Czövek, however, emphasised instruments, where Kodály's preference was for voices, and whilst she incorporated Kodály's exercises into her education programme, she suggested that an average student should not spend more than three or four hours on them. She also suggested that the names of notes should be learned after about six weeks of study (thus moving the pupil rapidly on from Kodály's principles of solfège).[52]

The distinction between Kodály's work and that of pedagogues such as Czövek would be argued more clearly in the next few years. When Ligeti reviewed a book by leftist József Gát in 1948, he proposed that *Bartók's* music offered a way of moving beyond recent disasters.[53] Praising Gát's application of relative solfège principles to the teaching of score-reading, Ligeti hinted at the political orientation of the book by warmly recommending it to 'progressively minded' pedagogues. Veress (by then his teacher) was surely one of the most prominent of these: his collection of didactic piano pieces, *Billegető muzsika* (*Fingerlarks*), took Bartók's *Mikrokosmos* series as a model because he found it fresh, full of folk song, and containing nothing alienating to a child (theory, system, method).[54] His music was intended to stimulate play, to prevent children from reading music mechanically, to encourage them to experiment with swapping hands and with playing notes not even in the score, and also to experiment behind the backs of parents and teachers in 'forbidden' areas. Ligeti reviewed it genially in *Music Pedagogy* in 1948. Intentionally or not paraphrasing Busoni's renowned comment about Bartók's *Bagatelles*, he closed his paean with the celebratory conclusion that since Bartók's 'The Marriage of the Cricket' from *For Children* there was 'at last – for the first time – something new'.[55]

After 1949, these gentle rivalries and individual projects would initially be swept aside by Soviet demands for music for the pioneers, demands that most composers met to some extent.[56] Some of Kurtág's very earliest compositions were for children: performed and reviewed in 1952, for instance, *Hej, ha galamb lennék* (*Oh, If I Were a Dove*) was a standard-fare song for pioneers;

---

[51] Czövek 1948: 4.   [52] Czövek 1948: 9.   [53] Ligeti 1948c.
[54] Czövek prefaced her book with a quotation from Sándor Veress, who took part in some of her workshops, which were associated with the circle that gathered around the Cserépfalvi publishing house. Maróthy 1975: 502. For Veress's remarks, see his preface to the first edition.
[55] Ligeti 1948a.
[56] Pioneer organisations attached to schools from 1946 onwards were based on the Soviet model, and were a means of instilling communist principles in 10–16 year-olds (the 'Little Drummers' was the equivalent group for 6–10 year-olds). As the groups gained premises outside the schools and expanded, they also organised summer camps and rallies: membership was already 600,000 in 1949, but would rise to one million by the mid-1950s. Romsics 1999: 286.

and his piano duet *Suite* was also known as *Táncdal* (*Dance Song*) and *Úttörő táncdal* (*Pioneer Dance Song*).[57] Ligeti too had composed a number of orchestral works for school ensembles, even if not explicitly labelled as 'pioneer', and had written his *Tunes from Inaktelke* – settings of folk songs he had collected himself – for a pedagogical volume.

The new climate made the Kodály ark rock. One of his fellow sailors, Bárdos, for instance, was attacked viciously at the Youth Music Days in 1952. Bárdos' *Tilinkó* (*Shepherd's Pipe*) and Ligeti's *Haj, ifjúság* (*Hey, Young People*), claimed the speaker for the Central Directorate of the Working Youth Alliance, did not resonate deeply with the young because they ruined their taste, were incomprehensible, awakened bourgeois feelings and were divorced from the beauties of current reality; furthermore they 'murdered' folk songs and distorted them. Honing in on Bárdos individually, the speaker delivered a full-blown denunciation of *Tilinkó* (judged as a distorted, autotelic, wild cacophony which young people could only characterise as jabbering mumbo-jumbo).[58] The criticism of Bárdos was repeated by the conductor of the group that had performed *Tilinkó*, who complained that both Ligeti's and Bárdos' pieces (especially Bárdos') were frequently wanton trickery, the product of a complete divorce from life.[59]

Yet whereas Bárdos and Ligeti were attacked with reference to problems surely emblematised by Kodály, the speaker for the Directorship of the Working Youth Alliance couched his remarks about Kodály himself in muffled tones. As if but a humble mediator of the great voice of the young, he intimated that 'Hungarian youth' would like to ask Kodály to write music that expressed their 'current lives, thoughts and battles'. Even in 1952, surely the apogee of Stalinism in Hungary, the request was understandable, because Kodály, his acolytes and a range of other composers were still disseminating repertoire that presented 'lives, thoughts and battles' entirely removed from the regime's primary interests. Yet in that year he was awarded the government's Kossuth Prize, decorated with the two titles of honour by the regime.[60] The regime thus drew on his authority as self-legitimation; meanwhile Kodály functioned within it.

The success with which he did so can be measured by the ongoing life of his pedagogical projects. Once he himself had been reinstated at the Liszt Academy following his brief banishment, he reinstated his solfège teaching, making it a compulsory subject for students. Furthermore, while a radical overhaul of the content of his Song Book would have been in line with the

---

[57] See Beckles Willson 2001: 4–11.   [58] Várhegyi 1952: 8–9.
[59] His comments were not printed in the *Új Zenei Szemle* summary of the post-Hungarian Music Week discussion, but were preserved in the minutes. MOL document 4.
[60] Hadas 1987: 486, endnote 24.

new ideology, it survived the political upheavals of 1949 relatively intact. The only change actually made was the omission of the religious material and the addition of an appendix of Soviet-Russian folk songs and mass songs, so the primary emphasis on Hungarian folk songs remained.[61] Thus the regime served to promote solfège and Hungarian folk song, but in combining them with Soviet materials could trigger a poignant nationalistic longing for independence. Nationalists were probably thus blind to the fact that the regime actually supported folk song very efficiently. Viewed by many as a last bastion of Hungary's musical hope, solfège remained an obligatory part of children's education throughout the communist regime and beyond.

Music of worship

Traditional religious devotion fared less well after 1949, when aside from a later-disclosed mass by Lajtha, sacred composition came to a standstill.[62] As the remarks Szelényi jotted down in 1946 while composing his *Symphony of a Factory* intimate, communist music would have new utopias to worship. At the heart of his particular vision was an Ideal factory:

> Not any old factory, but *the factory* that we see even with closed eyes; even someone who hasn't *seen* a factory. The embrace of machines and people in the fever of productive manufacture. Not tired, but determined, focused, proud people. The hymn of labour.[63]

Triggering, perhaps, at least a smile today, the glorification of the very bricks and mortar of the new society was a grim matter between 1948 and 1953. The new religion brought along new vessels of cantata and mass song that were ostensibly to be filled with tributes to one of the communist leaders, the Soviet Union, or an aspect of the new communist society. Where public spaces had furnished hymns to Hungary, God, or Mother Nature, the new political rallies were punctuated by Kadosa's *The Plan Will Triumph*, Szabó's *Song about Lenin*, or other such tributes. There was much ('determined, focused') work to be done, for composers were needed to orchestrate the great march towards Soviet-style modernisation.

Just as we have already traced above, however, the exchange of one set of ideals for another was by no means a clean one. Although God was taboo, another widely worshipped ideal – the Hungarian folk song – remained in

---

[61] Hadas 1987: 480.
[62] When his Catholic *Missa in diebus tribulationis 1950* was premièred in 1957 Lajtha was required to change the title to the more neutral 'Missa in tono Phrygio'. Solymosi 2002: 46.
[63] Among sketches for *Egy gyár szimfóniája*, subtitled 'Jelenetek egy gyár életéből' [Scenes from the Life of a Factory] and dated 7–10 August, 1946, Hungarian National Library. Underlinings in original rendered here as italics.

the centre not only of children's repertories, but a range of other ones too. It became a new site of contest, because the Kodályian line of Hungarian thought that celebrated the 'purity' of peasant life clashed irreconcilably with the modernising goals of the new regime; accordingly, the value attached to the so-called 'older' peasant songs conflicted with the new urbanising and industrialising agenda. We can map the contest in three areas, beginning with the folk-song suite. This genre was rooted in Kodály's inter-war dance suites and also *Singspiele*, which used chains of folk songs and dances to present idealised rural communities on the stage.

After the war the folk-song suite genre developed a more explicit function: as Ligeti explained to the readers of *Melos*, folk song and dance arranged for chamber ensemble assisted the dissemination of music in Hungary by providing for professional and amateur dance groups. The suites bridged the gap between light music and art music, propagating folk music as a living tradition:

> A new artform has been established: dances that have nothing to do with cheap, light music, but that recall the meaningful [*gehaltvollen*] dances of Viennese classicism . . . The *Tanzspiel* of István Sárközy deserves prominence among them, bringing a string of dances into a suite and adding a choir to the orchestra.[64]

Ligeti claimed that 'almost every Hungarian composer' had joined the 'movement', and that they wrote works drawing on Hungarian folk music just as Viennese classicism had drawn on German. His own *A bölcsőtől a sírig* (From the Cradle to the Grave), composed in November 1948, was presumably part of the project: the nineteen-section suite for soprano, baritone, flute, oboe and string quartet interleaves Hungarian folk-song arrangements with folk dances, creating a loose narrative from childhood to old age through the choice of folk texts.[65] His choice of folk song reveals a preference for the folk songs that were understood as 'older' and 'purer': by implication, the suite's narrative is thus a rural one.

After the regime change in 1949, two further folk-song suites reveal the new polity: both Szervánszky's *Honvéd kantáta* (*Soldiers' Cantata*, 1949) and Szabó's *Notaszó* (*Song Singing*, 1950) remained participatory and functional, but neither arranged folk song understood as 'old' or 'pure'. Szervánszky's *Soldiers' Cantata* was written to serve the newly founded

---

[64] Ligeti 1950a: 47. Ligeti identified composer György Ránki as the instigator of the movement, mentioning how exciting it was that the youngest composers – Halász, Maros, Sárközy, Kurtág and Lajos Vass – were all taking part.

[65] See Steinitz 2003: 49 for a musical extract of the work, which demonstrates Ligeti's development of motives from the folk songs in an instrumental interlude.

Soldiers' Orchestra: its four movements draw on the Hungarian recruiting dance, the *verbunkos*, throughout, using instrumental interludes to join up folk songs in different keys and portraying a day in the life of a soldier. Szabó's *Song Singing* is a great deal simpler in texture and more modest in forces, its title's incorporation of the word 'nóta' enacting an explicit reversal of the inter-war discourse that had castigated this popular art song type at the expense of 'pure' peasant song.[66]

The regime's concern to find a modern, progressive use for the national heritage led it to monitor the development of the mass-song genre. This genre was stylistically heterogeneous in Hungary, partly because many composers drew on (already diverse) inter-war repertories: some songs were indebted to earlier folk-song settings and sacred music, others drew on repertoire for choral societies and workers' choirs.[67] Meanwhile mass songs such as Kurtág's *Üdvözlő ének Sztálinhoz* (*Greeting Song to Stalin*) and *Már új világunk épül* (*Our New World is Evolving*) used melodic traits of Russian folk music, or refrain structures typical of mass songs from Russia.[68] But the main problem was the fundamental conflict between folk song's historical 'purity', and its application in the present regime. Predictably, then, when the job of assessing the situation fell to one of Kodály's most loyal followers, Járdányi, his inevitable complaint was that mass songs had insufficient pentatony – this being his marker of Hungarian character.[69] Equally predictably, at the meeting addressing the problem, the question was raised as to whether pentatony was the best measure of the mass songs' potential popularity. Finally, in an obfuscation that characterised most attempts to cope with the irreconcilable views, the closing statements of the Chair proposed that the mass song was 'on the way' to finding its national folk character. In fact, although the Hungarian mass-song genre was intensely conflicted, its life was short. The mass music department of the Union was disbanded in 1953 and demands for mass songs evaporated, as can be sensed from Bárdos'

---

[66] For an analysis of these pieces and attendant debates see Fosler-Lussier 1999: 292–316. Although Fosler-Lussier argues that Szabó's more utilitarian use of the folk song was a sign of his attempt to compose in line with new directives for defetishising Hungarian folk song's alleged 'purity', Szervánszky was by no means preservationist either. As Tallián has argued, his commitment to the party was at this stage devout, and *Honvéd Kantáta* is a utilitarian work, entirely divorced from the representation of history. Tallián 1999a: 52. Mapping selected party statements onto musical works is a rough tool at best: *Song Singing* was released on a record of alongside settings by Kodály, and the sleeve note introduced Szabó as a Kodály student and celebrated the 'virgin purity' of his folk-song settings. (Sleeve note by István Barna. Qualiton LP1572.)

[67] Bárdos' *Napfényes utakon* (On Sunny Paths) of 1948, for instance, was a product of his experience with sacred repertory, but could be used as a mass song once published with a communist text in four-part and unison melody versions.

[68] For a discussion of Kurtág's propaganda music see Beckles Willson 2001 and 2004a.

[69] The minutes documenting this debate, which took place at the Union on 27 November 1950, are summarised in Péteri 2003 (II): 241–2 (footnote 12).

successful and public extrication from the task of setting party-political texts on 28 December that year. In the place of a mass song he offered a (symbolically titled?) setting of a Weöres poem called 'The Harsh Winter Has Past', and the acceptance of this work was entirely uncontroversial.[70]

The cantata genre blended the national heritage with the Soviet directives far more successfully. Rezső Sugár's monumental *Hősi Ének* (*Heroic Song*) of 1952 was a celebrated success, for example, but it is nevertheless a blatant development of Kodály's *Psalmus Hungaricus* and Bartók's *Cantata profana*. Hungarian revolutionary and military themes provided the basis for many other cantatas, whether they focused on 'freedom' – and invoked Hungary's 1848 uprising – or alluded more generally to protecting the 'homeland'.[71] Even cantatas that were apparently less focused on the home were often claimed in terms of their explicitly Hungarian qualities: a review of Kadosa's *Stalin's Pledge* bridged the gulf between urban progressiveness and preservationist ruralism by asserting that the most convincing parts were those that 'spoke in the musical language of the workers', a quality that was 'closely linked' to the fact that they 'came nearer to the world of the Hungarian folk song'.[72]

Ligeti's *Ifjúsági kantáta* (*Cantata for a Youth Festival*) (1949) and Kurtág's *Korean Cantata* (1953) are suggestive comparative models in this light. Setting Péter Kuczka's text about the Soviet Union, Ligeti's work was part of his diploma portfolio, and was performed twice; Hungarian Radio recorded the first performance and broadcast it one week later. The performances triggered no press reviews, however, and at Ligeti's own request the recording was subsequently destroyed.[73]

Kurtág's *Korean Cantata* was far more in tune with concerns of the time and could contribute directly to the national question: when considered at

---

[70] At a meeting at which his Weöres setting, *Elmúlt már a vad tél* (The Harsh Winter has Passed), was evaluated by members of the Union, he stated that he had 'not been able to find' an appropriate text to fulfil his mass-song commission, so he had 'arranged with Szabó' that he would write a 'lyrical choral work' instead. MOL document 2.

[71] Composers could conceptualise their work in ways distinct from the regime in this way. András Hajdu's *Gypsy Cantata* (performed at the third Hungarian Music Week in 1956) was a product of Hajdu's ethnomusicological training and research, for Hajdu collected melodies from Roma communities throughout Hungary and used these in his work – a tradition predating communism. Personal communication, Jerusalem, January 2006.

[72] Maróthy 1950: 25.

[73] According to Ligeti's work catalogue it was performed at the Budapest Opera on 19 August 1949 (sharing a programme with Kodály's *The Spinning Room*) and three days later at the Municipal Theatre. (It is this source that indicates Ligeti had it destroyed.) An exhaustive search through newspapers has yielded only one short commentary in a magazine focused primarily on theatre and cinema. For Dénes Tóth the cantata was bold in scale, spirited and inventive. Tóth 1949. An overview of Ligeti's career in the *Új Zenei Szemle* in 1950 mentioned that its 'monumental choral sonorities' were a milestone in the composer's development, but noted that because he had written it in three weeks flat, it had some textural problems. Viski 1950: 41.

a hearing for the Second Hungarian Music Week in May 1953 one speaker asked whether it had really grasped the special Hungarian position in the Korean War. Its three movements for baritone, choir and orchestra narrated the imperialistic threat to Korea and the rise of a vast, committed partisan army coming to its defence, but the suggestion was made that Kurtág should have taken a less 'Korean' and a more 'Hungarian' view on the subject. Two speakers who had discussed the cantata with Kurtág on previous occasions vouched for his sincerity, and one insisted that the third movement was entirely Hungarian in intonation.[74] He could do this with ease, for Kurtág had characterised the rising mass of partisan fighters with pentatony. Indeed the review of the première offered special consideration to Kurtág, lavishing praise on him for his many artistic qualities but especially for the final march, which was 'almost a musical emblem of Hungarian and Korean unity'.[75]

The most representative Soviet/Hungarian cantata remains nonetheless Szabó's *Föltámadott a tenger* (*In Fury Rose the Ocean*) of 1955, the third in a triptych of works drawing on Hungarian literary themes. Using texts by the nineteenth-century poet Sándor Petőfi, a bridge structure reminiscent of Bartók, and manifestly Hungarian prosodic rhythm, it presents a rejoicing in the power of popular uprising and consequent freedom. 'Hungarians have become Hungarian again', proclaims the entire choir in movement 2, bouncing with its idiomatically *magyar* accents. And although the work makes no affirmation of the Soviet presence, its national celebration and its avoidance of pentatony makes its political point transparent. 'Hungarians have become Hungarian *again*' implies that Hungarians moved away from their earlier mistakes and have quite literally recovered themselves. *In Fury Rose the Ocean*, in other words, was an indictment of the past, and a tumultuous celebration of the present. It was an explicitly nationalist legitimation of the regime.

Instrumental music (Music without language?)

The demand that music legitimate and bolster the regime did not apply only to sung genres. Szabó's solo piano pieces *Felszabadult melódiák* (*Liberated Melodies*) were intended to portray the years after the war, and conformed to a broad swing away from generic titles to programmatic ones that took place after 1949. *Liberated Melodies* were the only piano works performed at the First Hungarian Music Week in 1951, and the programmatic emphasis

---

[74] MOL document 5. Imre Vincze and Lajos Keveházi were the advocates. Kurtág himself (unprompted) mentioned once how 'we' (friends?) believed in the partisan movement at the time. Informal conversation, April 1998.
[75] Csobádi 1953.

at the Second Hungarian Music Week in 1953 was similar. This festival offered a range of programmatic chamber music too: Endre Székely's Wind Quintet was connected to his experiences of the workers in the provincial town named Stalin City (Sztálinváros), for instance.

It was not sufficient, however, for composers to simply place a politically correct title on the front of their works, because at Union discussions many speakers pursued representational accuracy as absolute dogma. When the titles of some piano pieces by Kurtág were found to be arbitrary in 1952, discussants criticised the music (not the titles).[76] But such criticisms came, in time, to trigger little protests. Ligeti, for example, tried to lead discussion away from the programmatic aspect of Kálmán Halász's symphonic poem at an audition in 1953. Joined by András Szőllősy, he questioned whether a symphonic work should be judged exclusively on its programme, indeed whether music could really carry a programme at all.[77]

Such debates about the role of instrumental music were nevertheless only really heated when they touched directly on representations of the nation. Prior to the communist takeover, as I have argued above, composers' ideal instrumental music was a loosely defined divertimento or serenade type that was folk-song based, neoclassical, and somehow ethically progressive. Ligeti had constructed Szervánszky's *Serenade* in the image of this ideal: it was a product of the composer's 'noble humanity' and its use of tonality heralded 'a new way forward'.[78] But in 1951 this nationally conceived project came under fire when Szabó delivered a major attack on it, focusing particularly on Járdányi's *Divertimento concertante* and condemning the way that pentatony was being turned into the conduit of a 'reactionary, antiprogressive musical racism'. Given the history of the pentatony discourse, and the renewed political rationale for composers' adherence to it, it is unsurprising that the reaction was defensive. Pentatony, Járdányi countered, was both the most ancient layer of Hungarian folk music and the bedrock of more recent Hungarian art music.[79] Szabó had attempted to cut the nation from its 'Ur-granite', but Járdányi's response simply re-cemented the link.

Szabó's directive was clear: composers had to move away from the heritage of Bartók and Kodály and draw instead on the 'revolutionary' example

---

[76] The first piece, 'Spring', was problematic, for one speaker felt it was too insipid to evoke spring, while another argued vaguely that it did capture the season's restlessness (even if not its green trees). Only Ligeti – having, he said, heard the pieces three times already – attempted to speak of musical qualities distinct from the pieces' titles. He insinuated that nobody had gathered the music's significance, arguing that it needed hearing several times to be properly understood. MOL document 7.
[77] MOL document 2.   [78] Ligeti 1950a: 46.
[79] This is discussed in Tallián 1998: 160 and Péteri 2003 (II): 242–3. The latter includes quotations from Járdányi's and Szabó's remarks in July and at the festival in November 1951.

After 1945: a new empire forms

of Erkel and Liszt. The move did stem the flow of divertimenti, and it may have fuelled resentment about the repression of pentatony.[80] More importantly, however, it triggered at least one hostile musical response. Ironically, both this and a later analogous expression of hostility are in some measure a generic capitulation to revolutionary neo-romanticism: two composers strove to make bold statements, and an expedient way to do this was to incorporate poetry into large-scale orchestral works. But each work does, nevertheless, provide a key moment through which to trace the accumulating and increasingly brave expressions of opposition to Soviet doctrines.

First was Járdányi's *Vörösmarty Symphony*, performed at the second Hungarian Music Week in 1953, and providing what the composer termed 'a musical picture' for the romantic revolutionary poetry of Mihály Vörösmarty (1800–55). The first poem used is the *Appeal*, which as I mentioned in Chapter 1, was popular in the inter-war period as the lyrics of a nationalistic song ('Let fortune bless, let fortune curse, hence you shall not roam'). The *Symphony* uses the song as a musical theme, and at the close, presents it in an innocently pastoral setting. Járdányi's 'picture' was not of socialist triumph, but of national immolation.[81]

Szervánszky's *Concerto in Memory of Attila József* of 1954 was a yet more overt statement of protest, but was directed less at Szabó than at the situation more broadly. Much of its contemporary potency stemmed from the fact that Szervánszky had been a leading communist music journalist between 1945 and 1948 and had been a celebrated composer thereafter as well. Additionally, he used the poet Attila József (1905–37) very pointedly. József had been a communist in the inter-war years, but had been rejected by both the right-wing society in which he lived and even by Moscow; in 1949 he had been reclaimed by the Hungarian regime as a model communist, and many composers had set his socially committed poetry as a result. Szervánszky, however, selected not his political, but his unhappy personal poems as mottoes for the movements of his *Concerto*, a move that

---

[80] Tallián 1998 argues that instrumental concertos took the place of divertimenti. Actually, however, the concerto genre had been well represented on the programme of the First Hungarian Music Week and was already generally popular, as eclectic concerti by composers such as Gyula Dávid (viola, 1950), Rudolf Maros (bassoon, 1951) and Szervánszky (clarinet, 1950) make clear. Tallián also suggests that the influx of Soviet music and Soviet performers – and in particular the frequency with which Katchaturian and Kabalevsky concertos were performed after 1949 – may well have influenced Hungarian composers too, but mentions no actual influence of Russian concertos on Hungarian ones.

[81] Kodály drew on the melody again himself one year later in his impassioned and desperate choral work *Zrínyi szózata* (Zrínyi's Appeal), as if taking up and reinforcing his protégé's theme. See Tallián 1999a: 46–8 for a discussion of the *Vörösmarty Symphony* with reference to Berlioz's *Symphonie fantastique*.

symbolised a very public rejection of the regime's own move. Szervánszky's style in the *Concerto*, furthermore, contravened the aesthetic directives of the Soviet Union. The organisation of the five movements into a path from C to F♯ and back to C – with movements in E flat and A in between – referred to Ernő Lendvai's 'formalist' Bartók analysis (to be discussed in the next section). Hitherto banned middle-period Bartókian harmony is distinct in the first, third and fifth movements, and there are frequent allusions to *The Miraculous Mandarin*.

The thaw years in which Szervánszky's *Concerto* was completed witnessed a subtle relaxation in the policing of discourse, and writers turned increasingly to the forbidden elements of Bartók's style to articulate their desire for change: Szabolcsi used Bartók as a conduit for the sentiment that 'it is impossible to continue living like this' in 1954.[82] Thus the context for the *Concerto*'s première at the Third Hungarian Music Week in 1956 was one of swelling unrest and increasingly public dissent. Commentators were quick to observe that its tone was 'bitter', and Szabolcsi heard a world-shaking catastrophe in it.[83]

The increasingly frictional political atmosphere provides a context for both Kurtág's and Ligeti's instrumental compositions of 1953–4, each of which was patently focused on the Bartókian tradition. Kurtág's Brahmsian-cum-Bartókian Viola Concerto, remarkably, bridged the gulf between Járdányi and Szabó, for they both responded with compliments. Szabó even claimed that the work had a true depth of humanity and seriousness rare in a composer of Kurtág's age.[84] Kurtág was subsequently constructed in the press as having 'a significant place in Hungarian composition', because his Viola Concerto was like a premonition of the 'great world ahead', 'the sign pointing towards further artistic achievements'.[85] Ligeti's String Quartet, *Métamorphoses nocturnes* (1953–4), on the other hand, went unheard. It is transparently an extension of the elements of Bartók that were most at odds with Soviet demands and there is no sign that he even submitted it for consideration. By turn it imitates, intensifies, breaks up and juxtaposes alienated elements from Bartók's music. Additionally its title offers

---

[82] Fosler-Lussier 2004: 128, quoting from 'A zene történelmi hangváltásairól' [The Changing Sound of Music in History], in Szabolcsi 1954: 174. Fosler-Lussier's article analyses the discursive change in attitudes to Bartók in the context of the Western association of dissonance with 'truth'.

[83] These remarks were made in a discussion launched by a opening lecture delivered by Bence Szabolcsi. See Szabolcsi 1956: 44 and 31. Járdányi responded to someone else's comment that the work was bitter (a comment not included in the published version of the debate but traceable in the minutes of the discussion); and he defended the work's right to be bitter.

[84] It was generally agreed that the work was indebted to Bartók's Violin Concerto, but that as it did not merely *reproduce* Bartók, it was a praiseworthily individual composition. MOL document 6.

[85] Kovács 1955: 8 and 11.

homages to Bartók's *topos* of 'the night's music' and even the Bartókian event of metamorphosis itself, as if supplying a metaphor for a surreptitious compositional attempt at transformation.[86]

Ligeti's Six Bagatelles for Wind Quintet of 1953, however, were heard (shorn of one movement) at the Third Hungarian Music Week in April 1956. Their gently whimsical style could not trigger the sort of celebration that Kurtág garnered, nor could it provoke listeners in the way that could Szervánszky's monumental *Concerto*. The sole published review was simply appreciative:

> In terms of intonation, folk-song elements and the Hungarian musical language develop into an individual, ironic syntax, which is genuinely interesting and communicative. The first movement (Lamentoso) is of an urban tone. The dissonances – the result of an excellent feeling for instrumentation – are truly complaints, and reflect the title.[87]

It is not clear quite when or on what grounds the offending movement was cut, for the initial assessing panel was sympathetic in 1953.[88] As this review indicates, the movements heard could be negotiated very smoothly onto the stage and into the press in 1956. Aside from the final reference to the title, the review could well have been written ten years earlier. The thaw was under way.

---

[86] Bartók's music thematicises change, whether from human to puppet, human to stag (in a 'dark' forest) in *Cantata profana*, darkness to light and back in *Duke Bluebeard's Castle*, or even in the characteristic reinvention of musical materials in symmetrically arranged pairs of movements in his string quartets. Ligeti's interest in such dichotomies in terms both of musical material and imagery is also clear from the pair of choral pieces *Éjszaka* (*Night*) and *Reggel* (*Morning*) of 1955, to be discussed below, and his planned, but never finished, *Sötét és világos* (*Darkness and Light*) of 1956. See Steinitz 2003: 67 for a description of this manuscript.

[87] Csobádi 1956. See László 2003 for an analysis of the piece's debt to folk music.

[88] MOL document 2 (December 1953). Ligeti offered the bagatelles to the Union in the place of a state-commissioned string quartet and the panel 'voted unanimously' to consider them in the string quartet's stead. After studying the score, the committee also voted unanimously to allow them to be handled as the state commission. It was the accommodating attitude of this committee, presumably, that allowed the piece to be forwarded to another panel, and for it eventually to be considered for performance. At some further meeting (of which the minutes are unavailable) it was presumably decided that only five were suitable for the Hungarian Music Week. The five performed began with (what is now) Bagatelle no. 2, 'Lamentoso', omitting the last Bagatelle but closing with (what is now) the first. The panel (of twenty-five with Ligeti and the minute-taker) included Bárdos, Mihály, Hajdu, Halász, Kurtág and Szőllősy, all people he later referred to as friends. Szabó was not present. The absence of minutes of meetings in which Szabó commented on works of Ligeti is very striking and it is quite possible that the papers have been filtered by someone protecting his name. Certainly according to Ligeti's recollection, one of the judges on the panel, 'a member of the KGB', banned the last piece because of its dissonances. It is worth noting that its performance took place *two years and three months* after this meeting.

Formalism

Discussions about music's formal qualities clarify the political takeover and thaw even more neatly. They were simply blocked in 1949, the year that Bárdos had published an article called 'The foundations of Modal Harmony', in which he addressed a short piece of sixteenth-century music, taking a new perspective on repertoire that had hitherto been analysed only in terms of its polyphony.[89] He conceived it as a basis for his future research, but it was to be the last analytical publication for some time. Several harmony tutors appeared in the early 1950s, including two reprints, a collection of exercises by Bárdos in 1954, and Ligeti's tutor in that same year (the subsequent two volumes of exemplary extracts appeared in 1956).[90] Only in 1955 did further analytical – as opposed to pedagogical – literature come back into print.

There are two main analytical trends to map over the political change of 1949. The first, the study of folk music, was the more widespread. Given that this was engaged with a rather essentialised national definition associated with the inter-war years, it might have been doubly unsuitable. Kodály and Bartók's attempts to categorise the products of their fieldwork had founded the movement, adapting the Finnish ethnomusicologist Ilmari Krohn's system of classification and arranging their collections according to the relations between the final pitches of lines, rhythmic types and melodic ambit. They then analysed them according to cadential type, syllabic structure and melodic pattern. Bartók brought refinements to this system, categorised some of his collections according to genre, and even attempted to gauge the age – and thus the history – of the song types. His work is at the confluence of 'abstract' music and national definition.[91]

The regime would actually allow much folk-music research to continue along the lines that it had been doing for some time. Thus when Ligeti returned from a year in Romania and presented his research to the Hungarian Musicians' Union in 1950, he spoke both within the nation's tradition and the regime's own prerogatives. Romania, after all, was not only the residence of many Hungarians, but in the new political constellation was also a 'friend'. Focusing on the instrumental combinations, playing styles and harmonies of what he had discovered, Ligeti's lecture was a straightforward description of Romanian music in contrast to Hungarian, focusing on dissonance, and the varying reasons for its regular emergence in ensemble

---

[89] It was a four-part vocal piece by Joannes Gallus. Bárdos 1949.
[90] The reprints (both 1952) were tutors by Lőrinc Kesztler and Leó Weiner. Ligeti was evidently part of a community of musicians with analytical interests, referring with thanks to Bárdos, Gárdonyi, Járdányi, Halász and Molnár in his acknowledgements.
[91] See Erdélyi 2001 for an overview of Bartók's ethnomusicological work. Suchoff (ed.) 1997 is a valuable collection of his essays hitherto unavailable in English.

playing.⁹² In the more detailed exposition of his research published three years later, he described instrumental tuning systems, bowing style, melodic form, key and harmonic characteristics. Here too he devoted the most attention to this last area, providing detailed descriptions and musical examples of dissonances and their resolutions. Romanian music, he could conclude, had a different 'tolerance' of dissonance from Hungarian.⁹³

The other analytical thread to trace is equally concerned with the homeland, but intriguingly bound up with the (soon to be termed) formalist dimension of Bartók's music. The ongoing construction of Bartók against his 'other', Schoenberg, was a crucial influence. Molnár had suggested as early as 1937 that Bartók's choral works used 'the twelve-tone system' in a way that allowed folk-song motives to expand according to their 'inner laws'.⁹⁴ Analytical investigations effectively provided the technical evidence for Bartók's means of using of all twelve notes of the spectrum without renouncing tonality or modality.⁹⁵

In 1941, for example, a short article provided a description of Bartók's *Mikrokosmos* largely according to the series' pedagogical import, but also making some observations about its use of modes.⁹⁶ Initially identifying old church modes and pentatony in certain pieces and commenting on Phrygian cadences, the writer went on to discuss areas where two modes were combined in a sort of bitonality and then those in which more than two were combined. She pointed out how in these cases even 'chromatic' notes became 'main' notes, and how in combining Dorian, Phrygian and Lydian modes, Bartók had at his disposal all twelve notes of the spectrum. This extended tonality, she explained, was Bartók's revitalisation of form.

In the same month one of Kodály's students, György Kerényi, published a short article entitled 'Bartók's Key', an attempt to systematise Bartók's use of modes. If it provides but a glimpse, it nonetheless reveals that there were theoretical discussions going on. 'According to Lajos Bárdos' theory,' wrote Kerényi, 'the basic sonorous fabric of music can be arranged into twenty-one keys.'⁹⁷ He explained these through three scalar patterns of seven tones

---

⁹² MOL document 8.
⁹³ See Ligeti 1953. Ligeti 1950b, also addressing folk-song research in Romania, also refers to musical technicalities, but only in passing.
⁹⁴ Molnár 1937b: 66.
⁹⁵ Szelényi was an exception, for he also contributed to analytical literature, but not in nationalistic terms. His 1942 article entitled 'New Harmonic Systems' attempted to make inroads into the world of post-tonal harmony by identifying ways in which non-tonal chords were produced as a development of tonality (through proliferation of neighbour notes, use of suspensions, organ points), referring to a range of repertoire (*Tristan*, Debussy's *Ondine*, *Le Sacre*, Bartók's *Dance Suite*). In 1944 he wrote a short study comparing church modes with the tonal system. Szelényi 1942 and 1944.
⁹⁶ Hermann 1941: 54.   ⁹⁷ Kerényi 1941: 817.

and semitones (I, II and III). Each of the three could be used as a scale (or, therefore, a 'key') starting on any of its seven tones. Thus, each of the three linear patterns of intervals had seven keys.[98] Based on elements of the cycle of fifths and elements of modal thought, the system was one of the earliest attempt to theorise Bartók's harmony. Kerényi finally provided a few examples of scale 1 from Order II in Bartók's works and in folk songs, before proclaiming that this should be referred to henceforth as 'Bartók's Key'. This would become a staple of Bartók analysis under the name of the 'acoustic scale', as a consequence of another writer, Ernő Lendvai.

Lendvai's were the most path-breaking attempts to theorise Bartók's 'tonal' system, and they first appeared in print in 1947.[99] Rather than approaching the most obviously tonal or modal examples of Bartókian harmony, his first article tackled Bartók's Improvisations on Hungarian Peasant Songs op. 20, one of the composer's most chromatic works. The eight piano pieces allowed him to demonstrate, without mentioning Schoenberg specifically, that Bartók had built his own special division of the 'twelve-tone system' not through individual tones, but through intervallic constellations. Bartók had built pieces around a single interval, by piling up identical intervals (major second, minor third) to create new harmonies that divided the octave range evenly, by using centricity, and also a harmonic axis.[100] Lendvai's next article, a shorter piece on (the similarly chromatic) 'The Night's Music' from the piano suite *Out of Doors*, was less far-reaching in analytical terms, but far more evocative in metaphor. Whereas, he argued, Bach and Beethoven looked to God in their attempt to make sense of the world and Wagner looked to an ecstatic 'love death', Bartók, 'the heathen high priest,

---

[98] Pattern I was the white-note collection, which could give rise to the major scale, Dorian, Phrygian and so on. The two semitones of pattern II were closer together, so the pattern was 1 1 1 $\frac{1}{2}$ 1 $\frac{1}{2}$ 1 1 1 and so on; or, C, D, E, F♯, G, A, B♭ etc. The two semitones of pattern III were contiguous, forming $\frac{1}{2}$ 1 1 1 1 1 $\frac{1}{2}$. Kerényi – or rather, Bárdos's theory – generated these patterns partly according to analyses of Bartók's keys, whereby he transformed what would be tonal or modal keys of pattern I into keys of pattern II. As Kerényi explained in his footnotes, when Bartók used the key of G he provided a key signature of F natural (the fourth degree of the closely related key of C) and C♯ (the sharpened seventh from the other closely related key of D). When Bartók used pattern III, according to this theory, he transformed pattern I by taking elements of the key signature not of the closest keys, but of keys at one remove from them. Thus, when writing in C, he had a key signature of E♭ and C♯, generated through the process of taking the fourth from B♭ (one remove beyond F); and the sharp seventh from D (one remove from G). Kerényi 1941: 820.

[99] See Szabó 1994 for a brief biographical (and hagiographical) account of Lendvai. The earliest stages of his theoretical explorations (Lendvai 1947a and 1947b) are not available in English, but Lendvai 1948 is largely to be found in the English-language Lendvai 1999. His research has been rarely appreciated outside Hungary (Samson 1985 provides an exception), and is drawn on substantially only by Roy Howat, who focused almost entirely on Lendvai's application of Golden Section proportions. For an exchange between them, see Howat 1983, Lendvai 1984 and Howat 1985.

[100] Lendvai 1947a: 152–9.

philosophical materialist . . . who recognised only the laws of nature', needed 'strict form'.[101] Such 'strict form' was evidence of the music's natural, and even mystical, dimension: 'The Night's Music' was the music of the cosmos, thus a site of natural science, but also a realm of magic.[102]

Lendvai furnished these metaphors with the technical system that clinched Bartók's distinction from Schoenberg in the following year.[103] This was his now notorious division of the octave into three 'axes' (each comprising four notes divided by minor thirds) which, in a disarming appropriation of functional tonal theory, he termed 'tonic' (C, E♭, F♯, A), 'dominant' (C♯, E, G, A♯) and 'subdominant' (D, F, A♭, B). The language he used pointed to the rejection of all musical systems other than 'tonal' ones, and developed his earlier observations about piling up identical intervals and dividing the octave range equally (the 'distance principle').

While Lendvai undertook his construction of Bartók without mentioning the name of his big (atonal) 'other', that of his friend Ligeti was a touch more explicit. Ligeti's own analytical work, a single article on Bartók's 'Bear Dance', was at once less ambitious and less individual, attempting rather precariously to draw on Hindemith and Kurth, voice-leading and functional harmonic patterns. His underlying point was in line with Lendvai's concern to use 'tonal' language about Bartók, but in the case of 'Bear Dance' it was hardly controversial. Ligeti argued that Bartók's music was diatonic and pentatonic, and that even the most dissonant areas were simply compressed diatony. Bartók's chromaticism, argued Ligeti, was 'not, as some assume, an approach to the twelve-tone system'. Bartók's only gestures towards twelve-tone composition, he explained, were probably his violin sonatas.[104]

When, in the thaw, such discussions could be published once again, their claims about Bartók's individualism were further intensified. 1955 saw the publication of three analytical articles including one by Lendvai, whose book, *Bartók's Style*, was published in the same year.[105] Containing detailed analyses of Bartók's *Sonata for Two Pianos and Percussion* and his *Music for Strings, Percussion and Celeste*, this revealed for the first time his research

---

[101] Lendvai 1948: 217.   [102] Lendvai 1948: 218.
[103] Lendvai 1947b and Lendvai 1948.   [104] Ligeti 1948b: 252.
[105] 'Modális harmóniák Liszt műveiben' [Modal Harmonies in Liszt Works] (1955) in Bárdos 1969: 129–66; Gárdonyi 1955; and Lendvai 1955b. Bárdos' article observes harmonic motion in Palestrina and Lassus through the lens of the cycle of fifths. He comes to the conclusion that single harmonic steps typical of their music move through *two* fifth relations – as opposed to the functional system which moves most naturally in singular fifths. Thus chords shift from C to D (omitting G). Illustrating these steps graphically (almost identically to Lorenz's graphs of Wagner but on a much smaller scale) and then applying them to extracts of Liszt, Bárdos was able to theorise and illuminate the adventurous distances the Lisztian harmony travelled. Lendvai's book is Lendvai 1955a. Parts of it became available in English as Lendvai 1971, the entire book as Lendvai 1999.

about the Golden Section, and fleshed out a detailed account of how his various theoretical models could illuminate Bartók's harmonic processes. Running through the book is a binary model that emerges in a variety of contexts, each with symbolic resonance. The Golden Section, for instance, divides works and movements into 'positive' and 'negative' regions; chromaticism is polarised against diatonicism; asymmetry against periodicity, a proportional system against an acoustic system. One of the clearest uses he had for his binary model was to be able to conceive one movement as the mirror of the other by arguing that it was its inverse. Thus, the third movement of the *Sonata* was the resolution of the first, because it transformed all the negative (asymmetrical, chromatic, F♯-based) elements into positive ones (periodic, diatonic, C-based). On a symbolic level, the 'demonic' world was transformed into a 'joyful' one.[106] Bartók, according to Lendvai, was the great synthesiser of musical systems.

The book stirred up responses from Járdányi, Ligeti, Szelényi (plus Bárdos in response to Szelényi) as well as from two new writers, József Ujfalussy and Károly Sólyom, the last of whom levelled the gravest critique. Sólyom found Lendvai's attribution of functions 'tonic', 'dominant' and 'subdominant' to be arbitrary, because the chords they designated were not functional within the acoustic system, but to do with a 'distance principle'. Critical of Lendvai's construction of Schoenberg, he took the dramatic step of aligning Bartók *with* Schoenberg 'and others', pointing out that they had *all* broken off from the acoustic system. These two points led him to the conclusion that a notion of Bartók's unique synthesis of tonal and atonal systems was seriously flawed.[107]

Lendvai's responses to critics were uncompromising. He refused to be drawn into the topical world of hermeneutics from which Ujfalussy, concerned with 'form' and 'content', and the *meaning* of the dualities of Bartók's works, beckoned. He also claimed that Sólyom's view was 'dangerous', and reiterated his position as one who *knew* that Bartók and Schoenberg were fundamentally different.[108] He thanked Járdányi and Ligeti for their support too. And well he might. Járdányi had proclaimed that Lendvai had done what nobody had yet done, namely 'examine the *logic* of Bartók's rich and complex musical language'.[109] But the review that provided the most magnificent justification for Lendvai's position was the apologia by Ligeti.

---

[106] Lendvai 1999 (1955): 110.
[107] Sólyom 1955: 4–7. Szelényi, less competently than Sólyom, presented similar doubts: he questioned whether it was at all possible to bring the acoustic functional system and the twelve-tone together. Szelényi 1956a. Bárdos, misquoted by Szelényi, wrote a retort and correction that stimulated a further lengthy article from Szelényi. See 'Tonika, vagy nem?' [Tonic, or Not?] (1956) in Bárdos 1969: 187–92; and Szelényi 1956b.
[108] Lendvai 1956: 18.   [109] Járdányi 1955: 2313.

In an essay that is also a key to his own emerging interest in both Lendvaiesque musical polarities and consonance and dissonance, he celebrated the research and mediated a crystal-clear account of the way Schoenberg and Bartók were conceived in Hungarian thought.

The underpinning for his argument is by now very familiar. It constructed Schoenberg as a loser against the forces of historical development, and Bartók as triumphal winner. Ligeti did not engage with Lendvai's symbolic and metaphysical claims, but he defended him admirably in historical terms. On the one hand, the collapse of tonality and dodecaphony's ostensible freedom had led to a complete impoverishment of music.[110] On the other, Bartók's axis system rescued the principles of tension and release and even found an equivalent to modulation: it brought about a 'new system of relations within twelve-tonalism'. Lendvai could hardly have hoped for a better national apologist. And the national musical myth could hardly have hoped for a more energetically argued elaboration.

Silences

Public silence

While my arguments above indicate some of the ways Hungarian musical thought evolved in this very difficult period, the gaps in between can speak equally strongly. Several names had been missing for some time when Ligeti wrote his review of Lendvai, most importantly, that of his teacher Sándor Veress. Veress's national career had been building steadily since the later 1920s, and he was Bartók's research assistant at the Hungarian Academy of Sciences from 1934 and then Kodály's successor in the post of Professor of Composition at the Liszt Academy from 1943. He had more recently, however, sought international possibilities too. He made enquiries about emigration to Arthur Bliss as early as 1947, and thanks to his attendance at the International Folk Music Council Congress in Basel in 1948, he had established good Swiss contacts, Paul Sacher and Annie Müller-Widmann, who had supported Bartók some years earlier.[111] By this time Veress was also gaining international appreciation as a composer, thanks to which he attended premières of his ballet *Térszili Katicza* in Stockholm and Rome in February 1949. It was there that he lingered after the performance, neglecting to return to Hungary as officially expected. Within two years, he would have become a disseminator of Hungarian culture in Switzerland.

---

[110] Ligeti 1955: 42–3. Ligeti also revealed an awareness of more recent developments, arguing that Boulez's attempt to pursue the Schoenbergian path yet further had led to a complete loss of rhythmic, dynamic and instrumental contrast.

[111] Gerlich 2000.

Veress's struggles to find a way of existing outside Hungary can be traced in his various letters and diaries. Ottó Gombosi, Budapest's former editor of *Crescendo* who was by then Professor at the University of Chicago, was most important in the first years. He put Veress in touch with Hungarians established outside the country and Veress wrote to several of these, generating correspondences that provide us with traces of the Hungarian 'diaspora'.[112] Gombosi also secured Veress the use of a villa in Switzerland while Sacher conducted his *Transylvanian Dances* in Zürich, which provided a rationale for his official invitation to enter the country; at the same time the Végh Quartet performed his Second String Quartet in a private concert organised by Müller-Widmann. Thanks to Gombosi (working alongside Müller-Widmann and Sacher), Veress was employed to give some lectures at the University in Bern in the autumn of 1949, and in 1950 gained a permanent post at the Bern Conservatorium.[113]

In the next years Veress combined a transplantation of his Hungarian past into the Bern environment with a resolute attempt to take on some of the ideas around him. His teaching activity, at least, allowed him to maintain a certain continuity with what he had left behind. As he described his early teaching in 1987:

> I introduced a fundamental reform. The theoretical subjects included, alongside harmony, counterpoint and formal studies, solfeggio as well. I introduced the Hungarian method of Tonic sol-fa, previously unknown there. So, although there was a pressure of work, I spent my first few years at the Berne Conservatoire in a pleasant and harmonious atmosphere.[114]

His compositional reconstruction began with a major new work that bore the traces of his new life in Switzerland. *Hommage à Paul Klee* (1951), a suite of seven pieces for two pianos and string orchestra, is testimony to the art collection of Müller-Widmann. Yet whilst a breakthrough for him, in the Western European context the *Hommage* also revealed the extent to which his music depended on a Stravinsky-influenced, Hungarian type of neoclassicism. Indeed, as his diary reveals, he confronted the need to move out of his rather limited orbit even while working on the *Hommage*, reflecting on twelve-tone compositional practice as if it was something that was disturbing his work. He noted in Munich in July 1951 how 'exceptionally

---

[112] Conductor and composer Antal Doráti, Pál Gergely (Zürich Opera), Paul Láng (editor of the *Musical Quarterly*), for instance.

[113] Initially the paucity of Veress's musicological work triggered misgivings with Alphonse Brun, the Director of the Conservatorium; but the post metamorphosed, through Veress's own expertise and the sympathy of Brun, into a Professorship of Composition, Theory and Pedagogy. Gerlich 2000: 400–2. See also Traub 1986.

[114] Bónis (ed.) 1988b: 210.

dangerous' it was: apart from Berg, 'dodecaphonists' were all dogmatic. Perhaps, he thought, this obsession with determinism and regulation had a parallel with communism: where had the grand ideals of socialism gone, in the evolution of Soviet society, he asked himself.[115]

Weighing up dodecaphony critically was actually a background for finding ways in which to draw on it for his own work, however, and this signified a crucial step towards integration in the new environment. Veress would become a significant artistic presence in Switzerland – the celebrated teacher of Heinz Holliger, Jürg Wyttenbach and many other successful Swiss composers – and it was important for his teaching that he learned to be at least operative in the styles of the time. Yet it was also important for his reputation as a composer that his works shed any characteristics that might hinder their progress. In the striving for aesthetic absolutes that was taken to extremes in Western Europe in the early 1950s, he needed to rethink his compositional priorities quite dramatically. Consequently his Piano Concerto (1952), *Sinfonia Minneapolitana* (1952–3) and String Trio (1954) chart a sudden immersion in the dodecaphonic technique. These works enabled musicologist Andreas Traub to present Veress as a composer purged of folklore and *au fait* with abstraction. As Traub summed it up, 'in short, the row took the place of Hungarian folk music'.[116]

This successful 'exchange' of one type of musical material for another (or, more accurately conceived, the cross-fertilisation between the two) was not, however, paralleled in Veress's more practical attempts to extend himself. For his sights were set not on Switzerland, but rather on a move to the USA. Gombosi had recommended him for a post in Ohio in 1949 and also brought him together with two Hungarians at American universities with whom he developed lengthy correspondences. Historian István Borsodi mediated between Veress and István Csicsery-Rónay, who was relatively well established on the American political scene, in an attempt to help him gain a visa. But the political climate was not on his side. Letters to Veress from pianist Béla Böszörményi-Nagy reveal that in his own experience, the important thing for American officials was to decide whether a Hungarian was a Nazi or a Communist.[117] Veress, then, was quite a simple case: if he wanted to move to the USA, he would have to attempt to justify the 'unfortunate step' he had taken in May 1945.[118]

---

[115] Original at the Paul Sacher Foundation. Published in German translation in Traub (ed.): 1998, 29–34. This section at 30.
[116] Traub 1986: 63.
[117] Letters to Veress 2? 1949, 28 August 1949 and 4 December 1949. Paul Sacher Foundation (PSF), Sándor Veress Collection (SVC).
[118] Veress, in a letter to Borsody. 22 June 1952. In ring-bound file of mixed correspondence marked '1952–53'. PSF, SVC.

Borsody advised him in April 1952 that Csicsery-Rónay (with whom Veress had no direct contact yet) needed to know when Veress had joined the Communist Party and how long he had remained a member; he also needed him to make a declaration. This had to include the statement that joining the party had been neither an anti-American nor a pro-communist step but merely a formality; that because it served his artistic and personal beliefs it was not immoral; that there had been no political intent in it; that Veress never undertook party work; and that his aims were aligned only with the rebirth of Hungarian music.[119] Veress, however, sustained little hope in the proposed declaration, for he had never left the Communist Party.[120]

By this time, Veress's contact with Hungarians at home was virtually non-existent. As he reflected later, he lost touch with some of his closest associates because letters from him might have endangered the addressees.[121] Only one correspondent was to keep him in touch with events, and only in the initial phase of Veress's emigration. This was Colin Mason, an English composer and critic who was a student at the Liszt Academy until later on in 1949. Mason's letters – apparently smuggled out of the country in diplomatic postbags – offer glimpses of the terrorising society that Budapest had come to house. A letter from May 1949 mentions that Veress's apartment had not yet been searched by the police. Mason himself, we read, was attempting to extract all Veress's belongings from it before they noticed that they had gone.[122] These objects – it emerges from a list – were being gradually distributed around friends and family in the city (the piano with conductor László Somogyi, for instance, two pillows with composer Emil Petrovics).[123] Apparently Mason was also attempting to arrange the shipments of Veress's manuscripts – again, without any authorities noticing.

Mason's descriptions of the early months of the dictatorship also illuminate his own confusion about the dramatic metamorphosis of musical judgement around him. Veress would find it hard to fit in, he thought, because he couldn't write populist music like that of Szervánszky. He

---

[119] Letter to Veress from István Borsody in Pittsburgh, 7 April 1952. In ring-bound file of mixed correspondence marked '1952–53'. PSF, SVC.

[120] As he explained in his response to Borsody, there was 'no point' in writing the declaration. Letter to Borsody, 22 June 1952. In ring-bound file of mixed correspondence marked '1952–53'. PSF, SVC. As Breuer reveals from archival documents, Veress was not only a member of the party, but a member of the party's Musical Committee between 1945 and 1948. 'A "Párt" zenei bizottságának határozatai a Zeneművészeti Főiskoláról (1948–49)' [The Resolutions of the "Party" Music Committee about the Music Academy] in Breuer 2002: 221–32.

[121] The friendship with ethnographer and composer László Lajtha seems to have been the most painful loss to Veress. Bónis 1987 (ed.): 205–6.

[122] Letter to Veress, 21 April 1949. Mason wrote in English (although fluent in Hungarian and later to write to Veress in Hungarian) and avoided leaving traces of his letter's origin on the page. On this occasion it amounted to literally cutting the word 'Budapest' out of the paper. When he wrote on 25 May, he was extremely anxious that an earlier letter had been intercepted, although he gave it to 'N.' as usual. See Smalley 1972 for a memoir of Mason.

[123] This list is among family letters in a ring-bound file labelled '1950–52'. PSF, SVC.

himself didn't think that Szervánszky's *Serenade* was 'a solution to the problem of writing good communist music . . . it seems to me to some degree a retrogression, and a withdrawal. I'm sure that not even Szervánszky, with all his wholehearted idealistic desire to serve a regime which really looks after its artists materially, will be satisfied very long to write such music.'[124] Mason was also appalled by the new evaluation of Szelényi, whose *Symphony of a Factory* was 'one of the worst pieces of music I have ever heard', while he was now 'heralded as a great composer'.[125] Mason forecasted a descent into anti-formalism and despairingly described Szabolcsi as 'evasive': '[E]ven if one doesn't like Schoenberg, it is not enough to play a tuneless melody on the piano and dismiss it as trash . . . which is what Szabolcsi did.'[126]

Once Mason left Hungary in July, however, Veress's sources of information all but dried up. An undated letter from musicologist Dénes Bartha was presumably written once Szabolcsi had made his political metamorphosis: Szabolcsi, wrote Bartha, was now the only one who could achieve anything; Bartha himself was excluded.[127] In 1952 Veress received a number of postcards from former colleagues at the Hungarian Academy of Sciences, folklorists such as Gyula Kertész and György Kerényi, who were working alongside Kodály, Lajtha and Szőllősy on the publication of folk music. These cards present laconic, factual statements about research under way, equipment needed, or corrections to be made by Veress to the material on which they were working.[128] He also picked up a small amount of gossip from John S. Weissmann, a Hungarian writer, répétiteur and conductor who had lived in England since 1937.[129] But official communication with Hungary had ceased.

When he had failed to return to Hungary from his trip in 1949, his friend and pedagogical colleague Erna Czövek wrote to plead that he come home and continue their building project.[130] The Hungarian embassy in Bern wrote and asked whether he was going back; and even Communist leader József Révai recalled him urgently.[131] These admonishments and even the bait of a governmental Kossuth Prize that year making no impression, Hungary gave up. The ocean 'decontaminated' Hungary of his name, and drowned out discussion of his fate.

---

[124] Letter to Veress, 25 May 1949. PSF, SVC.   [125] Letter to Veress, 25 May 1949. PSF, SVC.
[126] Letter to Veress, 25 May 1949. PSF, SVC. Mason was describing a lecture Szabolcsi presented at the Eötvös Collegium.
[127] Undated. Ring-bound file labelled '1950–51'. PSF, SVC.
[128] 17 June 1952, 19 August 1952 and 6 February 1953. Ring-bound file labelled '1952–53'. PSF, SVC.
[129] A letter from János Weissmann dated London, 26–27 November 1950, reports on recent institutional shifts in Budapest. Ring-bound file labelled '1950–51'. PSF, SVC.
[130] Letter to Veress, 20 October 1949. PSF, SVC.
[131] Letter from the Hungarian Embassy, 22 February 1950. Letter from József Révai, 12 October 1949. PSF, SVC.

Private silence (music and language reconsidered)

To close this chapter, I will turn in more detail to what we might term the 'private' sphere of composition, that which could not be heard in public. Some indication of this area has already emerged above with reference to Ligeti's *Métamorphoses nocturnes*, but it is worth delving more deeply into one area of Ligeti's work that engages with an area of national debate – language – and exploring its intersection with the work of poet Sándor Weöres. Looking more closely at poetry and music allows us to trace some ideas discussed above within more specific material, and the poetry of Weöres in particular is an intriguing thread to set not only within the present chapter, but also against the backdrop of Chapter 1. Additionally, as is well known, Weöres was a source of inspiration for Ligeti throughout his Budapest years, and by looking closely at his early settings, we gain a new view of the works he composed after leaving the country. As should emerge in Chapters 3 and 5, it is not only the fact that Ligeti returned to the poetry of Weöres in 1983 that makes this the case. Rather, there are compositional ideas that surface for the first time in the Weöres settings that can be identified more generally in Ligeti's later works.

An introduction to Sándor Weöres is helpful at this stage. Born in 1913, he was recognised as a prodigiously gifted poet even as a child. Some of his early poems were published in a youth magazine in 1928 and were reprinted in a Budapest daily newspaper the following year; he published his first volume of poetry, *Hideg van* (*It's Cold*), in 1934. Kodály had set one of his poems in that same year and by 1940 had turned to him to request that he write more for children. Although the numerous letters it is known that Kodály sent to Weöres between 1934 and 1957 have not survived, we can see from Weöres' response in 1940, at least, what Kodály wanted.[132] Weöres enthused in agreement that there was indeed a need to 'eliminate the iambic hegemony from Hungarian poetry' and launch a 'counter-invasion'. He himself was keen to find ways of replacing the pervasive two-part rhythmic metres and creating something really Hungarian, he wrote. This interest in the Hungarian language and writing children's literature was part of a renaissance in children's literature analogous to the one described above in music.[133] Yet placing Weöres in this context illuminates but a fragment of his interests. The

---

[132] Kodály's letters are published in Legány (ed.) 1982. Weöres' letter to Kodály is reproduced in Domokos (ed.) 2003: 87–8.

[133] An overview of new children's literature in 1946 makes clear the perceived need for more, as well as the proliferation of publications for children, and the references to 'since the liberation' reveal the political motivation behind this 'need'. See Trencsényi-Waldapfel 1946, which refers to the work of Bartók's contemporary Zsigmond Móricz, who had died in 1942 (newly reissued), Attila József (who had died in 1937), and living poets Sándor Weöres, Gábor Devecseri, Ágoston Simon, Béla Balázs, Zoltán Zelk, among others.

divergences between his and Kodály's work reveal that very clearly. One later commentator remarked that the result of Kodály's encouragement, Weöres' groups of poems called *Rongyszőnyeg* (*Rag-carpet*) and *Magyar Etűdök* (*Hungarian Studies*) combined Kodály's 'musicality and sweet pain' with Weöres' 'cosmic universality'.[134] Yet that does little justice to their differences.

First, Weöres' poems reveal that he had his own 'musicality', which consisted of an exploration of language's acoustic properties with an endlessly inventive, rather than normative, approach. Alongside musical experiments with prosody, he wrote verses following rhythmic patterns from sources as remote from Hungary as rumba and rock 'n' roll rhythms. He also composed poems in entirely invented languages that were evidently conceived primarily in acoustics; and tried using musical forms and types such as fugue and symphony as models for poems. This virtuosically experimental tendency and the multiplicity of ideas that he included within a single volume concerned some critics, although before the Stalinist takeover none expressed doubt about his talent. Rather, they emphasised the parts of the multifarious volumes that they understood as fitting to the role of a poet; and looked upon his embrace of *poesie pure* and nonsense rhymes with mildly irritated bemusement.[135]

The second major difference from Kodály was that Weöres drew on a colossal range of spiritual writings (many of which he translated into Hungarian himself) in order to reflect on questions about the human predicament or, as he himself put it in an interview conducted in 1963, to 'cross the thresholds beyond the limits of everyday, practical, life'.[136] He was familiar with the ancient Chinese writings such as the Tshu-Tse collection and the Te King of Lao-Tse (which he himself translated); he also explored the Upanishads, the Bhagavad Gita, Egyptian hymns, Polynesian and Negro myths and Babylonian epic poetry. This richness of knowledge probably contributes to the intractable nature of much of his verse: the reader absorbs a set of hints and possibilities, but meanings are rarely spelled out. Weöres' interest in a range of intellectual traditions was by no means unique in Hungary, and he drew on the research of the scholar of myth, Karl Kerényi, and the ethno-linguist, Iván Fónagy. Yet there was possibly nobody else there who was able to use, so evocatively and suggestively, such a bewildering range of ideas. There was probably nobody else in Hungary whose work

---

[134] Kardos 1972: 574.
[135] See, for instance, Vajda 1947. On the Marxist side he was criticised for writing alienated, despairing poetry; a particularly vicious example of such criticism is found in a survey of contemporary poetry by József Szigeti. Summing up his tirade, he writes of Weöres: 'Hungarian Poet in 1947? No – just the versifier of the Hungarian reaction in 1947, driven into the counter-revolutionary position'. See Szigeti 1947: 761.
[136] Szabó 1989: 44.

suggests such an amusement about the contingency of the myths through which people live, either. In this respect, his thinking could hardly have been more different from that of Kodály.

It is also evident that his perspective on childhood was entirely distinct. Whereas for Kodály the child embodied innocence and opportunity, for Weöres, the world of the child was magical and fantastical. His children's verses conformed only sporadically to the established children's genres, rather crossing over between songs, rhythmic games, lyrical sketches, role-play and jokes. They also had (have!) a tremendous appeal to adults. Little wonder, then, that they appealed to so many composers who had broader interests than Kodály himself; and little wonder that Ligeti found them so intriguing.[137] What did he draw from them?

It seems likely that his first four settings, *Magány* (*Loneliness*) (1946) and *Three Weöres Songs* (1946) were triggered either by personal interest or tasks set by teachers. The study of prosody became obligatory for composers at the Liszt Academy from 1949, when Bárdos, having lost his position there when the Church Music Faculty was closed down, was invited back to teach it.[138] Bárdos's early post-war articles were concerned with the acoustic properties of national languages and his desire that music reflect them, thus both Kurtág and Ligeti were schooled in metrics and word-setting, analysed folk songs and Kodály's text settings in terms of prosody, and were made aware of the acoustic properties of the Hungarian language – as distinct from Indo-Germanic ones. They also analysed instrumental music in terms of its divisibility into poetic feet; and notated poetic metres as musical rhythms. In short, they immersed themselves in the possible technical parallels between music and language. Their student manuscript books provide detailed testimony of their studies, and one of these contains an early setting of Weöres by Ligeti, corrected by Bárdos.[139]

Later on Ligeti set three poems that remain unpublished to this day, suggesting that he acquired them directly from the poet, as a result of their

---

[137] Ligeti's teacher in Cluj, Ferenc Farkas, himself grasped some of such ambiguities of childhood when he set a group of Weöres poems in his *Gyümölcskosár* (Fruit Basket) of 1945. This light-hearted and witty group of twelve songs for soprano, clarinet, viola and piano does not shy away from eccentricity and grotesquery. The bizarre texts of Weöres ('Plumicorn playing conjures up wings on a piglet, sits on her, promises her kisses, and flies her away . . .') find suitably zany musical accompaniments that were surely of interest to Ligeti. His review of their publication in 1948 is admiring, and he may well have known them long before this date. See Ligeti 1948e.

[138] Szabolcsi had moved quickly to protect 'national intonation' when Stalin made his pronouncements on language, and sketched out a theory of various forms of 'false' musical intonation, which included – of course! – incorrect Hungarian prosody in music. But this followed the introduction of prosody teaching at the Liszt Academy. Szabolcsi 1951b: 1–2.

[139] For general prosody studies see Ligeti 'Skizzenbuch' 35 and 'Notizheft' 1; Kurtág 'Skizzenbuch' 2. Ligeti's setting of Weöres' 'Táncol a hold fehér ingben' (The Moon is Dancing in a White Robe), later to be included in *Three Weöres Songs*, is in Skizzenbuch 35, with corrections to text setting marked by Bárdos.

newly established friendship (*Dawn*, 1949–50). These songs and the ensuing ones in *Tél* (*Winter*, 1950) and *Pletykázó asszonyok* (*Gossiping Women*, 1952), nonetheless, were eminently suitable for use at the time, and *Gossiping Women* was indeed published in a compilation. Finally, *Éjszaka* (*Night*) and *Reggel* (*Morning*, 1955), would have needed considerable luck in finding performance platforms, indicating that Ligeti wrote them primarily to extend his technique and serve his own increasingly exploratory interests.

His first Weöres settings indicate his use of musical styles drawn from the choral heritage of Bartók, Kodály and Bárdos, but also indicate a quite singular distinctiveness from their work both in harmony and their texts' gentle subversion of child-related ideals. Weöres' 'Loneliness' was published in a poetry collection in 1944:

Sej, elaludtam,	Oh, I fell asleep,
sej, elaludtam	at the water's edge.
álló víz partján,	
álló víz partján.	
Fűvön fektemben	Whilst lying there on the grass,
ottan álmomban	in my dreams
nőtt liliomszál	a single lily grew.
nőtt liliomszál.	
Le kéne tépni	I should pick it,
mellemre tűzni	and press it to my breast,
az én rózsámat	I should kiss my Rose.
kéne csókolni.	
Sej, ellankadok,	Oh, I grow tired,
lassan bágyadok,	slowly fading away,
lassan bágyadok,	tomorrow I shall die.[140]
holnap meghalok.	

Ligeti's song gives the poem directional quality with dynamic shifts and interpolations of repeated text. The first line is mournful and slow; the second, lively and extended with melisma – as if, madrigal-like, imitating a growing plant. The central two lines are set to a quicker tempo and with evident determination, as well as being extended with repetitions of 'I should kiss' and 'kiss'. 'Oh, I am getting tired' then interrupts, returning to the slowness of the opening. Additionally, at this point there is a reprise of the

---

[140] Weöres (1940) 1975 (I): 493. Unless otherwise indicated, the Weöres translations are my own.

very opening line 'I fell asleep on the banks of a lake', and the final line of 'getting tired', 'getting weak', and 'die', is set in a musical sequence.

Thus far, the song constructs a dramatic frame in a more obvious way than does Weöres' poem itself and is in line with the types of setting typical of Kodály and Bárdos. Yet the song is not articulated firmly in harmonic terms. Points of rest in the outer sections are found only in fleeting moments of relative consonance in a texture of shifting contrapuntal lines; semitone clashes overstep the conventions of contemporary choral repertoire too. The central part has more triadic parallel motion, but the chain of resultant consonance, even if less poignant, allows for no more sense of a tonal centre.

If overlaid with the narrative in which the poem was first conceived, moreover, the musical ambivalence gains further significance: within Weöres' puppet play entitled *Lunar Boatsman* (1941) it is a song sung by a mournful princess. The play elaborates what first appears to be an archetypal children's story of a princess courted by various rulers from afar, but which destabilises and energises the conventional princess model. The trigger is a fortune-telling falcon. From this bird the princess learns the intentions of the various suitors gathering around her. Fleeing in search of her own true love, her consequent coming of age leads her to realise that love is not the idealised thing of which she had dreamt at all. It brings much sadness, even a sort of death: this she expresses by singing 'Loneliness'.

This disillusion and gentle critique of both idealised princesses and romantic love emerges much more strongly in Ligeti's 'A Merchant Came with Giant Birds' from *Three Weöres Songs*. But here the ideal is renounced altogether. The poem itself seems to be a skeleton of a fairy tale, notwithstanding its gently provocative portrayal (again) of a princess. If the first two strophes portray her as a typically walled-in beauty in the first two strophes, the third reveals that she has more to her than meets the eye.

Kalmár jött nagy madarakkal,	A merchant has come with giant birds,
a hercegkisasszony meg ne lássa,	the princess should not see,
őrizzétek a hercegkisasszonyt!	protect the princess!
Kalmár jött nagy madarakkal,	A merchant has come with giant birds
a gyerekek kiabálnak,	the children are screaming,
a hercegkisasszony meg ne hallja!	the princess should not hear!
A hercegkisasszony sápadt, sose szól,	The princess is pale and never speaks,
Szívében sok nagy madár rikácsol,	in her heart giant birds shriek,
őrizzétek a hercegkisasszonyt!	protect the princess![141]

---

[141] Weöres (1941) 1975 (I): 423.

After 1945: a new empire forms 69

The poem leaves much suggested, but nothing explained; nevertheless the birds are clearly central to the possible stories behind what we read. At the opening they are apparently something from which the princess should be protected: they seem dangerous to her, as if metaphors for a kind of knowledge from which she is barred. While this recalls the fortune-telling falcon, however, by the third verse giant birds emerge as already in union with the princess's heart. It turns out that secretly, she has already acquired the knowledge that the dangerous birds (falcons?) might have passed on.[142] Moreover, the birds are *shrieking*, against which her silence is in great contradiction. Attempts to protect her from birds seems to be too late: after all, she already has her own big noisy ones. This princessly innocence is superficial: it coexists with a more violent reality within.

Where Weöres' poem is mysterious, Ligeti's setting is just about as straightforward as music can be, because it stresses one type of music so consistently. Although he might have drawn on this fairy-tale paradox and played with images of light and dark, or created a structure in which the revelation of the princess's inner nature effects a musical change, the song presents only hideousness. Menace is present throughout. Much the most dissonant piece Ligeti had ever written at this stage, its crudely declamatory vocal line makes no attempt at melodiousness; and the ostinato's rhythmic irregularity sets up an unmistakable ugliness. Only a heightened vocal treatment draws attention to the shrieking birds of the princess. Thus, there is no music for an innocent princess, and 'his' birds are no different from 'hers'. It has been suggested that for Weöres, childhood and the childlike represented a common past akin to myth; Ligeti, on the other hand, made no attempt to portray any of that common past with romanticised innocence.[143] His song eradicated the notion of childhood purity altogether: the repetitive thrusting crescendi of the piano part make the covert sexual innuendos of the text as musically explicit as they are likely to become.[144] (See Ex. 2.1.)

---

[142] Weöres often drew on familiar romantic notions of birds residing in the heart, and thus suggesting love entanglements. See 'Rag Carpet' no. 16, 'On my heart a peacock walked, now a bat is hanging there, a sparrow will nest on my heart'; and no. 22, 'A beautiful bird knocks on my window and has already flown. Like a rose of stone still in my heart a beautiful bird'. *Rongyszőnyeg* (*Rag-carpet*). Weöres (1941) 1975 (I): 383 and 385.

[143] Kenyeres 1983: 163.

[144] Only one source traced so far might bring us towards confirming the tantalisingly intangible narrative. This is a reference from ancient Vogul poetry, a source of mythology, ritual and custom with which Weöres himself would have undoubtedly been familiar. Vogul is a relation of the Hungarian language, and extensive collections of Vogul poetry were published in a bilingual version at the end of the nineteenth century and early in the twentieth. It is the Vogul word for 'bird' ('Kāk') which is suggestive here, for it also means 'penis'. 'Kāk' is a type of word associated, in its simplicity, with children. (The female equivalent is 'nun'.) The verb to copulate is taken from this word of dual meaning: 'kākti, kāktaxti'; and in some Vogul poetry copulation is expressed with the phrase to 'prod/poke/prick [!] with a bird' (madarat bökdösni), in a style which appears distinctly childlike. Munkácsi & Kálmán 1986: 218. I am grateful to Peter Sherwood for drawing my attention to this.

Example 2.1. Ligeti 'A Merchant Came with Giant Birds', from *Three Weöres Songs*, close

After 1945: a new empire forms

When Ligeti returned to Weöres in the mid-1950s in order to experiment with music (as opposed to write music for official platforms), he took a different line, one that heralded his future work very distinctly. By this time he had entered his more adventurous phase, and had completed *Musica ricercata*, Six Bagatelles and his first string quartet. He was to recall later that he wrote these Weöres songs just at the moment when he began to move away from Bartók's influence, which prompted Sallis to address them from two perspectives in particular: Adorno's *Philosophie der Neuen Musik* and Weöres' poetry. For Sallis, Ligeti captured Weöres' demand for a poem's 'unity of mood', and employed a technique analogous to Adorno's 'complementary harmony'.[145] Yet with the benefit of a broader background in Hungarian thought, we can look once again at what Ligeti did with the poems.

He selected them from collections Weöres had published after he had shifted from the aesthetic position represented by 'Loneliness' and 'Merchant'. Commentators – and Weöres himself – described the change as a new emphasis on an 'Orphic', spiritual writing that the poet strove for in direct response to criticism from the highly regarded metaphysical writer Béla Hamvas.[146] *Éjszaka* (*Night*) was published in the first volume after his change. Almost mystically, the poem first evokes darkness, solitude in nature, and quietness. It then turns into a supplication, invoking music and Biblical symbols of goodness and nature, before returning to the darkness, nature and solitary quietness.

Rengeteg tövis: éjszaka!	Masses of thorns: night!
rengeteg csönd: tücsök-cirpelés!	infinite silence: cricket-chirping!
én csöndem: szivem dobogása!	my silence: my heartbeat!
Tejről, mézről szóljon az ének.	Of milk, of honey, let the song sing
Virágról szóljon az ének.	Of flowers let the song sing
Sok, nagyon sok virágról.	Of many, very many flowers
Anyáról szóljon az ének.	Of mother, let the song sing.
Rengeteg tövis: éjszaka!	Masses of thorns: night!
rengeteg csönd: tücsök-cirpelés!	infinite silence: cricket-chirping!
én csöndem: szivem dobogása!	my silence: my heartbeat![147]

Ligeti's setting, however, cuts out the most intimate inner pleas for goodness, even cuts out the setting in nature. It uses only the following extracts:

---

[145] Ligeti's 1984 recollection cited in Sallis 1996: 168. See also 189–92.
[146] Béla Hamvas, 'A *Meduza* (1947)', in Domokos (ed.) 1990: 213–17.
[147] Translation by Sallis. Sallis 1996: 189. Original published in Weöres 1975 (I): 617.

> Masses of thorns [many repetitions]
> silence! silence! masses of masses of silence!
> my silence
> masses of silence
> my heartbeat!
> silence
> Night.

Rather in the way he reviewed Lendvai's work in the same year, here Ligeti took one specific aspect of the poem only. The parallel refers not only to the selectiveness, but to the very selection: just as he bypassed Lendvai's symbolic system, he cut out Weöres' spiritual metaphysics. Indeed his intriguing response to Lendvai alerts us to an important aspect of these settings.[148] The pair, 'Night' and 'Morning' (*Reggel*), are just the sort of opposites that appealed to Lendvai. The internal binary structure of 'Night' itself is even more interesting. 'Masses of thorns' spreads up from a low C until the proliferating voices occupy all seven notes of the white collection; at 'silence', all the voices sing on the 'black notes'. The final chord is a C major triad. Harmonically, then, Ligeti plays with a very simple opposition. Although Sallis identifies this as Adornian, its simplicity is archetypical of Bartók, especially as mediated through Lendvai. This is also true of much of *Morning*. No matter what Ligeti saw in the piece that was moving away from Bartók, the heritage remains profound. *Morning*'s ostinati and the modal segmentation of sections are unmistakably reminiscent of Bartók's choral writing.[149]

Yet a number of elements suggest that the songs are looking forward, beyond Hungary – if still from within it. These are all linked to the vocal style and treatment of language. First, Ligeti 'interfered' with the text rather than treating it as a sacred whole. He largely stripped it of its romanticism and treated it as a less emotive set of images to depict. Second, he explored the acoustic properties of the verses as abstractions, toying with them as musical objects. The more appropriate setting of the time would surely have done what another composer, Hajdu, had done in the same year with precisely this verse, namely striven to pin down its 'true' prosodic contour.[150] Ligeti, rather, set it in an 'unorthodox' metre, and then tossed repeated segments around so that they overlapped, distracted one another and cut across the bar lines. Third, he interpolated into *Morning* wild shrieks that, although

---

[148] Sallis also suggests Lendvai may have influenced these pieces, but he makes a regrettably unrewarded attempt to trace Ligeti's use of the axis system and Golden Section. Sallis 1996: 183–8.

[149] Twenty-Seven Choruses for women's and children's choir in particular. See Vikárius 2004 for an introduction to Bartók's writing for choir.

[150] See András Hajdu's 'Bóbita ritmikája' [The Rhythmic Pattern of Bóbita] in Domokos 1990: 307–22 at 308–9. (Originally published in *Csillag* 1956/10.) Hajdu analyses the prosody of several Weöres poems, using musical notation to indicate his interpretations.

Example 2.2. Ligeti, *Night*, bb. 39–44

familiar from Bartók's *Village Scenes*, were more provocatively bizarre than anything else written in this period (they would resurface later on in his work).

These three aspects of *Night* and *Morning* come together in a highly physicalised music, a music that intrudes on the listener invasively. A fourth aspect of *Night* makes this physical quality even more apparent, namely its polarisation of two basic types of harmony and texture. Creating a sense of the 'masses of thorns' by repeating the text to a steady rhythmic formula, these unvaried reiterations evoke a dense, oppressive and impenetrable mesh of vegetation around the listener. Then as if sweeping away the thicket, a detached word of rest, 'csönd' (silence), emerges on the pentatonic collection. The 'presence' of (pentatonic) silence – just briefly – makes the thick swathes of sonorities absent (see Ex. 2.2). The dualistic mysteriousness of *Night* becomes less a critical extension of music in Budapest, than a somewhat fluid ambivalence that intimates Ligeti's anxious but also contradictory longing to step away. The particular 'silence' of pentatony would be fleetingly present in future years, as well.

PART II

3 After 1956: the parting of ways

1956 is a year that Hungarian history can never forget. Yet the uprising and its bloody repression in October 1956 were, we should nonetheless remember, only the final events in a series of political switches following Stalin's death three years earlier. At that point the Kremlin had initiated military détente and general de-Stalinisation in the Soviet Union, and the installation of Imre Nagy and his consequent reforms led to a political thaw in Hungary. Nagy had then been dispensed with in line with a new re-Stalinisation in 1955, but this phase was brief: in February 1956, the tide turned back towards thaw and he became Prime Minister again. In the following months he had pushed through more reforms, and public determination to regain independence, arrange political and economic reforms and allow freedom for the press and religious worship culminated in a vast uprising. The violence that followed, and the many thousands of Hungarians fleeing the country, gave 1956 its historical status.

Political change could only come into effect later. The transition phase saw the new leader János Kádár dealing out vicious retribution to those who had had a prominent role in the thaw years or in the uprising – by then termed 'counter-revolution'. Meanwhile the Vatican condemned the brutal Soviet tactics, and there were mass protests by workers' councils and groups of intellectuals. The Writers' Association and the Journalists' Club – established in the Nagy years – formed a Revolutionary Council of Hungarian Intellectuals, of which Kodály was the Chair.[1] Kádár could thus achieve real consolidation only after these independent groups were disbanded: he abolished the Revolutionary Council and suspended the associations themselves at the end of November. But his government found firm ground only in the year that Nagy and three of his associates were executed, 1958.

Had the terrorising tactics not been counterpointed with enticements, this firm ground would very likely not have been long-lasting. Kádár arranged pay rises and tax cuts, however, and made promises that his government would not return to Stalinism. His effort to disperse Catholic hostility resulted in a tense but ultimately productive relationship between church and state (the latter provided the church's main income and supported

---

[1] Romsics 1999: 316–17.

religious instruction in schools). And he secured an agreement with the Vatican in 1959, after which priests newly appointed by Rome swore allegiance to the Hungarian constitution.[2] Taming the intelligentsia with new journals and Kossuth Prizes, with the help of György Aczél (Deputy Minister for Cultural Affairs 1957–67) in particular, he also established a new arts policy which stated that cultural diversity was a crucial part of socialism. Although the government would still favour the category of 'socialist realism', it would, from then on, also tolerate other arts so long as they did not undermine party principles.[3] Prior to all this negotiation Kádár even offered amnesty to émigrés. Ligeti, who had departed shortly before Christmas in 1956, was not one of them, but between thirty-five and forty thousand of those that had fled chose to return.[4]

Hungarian contexts

In this next section, I plot three paths, initially examining the institutions and printed discourses that shaped music in Budapest, and then tracing the private worlds of Kurtág and Ligeti. These private worlds can be constructed only with frustratingly fragmentary archived letter collections. But they do offer some intriguing insights.

Budapest

1956 was certainly an end for much of Budapest musical life, but revitalisation did proceed in the following year. The government disbanded the monolithic Hungarian Musicians' Union and its journal after the uprising; but it re-established the Union in 1959, and underwrote its new journal, *Magyar Zene* (Hungarian Music) in the following year. *Muzsika*, another new state-sponsored music magazine, was already in circulation in 1958; and the Hungarian Academy of Sciences established a new journal for musicology, *Studia Musicologica*, in 1960.

---

[2] The state regarded the church (and in particular the Catholic church) as a threat, but its strategy was to pressurise its members into state collaboration on various levels; this included coercing a large number of priests into becoming secret agents.

[3] Two well-known catchphrases sum up this new situation. First, Kádár's remark that 'Those who are not against us are with us' (a reversal of Rákosi's slogan in the previous regime), and second, the categorisation of art into what was to be 'boosted', 'bearable' or 'banned' (*támogatott*, *tűrt*, and *tiltott* – the 'Three Ts'). See Ignotus 1972: 263–4 and Romsics 1999: 389. Révész argues in more detail that the boosted category was reserved for socialist realism (understood as the most 'modern' art), the bearable was 'humanist' and non-oppositional, while the banned was art that was understood to be damaging to the People's Democracy. Révész 1997: 101–2.

[4] Romsics 1999: 322.

The Soviet Union continued to shape not only the selection and coverage of events in these publications, but also events themselves. It sent Hungary a veritable stream of performers, organised the unfortunately titled 'Month of the Hungarian–Soviet Friendship' in 1959, and arranged three concerts celebrating the tenth anniversary of the foundation of Hungary's People's Republic in that same year. But the balance had shifted, and the music press offered only minimal coverage of debates from the Soviet Union. In the whole of its first year *Muzsika* only included one short exchange between Shostakovich and Khachaturian about the 'democratisation' of music, and a single article by Tikhon Khrennikov about the new Central Committee Resolution. Soviet rhetoric had been largely expunged, moreover: despite the government's favouring of 'socialist realism', the concept barely figured in *Muzsika* and *Magyar Zene*, and 'formalism' was similarly absent.

Given that Kodály had had a prominent role in the Revolutionary Council and that the chasm between essentialised folkloric and party views remained intact, the question of the national heritage should have been explosive. Neither side, however, addressed it. Instead, the government made a point of entering a new dialogue with Kodály, trying to win his support for its plans and wooing those it termed 'the other group captains of the Hungarian Parnassus'.[5] Kodály gained a third Kossuth Prize, Presidency of the new Hungarian Musicians' Union, and large-scale seventy-fifth birthday celebrations in 1957. *Muzsika* was launched just in time to cover these events, and to devote nearly two thirds of its first issue to tributes and articles about him. Kodály himself, moreover, was apparently equally keen to avoid conflict, and in the early post-uprising years his published statements were carefully ambiguous. Later on he became more straightforward: while on a tour of the Soviet Union in 1963 he played down the impact that early folklorists in Hungary had had on his work, emphasising, rather, the formative influence of the Russian Revolution.[6] On returning home after his trip (during which his *Singspiel, Háry János* was redesigned along party political lines) he reiterated his earlier claim that Hungary had much to learn from the Soviet Union. On both sides, then, there was a new obfuscation of the relations between musical nationalists and communists, Hungary and the Soviet Union.

---

[5] Révész 1997: 109. Many leading individuals who had been involved in the revolution were interned or imprisoned for several years: Kodály's position was exceptional.

[6] The government watched Kodály with some anxiety, even while it allowed him to travel outside and represent Hungary. Péteri 2002 reproduces an extended report prepared for the Ministry of Culture by Tibor Sárai, secretary of the Musicians' Union, in which Kodály's conduct in the Soviet Union was described in detail.

The situation was rather different in another area of potential antagonism, modern music from the West. Here major practical changes were in order, for the government would be pressed to placate musicians desirous of both individual compositional choice and access to new music. Thus although the Musicians' Union and its journal continued to provide fora for debating some works, formal submission and vetting procedures were almost entirely eradicated. For the first time since 1948, moreover, new music from Western Europe could be heard in concert and discussed in the media. Hungarian Radio broadcast a new work each month in a programme entitled 'In Hungary for the First Time' (*Magyarországon először*) and in 1965 established a broadcast series called 'Concert Cycle of Music from Our Century' (*Hangversenyciklus századunk zenéjéből*); the central agency for concert organisation, the National Philharmonia (*Nemzeti filharmónia*) collaborated with the Union to run a series called 'Chamber Music of Our Time' (*Korunk Kamarazenéje*) from 1962. *Magyar Zene* and *Muzsika*, as well as the National Philharmonia's booklets and the daily press, published critical commentaries. They also published articles addressing recent music history, aesthetics and contemporary music, and reported on festivals of new music such as those at Darmstadt and Donaueschingen.

Nevertheless, and despite the government's apparent diversification, there were often spurious bureaucratic obstacles that prevented composers from travelling to such festivals, and the representation of new music in Budapest was actually very small and selective. 'In Hungary for the First Time' concerts usually presented only Hungarian works. Chamber Music of Our Time comprised only five concerts each year and was discontinued in 1965. Moreover, only a limited number of works that were performed were actually explored in printed discourses. The Western works from the twentieth century to be heard in the first six years after 1956 that were also discussed in *Muzsika* were Berg's Chamber Concerto, Britten's *Sinfonia da Requiem*, String Quartet no. 2 and *Albert Herring*; Hindemith's Septet and *Des Todes Tod*; Honegger's Symphony no. 2, 'Symphonie pour cordes', Symphony no. 5 (1950), *Le roi David* and *Jeanne d'Arc*; Orff's *Catulli Carmina*; Seiber's *Besardo Suite* no. 2, String Quartet no. 3 (1948–51) and Clarinet Concertino (1951); Schoenberg's *A Survivor from Warsaw* (1947); Stravinsky's Octet, *A Soldier's Tale* and *Oedipus Rex*. Only four of these had been written after 1945 (and of those four, two were by the Hungarian Seiber, and one was an explicitly anti-fascist work), and the profile and quantity of post-war music performance from the West barely improved for the rest of the decade. In fact, then, composers concerned to learn about contemporary Western music were dependent on new music procured privately. In this sphere shipments from Ligeti were of help, and musicians gathered around people who had record players, such as composer Rudolf Maros.[7]

It is worth making a brief comparison with the situation of writers, who were better served insofar as they had access to a very rich variety of foreign literature in the periodical *Nagyvilág* (Great World) from the spring of 1957 onwards. Composers had no equivalent access to new music.[8] Many writers deemed to be treacherous, however, were barely allowed to appear in print themselves: Weöres' 'Wells of Fire' (*Tűzkút*), for instance, came out in France in 1963, and in Hungary only the following year.[9] Composers heard their new works within orchestral programmes (Farkas' quasi-dodecaphonic Praeludium und Fuga for orchestra of 1947 was finally premièred in 1957, for instance) or in the series of composer-portrait concerts organised by the Musicians' Union. That said, provocative pieces were not heard more than once.

Meanwhile printed discourses reflected the government's line that the country was to make a complete break with Stalinism and create a new order. Writers sought a new style for the new time, and already in 1958 Ujfalussy detected positive signs that Hungarian music was going to move beyond the utter tedium of its past mannered style and become more 'European Hungarian'.[10] Writers also followed the government's embrace of 'diversity': when Szervánszky's pointillist *Six Orchestral Pieces* were premièred in January 1960, nobody in the press denied that they deserved to be heard (once!) and considered along with everything else.[11] And although writers did not respond to the government's favouring of socialist realism, they did respond to its tolerance of so-called 'humanism', commending composers who had 'something to say' (mondanivaló), and sometimes attempting to justify highly provocative pieces with notions of composers' 'honesty'. Jemnitz, for instance, attempted to legitimate Szervánszky's *Six Orchestral Pieces* in just such terms: notwithstanding the work's unmelodic, splintery

---

[7] As composer András Szőllősy (b. 1921) wrote to Ligeti, 'We're cultivating ourselves with Rudi, we go to see him a lot ... we miss your presence. Rudi's got hi-fi, so we can listen to all the new music we get on record or tape from the radio *repetitio ad libitum*. In this respect we are nothing like as uninformed as we were, but in the field in which you're working we have very little acquaintance. We know only one electronic music record – the one with works by Berio, Maderna and another chap – and that's too little for us to form an opinion about it ... I'll go and collect your Boulez article from your mother in the next days ... whether or not I'll understand it, knowing only one Boulez work, *Le marteau sans maitre* ...' Letter Szőllősy to Ligeti, 7 July 1958, PSF, GLC.

[8] Révész 1997: 104–5. Moreover, having the score of a new work cannot be compared with having a copy of a poem, or a novel. Composers often had to imagine what music actually sounded like.

[9] Romsics 1999: 389–91. The publication of Pilinszky's 'On the Third Day' (*Harmadnapon*) in 1959 was a significant exception. I discuss Pilinszky further in Chapter 4.

[10] Ujfalussy 1958a: 31. Ujfalussy had worked in the Ministry between 1950 and 1955 and had become professor at the Liszt Academy in 1955: he was not a politically oppositional figure.

[11] Kovács 1960; Jemnitz 1960; Pernye 1960b.

and fractured character (it could easily have been categorised as 'formalist'), Jemnitz contrived to attribute its style to the composer's 'inner voice'.[12]

Composers, of course, were keen for a new order as well. But their main concern in the later 1950s and early 1960s was neither 'diversity' nor 'humanism': they simply wanted to study the technique they most associated with the West, namely dodecaphony. There was consequently a significant conflict between composers and commentators. For leading broadsheet critic András Pernye, Szervánszky's new work was just a rehash of inter-war modernism, and thus couldn't hope to speak to more than a small group of avant-gardists.[13] Others laughed at how young composers could be entranced by the fifty-year-old technique of dodecaphony. More than one discussed the historical fallacy that blinded young composers into thinking that dodecaphony was more advanced than the music of Bartók.[14]

Despite the putatively 'diversified' and 'new' regime, then, writers held deeply entrenched positions. Of course these were partly a consequence of the government's covertly restrictive directives, but they had a long history behind them: as we have seen, these particular views were common currency in the inter-war and post-war periods and fed directly into the dogma of the regime in 1949. Resurging in the late 1950s, they were laced with an alarmist rhetoric that hinted more knowingly about links between dodecaphony and fascism.[15] In other words, the regime's directives functioned to extend and justify national self-censorship along very traditional musical lines. Ujfalussy warned Ferenc Farkas away from 'deep serialism', contrasting it with the world of the 'day' and referring darkly to an 'apocalypse'.[16] Pernye proposed that composers who wrote dodecaphonic music 'did nothing but fear and tremble' and 'retreat into death'. He too referred to an 'apocalypse', describing how Schoenberg, Berg and Webern brought forth 'only irresolvable problems, the horrors from which there is no way out and within which even death seems a transfiguration'.[17] When critics heard Schoenberg's *A Survivor from Warsaw* in 1961 they were confirmed in their long-held views about dodecaphony: one asserted that the 'terror, death and apocalyptic horror' of the work was revealed because its primary compositional principle, dodecaphony, was 'above all suited to portraying darkness, and shocking the listener'.[18]

---

[12] This is particularly clear in Jemnitz 1960: 34; but see also Kovács 1960 and Pernye 1960b.
[13] Pernye 1960b.
[14] Gergely 1965: 37; V. 1963: 19. Ujfalussy pointed out that mainstream Europe had already moved beyond dodecaphony into *musique concrète*. Ujfalussy 1958b: 27.
[15] Concert reviewers did not mention Adorno's related suggestions of the same period. See note 23 below.
[16] Ujfalussy 1961: 82.   [17] Pernye 1961c (part II): 29–31.   [18] Breuer 1961a: 37.

Additionally, however, writers were still clinging to the moral of Thomas Mann's novel *Doctor Faustus* to which I referred in Chapter 2 above. When they discussed dodecaphony's 'hedonism', 'speculation' and 'unrestrained, irrational intuition', they were drawing directly on that allegory, invoking the tragic end of Mann's anti-hero Adrian Leverkühn.[19] The ongoing importance of Leverkühn can partly – but only partly – be explained by the limited alternative resources in circulation. To be sure, one critic remarked of the country's first post-war monograph about music from the twentieth century that until reading it, all his knowledge about dodecaphony had been gleaned from *Doctor Faustus*.[20] But the novel's pervasiveness overflows this explanation: it was actually a product of Hungary's long-established reverence for its author. Mann had been a vital symbol of anti-fascist hope for Hungarian intellectuals in the 1930s, and his three unofficial visits in that decade had tremendous political resonance. He was then (and for many remained) a voice of irrevocable 'truth': one commentator described him as 'the voice of the future humanism, the voice of reason', and proclaimed that 'from [Mann] we learned the truth of the everyday and the great truths'.[21]

Yet not only the iconic esteem of Mann was at play in the late 1950s, but also the teaching of former Professor of Philosophy Georg Lukács, whose article on Mann (also mentioned in Chapter 2) was geared towards speculation about the future.[22] Lukács had read *Doctor Faustus* not merely as a condemnation of a Faustian composer, but also as a vision of an alternative life. Mann's epilogue, said Lukács, was 'also a prologue', for Leverkühn instructed his audience to learn from his lesson and never to turn away from the good and humane in the world.[23] Thus in 1960 (his student) aesthetician Dénes Zoltai used *Muzsika* to claim of the closing pages of *Doctor Faustus* that:

---

[19] Pernye, 1961c (part I): 21. In 1961 Ujfalussy warned Farkas that he was actually becoming 'like Leverkühn'. Ujfalussy 1961.

[20] Keszi 1961 reviewing Fábián and Kókai 1961. Their interest in technicalities notwithstanding, Fábián and Kókai also remark that Schoenberg's true significance is to be found in Thomas Mann's novel *Doctor Faustus*, in which he is 'emblematic not only of modern music, but of the whole of modern art'. Fábián and Kókai 1961: 98. His true significance, surely, was providing a negative model.

[21] Pál Ignotus, 'Thomas Mann' (1937), reprinted German translation in Mádl and Győri (eds.) 1977: 129–32. These references at 130 and 132. It is worth noting that in the same year, Molnár considered Kodály to be a musical equivalent of Mann in his renewal of a 'great artistic ethos'. See Molnár 1937: 14.

[22] Lukács' esteem on returning to Budapest from Moscow in 1945 had been high, and he became Professor of Aesthetics and Philosophy at the University in Budapest. Although he was stripped of this position after taking a leading role in the Revolutionary Council in 1956, by that time his teaching had been absorbed by a significant number of young writers on music, János Maróthy and Ujfalussy included.

[23] Lukács, 'The Tragedy of Modern Art' (1948), in Lukács 1964: 47–97, at 97. At the time of writing, he was attempting to bring about a Plebeian democracy in Hungary, a (Marx-inspired) government that would be distinct from the Soviet Union.

> Herein [in Leverkühn's dying words] lies the only way out . . . If the modern artist places his heart and art at the service of the triumph of future humanity . . . then he can move beyond the alienation and materialism that enchains avant-gardism. Only thus can there be a way back from the depths of hell into the humane world, where art testifies not only to the unutterable sufferings of mankind, but declares its faith in the justice and the coming triumph in the battle against barbarism.[24]

Mediated by Lukács, *Doctor Faustus* thus remained a perfect bolster for the entrenched national musical mythology. Zoltai reiterated the tale according to which Schoenbergian types had 'merely accepted' the horrors around them and had represented them in music while Bartók had looked beyond them, but he drew on Mann to assert that if an artist withdrew into individual suffering and subjectivity, he might be tempted *by Mephistopheles himself* to construct an over-rationalised means through which to organise his art. Because for Mann such means symbolised both 'bloodless intellectualism' and 'bloody barbarism', Zoltai too argued that artists should not be allowed to withdraw into isolation, but must remain in contact with the human world around them.[25]

But Zoltai and all the other writers taking this line faced a conflict that was more fundamental than the one between state-tolerated 'humanism' and composers' concern for dodecaphony. Essentially their narratives were only useful for rehearsing a national myth, and that myth had no appeal to the new generation. Young composers had responded to the government's tolerance of diversity and embraced the technique that symbolised the country's musical 'other'. Their music was thus in such conflict with the national ideal that commentators struggled to articulate an identity for it, let alone affirm a national renaissance.

The absent national discourse is revealed most acutely in the reception of *C'est la guerre* (1961), an opera by the young Emil Petrovics (b. 1930). *C'est la guerre* is an unmistakable product of the period, because it uses an apparently dodecaphonic opening to set the scene of fascist Hungary during the Second World War. It nonetheless provoked a furore in the Hungarian Musicians' Union, because it was politically delicate. The historical resolution to fascism

---

[24] Zoltai 1960: 29. Zoltai might have drawn usefully on Adorno's own suggestion of a parallel between integrated serialism and totalitarianism in 'Das Altern der neuen Musik', first published in *Der Monat* in 1955, later extended in 1956 in *Dissonanzen: Musik in der verwalteten Welt* (Göttingen: Vandenhoeck and Ruprecht, 136–59). It seems that he had read it, because although he did not identify his source, a few months later he discussed Adorno's critical discussion of Bartók that appears within it (see Zoltai 1961). Indeed this was his main interest, because rather than engaging with Adorno's proposal about dodecaphony, he simply defended Bartók against Adorno's 'bourgeois' criticisms, and rehearsed a defence of the use of folk music as a compositional resource.

[25] Mann 1961: 126.

in Hungary had been the Red Army's 'liberation' of the city from German occupation, but the opera did not include the liberation at all: it closed instead with the arrest of the two leading male characters and the suicide of the heroine.[26] Additionally, it touched on a barely addressed national shame: the soldiers in the opera, although depicted with a note row, were evidently not German at all. They were Hungarian.

Had the opera been written ten years earlier, it would surely have been attacked for not presenting the Red Army's glorious liberation of 1945. By 1961, however, even while that event was no longer celebrated so vacuously, it could not be discussed critically any more than could the repression of 1956. Thus, silenced on the subject of the Soviet actions, speakers were forced to engage with the opera's suggestion that Hungarians had been too passive to resist their (compatriot) fascists. On one level, the opera confronted them with a historical parallel for the situation in which they themselves lived, namely a partial gagging under occupation, and a violently negotiated impasse. On another, as they faced an opera about one of the most vile episodes in the country's history, they lacked the impetus to construct a strong narrative about the nation's music.[27] In response they intimated a desire for something positive, a longing for something sincere, and asserted vaguely that the opera should have drawn on musical techniques other than dodecaphonic ones. In other words, they avoided the conflicts presented in the libretto, and camouflaged themselves in the obfuscatory rhetoric of humanism.

Kurtág, at home

The personal recollections that Kurtág has offered since 1956 can only really hint at how he passed the revolution and made the musical transformation that his String Quartet op. 1 reflects. We gather he had something like a nervous breakdown in the wake of the uprising and the subsequent clampdown (as if the nature of the Soviet Union became suddenly clear to him for the first time), and that he reconstructed himself with great difficulty while studying with Messiaen and working therapeutically with Marianne Stein in Paris in 1957 and 1958. Famously, he stopped off to visit Ligeti in Cologne on the way home and heard recordings of Stockhausen's *Gruppen* and Ligeti's *Artikulation*, experiences that he felt made a yet more powerful impression than had his studies.

---

[26] I discuss responses to this opera in detail in Beckles Willson 2003.
[27] The exception was András Pernye's hollow claim in the press that the opera was the 'birthday' of Hungarian opera. I return to this in the Epilogue.

We can thicken out this account only fractionally with remarks made by Ferenc Sulyok (a friend of both Kurtág and Ligeti who had moved to Paris in 1949) and Ferenc Farkas (with whom Ligeti studied in Kolozsvár, and Kurtág, in Budapest). Writing to Ligeti in 1958, Sulyok mentioned hearing that the Kurtágs were looking terrible. He blamed what he called 'Gyuri's masochism', presumably a reference to Kurtág's crisis of conscience of 1956.[28] Then in the following year he asked Ligeti whether the rumour was true that Kurtág had written a string quartet and sent it to him.[29] Farkas also mentioned the string quartet to Ligeti when he wrote in 1961, yet he referred only tantalisingly briefly to the 'scandal' that it had created.[30]

A single letter from Kurtág to Ligeti that he wrote while composing the quartet adds a little further background.[31] Apparently responding to a question from Ligeti regarding which Universal Edition scores he possessed, Kurtág wrote that he had only those already provided by Ligeti, namely Webern's Variations for Piano, op. 27 and Stockhausen's Piano Pieces I–IV. He had also copied out Webern's opp. 5, 6, 10, 21, 22, 28 and 30, however, and had four volumes of *die reihe*. In passing he mentioned that one composer was causing a great deal of excitement: Rudolf Maros, about whose talent Kurtág himself was sceptical.[32] (As mentioned above, however, Maros was important for his possession of a record player.)

The most striking part of the letter is the section addressed to Ligeti directly. Kurtág's devoted admiration combined with his genuine sense of inadequacy bespeaks a complex friendship indeed:

> I know how busy you are, but if you had time occasionally to write about what you're composing, in the way you described your compositions in Paris, that would be a great help. And if there are any drafts of your lectures

---

[28] Kurtág became strongly critical of the Soviet regime only at the time of the 1956 revolution, and became deeply self-critical thereafter in consequence. For his own recollections see Dibelius (ed.) 1993: 108, and for further discussion, Beckles Willson 2001 and 2004a. Sulyok letter to Ligeti, 22 July, no year provided. References to Cologne and Ligeti's Webern book suggest that it is 1958. PSF, GLC. Ligeti entertained the idea of turning his Webern radio lectures into a book at this time. See Borio's discussion of Ligeti's Webern reception in 'Strukturen im chromatischem Raum: die Webern-Seminare von Pousseur und Ligeti', in Borio and Danuser (eds.) 1997: 249–66, at 261–66.

[29] Sulyok letter to Ligeti, 16 October 1959. (The year is not provided, but references – such as to the sudden death of violinist Ede Zathureczky – indicate that it is 1959.) PSF, GLC.

[30] Farkas letter to Ligeti, 12 April 1961. PSF, GLC.

[31] Kurtág letter to Ligeti. PSF, GLC. It is not entirely clear, but it seems that Ligeti had written to Kurtág, who provided him with an address and some information he had requested. There is no trace of letters from Ligeti to Kurtág.

[32] Kurtág letter to Ligeti. PSF, GLC. Kurtág referred to Maros as 'the Hungarian Dürrenmatt', drawing on Ligeti's thoughts about Dürrenmatt (these are untraced, but it is clear that they were at the very least mildly derogatory). Kurtág used a Romanian proverb to suggest that although Maros was being praised for his boldness and really was writing in a comparatively fresh tone, the change was superficial. ('*Vulpea îsi schimbă piclea, dar naraval-ba*', translatable literally as 'a fox can change its skin but it will keep its old habits'.)

(even the hundred-minute radio introductions would be helpful, like the one for Boulez's Third Sonata) those would be useful, please send them too. Once the string quartet pieces are finished I definitely want to show them to you. You certainly won't like them, I think they come together better than the Paris pieces, what I heard in Cologne didn't fail to make an impact, but I think it will be a long time before I am capable of writing an acceptable piece of music. I saw a couple of your letters at your mother's, in contrast to her and you I am not anxious about your future, I feel everything will work out just as I've foreseen for many years, before long some kind of acceptable solution will emerge of its own accord.

I won't write more now, and I've just realised that I still haven't thanked you for your hospitality in Cologne. I still love you very very much, but I can neither say it nor write it.[33]

Ligeti, escaped

Kurtág was, of course, right to be confident about his friend. Ligeti rapidly switched from being an anonymous refugee to a significant and popular teacher at the Darmstadt Summer School. His compositions caused tremendous excitement, and his essays – published in the most important specialist journals of the time – provoked prestigious controversy. Karl Woerner's notorious description of his arrival in Cologne does little to complicate this success story: the tale of a man refusing food, losing consciousness, awaking in a frenzy of speech about new music and collapsing back into a twenty-four-hour sleep is simply an entertaining caricature. Nevertheless, and despite Ligeti's complaint that Woerner had been 'unnecessarily dramatic', it would be impoverishing to dismiss the impact of emigration when we reconsider these years, especially as Ligeti's letters to compatriots suggest a prolonged moment of in-between-ness, a struggle to find the future amidst an obliteration of the past.[34]

The correspondence is not extensive, but it is diverse. Sulyok, mentioned above, sent letters that were often gossipy about his and Ligeti's mutual friends, and he made romantic liaisons a regular theme. Sulyok followed Ligeti's work with great interest, and Ligeti sent him his scores as soon as they were published. Kálmán Halász, another friend from Budapest, was in Paris between 1956 and 1958, and wrote a number of times from Texas between 1958 and 1960 about his subsequent struggles there. Ligeti also exchanged

---

[33] Kurtág letter to Ligeti. PSF, GLC.
[34] Woerner 1973: 237. (German edition published in 1963.) Ligeti quoted in Nordwall 1971: 61. (Swedish original 1968.)

letters with more senior, relatively established Hungarian émigrés. Sándor Veress was one, UK-based composer Mátyás Seiber was another, but his most consistent correspondent was John S. Weissmann (already mentioned in Chapter 2 as a correspondent of Veress).

Weissmann, like Seiber and Veress, provided letters of recommendation and also personal introductions wherever possible, and additionally, some journalistic coverage. Visiting Budapest to report on a Bartók Festival for *The Music Review* in October 1956, he had taken the trouble to seek out young composers absent from the programme. He had thus used his review not only to praise Szervánszky's *Concerto In Memory of Attila József*, but also Halász, Maros, Béla Tardos and Ligeti for their fluency, liveliness and – in the case of Ligeti – individuality.[35] He would go on to write more about Ligeti in *Tempo* some time later.[36] But to assume that professional advancement was Ligeti's sole concern in their exchanges would be a mistake. The letters were also an outlet for his more personal reflections about emigration. Writing in Hungarian, to a Hungarian who knew Budapest, allowed him a dialogue that was impossible with new friends. As he wrote to Weissmann in July 1957, 'I'd also like to ask you to write to me if time allows. You can't imagine how good it is in this foreignness.'[37]

At the risk of oversimplifying what was surely a complex process of negotiation, we can map two basic threads in Ligeti's letter writing. Initially there was a discussion of the loathsomeness of Hungary, which involved a sort of self-purgation, something immediately evident in both Sulyok's and Veress's letters too. Sulyok told Ligeti he had bought a score of János Viski's Piano Concerto, just to check that he wasn't becoming like Viski himself.[38] Veress applauded Ligeti's initial step out of Hungary, and unleashed a torrent of criticism about the state of music back home, where even without the crushing influence of the mediocre Szabó, he said, the 'provincial . . . pentatonic running on the spot' was so intolerable.[39]

Ligeti's six-page response to Veress was yet more cutting. He located the key to his own intolerance of the situation as claustrophobia, and he made it clear that things had become far worse after the older composer had left in 1949:

---

[35] Weissmann 1957a: 54–6. By the time it was published, Ligeti was out of Hungary, and responded enthusiastically, claiming to 'agree with him 100%'. Ligeti postcard to Weissmann, 24 April 1957. GLC, PSF. Microfilm 109.1: 001173. One senses that Ligeti was practising a diplomacy that preserved his contact with Weissmann, for the latter praised many aspects of Hungarian music (in particular music of the communist Tardos) that were obviously anathema to Ligeti.

[36] See Weissmann 1958: 28–9. This is the last in a series of four articles surveying Hungarian composers of the twentieth century.

[37] PSF, GLC, Microfilm 109.1: 001181.

[38] Sulyok letter to Ligeti, 6 June 1963. PSF, GLC. János Viski was a minor composer whose name has surfaced above as a speaker in debates at the Union.

[39] Veress to Ligeti, Bern, 19 December 1956. PSF, SVC.

After 1956: the parting of ways

> Life at home [in Hungary], the horrors of the everyday, the delicate mechanisms of the regime, the way one is not simply a victim, but is at once involuntarily a part and practitioner of the tyranny . . . the unstoppable inhuman automatisation, this you can sense fully only inside, in the inner recesses of the machine.[40]

His letters to Weissmann were also quite detailed. He explained a little about the conditions in Budapest as follows:

> It's no coincidence that it was Halász and I that left. We didn't toe the official Soviet Szabó line, but nor did we belong to the clique of conservative 'magyaros' Kodály followers. From an artistic perspective our situation was impossible quite beyond the political pressures which dominated everything: not merely because we were kept in the background without performing and publishing opportunities, but because we suffered in an unbearable airlessness, shut away from European music and culture. My departure isn't a 'little expedition' to Europe. Naturally I'd be happiest if I could live in Hungary – were it possible.[41]

And six months later:

> The primary reason that I left – and I have, nonetheless, dreadful homesickness – abandoning my 'prestigious' teaching post at the Academy with its secure existence, leaping into complete uncertainty, was that I found the parochial self-satisfied lack of atmosphere unbearable.[42]

And with Weissmann he also had some candid exchanges of view about the future of music, because Weissmann continued to cherish hope in Hungarian music on the Soviet path:

> Another way out, and it's a truly important one, is the Soviet model, the socialist realist path, if you like. I can see already you're throwing away this letter, or smiling sourly: 'so they were right when they held W. to be an *agent provocateur*' etc. But I'm serious; although I take things much more seriously than the late comrades. For I think it's crucial that today's composer find the path to the 'broad masses', or abolishes the gulf separating the creative musician and the audience . . .
>
> I don't entirely share your view about Hungarian music at home, that it's epigonism. A large part of it is, that's true, and it's not even good quality epigonism – which would be the Bartók style – but the heavy and completely outdated Kodály stink![43]

---

[40] Letter to Sándor Veress, dated '1956 Christmas'. PSF, SVC.
[41] Ligeti letter to Weissmann, 25 January 1957. PSF, GLC, Microfilm 109.1: 001167.
[42] Ligeti letter to Weissman, 12 July 1957. PSF, GLC, Microfilm 109.1: 001185–86.
[43] Weissmann letter to Ligeti, 9 July 1957. PSF, GLC, Microfilm 109.1: 001182. In spring 1957 Weissmann attempted (unsuccessfully) to gain information about composers there in order to write about them in *Tempo*: in a letter dated 30 May 1957 he complained that the composers

Ligeti took the opposing position:

> I can't agree with you with respect to the 'soc. rea.' way out. There are some who can do that sort of thing well, on a high level (like Britten and Orff frequently do) but one either has this capacity or one doesn't.[44]

Nevertheless, it was far from easy for Ligeti to find a place in his new environment, and this concern offers the other main thread to map in his writing. It was simple to oppose socialist realism, and criticise the 'spineless' way in which Hungarian intellectuals compromised themselves and were contained by the regime (Kodály came into this category for shaking hands with the new President once the uprising had been beaten down and – without comment – accepting a government Kossuth Prize).[45] But identifying his own way forward was more tricky. First, he still felt part of the mess he had left behind:

> The tragedy of recent Hungarian music is that not only the officials, but even composers themselves have overstressed 'accessibility', and a freakish product has emerged which interests neither the 'broad masses' nor the *Fachidioten*... Of course I can't pass judgement about Hungarian music in this way, because I'm swimming in it myself, and to this day haven't really clambered beyond epigonism. I was different from the others only in so far that I sensed there was a problem, and didn't sit self-satisfied on my special bonuses, content with the fact that I was played.[46]

Second, even though he had shifted himself out of that unpleasant milieu, the new environment was far from inviting. Moving temporarily from Vienna (where 'every third person' was Hungarian[47]) to Cologne, he found the post-war landscape disturbing and 'foreign': it established an 'atmosphere' (significantly, he used this word repeatedly) that was 'surrealistically bizarre'. In his description, 'the more mushroom-like hypermodern neon blocks spring up, the more the ruins emanate their mood of death – the corpses and the living... it has a peculiarly acrid flavour'. Cologne Cathedral, in the midst of this space, was 'like a dream'.[48]

Furthermore it was not only the architecture that disturbed him, but also the people. Reflecting on his career options to Weissmann, he could see that the country had a lot to offer, but wrote with some desperation, 'If

---

didn't recognise the help he could give them, and in another, dated 9 July of the same year, explained (at Ligeti's request) in more detail. Composers had turned against him as a result of his (alleged) opinions about works he heard at the Bartók festival, and refused to cooperate. See PSF, GLC, Microfilm 109.1: 001176 and 001183.

[44] Ligeti letter to Weissmann, 12 July 1957. PSF, GLC, Microfilm 109.1: 001185.
[45] Ligeti letter to Veress, 1 April 1957. PSF, SVC.
[46] Ligeti letter to Weissmann, 12 July 1957. PSF, GLC, Microfilm 109.1: 001185.
[47] Ligeti letter to Veress, Vienna, Christmas 1956. PSF, SVC.
[48] Ligeti letter to Veress, 20 February 1957. PSF, SVC.

After 1956: the parting of ways

only I didn't hate Germany so much! I couldn't live here for long.'[49] Yet his attempts to settle elsewhere were fruitless for some time. He asked for Veress's help in getting work in Switzerland (where he had the possibility of gaining residency), but this was to no avail. Indeed while Veress had been apparently sympathetic initially, he ultimately rejected the work of the postwar avant-gardists (later he would denigrate Ligeti's *Volumina* in particular).[50]

In these unsettling circumstances, however, Ligeti was nevertheless finding his feet by investigating the music of Boulez and Stockhausen, and marking out his difference from it. 'If they're like Mondrian, I'd rather be like Klee,' he wrote to Veress.[51] By April 1957 he was enthusiastically 'up to his neck' in electronic composition, while maintaining what he called 'a certain feeling of distance'. At the studio, he explained, 'the view of music is rather one-sided'.[52] As he wrote to Weissmann in July:

> I've had the occasion to get to know all these works (meaning everything by Boulez, Nono, Stockhausen, Berio, Maderna etc. etc.) . . . in particular I feel Nono to be significant (his most recent work, for instance, the 'Canto sospeso'). I think Boulez's 'Marteau' is a very beautiful work too. But I feel the great importance which the composers (Stockhausen in particular) ascribe to themselves is a bit exaggerated. I think, as do you, that the father of the whole movement is Webern, who is by far the greatest, in fact he's incomparably greater than his young followers. I feel the importance of the movement is that it is the only way out of the stagnation into which music had descended.[53]

By this time he had made the analysis of Boulez' *Structures Ia* that would position him in the pages of *die reihe* in the following year, and he was also working on his own electronic compositions.[54] It is perhaps unsurprising

---

[49] Ligeti letter to Weissmann, 12 July 1957. PSF, GLC, Microfilm 109.1: 001185–86. See also Ligeti letter to Veress, 1 April 1957. PSF, SVC.

[50] Veress letter to Ligeti, 3 October 1958, in response to Ligeti's letter explaining that he had everything he needed for Swiss residency apart from employment (10 September 1958). For Veress's opinion of the postwar avant-garde and of Ligeti, see his letters to János Demény, 17 March 1962 and 2 May 1968. PSF, SVC. As a recently published letter reveals, Ligeti wrote to Varèse in the USA and asked for his assistance in what he termed 'the re-establishment of my life', but apparently received no answer. In Meyer and Zimmerman (eds.) 2006: 403.

[51] Ligeti letter to Veress, Vienna, Christmas 1956. PSF, SVC. This was conceivably an attempt to charm Veress, whose *Hommage à Paul Klee* was a sign of his own enthusiasm for the painter. See Chapter 2 above.

[52] Ligeti letter to Veress, 1 April 1957. PSF, SVC.

[53] Ligeti to Weissmann, 7 July 1957. PSF, GLC, Microfilm 109.1: 001179–80. Ligeti wrote somewhat differently to Veress and Weissmann, for to Veress he *complained* that the only composer to be recognised at the Cologne studio was Webern. Conceivably, again, he attempted to ingratiate himself with Veress, for whom Webern was uninteresting. (See footnote 51.)

[54] As he wrote to Veress: 'I haven't composed for a while because I was asked to write an article on Boulez. It wasn't musical, but rather like a decoding . . . the new techniques open up a lot of possibilities, but the creativity begins only after the automated processes.' Ligeti letter to Veress, 1 April 1957. PSF, SVC. See Ligeti 1958.

in this light that his exchanges with Weissmann – whose interests clearly lay elsewhere – dwindled thereafter, as did the patchier correspondence with Veress. He lost another Hungarian contact in 1960 with the death of Seiber; and his communications with Halász seem to have fizzled out at about that time; those with Sulyok, in 1963. Ligeti had a new circle of contacts by then. Had his Hungarian past become useless to him?

Juxtapositions

On the most obvious level, of course it had, so there is little point in attempting to read Ligeti's music in the context of Hungary's parallel musical development. And to read Kurtág's music against this context would offer nothing new.[55] Instead, what follows is an alternative and parallel history, a construction of their works as outgrowths of the previous era, using three basic ideas central to discussions of Hungarian music historically – music in language, language in music, and music as 'language' (reflecting darkness and light). Juxtaposing Kurtág and Ligeti under each of these headings can suggest how each moved forward through their specific pasts (even by attempting to obliterate them) and how their very different solutions – mediated by their different environments – may set one another into relief.

Language as music

Recalling the training that they shared, and acknowledging that – even if introduced by the regime – prosody was taught in interesting ways by a musician whom they both respected (Lajos Bárdos), it is perhaps unsurprising that both Ligeti and Kurtág retained a sensitivity to the 'music' inherent to language. But it was not prosodic text-setting that would be a feature of their work, nor a concern with setting texts that respected their inherent music and rendered them comprehensible to the listener. Least of all was it an ethnographic concern, or a national political one. Rather, some of their abstract works contain rhetorical moments, 'embodied' rhythms, folk-music types and discursive textures. These moments can be traced not only in Ligeti's *Metamorphoses nocturnes*, but also in his String Quartet no. 2 (1968), bespeaking an understanding of music as something akin to talking. As Borio has argued, implicitly drawing on Adorno's work on Bartók and his conception of rationality versus mimesis, they distinguish Ligeti's music from that of the abstract serialists and secure it a 'human' quality.[56]

---

[55] See Beckles Willson 2004a for a discussion of the context for, and reception of, Kurtág's work of this period, *The Sayings of Péter Bornemisza* in particular.
[56] Borio 1984.

Example 3.1. Kurtág, String Quartet op. 1, movement 1, bb. 1–5

Adorno's notion of such 'human' music might be used to illuminate Kurtág's conception of speech patterns as compositional armatures, because his concern with musical rhetoric stimulated him to analyse both his own music, and that of others, in terms of poetic feet. He observed, for example, that the opening of his String Quartet (see Ex. 3.1) was basically a dactyl;

Example 3.2. Kurtág, analytical note to Ligeti's sound blocks

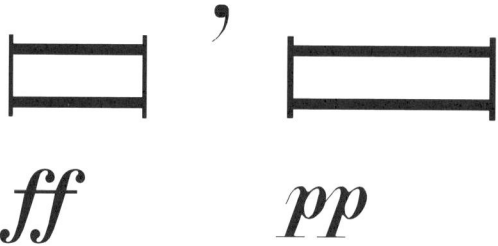

and the opening of *Signs*, op. 5, was a trochee.⁵⁷ Noting down his thoughts on what were for him the basic units of music, he also observed that:

> in fact with Ligeti, a sound mass connects immediately to the succeeding one – one plus another, or one plus more than one other becomes a group, or the succeeding one instantly becomes the second part of the basic unit, thus [see Ex. 3.2] . . . can be perceived as a spondee or trochee.⁵⁸

The use of the phrase 'can be perceived as' indicates the way the thinking was to do with realisation in sound, rather than abstract structural armature. Kurtág was concerned, then, with precisely the sort of enacting, living mimesis that Adorno regarded as critical in the preservation of the artwork in over-mechanised modernity.

One might explore this tendency in the first of the Eight Piano Pieces op. 3, in which an ostinato provides a sort of grid within which rather less methodically arranged elements are situated and allowed to erode. Diffuse registral positioning of symmetrical and twelve-note constellations, as well as the rapidity of pitch change, create an sense of instability; they also ensure that the pitch organisation is masked to the extent of being inaudible. (See Ex.3.3.) The ostinato is further destabilised by indeterminate rhythmic elements: rests between the groups are lengthened by two unmeasured commas (one before and one after a silent barline), for instance. The top two staves' entries are also notated without specific temporal values. Pre-publication sketches for the 'Key to signs' demonstrate that each comma was originally to be understood as 'like a breath'.⁵⁹ The groups of grace notes were to be played 'always melodically, not fast, but in the context of the *espressivo* or more deeply struck notes merely *as if spoken in brackets*'.⁶⁰ The

---

⁵⁷ Sketchbook q to op. 7, p. 13. PSF, György Kurtág Collection (GKC).
⁵⁸ Sketchbook q to op. 7, p. 15. PSF, GKC.
⁵⁹ PSF, GFK. Loose sheets in folder labelled 'Jelmagyarázat' [Key to signs], in sketches to Eight Piano Pieces op. 3, page 1r.
⁶⁰ PSF, GKC. Loose sheets in folder labelled 'Jelmagyarázat' [Key to signs], in sketches to Eight Piano Pieces op. 3, page 2r. [my italics].

Example 3.3. Kurtág, Eight Piano Pieces op. 3, movement 1, extract

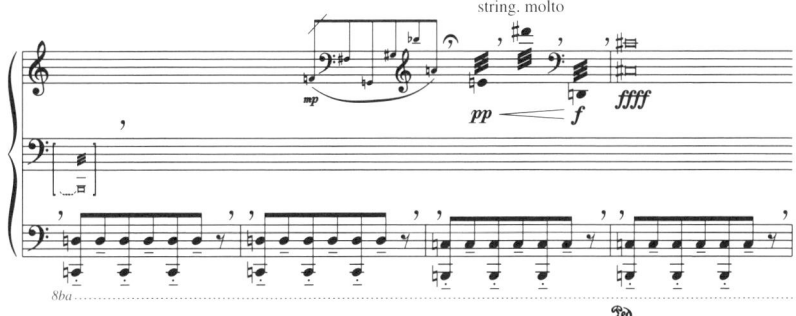

monotone passage *come campane* was also given expressive indications – prosody signs – so that musical imitations of gasps and gestures can transform this otherwise mechanical ostinato into something rather rugged and animalistic.

′∪ | – – ∪ | – – ∪ | – – ∪′.[61]

It is doubtful, however, that the rather minimal structure into which these mimetic gestures are placed creates anything approaching the tension that Adorno sought between the two. Rather, the emphasis on the gestural mimetic quality of the music renders it unextendable: it longs for music to sigh, gasp and have convulsions. Then it ends. It manifestly fails as an Adornian social critique, hovering, rather in a space resistant to appropriation for narrative utopia. (This was clear to Hungarian critic Pernye, who would argue that Kurtág's music spoke only of his own suffering rather than lighting the way forward for others.[62])

---

[61] PSF, GKC. Loose sheets in folder labelled 'Jelmagyarázat' [Key to signs], in sketches to Eight Piano Pieces op. 3, page 2r.
[62] Pernye 1962.

That Ligeti's *Aventures* – a far more overt use of linguistic mimesis – could be a channel for Adornian utopia was clear to many who wrote about it early on. Indeed the Frankfurt School view overwhelmingly characterised its reception. Linguist Hans G. Helms, for example, argued that *Aventures* staged the reified gestures of modern society and then attacked them with historically reflective compositional materials. For Helms the work was important for its critique of the dehumanising processes of an anonymous, cliché-ridden world.[63] Klüppelholz was as keen as Helms to argue for the work's social meaning. Drawing on linguistic theory, he attempted to translate the meanings of the singers' 'texts' according to elemental shifts in pitch, and argued that there was a movement from speech to music and back to speech that underlay the large-scale form. He suggested that it tried – by removing the semantic element in vocal music – to make music say the unsayable.[64] In other commentaries *Aventures* emerged as a sort of culmination and critical summation of contemporary music theatre.[65] Alternatively, writers focused on its rationalisable complexity: Kaufmann analysed *Aventures* in terms of its disruption of logical structure and its creation of absurdity thereby. His emphasis on structural layers draws on Ligeti's own introduction to the piece, and resonates with the need to assert the work's planned, non-arbitrary basis, as well as to justify its traditional formal underpinning.[66]

All these critical structuralist arguments, however, bypass the equally notable – if unsettlingly embarrassing – fact that *Aventures* begins with overt gasping and panting. Could it be that *Aventures*' provocative pantomimicry triggered these urgently rationalising responses from its listeners in an automatic gesture of repression? Is it not possible that the overtly visceral aspect to the piece was unsettling to the extent that it needed to be put instantly into a political, historical or abstract framework? For does the presentation of singers making all these carefully directed sounds ('ironically', 'affectedly' and 'coquettishly'), not grate against our expectations that they will sing words? Do these noises not invade us with their blatant corporeality, make themselves disturbingly *felt*, and remind us of language while also failing to provide us with the concepts that language is supposed to transmit?

---

[63] Helms 1999 (1966): 343.   [64] Klüppelholz 1995 (1976).
[65] Helms 1999 (1966): 343. Paul Op de Coul's article about *Lux aeterna* attached a section on *Aventures* at the end, so that it represented a sort of exceptional extreme within his framework. Op de Coul 1974: 68–9. Werner Klüppelholz drew the piece into the debates about music's relation with language and when his article was collected into a book it formed the end of the final section entitled 'Music as Language'. Klüppelholz 1995 (1976): 120 and 142.
[66] 'Ein Fall absurder Musik: Ligeti *Aventures* und *Nouvelles aventures*', in Kaufmann 1969: 150–8, at 136–8. This article, although its technical expliqués may seem somewhat worn, is exceptionally and illuminatingly thoughtful.

They are 'there', hideously, but conceptual meanings are quite outside them.

The libretto for a scenic version, which Ligeti wrote while composing, might argue otherwise, for it contains a sort of plot, with dancers and mime artists.[67] Yet this scenic version is most suggestive of a parallel bizarre play on meaning and its puzzling deficit. Within bar 47, no fewer than four characters will seem to embody the baritone (who hides behind a screen): an Olympic runner who rushes onto the stage and gesticulates as if singing the baritone's first phrase; a mime artist who looks like and acts like the still-invisible, singing, baritone, i.e. a Doppelgänger; a Doppelgänger of the Doppelgänger who does the same; and then finally the baritone will leap out from behind his screen, as if doubling himself by some trick. Meanwhile a monster, and no ordinary monster but a *golem*, has walked onto the stage.

Of all literary figures, this monster of Kabbalistic legend is the one most associated with language. It is told traditionally that golems were made from clay and might be brought to life with the magical letters spelling out 'emeth', the Hebrew word for 'truth'; their life could be drained away again by erasing the 'E' inscribed on their foreheads so that 'emeth' became 'meth', meaning death. According to Kabbalistic mysticism, God created the universe itself from the *sefiroth*, or numbers, combined with the twenty-two consonants of the Hebrew alphabet: the creation of a golem was a parallel act of creation, and the invocation of the name of God would be an animating force in that act.[68]

And yet Ligeti's golem has minimal impact; and even what impact there is, is disjointed, not timed to follow on as if causal. Other than the Olympic runner who collapses in terror, nobody notices it arrive; and nobody notices that the Olympic runner has collapsed. There is no musical registering of these events at all. Somewhat later, the two mime artists notice the golem. But they then forget about it almost instantly. Once again, there is no musical registration. Finally everybody notices the golem and the singers start shrieking. The golem disappears.

Where is the mysticism of the golem? Where is its weighty symbolism, its mysterious connection to creation? Where is the stuff of legend for us to contextualise, historicise and theorise? It is simply not there! Neither, more importantly, is a language that we could subject to Kabbalistic scrutiny. As if in direct *opposition* to Kabbalistic analysis of the alphabet, to exegesis

---

[67] This libretto is included in Peters Edition's German catalogue, but not its English one. See UE5935.
[68] 'The Idea of the Golem' in Scholem 1965: 158–204.

and explication of its layers of meaning, Ligeti's 'language' of phonetics is actually not a language at all. One regards it as if it were language – and yet it is merely *instructions for the production of noises*.[69] The noises contain no conceptual meanings, and carry no mystical symbolism. The text is not conceptual, so there is nothing 'behind' it, there can be no 'uncovering' of its meanings, no joy in interrogating it with deep, close readings, and no penetration of the ultimate truths that lurk behind obscure and complex texts.[70]

Rather, *Aventures* thrusts itself at us as if it were language, but what we hear and feel is not linguistic at all. As Kakavelakis has argued, the earthy corporeality of the gestures is so intense that we empathise to the point of rather uncomfortably feeling they are their own.[71] We are invaded by the gestures and noises. Moreover, as Kostakeva has pointed out, the density of the consequent sensations (particularly when accompanied by the scenic realisation) precludes their absorption and rational understanding.[72] *Aventures* takes us over. We can only retaliate with concepts after we have recovered.

Language in music

Ligeti and Kurtág were in very divergent circumstances after 1956, and in contexts in which the placing of language into music was discussed in very different ways. Patently, then, it would be difficult to claim that their refraining from text-setting for nearly seven years thereafter had anything to do with the crude ways in which music and language had been discussed when they were together in the preceding years. Nevertheless, they returned to text-setting at about the same time, which does trigger momentary pause for thought. Moreover, they each reached for archaic Christian texts when they did so, thus making a move that had a significant tradition in Hungary. Kurtág began setting extracts from the sermons of the sixteenth-century Lutheran preacher Péter Bornemisza in 1962, finishing *The Sayings of Péter Bornemisza* op. 7 in 1968, while Ligeti began setting the Latin requiem mass in 1963, concluding his partial setting, *Requiem*, in 1965 (also setting a further text from the mass in *Lux aeterna* in 1966).

The Sayings and *Requiem*, furthermore, have strikingly similar textual structures, each of which situates human death in a mythological framework. The first three parts of Kurtág's four-part work, 'Confession', 'Sin', 'Death',

---

[69] Op de Coul 1974: 69.
[70] In the end, we realise, it is not just Kabbalistic interpretation that *Aventures* scorns, but the practice of interpretation in general.
[71] Kakavelakis 2000: 108.
[72] Kostakeva 1996: 134–5. Kaufmann makes a similar point when he compares the materiality of *Aventures* with the intransigence of *Atmosphères*. See reference above.

are mirrored in Ligeti's 'Introitus', 'Kyrie', 'Dies Irae'; but Kurtág concludes with 'Spring', while Ligeti – after some hesitation – allowed his *Requiem* to close with only a 'Lacrymosa'. The simplistic reaction to this is to regard them as musicalisations of Hungary's desired textual projections of 'hope', and the avant-garde West's statement of non-affirmation and 'critique', but (as will emerge below) this is not how they were understood at the time. More intriguing is to move beyond this dualistic model and take a closer look at each work's entanglement of music and language, for each uses music to overflow and challenge the more obvious presentations of the texts set. In fact, each might be read as an argument against regarding music as a vehicle for the conceptual statement suggested in the text.

The very title of *The Sayings of Péter Bornemisza* points precisely to the spoken form of language, suggesting that the work enshrines an invocation of the historic minister's words. At times, indeed, the texts are distinctly predicatory, such as in Part II ('Sin'), movement 10:

Az igék olyak, mint kemény, erős, éles kapák, kikkel bekapálta János az vakmerő, gonosz és kemény lelkű szíveket, hogy megismernék az ő belső, meggyökerezett gonoszságukat.	The Word is like the strong, sharp hoes with which John weeded audacious, evil, hard-souled hearts, so that man recognises his own inner, ingrained corruption.[73]

The piano accompaniment to this statement apparently affirms its determined adherence to ecclesiastical matters: it is canonic (although the lines are splintered by a percussive, staccato texture that may resemble violent hoeing) and beneath 'his own inner', three chords evoke a fragment of a chorale. This detached mode of address is also apparent in Part III ('Death'), movement 6:

Senki nincs oly tudatlan, ki ne tudná hogy neki valaha meg ne kellene halni. De mégis, midőn az halálhoz közel jött, csavarog, búsong, ordít, jajgat . . . Mit sirsz, nyavalyás? Mit rikoltsz? Mindenek tartoznak ezzel, te is oda mész, azhová egyebek mennek, ugyan erre születtél volt.	There is no one so ignorant who does not know that at some time he will have to die. But still, as the time draws near, man wanders sadly, howling, wailing . . . What are you crying for, wretched one? Why are you screeching? Everyone has this debt; You too will go there, where the others are going; to this you were born.

---

[73] Bornemisza texts are in my translation.

The musical setting of this text, however, indicates the lability of the narrating voice, for it dramatises the textual change from an observation of fact to a reprimanding question by suddenly becoming shrill. The change is so abrupt that the voice is destabilised, seeming to come from a different source. 'Sayings' no longer import the authority that the title suggests they will.

In fact the question of the Sayings' ministerial authenticity is placed in question by the voice itself, the female singer. Moreover, the very opening movement, 'Confession', conjures up a visitation upon a woman from the devil himself, fundamentally disestablishing the idea that she might represent a ministerial pillar of goodness. The music of this movement, meanwhile, is the sole movement by Kurtág (in any work) that uses the dodecaphonic method in such a way that the rows regiment musical processes.[74] Explicitly drawing on Mann's *Doctor Faustus*, then, it presents Bornemisza's sayings within a musical fabric that is part and parcel of a demonic temptation.

As the rest of the work unfolds, the voice's ongoing entanglement with the visiting devil may be mapped in sporadic appearances of twelve-note rows and descriptions of the devil's activities. There is also a distinct narrative line in the texts through which death brings a disengagement from the devil, and a new concern with the goodness, and Godliness, of nature. The musical style evolves in a manner that is attuned to this shift, and in the last movement, both the vocal and piano parts use musical symbols to represent the coming of spring, and imitate the sounds of animals. These emphasise the goodness of life on earth, as opposed to a diseased and lonely despair. On one rather obvious level, then, there is a motion from unstable temptation and withdrawal towards newly discovered stability and the embrace of humanity.

And yet that is only one level of the work, because the musical interactions with the 'sayings' are far more disturbing than I have indicated so far. In fact the metamorphosis of the voice is luridly *enacted* through the singing voice, rather than described or represented. Recounting a series of instances in which the devil may sway humanity from its Godly purpose in Part II ('Sin'), the singer even breaks into a bark, as if living out the vileness of sin, actually uttering animalistic sounds. She then provides a horrifying account of death, before – in a dramatic shift of tone – breaking out into an

---

[74] See Halász 2002 for a discussion of Kurtág's far more subtle use of row technique in the String Quartet op. 1 and Wind Quintet op. 2. The hidden character of the twelve-note collections in these pieces has surely contributed to the fact that for many years the consensus was that *The Sayings* contained Kurtág's only dodecaphonic movement. (See Margaret McLay's analyses in McLay 1986 and Hoffmann's remarks in 1992: 131, for instance.) Halász points out that in Hungary dodecaphony was understood as being a restriction on creativity, while Kurtág was celebrated as freely expressive, thus Kárpáti and Kroó sidelined this aspect of his music when they wrote their studies in the 1970s. Halász 2002: 236–7.

aria-like movement celebrating the forgiveness of God in Part IV ('Spring'), movement 1.

The musical vessel for her 'sayings', then, suggests that she is living out these changes during her performance: we are actually witness to her struggles. To understand this we might reflect again on the apparently Faustian visitation at the opening but suspend, for a moment, the now incongruous idea that she represents Péter Bornemisza, or even Adrian Leverkühn. A woman singing (and occasionally barking) of visitation is most evocative, after all, of historical demonic possession, just as are the multiplicity of voices in which she seems to sing, and the very archaism of her language. The nuns of early seventeenth-century Loudun (to take one of the most famous cases of possession) were subject to visions and violent physical convulsions. They spoke in the traditional language of the church, Latin (even if they did not normally know it), but rendered it 'diabolical', by using it to reject God. The nuns' utterances were thus understood as demons speaking through the nuns.

If this is an apposite way to interpret the behaviour of the singer in the early, bedevilled parts of *The Sayings*, then it also leads us to a vivid way of conceiving both the close, and the music's entanglement with language. In historic cases of possession, the nuns' instabilities could be drawn out of them through ritualistic exorcism. In such rituals, a nun's apparent evil could be circumscribed in the rhetorical form of the 'devil'. This devil was understood as occupying a space within her, yet it is also extricable from her: it is (only) in her unconscious, 'an elsewhere that [she lets] slip that is not [her]'.[75] Delimiting the devil in language offers the opportunity for it to be contained and expelled, a process for which the title of *The Sayings*' Part I, 'Confession', can be read as emblematic. It points to that purgative, even cathartic, process through which cleanliness and holiness may be regained through speech.

At the other end of the cycle, the absolute *transformation* of the singer's voice in Part IV ('Spring') is indicative of a fundamental and internal shift within her very being. It is suggestive of the cases of exorcism in which the purgative process would transform a nun so that she experienced another extreme of possession, namely divine illumination. After the possessions at Loudun, for example, Sister Jeanne des Anges, her hand mysteriously inscribed with the names of the demons that had inhabited her, 'reappear[ed] as a martyr of Christianity'.[76] At the close of 'Spring', (Part IV movement 1), the soprano gives voice to a soaring chain of thirds as she sings of the belief in redemption, closing with the resonance of a C♯ major triad.

[75] De Certeau 2000: 100.   [76] De Certeau 2000: 7.

Example 3.4. Kurtág, 'Spring', movement 1 from *The Sayings of Péter Bornemisza*, close

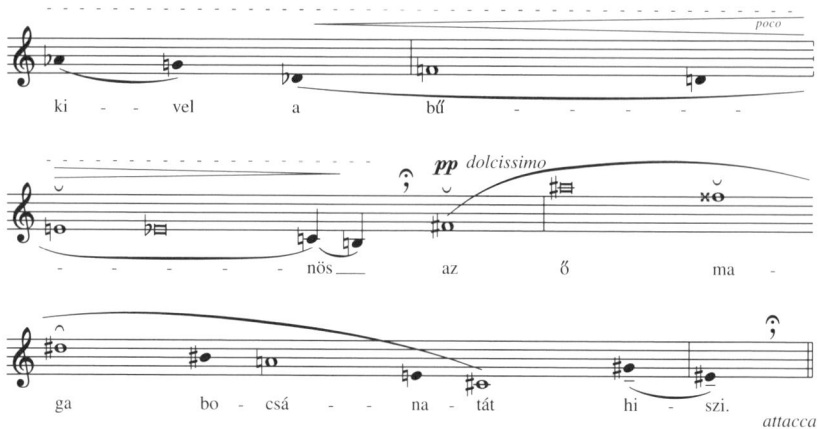

attacca

(See Ex. 3.4) In the context of the rest of the work, this is a moment of exceptional consonance – and the sympathetic vibrations of the undampened piano strings ensure it rings on around and beyond any of the individual tones sung.

In some fashion, then, this violently dramatic work makes a comment on the power of language and thus suggests a new dimension to the significance of the title 'sayings'. The cycle's unfolding vicissitudes, its horrifying reflections on sin and death that give way to more hopeful affirmations of goodness, celebrate that releasing the actual sounds of language can have a healing effect on the physical and spiritual being.

Yet at the same time, the very nature of spoken language is questioned within the cycle, for there is such a tension between the early utterances (ostensibly emerging from the innermost – 'Truest'? – realms of the singer) and those at the end (emerging through the same mouth). Can there be any certainty about the teleology of this apparent motion into light? After such violent and uncontrolled eruptions from the singer, such explosions of noises (music?) into her 'sayings', can we really trust in this motion towards the community, towards nature, towards God? As reviewer György Kroó asked critically, his question arising from a distinct sense of lack in the musical realisation of the textually positive redemptive message: 'isn't there a deficiency of authentic prosody in the melodic, singing, wonderful melodic waves of the third and fourth parts? The Webernesque shadow is not lost even with the arrival of morning, of Spring.'[77] The doubt was key, for *The Sayings*

---

[77] I discuss this in detail in Beckles Willson 2004a: 129–46.

related a redemptive passage, but also enacted a musical loss of control that was never quite resolved. It sat ambivalently, then, amid unproblematic searches for sincerity in human actions and speeches.

Ligeti's *Requiem* – odd as it may seem at first – was understood in the West in ways that are distinctly similar, but reversed. Predictably, supportive critics were concerned to distance it from affirmative religious statements, and yet they were nonetheless equally concerned to suggest that it did, actually, offer a redemptive promise. Salmenhaara, for instance, described the four parts as a monumental journey from darkness into light, in which the opening text 'let perpetual light shine on them' and its setting provides a microcosm of the whole. Symbolically, this constituted a motion from hell to heaven, within which the 'Lacrymosa' was a consoling closure. The sliding from the lower registers into the higher, as well as the increasing presence of tonal elements, seemed to Salmenhaara to offer a musical enactment of this journey.[78] Ligeti, too, suggested that the 'Lacrymosa' concluding the work 'rejoins', tentatively, the forces that are shredded in the tempestuous 'Dies irae' sequence.[79]

There is little doubt that the music is used to map out quite clear trajectories at the opening. The sonorities of the 'Introitus' move from 'dark' male voices in the depths, to 'light' female voices high up. That is the basic curve of the opening movement. Yet it is difficult to agree with Salmenhaara that those voices actually 'shine down': there is no union of the upper with the lower. Rather, it is as if a question is posed and a plea is made, the rising contour of which emphasises its openness. The horrific violence and bleakness of the 'Dies irae' leads us into confusion and shock: it is a terrifying confrontation with the Day of Judgement. The final 'Lacrymosa' ends in a poised, breaking silencing. It weeps, and stops. There is little sign of illumination, transcendence, or promise.

This uncertainty did not go unnoticed: as Nordwall remarked, 'the elemental conflict is not resolved or overcome', and the 'Lacrymosa' is actually just a 'simple epilogue'.[80] Salmenhaara, despite his sense of a motion from hell to heaven, could finally only argue for the ultimate sense of the *expectation* of eternal light.[81] Kaufmann, too, acknowledged that the *Requiem* was a 'fragment'. All these qualifiers bespeak the fact that the work is by no means balanced towards an unambiguously positive message, something that most writers were not keen to explore. After the horrors of the judgement day, the pleading for mercy and the begging for eternal rest, there are actually no answers provided at all: the work dissolves in silence. In the silence that

---

[78] Salmenhaara 1969: 144–5.   [79] Quoted in Steinitz 2003: 145.   [80] Nordwall 1966: 110.
[81] Salmenhaara 1969: 145.

follows, there is still no answer, but writers seem to have felt like Thomas Mann's Zeitblom in *Doctor Faustus*, who conceived beyond Leverkühn's *Lamentation* a 'hope beyond hopelessness'. Surely, they seem to have said to themselves, 'out of the sheerly irredeemable hope might germinate'.[82]

Setting the *Requiem* into comparison with two of Leverkühn's works somewhat illuminates the nature of its ambiguity. Moreover, it is far from impossible that Ligeti was (even if subliminally) influenced by these fictional works, for as we know, Mann was widely read in his Budapest years. His own description of the *Requiem*'s 'secret construction principle' that embraced every single aspect of the piece, 'every pitch, every interval, every complex of intervals, every unit, subdivision and ratio of duration', is like Zeitblom's fearful description of the rationalised system of Leverkühn's *Lament*, in which a 'magic square' determined everything, so that no note was admitted that 'did not fulfil its thematic function . . . there was no longer any free note'.[83] A yet richer link can be made with Leverkühn's *Apocalypsis cum figuris*. Ligeti cited Bosch and Breughel as influences on his conception of the last judgement, whereas Leverkühn's starting-point was Dürer's series of woodcarvings depicting the Apocalypse; but each work explores the final reckoning. Additionally, each draws on a type of quasi-fugal writing that rather predates the fugue (Ligeti cites Pérotin, Machaut, Ockeghem and Palestrina as inspirations; Zeitblom refers to Palestrina and Monteverdi). Each depicts vast masses (Ligeti), or a 'great multitude' (Zeitblom), through choral writing that is dramatic in its complexity and individuality.[84] Each constitutes a horrific journey to Purgatory.

The comparison between the Leverkühn works and Ligeti's *Requiem* may also help conceive the significance of what Ligeti termed a 'black light'. This paradoxical notion is identified by Nordwall as occurring at the 'Lux perpetua', where 'we reach the darkest moment in the whole work, a black eternal light'.[85] Might this be the blackness of Leverkühn? For Leverkühn, there was an interpenetration of good and bad: he revoked humanity, hope and expression to the extent that – as Patrick Carnegy puts it – black becomes white, and vice versa.[86] And yet this suggests only 'relentless theological negativity', the pitilessness of his *Apocalypsis*, whereas Ligeti does not use consonance for evil and dissonance for good.[87] Rather, he preserves quite

---

[82] Mann 1968: 417. In György Kroó's 'Les "Dits de Péter Bornemisza" de György Kurtág' (originally published in Hungary in 1974), Kroó makes brief reference to *Doctor Faustus*. His tentative and fleeting suggestion is that the deepest core of the work consists of a modern working of the Faust legend. He closes his article with his own 'hope beyond hopelessness', asserting that Kurtág's work proposes that one *can* renounce the pact with the devil. Albéra et al 1995: 211–53, at 252–3.
[83] 'Requiem' in *Wort und Wahrheit* (1968), cited in Lobanova 2003: 114–15. Mann 1968: 467.
[84] Mann 1968: 358.   [85] Nordwall 1966: 110.   [86] Carnegy 1973: 130–1.
[87] Mann 1968: 347.

traditional symbolism for forces of good and evil; and hellish laughter is not revealed to be equivalent to purity in the *Requiem*.[88] There is even a sort of transformation to lighter, higher sonorities in the 'Lacrymosa'. But they are dauntingly pallid.

Kaufmann's subtly argued suggestion was that the *Requiem* cites theology, allows it to dissolve, and then also to re-emerge in a transformed state in the background. Ligeti, he suggested, achieved an elevated sort of emptiness in which a new place, free of fear and terror, might be possible.[89] Indeed it 'might be possible', perhaps, and such a sophisticated conceptualisation sets it apart from Leverkühn's intention of *revoking* hope in his own *Lament*.

Yet we might also stand back, for a moment, from these attempts to use the *Requiem* as a medium for utopian hopes. There is no better place to look for an alternative than its première, in which it was programmed before Beethoven's Ninth Symphony, that very joyful work Leverkühn desired to obliterate with his *Lament*. The programming, then, is nothing if not uncanny. And it is surely paradoxical that, although Beethoven's Ninth Symphony was heard *after* the *Requiem* in concert, a critic was heard to say of the *Requiem* somewhat later: 'for a while all other music seemed impossible'.[90] Did the impact of the *Requiem* obliterate, in advance, the joyful message of Beethoven's Ninth? The critic's remark echoes Adorno's claim that there could be no poetry after Auschwitz, yet it was not prompted by multiple death, but merely by a musical evocation of multiple death. Surely, this reminds us of the elementally grieving negativity that this work can also awaken?

It would be crass to mock the way writers found a utopian, redemptive meaning for the *Requiem*'s evocation of death and mourning. Yet we do well to realise that such meanings tend to be found under intense duress: the need to find meanings may be in direct relation to the intensity of the experiences themselves. We can argue that the *Requiem* is a message of hope. But if we are doing that, we have probably already shuddered in its post-Apocalyptic glow.

Music as 'language' (Darkness and Light)

The further one shifts away from music that is in any way linguistic, the closer one may come to the more abstract, yet also elemental quality that it may convey. Already emerging in Chapter 2 was a polarity in Ligeti's

---

[88] Mann 1968: 364.
[89] 'Betreffend Ligetis *Requiem*' (1970) in Grünzweig and Krieger (eds.) 1993: 134–48, at 134 and 148.
[90] Nordwall 1966: 110.

works that could be understood as an outgrowth of a Bartókian syntax and musical symbolism. Concepts of 'light' and 'dark' were key. How curious it seems, from this perspective, that Kurtág's String Quartet op. 1 (1958–9) has never been compared with works by Ligeti. Central to the well-known 'programme' of Kurtág's work, the idea of a cockroach in search of the light,[91] or the transformation of 'mould and suppurating wounds' into 'beauty', is a tension between 'dark' and 'light' sonorities. These, indeed, have informed most interpretations of the quartet, drawing particularly on Kurtág's own remarks from the 1980s.

As Peter Hoffman has argued in the most detail, for example, Kurtág's association of particular chords with light and purity, and his parallel concern with Kafka's *Metamorphosis*, can furnish a narrative for the piece.[92] The first movement's (dirty) chromatic chords and (clean) harmonics encapsulate Kafka's filth-surrounded human-turned-insect, Gregor Samsa, trying to reach the window of his bedroom. As Ex. 3.1 shows, the polarisation is present even in the very opening gesture, between the parallel thirds (B♭–D and B–D♯) and the low-register cluster. Each of the groups of chords presents manifestly 'open' or 'closed' sonorities, whether this is achieved through spacing, register or harmony. The movement's closing arpeggiated harmonics symbolise 'heaven'. Hoffmann, noting that Samsa dies after a long night awake, just as he sees the light of dawn, understands the sixth, final movement as the fulfilment of Samsa's fate (i.e. his death). It is unmentioned, and yet absolutely transparent: reading Kurtág as Kafka constructs the String Quartet as a variation on Ligeti's first string quartet, *Metamorphoses nocturnes*. Samsa was transformed, overnight, into an insect and would be transformed, at the end of another night, into dead matter.

The symbolism of such a transformation, clearly, was also a prominent concern in the reception of music in Budapest in exactly the period in which Kurtág's quartet was written. The basic relations between consonance and dissonance were crucial to critics' and musicologists' understanding of community and alienation, light and dark, and the transcendence of suffering. Understood through Hoffmann's reading, the String Quartet's striving for 'light' could be positioned as the inverse of the positive striving sought by realist critics in Budapest: movement towards light was ultimately a motion into death.

---

[91] As musicologist Péter Halász has pointed out, there is perhaps something ironic in the 'programme': cockroaches always flee light. Personal communication, 22 November 2005.
[92] Hoffmann 1991.

After 1956: the parting of ways

Yet the polarity is not merely a symbolic tool, but also a primary structuring device in two other abstract works in this decade. The first movement of the Wind Quintet op. 2 (1959) is an interesting example, in that it seems to combine the intricate, 'crystalline' shifts that characterise some of Webern's writing with the sorts of harmonic thinking closer to Bartók and Ligeti. As Ex. 3.5 shows, the movement comprises three phrases, the latter two of which open with dissonances but resolve onto G, A and B, that is, onto a whole-tone fragment. The final phrase is underpinned by a low-register C (in the horn) which, combined with the E in the bassoon, suggests a resolution. The upper instruments colour this somewhat with dissonance, but do not fundamentally disturb it. In a very loose sense, then, the movement rehearses a perfect cadence in C major.

The seventh movement of Eight Duos for violin and cimbalom (1961) offers a yet looser notion of consonance, establishing groups of notes as 'stable' less through their harmony, than through their repetition and euphonious distribution (see Ex. 3.6). The two lines are almost, but not quite, black-note against white-note collections and the momentary invasion of one into the other (bars 6–7) creates the point of tension around which the piece is shaped.

It is in *The Sayings of Péter Bornemisza*, however, that these Bartókian, or Ligetian, polarities are put to the most dramatic use. The depiction of sin and death, for instance, is dark and chromatic, while faith and natural renewal are based in relative consonance, and this shapes, in very broad terms, the harmonic contours of the twenty-four-movement work. It contributes greatly to the elemental impact of the transformation discussed above, two extremes for which would be the opening of Part III ('Death'), and the opening of Part IV ('Spring'). The solo piano opening of 'Death' is harsh, chromatic, and deep in register; the solo vocal close of 'Spring' is ravishingly lyrical, harmonious and arc-like in its registral sweep (as already mentioned above, and see Ex. 3.4). But other key moments in the cycle pinpoint this illustrative layer equally clearly: the chromatic, funnelling melodic motive associated with the concept of sin (see Ex. 3.4 again), contrasting with the towering perfect fifths presented at the invocation of God, for instance, shown in Ex. 3.7.

Whilst the background to these dichotomies can be mapped onto the sort of hermeneutics prevalent in Hungarian musical thought, they have a more specific and technical context too. Kurtág generated a considerable body of compositional sketches for *The Sayings* in tandem with analysing music and studying published musical analyses, many of which were by Lendvai, and most of which were concerned with harmonies in the music

Example 3.5. Kurtág, Wind Quintet op. 2, movement 1

of Bartók. One approach he took was the verticalisation of certain passages, and the labelling some of the chords, within which 'w' – Lendvai's label for the whole-tone collection – has a prominent place.[93] Another was the division of the pitches into two opposing whole-tone collections (again, an

---

[93] See, for instance, Skizzenbuch n zu op. 7, where Bartók's Sixth String Quartet is treated in this way.

Example 3.6. Kurtág, Eight Duos op. 5, movement 7

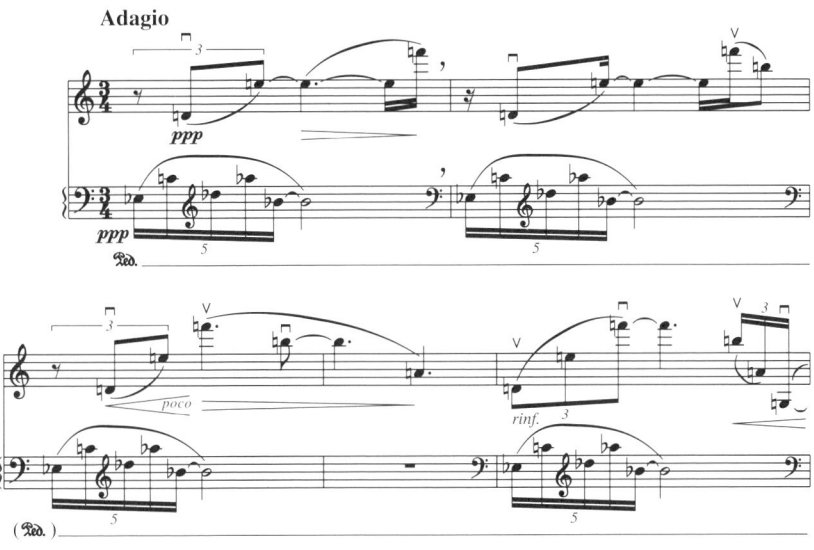

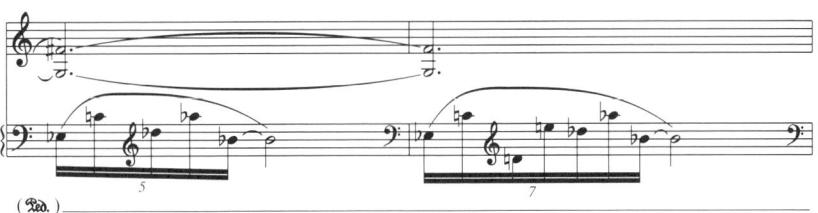

influence of Lendvai), as seen in extended work on 'From the diary of a fly', 'Minor seconds, major sevenths' and 'Chromatic Variations' (*Mikrokosmos* Volume VI).[94]

In terms of working practice, the link between composition and analysis seems clear: the activities are noted within the same books, and in some cases one almost flows into the other. On 17, 18, 20 and 21 February 1967 Kurtág made compositional sketches, but on the last of them wrote 'let's throw everything out' and on that same day began to analyse again.[95] Some months before, his days seemed to alternate between analysis and composition: on 15, 18, 22 and 27 September 1966, for example, he sketched towards part of *The Sayings*, but on 25 September he worked analytically

---

[94] PSF, GKC, within 'Kapitel 5', Analytishe Notizen, Skizzenbuch (1965) 12v. and 13r.; and Analytische Notizen (1965?) zu Quartet Nr. 6, 33v.–37r. inclusive.
[95] PSF, GKC, within Sketchbooks p and q to op. 7

Example 3.7. Kurtág, 'Sin', movement 1 from *The Sayings of Péter Bornemisza*, close

on Bartók's String Quartet no. 6.[96] On 3, 5, 6, 16 and 17 January 1967 he sketched; on 19, 20, 21, 22, 23 and 30 he analysed. Then on 30 and 31 January, 2, 6, 7, 8, 9 and 10 February he sketched and on 15 February he analysed.

Whilst there is no sign that analysis fed into composition in any simple sense, the whole-tone collection emerges in one movement in particular, 'Death', movement 7, which repays a brief examination here. The first section is underpinned by a silently depressed, but increasingly resonant, whole-tone collection built upwards from G♭ (see Ex. 3.8). The rest of the movement is also engaged with a variety of consonances and their gentle, dissonant elaboration. But there is no simple polarisation in the harmony. Rather, the music offers a more intractable and contradictory sense of these qualities, even though the text is describing a metamorphosis – that from life to death.

The famous motto of Part III ('Death') movement 3, 'Virág az ember' ('Flowers we are'), offers the simplest example of this subtle treatment, as it sets up a consonant resonance and then sours it with one note, the D

[96] PSF, GKC, Sketchbook n to op. 7 contains the analysis; the sketches can be seen in Sketchbook l to op. 7.

Example 3.8. Kurtág, 'Death', movement 7 from *The Sayings of Péter Bornemisza*, bb. 1–4

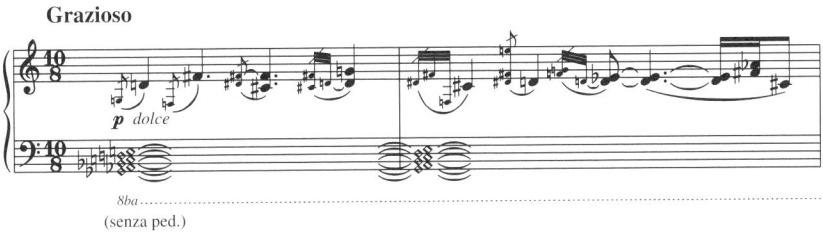

(see Ex. 3.9). If we separate the notes of this motto into the two whole-tone collections, it is clear that the four notes directly preceding the D – i.e. E♭, G, F and C♯ – comprise four notes of one whole-tone collection, the one to which the D does not belong. In that sense D is oppositional, a dissonance. On the other hand, bar 1 provides a consonant field of consonance for it with G♯ and E, and the F♯ in the bass that joins the D is of the same collection, so it should be well supported. The harmonic ambiguity here throws the apparent 'flowering' that the mottos represent in Part III ('Death') into doubt. In the movement following this first flowering, which evokes physical death in terrifying corporeal detail, the doubt is confirmed: dense chromatic micropolyphony seems to expand the hints of dissonance scarring the flower into something all-pervasive, overriding. Thus 'flower' conjures up birth, and yet with that birth, an inevitable withering, death, and remembrance. It is 'present', only to be 'absent'.

Juxtaposing the harmonic and textural dichotomies of Kurtág and Ligeti is very striking. Let us recall the extract of Ligeti interpretation in which the writer described a sense of musical 'presence' in *Lontano*:

Example 3.9. Kurtág, 'Death', movement 3 from *The Sayings of Péter Bornemisza*

Vi - rág,   vi - rág,   az   em - - - - ber.
Flow-ers,   we are,   frail flow - - - ers.

ppp

> When the micropolyphony evolves into a homophonic surface, the constitution of the sound shifts from indistinctness to an increasing presence and clarity until it seems to stand there right in front of the listener.[97]

Here the presence is understood as a product of harmonic clarification, the creation of homophony out of polyphony, consonance out of dissonance – in fact a reverse process of the scarring and polyphonic destruction of the 'flower' in *The Sayings*. Yet it is not only this musical polarity that encourages us to set the two alongside one another. Several of Ligeti's works have a corresponding metaphorical fascination. When Harald Kaufmann, with Ligeti's guidance, introduced *Atmosphères* (1960) in the first article to be published on it, he discussed the shifting textures and sound masses as a ritual celebration of death. Ligeti, he said, conceived it in memory of Mátyás Seiber, and as a distant, submerged, Requiem mass.[98]

As the correspondence between Ligeti and Kaufmann reveals, it was explicitly the polarities in register, dynamic and sonority that Ligeti heard symbolically.[99] Then building on Ligeti's suggestion, Kaufmann made parallels between stages of the mass and *Atmosphères*' instrumental textures to argue that the abrupt replacement of top-register piccolos with lower strings could be understood as a fall into the infernal depths of hell.[100] He also argued that the consonant diatonic chord following the 'Dies irae' section be understood as a reconciliation after terror, an 'Agnus Dei'. But perhaps most interesting, from the perspective of Kurtág's String Quartet of

---

[97] I mention this in the Introduction. Britta Sweers, 'Raum und Zeit' in Engelbrecht, Max and Sweers 1997: 67–88, at 78. The reference is to a section beginning in bar 41. 'Presence' is translated from 'Präsenz', 'constitution of sound' from 'Klanggebilde'.

[98] Kaufmann 1969: 107–17. Also Ligeti, 'Über Atmosphères' in Lichtenfeld (ed.) forthcoming. This aspect of the work was exorcised by Floros in 1996 (who established with Ligeti the fact that it was not valid). See Floros 1996: 100.

[99] 24 June 1962. Grünzweig and Krieger (eds.) 1993: 199.   [100] Kaufmann 1969: 115.

Example 3.10. Pascal Decroupet and Inge Kovács, Analysis of Ligeti's *Atmosphères*

the previous year, is the ending of *Atmosphères*. Kaufmann portrayed it as analogous to a redemptive death:

> Thus the actual standing cluster resonance, with which the piece opens, recalls a distant murmur of the Requiem aeternam; the 'funnel' of the now narrow pitch range where fear reigns no more, could be understood as a consoling Lacrymosa.[101]

It is not only dynamics and register that link these elemental ideas with Kurtág and Ligeti's past Hungarian system of reference, but also harmony. Ligeti adjusted Kaufmann's harmonic analysis in one area, suggesting that it was but a passing detail that one particular chord was pentatonic. But there is another moment in the work in which pentatony is used to particular effect: at bar 19, the winds swell in volume in order to reveal their hitherto obscured pentatonic cluster with tremendous luminosity. In fact it is instructive to observe how much such pentatonic groups underpin the dense clusters generally: instrumental groups are frequently divided into such 'black note' and 'white note' collections, and the underlying construction of chords is frequently whole-tone. The consequence of separating out the parts of the clusters that resound through dynamic emphasis is plain, as Ex. 3.10 shows: the basis is a chain of major seconds. One might be forgiven for mistaking Decroupet and Kovács's analysis for a piece from Bartók's *Mikrokosmos*.[102]

Rather than eradicating this basic exploration of consonance and dissonance (and its association with light and dark) from his resource base over the ensuing years in the West, Ligeti returned to it several times. That he drew it partly from Bartók seems indisputable: in one of his Bartók lectures for the Bayerische Radio in Munich he discussed precisely these dichotomies.

---

[101] Kaufmann 1969: 116.
[102] Borio and Danuser (eds.) 1997 (Vol. II): 292. The analysis appears within Pascal Decroupet and Inge Kovács, 'Erweiterung des Materials', 277–332. Petersen 1991 juxtaposes moments from works by Bartók, Lutoslawski and Ligeti to argue that their treatment of the twelve-tone spectrum differs fundamentally from that of Schoenberg, in that it preserves an 'inherent tonality'. He too describes *Atmosphères* with recourse to consonance and dissonance. Petersen 1991: 297–8.

Recalling Lendvai, he pointed to Bartók's individual use of classic polarities, demonstrating the flux between diatony and chromaticism, whereby a theme might appear in two forms. The diatonic one was a spread-out version of the chromatic, and the chromatic was simply a compressed version of the diatonic.[103] Building up his argument from a division of the chromatic space into two whole-tone collections, he also demonstrated how Bartók used these oppositionally, so that in some pieces, 'in harmonic terms, little occurs apart from the constantly fluctuating exchange between the two surfaces. Everything else is figurative decoration.'[104]

One might wonder whether his lectures on Bartók were simply convenient ways of making money, and assume that he drew on old knowledge in order to do that. Yet his commitment to these basic ways of achieving contrast, and engineering tension and release, was not limited to his lectures, but was spread through his own compositions. *Lux aeterna*, for example, plays on a tension between consonance and dissonance throughout. It contains very distinct moments of consonant repose, one of which is a simple diatonic triad, but most of which are incomplete whole-tone collections. Combined with iconic uses of register, symbolic words from the text such as 'Domine' and 'light' gather just the associations that he was concerned to represent in submerged form, in *Atmosphères*. By this time, he had already developed them very explicitly in *Requiem*, and would employ them again before too long: it was not by chance that a reviewer of *Lontano* in 1968 described the work as a glowing lamp, to be extinguished at the end.[105] *Lux aeterna*'s surges from dissonance to consonance (C major triads!), lower register to high register, obscure textures to clear ones, trigger these basic associations of darkness and light.

If these are 'basic associations', however, one question becomes pressing: do we need to read the harmonic dichotomies realistically, or symbolically? Are they necessarily to be comprehended in terms of life and death? And the answer is, of course, 'no'. We can also attune ourselves afresh to their elemental impacts, impacts that are – one hopes – somewhat unpredictable. To this end, it is perhaps apposite to do as Nancy proposed, to let things 'present – lose' themselves, and here to do so with a final juxtapositioning. The textual representations perhaps obscure their similarity (see Exx. 3.11 and 3.12). Yet the close of Kurtág's String Quartet op. 1, movement 1 (1959), and the close of Ligeti's String Quartet no.2 (1968), have an analogously evanescent and luminous 'presence – absence'.

---

[103] 'Über Bartóks Harmonik', in Lichtenfeld (ed.) forthcoming.
[104] 'Über Bartóks Harmonik', in Lichtenfeld (ed.) forthcoming.   [105] Evarts 1968: 42.

After 1956: the parting of ways   115

Example 3.11. Kurtág, String Quartet op. 1, movement 1, close

Hungarian contexts revisited

I have pointed to Ligeti's distant view of Hungary in his early years of emigration, and in the section above I identified elements in Ligeti's immediately ensuing work that suggest an ongoing dialogue with his Hungarian past. It remains now to bring these together, and to examine his verbal reflections at the end of the decade. To what extent had his views on Hungary changed? How might this affect our thoughts about his music? A similar process for Kurtág is called for too. And whereas our sources for Kurtág's construction and self-construction at the beginning of the decade are extremely thin, the situation is rather different towards the end. In this final section, then, I attempt to close the circles.

Example 3.12. Ligeti, String Quartet no. 2, close

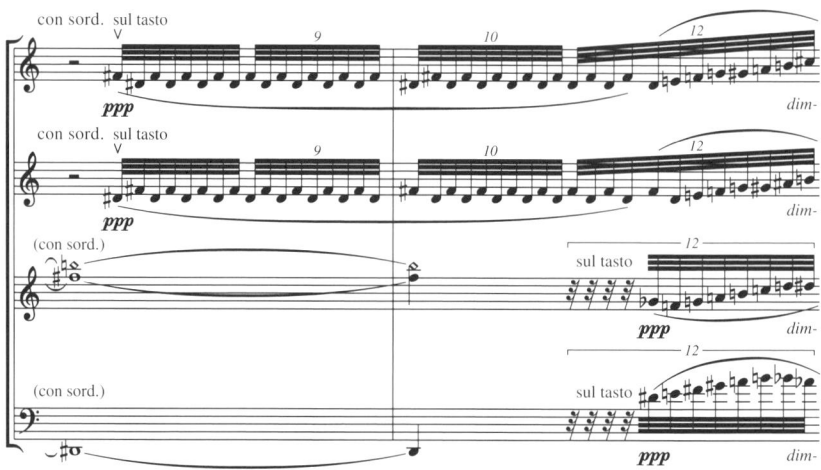

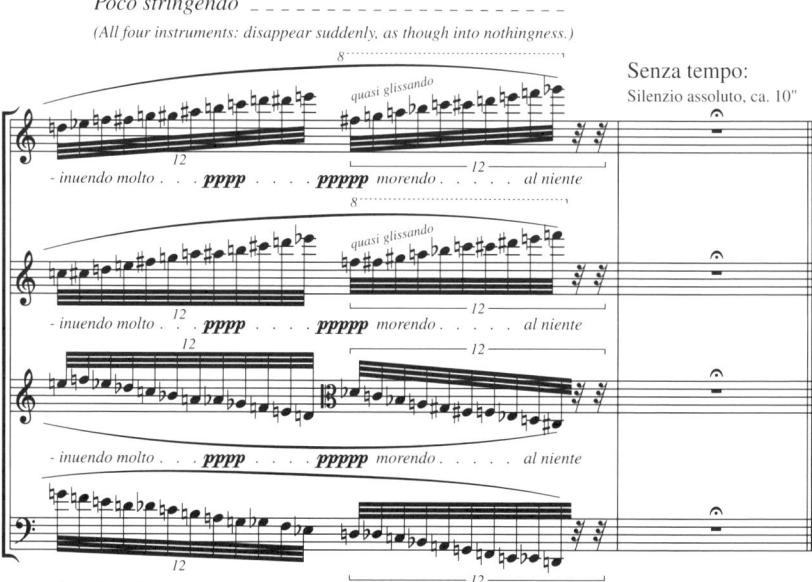

Ligeti as longing

Two particular points of reference may offer a frame for re-engaging with Ligeti's relationship with his past. First, the sense that in the summer of 1957, while no longer part of Hungary, he still struggled intellectually with its culture in ways that he conceived very physically ('I'm swimming in

After 1956: the parting of ways

it ... and to this day haven't really clambered beyond'[106]). Second, the rather more intractable, yet nonetheless fascinating fact that despite deciding to leave the *Requiem* as a fragment in 1966, shortly afterwards he was seriously ill and – in what he claimed was an extreme state of morphine-induced euphoria – composed his radiant, luminous *Lux aeterna*.[107] In this delay to the provision of an 'eternal light', and in the unwillingness to use it to resolve the *Requiem*, we can construct the ongoing tension, the prevailing 'in-between-ness' that was his stateless condition. If he still felt intellectually – or even corporeally – imprisoned in Hungarian culture, he was also just floating in this new place. He remained intensely sensitised to the 'atmospheres' around him that he mentioned so frequently in his letters. The gap between what he had left behind and what he had attained in the West was vast.

In making this observation we gain a new filter for reading the titles of his works. Although in the context of the Western avant-garde's abstractions, many were regarded as 'concrete' and 'human',[108] on closer inspection they turn out to be quite the opposite. The intangible quality of *Atmosphères* needs no special pleading (especially with reference to Ligeti's letters), but it is not the only one that is suggestive of an unsettled condition. *Glissandi* evokes an indefinable location: it is neither 'here' nor 'there', but somewhere moving in between. *Volumina* evokes, without defining. Most suggestively, not only does the title of his incomplete *Visions* (1956) invoke something absolutely other-worldly, but when the same ideas fed into a new work in 1959 Ligeti called it *Apparitions* – another word for 'visions'. He chose the word 'visions' to capture weird sounds heard from afar (those of Western European electronic music heard on the radio from Hungary); but 'apparitions', in this case, suggests that the sounds remained other-worldly to him even though he was in their midst. Toop describes *Visions* as '*the* turning point in Ligeti's creative life, the moment at which he resolutely set out to find and enter a Promised Land'.[109] But as he came to know the 'Promised Land' itself, the gulf remained intact.

We can trace his continuing sense of physical struggle ('swimming') and of a haunting sense of distance for some time thereafter. In a famous interview, for example, he explained the ideas behind his 'textural' compositions, and the very personal quality of his recollection is striking. The origin he found for his work was not a daytime experience, but a dream. Additionally, his recollection of the dream contained the recollection of a place, a place of safety (and light!) to which he longed to retreat, but from which he was barred by the entanglements of an imaginary mesh:

---

[106] Ligeti letter to Weissmann, 12 July 1957. PSF, GLC. Microfilm 109.1: 001185.
[107] Steinitz 2003: 150.   [108] Nordwall 1971: 18–19.   [109] Toop 1999: 43. Italics original.

> *In my early childhood I once dreamt that I could not make my way to my little bed (which had bars and for me signified a haven)* because the whole room was filled with a finely spun but dense and extremely tangled web . . . Besides myself, other living creatures and objects were caught in this immense web: moths and beetles of all sorts, which were *trying to get to the weakly flickering candle in the room*; and enormous damp, dirty pillows, whose rotten stuffing was bulging out through the rips in the covers.[110]

There is a tremendous fragility in the dream thus far, but in the next section it intensifies yet further though the introduction of time. The texture of the seething web shifted continuously, but:

> These transformations were *irreversible*; *no earlier state could ever recur*. There was something *inexpressibly sad* about this process: the *hopelessness of elapsing time and of the irretrievable past*.[111]

The words conjure up a profound longing to retrieve something lost. Of course by framing that loss in a childhood dream, it appears to be simply a charming memory of childhood, detached from Ligeti's present experience. It thus leads readers to imagine an enchanting past: it masks the present. His explanation of *Poème symphonique* that combined a recollection of his uncle's printing works in Dicsőszentmárton with a fictional tale by Gyula Krúdy is similar in effect.[112] Memory is again packaged entrancingly, and, furthermore, is detached from any conceivable pain by becoming a parody of musical practice (it is scored for 100 metronomes). These examples point to a constant presence of memory, but also a strategy of transforming memory into play. One might go so far as to say that Ligeti avoided taking the memories seriously in public, to avoid become a typical exile, a 'pitiful monument' to his grief.[113]

Several other works can be read as more focused reflections on his journey's irreversibility, and of the more general 'impossibility of mythical return'.[114] The overt satires of *Aventures* and *Nouvelles aventures* suggest wild, estranged journeys into the irrational, from which there is no way back. As Nordwall bleakly observed, *Aventures* ends with a *Trionfo della morte*.[115] *Requiem* grasps an ultimate position of 'in-between-ness', Purgatory, and uses it as an alienated vehicle of memory and reflection on loss. But as I have suggested above, it evokes only the *idea* of hope beyond. It revisits the *memory* of hope, rather than hope itself. Even though Ligeti claimed that there was a 'rejoining' of forces in the 'Lacrymosa', he also said that

---

[110] Ligeti 1993 (1960): 164. My italics.   [111] Ligeti 1993 (1960): 165. My italics.
[112] Steinitz 2003: 129.
[113] The phrase is Svetlana Boym's, from her discussion about the modern taboo on nostalgia. Boym 2001: xv.
[114] Boym 2001: 8.   [115] Nordwall 1961: 76.

similarities to the 'Introitus' did not signify a return, but rather a 'spatially distant backward look', 'offering listeners "an impression of *déjà vu*", in twilight'. The light was not in the present, but 'already ... in the past'.[116]

In the title of *Lontano* (1967), it is as if Ligeti could at last name the remoteness and accept the irreversibility of the journey taken, and two subsequent titles, *Harmonies* and *Continuum*, evoke a more settled understanding of the distance travelled. And as if responding to a new-found stability, Ligeti returned to familiar generic types thereafter: Cello Concerto (1966), String Quartet no. 2 (1967–8) and Wind Quintet (1968). These works continue to suggest musical polarities and gulfs too wide to be straddled, but they handle such symbols of the incommensurability between lost and found within solid, recognisable generic frames.

It is towards the end of the decade that we can most clearly identify Ligeti establishing some material sense of belonging, for in 1967 he became an Austrian citizen and in 1968, Harald Kaufmann wrote a dictionary entry for him.[117] By then professionally and legally established, in constructing his past and his present for the benefit of Kaufmann, he passed through reflections that hint at an unquenchable desire for a (cultural) historical origin. This could not be, and was not, Hungary. After all:

> I am not viewed as a 'Hungarian' composer in Hungary, where lately (until recently I counted as a *persona non grata*) I have been apostrophised as a 'composer of Hungarian provenance living in the West', in no way 'Hungarian'.[118]

Furthermore, although the Hungarian language and literature had influenced him 'entirely', it had never been the case with music, he said.

> Not Hungarian music: Mahler or Berg are nearer to me than Bartók, despite my 'Bartókian period(s?)' in student days. But the impact of Bartók became faint, in the meantime, whereas the impact of Hungarian literature remained equally intense.[119]

---

[116] From 'Requiem' (1968), cited in Lobanova 2003: 137. Moreover, while obviously a vehicle for exploring Purgatory through an established historical genre, it is also a recollection of Ligeti's own compositions specifically. His two early cantatas explored all-too-close encounters with death in 1945: 'Tenebrae factae sunt' describes the crucifixion and was dedicated to his mother and girlfriend in January; 'Angelus Domini descendit de caelo' describes the resurrection and – symbolically – was dedicated to the 'home-comers' in March. Ligeti had tried to set Weöres' poetic reworking of the epic of Gilgames, 'Istar's Journey to Hell' in 1955, and *Requiem* revisited this notion of a journey into death.

[117] According to Werner Grünzweig and Gottfried Krieger, this was the *Dutton Dictionary of 20th Century Music* eds. Eric Salzman and John Vinton (Grünzweig and Krieger (eds.) 1993: 260). See footnote 122 below, however.

[118] Grünzweig and Krieger (eds.) 1993: 231–2.

[119] Letter dated Vienna, 25 July 1968. 'Briefwechsel György Ligeti – Harald Kaufmann', in Grünzweig and Krieger (eds.) 1993: 185–262. See 231.

His references to Bartók – and Hungary – were similarly cautious when he was interviewed in the same year about his new String Quartet. He did not wish to 'deny' Bartók's influence, he said, and ambivalently admitted that there were 'more or less clear allusions to Bartók's string quartet style', while later on in the same interview claiming that the only connection with Bartók was in fact a use of pizzicato.[120] In the same interview he made a remark about domestic music-making, using the word 'alien' to describe his relation towards it. He thus sliced through the links with his activities as a young man in both Cluj and Budapest, and his published celebration of *Hausmusik* in the *Zenei Szemle* in 1948.[121]

By shedding his musical links with Hungary he was able to locate himself firmly in Vienna and position himself in a historical trajectory of Viennese composers. His recommendations were that Kaufmann should identify him as an 'Austrian composer from Hungary', and minimise his journey and arrival there. Playing his past down as if to ease his assimilation, in response to Kaufmann's first draft text he wrote:

> Perhaps 'emigration' is not the right word. ('Flight' would be far too dramatic on the other hand, so not recommendable either.) I'd simply suggest: 'Since 1956, permanent residence Vienna'.[122]

There was another emigration behind him, of course, for he lived in Hungary for only eleven years (many months of which he spent back in Romania). So he also mentioned to Kaufmann that while of Hungarian origin, he was actually born in Romania, even if he had 'really no connection' to that country. This erasure was perhaps the easiest of all to perform, but it led him to touch on something he could not express with such ease, namely his lack of any link with the Jewish heritage. He did not merely tell Kaufmann he was 'of Jewish origin', but wrote that he was 'of *guaranteed* Jewish origin', thus using a tone for his Jewishness entirely different from either his Hungarian

---

[120] Interview with Josef Häusler (1968/1969), trans. Sarah E. Soulsby. See *Ligeti in Conversation* 83–110, at 104 and 107. His responses to observations from Nordwall that his String Quartet was Bartókian were that he himself hadn't conceived the work in that way while composing. Nordwall 1971: 25.

[121] Interview with Josef Häusler (1968/1969), trans. Sarah E. Soulsby. See *Ligeti in Conversation*: 107. See also chapter 2 above.

[122] 16 August 1968. 'Briefwechsel György Ligeti – Harald Kaufmann', in Grünzweig & Krieger (eds.) 1993: 237. The dictionary was never produced as described above in footnote 117; rather, it finally emerged in 1971 as *Dictionary of Contemporary Music* (US: E. P. Dutton and Co.; UK: Thames and Hudson in 1974). In the 1974 UK edition the entry for Ligeti is ostensibly authored by Monika Lichtenfeld (trans. Jeanne Wolf). It contains the statement: 'Since 1956 his permanent residence has been Vienna.' Lichtenfeld was mentioned by Ligeti in a letter to Kaufmann on 5 June 1963 as a gifted musicologist whom he would like to assist gaining a post somewhere. See Grünzweig and Krieger (eds.) 1993: 202–3.

or his Romanian background.[123] He adhered to it, then, and made a claim about its authenticity. Herein, quite possibly, lay the most fundamental sense of loss of all, the sense of missing something that he had never had but on some level 'could' have had:

> Unfortunately I have very little to do with the Jewish tradition (probably less than Mahler and Schönberg), for my parents were by and large already what they called 'assimilated Jews' in the K. u. K. monarchy. I regret now as an adult, it's almost unpleasant to me, that I observe the Jewish tradition as something exotic, as if from a distance. This is a sort of disguised Jewish complex.[124]

His final request to Kaufmann was to strengthen his link with Vienna yet further, and for specific career reasons:

> If you have nothing against it, I'd prefer it if rather than 'Composer resident in Austria of Hungarian origin' it said 'Austrian composer of Hungarian origin', for reasons of which I've already written. I don't attach *so* much value to 'national' affiliations myself, but *others*, however, by and large regard it as important. In that I don't count as 'Hungarian' and that not only in Austria but also abroad, people tend to assign artists to a state (see the *Musical Quarterly*: European Music, 'French weeks', Unesco perspectives etc. etc.), it's a decided handicap not to be attached to one state or another. So it facilitates the dissemination of my music considerably when I count as 'Austrian', and even the minor difference of 'living in Austria' is sufficient for me to be swept into an artistic no man's land – which I have, to my own cost experienced all too significantly for some years . . . Don't have any scruples, I'm an Austrian citizen *de jure*, and all my compositions which count (apart from *Artikulation*) were written in Vienna. So just as Joannis Avramidis, Wander Bertoni and others are 'Austrian sculptors', it would be simply practical for me to be an 'Austrian composer of Hungarian origin'.[125]

He concluded these reflections about practicalities by offering an idea to which he did actually feel attached. Rather than modern Austria (where he was dissatisfied with his professional recognition), this was a place well and truly of the past, the place in which his parents were assimilated Jews and which was lost in 1919. Drawing on Robert Musil's renowned nickname for old Austro-Hungary, he wrote to Kaufmann that:

---

[123] 25 July 1968. 'Briefwechsel György Ligeti – Harald Kaufmann', in Grünzweig and Krieger (eds.) 1993: 231–2.
[124] 'Briefwechsel György Ligeti – Harald Kaufmann', in Grünzweig and Krieger (eds.) 1993: 231–2. 'K. u. K.' is an abbreviation of 'Kaiserlich und Königlich' (Imperial and Royal), a semi-ironic name for the Austro-Hungarian Monarchy.
[125] 16 August 1968. 'Briefwechsel György Ligeti – Harald Kaufmann', in Grünzweig and Krieger (eds.) 1993: 239. Ligeti had been granted Austrian citizenship in 1967.

> If I had a musical home somewhere, then it would be old (not today's!) Austria, only and exclusively Kakania. (Can one put 'Kakanian composer' in a dictionary?)[126]

But would it be too speculative to read this dream of Kakania, his musically floating 'in-between-ness', and his sense of detachment from the present as a rather artfully suppressed, but more problematic longing for home? Did he actually, in private, feel like an archetypically wandering Jew? The question will resurface in Chapter 5.

Kurtág as object of longing

Kurtág's position at the end of the 1960s can be illustrated rather neatly with an anecdote about a book of interviews. Compiled by musicologist Imre Földes, this volume attempted to give voice to a new generation of composers including Kurtág.[127] Kurtág was one of two whose year of birth actually fell outside the nominal bracket (the 1930s), but he stood apart from the rest for a more striking reason too. He simply did not take part. Instead, in a way that is symptomatic of the way his professional persona evolved, three performers conversed with Földes about him in his absence. He was at once crucial to the publication and brought within its pages, but meanwhile silent in person.

The silence with which this leaves us now is somewhat deceptive, for Kurtág was well established as an instrumental coach and teacher and thus had a semi-public role in which he talked a great deal. Nonetheless, in a context within which composers were giving voice to their individual compositional aims, and within which public conceptualisations of music had such a charged political significance, his reticence is worth noting. As will emerge in subsequent chapters, it would contribute to the way his music was constructed by others. What follows here is an account of how it began.

At the beginning of the decade Kurtág's position was by no means prominent. When his Viola Concerto (of 1954) was performed in 1961, for instance, it could not contribute to discussions about the future of music, because, as discussed above, writers were in search of progress, diversity and humanism.[128] When, however, his String Quartet op. 1 was premièred later

---

[126] He followed this with an ironic and humorous passage written in the letter style of Mozart, clearly playing with the idea (having just finished his string quartet) of being a composer of Viennese descent, a 'Hofcompositeur' – as Mozart called himself at such times. 25 July 1968. 'Briefwechsel György Ligeti – Harald Kaufmann', in Grünzweig and Krieger (eds.) 1993: 232.
[127] Földes 1969: 6.
[128] Breuer embraced it like an old friend, precisely because it was no longer novel. Breuer 1961a.

After 1956: the parting of ways 123

in the same year, it triggered a marked shift in his renown. Programmed within a concert organised by Ferenc Farkas, it was summarily dismissed in the single published review as a Webernian dead-end but, revealingly, the reviewer also complained that the première was a 'sensation'.[129]

Reconstructing the 'sensation' is not a straightforward matter, for there are no other textual sources illuminating it. Recollections suggest, however, that an official committee had rejected the quartet in the previous year, and that Farkas' programming was thus a provocative intervention.[130] The preparation for his concert was necessarily equally interventionist, for most performers had never even seen such scores let alone heard such music: it required extraordinarily protracted rehearsals (the players were coached by András Mihály). Moreover, these rehearsals were open to curious auditors, who discovered a truly rare space in which Webernian music could be heard under gradual sonorous construction. Consequently Kurtág became a vessel of sounds that were otherwise still suppressed and, by extension, it became important for official rhetoricians to emphasise his undesirability. They even did this one year later, not only by invoking the datedness of his music, but also its lack of social responsibility. Even if 'honest', Kurtág's Eight Piano Pieces op. 3 succeeded in portraying only loneliness and despair, according to the two critics who reviewed their premières in 1962. Kurtág, they argued, neglected his duty to make the world a better place: he was stuck in darkness, unable to move to the light.[131]

By 1963, in the second year of Chamber Music of Our Time (in which the music of Webern himself had a place), Kurtág's music was no longer so inflammatory. Critics were able to account for his Eight Duos for violin and cimbalom op. 4 and Wind Quintet op. 2 by arguing that while he drew on fashionable musical techniques (read: dodecaphony, for as one put it, 'the devil' was lurking at the concert series), he was now evoking not only suffering but also joy, and demonstrating a desire to reach out to people.[132] This was a considerable shift, but it reflected a broad trend towards political and

---

[129] Breuer 1961b: 36.
[130] Although no documentation has been traced, Kurtág recalled in 1998 that a three-member committee at the Hungarian Radio rejected the work. I discuss this in more detail in Beckles Willson 2004a: 40–3. Kurtág remembered on the same occasion that even after the performance at Farkas's concert, the Ministry rejected the string quartet. See further reference to this above, referenced in note 30.
[131] Breuer 1962; Pernye 1962. The fact that the work in question, Eight Piano Pieces op. 3, had already been performed in Darmstadt surely heightened its political significance. According to Kurtág's recollections in April 1998 (private conversation with the author), when dissident Andor Losonczy performed these pieces in Darmstadt, the festival organisers requested more of his scores. The Ministry in Hungary refused to allow scores to be sent; and they called Kurtág up for two months' military service that effectively prevented him from going to Darmstadt that year. Documentation to confirm this has not been traced.
[132] Pernye 1963a; Breuer 1963. Pernye 1963b; Breuer 1964.

musical consolidation. Pernye's justification of Kurtág, for example, was a simple legitimation of the new political order. Kurtág's initial turn to 'lonely' methods of composition, he explained, was a consequence of an uncontrollable 'inner need' to make a radical break from the path represented by the *Korean Cantata* and the Viola Concerto.[133]

Thus, in a free variation on progressive humanism, Rudolf Maros was soon acknowledged for drawing techniques learned from Polish sonorists (revealed in his *Euphonia I–III*), and celebrated because his 'striving for sonorous beauty speaks of the desire for the *psyche's deep and honest* statements'.[134] Zsolt Durkó (1934–97) made a particular impact with his violin concerto *Organismi* (1964), which was regarded as path-breaking but also – in the words of one leading establishment critic János Breuer – 'filling apparently speculative forms with *true emotions and content*'.[135] Durkó even drew explicitly on Hungarian styles, thus his *Una rhapsodia ungherese* for two clarinets and orchestra (1965) and *Fioriture ungherese* for chamber choir and orchestra (1966) heralded a new integration of recently acquired techniques with more traditionally approved musical elements. These contributions reinforced the principles of the new 'diversified' regime and married it with emerging ideas about a national musical corpus.

The book of interviews that attempted to present a new compositional generation is another trace of this process. And as if a cipher for the new situation, Kurtág emerges within it not only as a composer with a profoundly admirable moral stance but also, suddenly, as a reflection of current Hungarian society. One pianist referred to him as '*our* composer of the time'.[136] Relinquishing his secure professional existence, the pianist proposed, Kurtág had practised the 'strictest honesty' and a 'self-reproaching statement of truth', while the interviewer suggested that because Kurtág had such a 'responsible' attitude to musical materials and a 'merciless search for truth', he spoke directly to 'the Hungarian person today'.[137]

---

[133] Pernye 1963b.   [134] Raics 1966. My italics.

[135] Breuer 1965b: 6. My italics. Walsh 1968 provides an introduction to the work of Durkó. See Walsh 1969 for a more general overview of Hungarian music of the decade. The special issue of *Tempo* in which it was published also includes articles on individual composers by Hungarian writers.

[136] Ádám Fellegi. Földes 1969: 193. Italics original.

[137] Ádám Fellegi. Imre Földes. Földes 1969: 194. It is not actually clear that Kurtág would have had a blossoming public career had he continued to write in the styles of his *Korean Cantata* and Viola Concerto, but he was indeed sidelined by official organisations subsequently: his music was never featured in a 'composer portrait', for instance. It might be argued that he had not composed enough to warrant such exposure, and that there was no reason for his exclusion from the series other than that. Many such portraits were divided between several composers, however, and whether or not people ever stood in its way, the very fact that such a composer portrait never did take place is representative of Kurtág's situation on the edge. In other words, he was not celebrated 'as Kurtág' – unlike older composers such as Farkas, Kadosa and Ránki,

The high point of consolidation was reached in 1968, when Mihály founded a new-music ensemble (the Budapest Chamber Ensemble), Kurtág completed his first work for some years (*The Sayings of Péter Bornemisza*), the new ensemble visited Darmstadt for a concert at which *The Sayings* was premièred, and a repeat concert was organised in Budapest. A substantial number of critics regarded the Budapest concert not only as a turning-point, but also as a moment of redemption for the nation. Kurtág's *The Sayings of Bornemisza*, moreover, was understood as metonymic of that redemption, either because of its reported success in Darmstadt, or because of its extension of the musical tradition from Schütz to Bartók.[138] Just as Kurtág's composition represented a rough ride into light (the programme note for the concert described it with the Latin motto 'per aspera ad astra'), so too could both Kurtág's own development, and the development of the nation, be understood as such.[139] Most importantly, *The Sayings* heralded Hungary's re-integration with the western world. As one writer expressed it, *The Sayings* contained a quality that since Homer, had been known as 'European'.[140]

Where *C'est la guerre* captured a moment of national despair, then, *The Sayings of Péter Bornemisza* caught one of national hope. But just as the situation in 1960 had been painfully ironic, there were considerable contradictions in the situation of 1968. Hungarian assertions about the Western European press acclaim were highly distorted: Kurtág's music actually received very tentative recognition in Darmstadt, much of the music on the programme was slated, and the concert created no lasting links between Hungary and Western Europe at all.[141] Additionally, Kurtág's own view of his position was entirely at odds with those of his celebratory critics, as one of his jotted notes reveals:

> The experience of Ligeti's pieces. Classics of the second half of the century. Me, nowhere and last night I managed to say it to Márta – like Csontváry giving up painting the poor reception of his Paris exhibition in 1908 [*sic*], there's something connected, the Bornemisza was something like that for me.[142]

He was probably referring to a text by painter Kosztka Tivadar Csontváry (1853–1919) that describes what he did following his exhibition in Paris, namely withdraw and reflect that his life was in vain:

---

or the younger ones such as Bozay and Durkó. It was not until 1978 that he would have a LP recording dedicated to his works, whereas Balassa, Bozay, Durkó, Petrovics and Láng each did rather earlier on.
[138] See Beckles Willson 2004a: 129–46.   [139] Várnai 1968: 21.   [140] Homolya 1968: 22.
[141] Beckles Willson 2004a: 129–46.
[142] Notebook. 'Zeichnungshefte klein', no. 2. PSF, GKC. Undated.

I withdrew to the peaks of Lebanon and painted cedars. Quietly, in my loneliness and my hair already turned white I wondered what the point of the great battle had been, when nobody can in any case enter heaven with the trappings of power or wealth. And yet without God, I ask, what is the point of living on this earth?[143]

Now if Kurtág suffered comparable doubts about his life as a composer (and his letter to Ligeti discussed above underscores those), it is little wonder that he did not take part in public interviews. But his identification with Csontváry triggers several further questions, for Csontváry's fanaticism about having a prophetic mission is clear from the preceding part of the text (he was fully psychotic at the time of writing). It was precisely because his divine message had gone unheard that he was so downcast.[144] Did Kurtág share a sense of prophetic mission? Was Csontváry's mystical madness something with which Kurtág identified? These questions will accompany us in Chapter 4.

---

[143] Gerlóczy and Németh 1976: 103. This text was published in 1973 in the literary journal *Forrás*. See 'Csontváry írásaiból' [From Csontváry's writings], *Forrás* 4/ November–December 1973, 155–60, at 155. Kurtág may well have seen it sooner. Pilinszky clearly had access to Csontváry's manuscript in 1962, for he wrote about it briefly then. See 'Csontváry olvasásakor' [While reading Pilinszky] in Pilinszky 1999: 264–6.

[144] In the year following the exhibition Csontváry reported that Pierre Weber, critic for the *New York Herald*, had acclaimed his paintings as transcending all other work in the world. Subsequently it has emerged that nothing at all was published about the exhibition in the *New York Herald* or anywhere else. It is possible that someone (whether or not Weber) made some such comment to Csontváry in person, but it is also possible that the comment was made with irony. Csontváry – who was on the brink of the psychosis that would accompany him for the rest of his life – may have been aware of this (indeed his later references to the event indicate precisely that). But he nevertheless used it to argue in no uncertain terms that his divine national genius had been recognised, and that he would continue on his path as God's chosen one. Németh 1970: 181–2. For the extended text that he wrote later (date unspecified), see Gerlóczy and Németh: 103.

4 After 1968: Budapest, Kurtág, and events

First, a brief disclaimer. 1968 has nothing like the significance of 1956 for Hungarian music, even if Mihály's Darmstadt pilgrimage and the première of *The Sayings of Péter Bornemisza* that year were understood as events of weighty historical importance. Even the deaths of two major figures in the years flanking 1968 – Kodály in 1967 and Szabó in 1969 – were of symbolic, rather than practical significance.

There was little sign of real change in the global power struggle either. Soviet expansionism led to Cambodia, Laos, Ethiopia, Mozambique, Nicaragua and Vietnam turning communist during the decade. And several of the Eastern Bloc governments proved particularly vicious in 1968. In March the Polish regime cracked down on student unrest, the radical-liberal intelligentsia and what it termed 'Zionism'; then in August the Soviet Union harnessed its satellites to march into Czechoslovakia and obstruct liberalisation.

At the same time, nevertheless, some détente processes were under way. The USA's President Nixon visited China (where he met President Mao Tse-tung) and Moscow (where he met Communist Party General Secretary Leonid Brezhnev) in 1972, and made new agreements on nuclear armaments in 1972 and 1979. German Chancellor Willy Brandt's policy of *Ostpolitik* reduced aggression between Germany and Poland. Regimes in countries of the Eastern Bloc were forced to grant their dissidents legal opportunities for political disagreement when the Helsinki Accords were passed in 1975. These liberalising movements, rather than the oppressive ones, are the best context for Hungary, for its position in the Eastern Bloc was rather favourable.[1]

Politics and culture in Budapest

Put into place in 1968, Hungary's New Economic Mechanism made private enterprise possible for the first time since 1949, and the country's subsequently evolving hybrid economy – part state-controlled, part market-dependent – was highly successful.[2] The main strength was agricultural

---

[1] Bideleux and Jeffries 1998: 566. Only Yugoslavia was comparably progressive in economic reform.
[2] The country's growth outstripped that of many Eastern neighbours, as well as many countries in the West. Romsics 1999: 346.

production, but this was supported by investments in infrastructure and new trade agreements with the West. The consequence was a higher standard of living than in most Eastern Bloc countries.

This material background goes some way towards explaining the dearth of public opposition to the regime, but the government's increasingly tolerant policies were also significant. When in January 1977, 230 prominent Czech intellectuals published a statement in the West arguing that the Helsinki Accords had brought but the façade of free speech, only thirty-four Hungarians signed the supportive letter organised in Budapest three days later.[3] And the government did not take any action at all in response. To be sure, a few individuals had entered into direct confrontation with it in the previous decade, and they continued to provoke.[4] Miklós Haraszti became the most notorious: forming a Vietnamese Solidarity Committee in 1965, he was expelled from university in 1966, readmitted in 1968, but expelled again in 1970. Using his resultant spare time to work in a factory, he then wrote a study in which he presented his experiences in the form of a critique of state socialism. His attempt to publish it cost the editor of the journal *Szociológia* (Sociology) his job.[5] But such attempts to challenge the system were far from widespread.

Changes that developed somewhat surreptitiously in tandem with government policy were more characteristic. During the late 1960s, for example, the Catholic church had begun to expand its use of music in services. Seminarists were able to study plainchant at a summer school set up in 1967, and this annual event subsequently led to the establishment of parish scholas and choirs.[6] Throughout the decade Cardinal József Mindszenty had been living in refuge in the United States Embassy, refusing to leave the country until the government revoked his conviction for treason (of 1948), and refusing to acknowledge the rapprochement between church and state agreed in 1959.

---

[3] The list is reproduced in Csizmadia 1995 (I): 75. Pianist Zoltán Kocsis, the one musician who signed this *Charter 77*, as it was called, was awarded the Kossuth Prize two months later. Csizmadia 1995: (II): 172–3. There were two further protests about the same matter in 1979. Composer Zoltán Jeney signed both; Attila Bozay, another composer, signed one: Zoltán Kocsis signed neither. Csizmadia 1995 (I): 82–3, 86–8. There are always complex reasons behind decisions whether or not to sign such documents; the aim here is merely to point to the main trend whereby musicians took no part in overt political resistance.

[4] They were mainly students at the Eötvös Lóránd University in Budapest, where the humanities faculty, the law department and the university theatre – along with various artists' clubs and youth clubs – became meeting points for resistance activists. Révész 1997: 163–4.

[5] It was published a few years later in several languages as *A Worker in a Workers' State: Piece-rates in Hungary*: see Haraszti 1977 and Michael Wright's 'About the Author', 11–17.

[6] Dobszay 1998: 4, 7–8. It will be some time before the circumstances of this new movement can be fully weighed up and contextualised within the shifting relations between the USSR and the Vatican. Dobszay, who led it, plays down the explicitly political problems he encountered in his publications, arguing that there were plenty of other ones to deal with first.

In 1971 the government finally revoked his conviction and he departed.[7] By 1972, the study of plainchant had been introduced to the Liszt Academy curriculum.

Other government policy changes had visibly direct consequences for cultural activities. *Ostpolitik*, for instance, made available a large number of German scholarships for Hungarians.[8] Kurtág was supported for half a year in West Berlin as a result, although whether the visit actually made any impact on either his work or the Budapest scene is highly questionable. Others benefited more from increased freedom to move about, and poet János Pilinszky's reports on his travels in the West were widely disseminated (even if primarily in the organ of the Catholic Church, *Új Ember* (New Man)).[9] Composers studying abroad and travelling to Darmstadt and Warsaw brought in further new scores and recordings, and also encouraged people to organise platforms for new music at home. Hungarian Radio, for example, established a new series for modern music in 1977 called 'Reformed Music' (*Megújhodott Muzsika*), but the most significant development was made by the national concert agency Philharmonia, which inaugurated a major festival under the title of 'Music of our Time' (*Korunk zenéje*) in 1974. This was to be an important annual event, and provided the official focus for Budapest's new music scene subsequently.

The expansion of Westward-looking activity in Budapest occurred simultaneously with new concerns for and interests in life outside the metropolis. These took two main forms, one of which was a folklore revival known as the Dance House movement, witnessed in the early 1970s as a number of people began gathering music and dance practices from rural areas in order to lead folklore workshops in towns and cities.[10] The other was a revitalised political concern about Hungarians outside the country's borders. A new Patriotic Popular Front began to campaign on their behalf in 1968, and the affiliated 'mother tongue movement' set up a series of conferences in 1970 to address the preservation of the Hungarian language in Romania.

This resurgence of nationalist expression was probably less a consequence of anxiety about the East, however, than of increased contact with and ambition towards the more prestigious world of the West. In the music

---

[7] Firmly opposed to détente, he obstructed the appointment of a successor to himself until he died in 1975. Romsics 1999: 409–10.
[8] Romsics 1999: 409.
[9] He devoted several essays to descriptions of and engagement with the work of Robert Wilson, in which he emphasised the way the ritualistic style, through slow-motion and silence, evoked a universal 'rebirth' of theatre, in the most mystical and metaphysical sense. See, for instance, 'Új színház született' [A New Theatre Has Been Born], *Új Ember* 8 August 1971 and 11 September 1971, reproduced in Pilinszky 1999: 651–3 and 660–4. See also his book about Sheryl Sutton, first published in Hungarian in 1977: English translation, Pilinszky 1992.
[10] Széll 1981. See also Frigyesi 1996.

world, the 'musical mother tongue' resurfaced in two areas, one of which was minor journalistic coverage of a musical parallel to the Patriotic Popular Front. Reports in *Muzsika* expressed anxiety that the musical mother tongue associated with Kodály had a battle to gain legitimacy in Romania.[11] The other was ethnomusicologist Bálint Sárosi's prominent radio programme 'Our Musical Mother Tongue'. Sárosi's work subsumed gypsy music into the same category as Hungarian folk music (as part of the mother tongue, that is), and resulted in book publications catering not only for the Hungarian market, but for the English and German-reading ones too.[12]

Most obviously, when in 1967 a new summer music festival entitled 'Bartók Seminar' was established in the Western Hungarian town of Szombathely, its main goal was to provide non-Hungarian performers with a means of grasping Bartók 'authentically'. As musicologist József Ujfalussy explained, the key was in the Hungarian language:

> Diverging from Western European languages, the structure, intonation, stress-pattern, melody and tempo of the Hungarian language is the pulse and heartbeat of Bartók's music. It was not for nothing that Bence Szabolcsi alerted us to the way that when lacking these characteristics Bartók's music sounds foreign, its interpretation is distorted. Often have our ears been struck by foreign emphases, misunderstood agogics and phrasing even in the most outstanding interpretations. Our task is to guard the correct interpretation especially when Bartók's text and stage works are published without the original Hungarian texts.[13]

Ujfalussy's arguments echo with mythological narratives about national preservation, and were clearly rehearsed to bolster Hungarian identity in the international sphere of musical performance.

These new forms of nationalist expression were a consequence of the government's retreat from direct intervention, and also its provision of support

---

[11] In 1972 *Muzsika* summarised articles from the journal *Korunk* (Our Time), published in Cluj (Romanian home to a large Hungarian population).

[12] Sárosi's radio programmes fed a book called *Our Musical Mother Tongue* (see Sárosi 1973), but his *Cigányzene* [Gypsy Music] (published in Hungarian in 1971) would be released in German in 1977, and in English in 1978.

[13] Ujfalussy 1967: 2. This is a printed version of a lecture he gave at the seminar, the title of which is 'What Can the Bartók Tradition Give the World?' Erna Czövek and János Breuer had both attempted to grasp what the 'ideal performer' did with the score in 1965, Breuer positioning the true 'Hungarian' performer between two negative extremes, the objective (read: modernist, formalist) and the over-subjective or indulgent (read: Romantic). Czövek 1965, Breuer 1965a. The new trend would feed into research in performance practice by both Breuer and László Somfai, whose work explored Bartók's recordings as a pianist. Somfai's first proposals regarding the importance of Bartók's recordings to musicology were presented at the second Bartók Seminar in 1968 and published thereafter. See Somfai 1968. See Beckles Willson 2004d for a discussion about his later work (1990–2000), in which related issues are explored with particular emphasis on language.

for a more diversified range of cultural forms. Many artists were to experience a consequent sense of empowerment. Although, for instance, it was the government that provided institutional frameworks for the Dance House movement (its very name was drawn from the state-sponsored 'Tánzház' facilities in which it operated), participants regarded their work as an independent grassroots response to urban desire for authentic village culture. And when musicologist and critic Tibor Tallián used *Muzsika* to express ruthless scorn for Durkó's grand opera *Moses* (1977) without apparently having recourse to any predetermined, monitored state position, it was indeed clear that there was room for strong public disagreements about the value of music, in the absence of any governmental interference.[14]

Tallián's review is worth examining because it was in tune with the most important artistic change of the decade. His main claim was that neither the tragic prophetic tone of the opera, nor its recourse to totalising mythologies, had any resonance with the complex world of the present. On one level this was a simple attack on the musical establishment: from 1971 until 1976 Durkó had been Professor of Composition at the Liszt Academy, and in 1974, the newly inaugurated festival 'Music of Our Time' had devoted a whole concert to his works, an accolade that positioned him at the top of the new Hungarian musical life. On a deeper level, however, Tallián's review was expressing the new desire for less fixed and monumental forms of artistic expression. Another reviewer remarked what a worthy task Durkó fulfilled in building a bridge between avant-garde asceticism and the Hungarian tradition, but this dichotomy had long had its day,[15] because such rigid ideas about what constituted 'Hungarian traditions' and the supposedly 'ascetic' avant-garde were irrelevant to most younger critics. Those celebrating Attila Bozay's (b. 1939) *Improvisations* for zither (1972), for instance, admired not only his use of a traditional (folk) instrument, but also his formal flexibility and his development of an individual virtuosic style. The new move towards artistic experimentation is summed up by the very title of his work. And although a backlash would ensue, it came not from the government, but from the musical establishment itself. The case of another representative formation, the Budapest New Music Studio, makes this particularly clear.

The New Music Studio was Western in influence, but occupied a political position analogous to that of the Dance House. Its initial members, composers Zoltán Jeney (b. 1943), László Sáry (b. 1940) and László Vidovszky (b. 1944) had met regularly as students to discuss modern music and compare compositions. When they purchased Chinese gongs, however, and when they were invited to play them at the Communist Youth Alliance, the Director

[14] Tallián 1977. [15] Somfai 1974: 1; see also Tallián 1974.

of arts ensembles at the Alliance was impressed to the extent that he offered them a residency there.[16] Henceforth working at the Alliance with the resident conductor Albert Simon, the new 'Studio' operated initially within the sphere of education. Thus it provided two-part concerts presenting and discussing a major work from the first half of the twentieth century (by Varèse, Berg, or Webern, for instance), and performing a new piece by Jeney, Sáry, Vidovszky or part-member Péter Eötvös (b. 1944).[17] But when Vidovszky returned from studies in Paris in 1971 bearing scores and writings of John Cage, the Studio took a more experimental direction. The discovery of Christian Wolff (at Darmstadt in 1972), and then minimalism (in 1975) shaped its explorations further.[18] It attempted to wipe the historical slate clean, and develop new approaches to music's most basic pitch materials, timbres and temporalities through collaborative improvisation.

The government was unconcerned about all this experimentation, but when senior music reviewers and some established composers were confronted with it they exploded with a Hungarian protectionism that echoed decades of nationalist rhetoric. Breuer attacked Jeney's music in 1973 for its 'fashionable Zen Buddhism'; three years later he concluded a damning review of music by Jeney and Sáry by questioning the value of a workshop or laboratory that even after such a prolonged period brought not results, but merely additional experiments.[19] Composers such as Petrovich, Szokolay and Durkó had entered a phase of consolidation in these years, and they identified the Studio as a danger to the national interest. Petrovich proposed superciliously in 1975 that Hungarian music was now safely *beyond* its childish experimental years and had grown up.[20] Durkó was probably alarmed by the cult popularity of the Studio's events when he remarked in 1976 that audiences only liked the newest music because it was completely vacuous.[21] For Szokolay, it was crucial that Hungarian music unite stylistically, so that it could find a place on the international scene thereby. This view was shared

---

[16] Jeney and Sáry were initially invited to play by the conductor Albert Simon within a concert of new music he was presenting with the resident ensemble. The director of the arts ensembles was Pál Szigeti (a Moscow-trained communist). (Conversation with Jeney, June 2004.) The New Music Studio documentation housed at 'Artpool' (see Archives in Sources) includes concert programmes from December 1962 to June 1966 organised by the student composers' circle. See also Vidovszky and Weber 1998: 9.

[17] Eötvös, from 1966 onwards resident in Cologne – where he was variously a student, copyist, performer in Stockhausen's ensemble and assistant in the electronic studio of the West German Radio – travelled to Hungary regularly.

[18] Szitha 2000 analyses the impact of minimalism through an account of American minimalist works performed, visits from Rzewski and Reich (1977), and musical compositions by studio members. For a broader account in English, see Williams 2005.

[19] Breuer 1973b. Breuer 1976c.

[20] Interview with Mária Feuer (published in November 1975), Feuer 1978: 11–13.

[21] Interview with Feuer (published in January 1976), Feuer 1978: 21–3.

by Mihály, whose Budapest Chamber Ensemble had a rival in the Studio, and who felt that there was a need to clarify to foreigners just which music was a valuable representation of Hungary.[22]

The Studio, however, took advantage of the regime's new tolerance and support to sidestep nationalist protectionism. In doing so it was typical of a very broad shift in artistic trends, and it is particularly valuable to position it among some other new arrivals on the scene, starting with poet Dezső Tandori (b. 1938). Tandori had been a legend even before his first poetry volume *Töredék Hamletnek* (*Fragment for Hamlet*) emerged in 1968. Once published, the philosophically doubting tone of this volume had established him as a figure who polarised opinion.[23] His next volume *Egy talált tárgy megtisztítása* (*The Cleaning of an Objet Trouvé*, 1973), however, took him into what one reviewer recognised as 'non-art'.[24] The loss of the lyrical subject had turned into irony, and the volume triggered 'shock and embarrassment' in its presentation of visual symbols, empty pages and broken syntactical games.[25] Within the pages of *The Cleaning of an Objet Trouvé* the Hungarian language was deconstructed for the first time, high art collided with low, and Jesus jostled with everyday objects. Tandori's rejection of the unified subject, combined with a lack of interest in expressing emotions conventionally borne by poetry, meant that his work was read – even when sympathetically – as 'entirely foreign to the Hungarian tradition'.[26]

Tandori evidently had some interest in the New Music Studio, for he wrote a poem in reaction to *Schroeder halála* (*The Death of Schroeder*) of 1975, a piece for one pianist and three assistants by Vidovszky performed at a Studio concert.[27] By this time Jeney had encoded some of Tandori's linguistic experiments in pitches, and used them to produce partially automated compositions with permuting patterns in *Orfeusz kertje* (*Orpheus' Garden*, 1974), *Arthur Rimbaud a sivatagban* (*Arthur Rimbaud in the Desert*, 1976) and *Kiegészítések* (*Complements*, 1976).[28] Subsequently Tandori wrote

---

[22] Szokolay and Mihály interviewed by Feuer (published in March 1976 and December 1975 respectively), Feuer 1978: 38–40 and 19–20.

[23] Ferencz 1993: 84. These poems dated from 1959. I know of no research into any attempts made by Tandori to get his work published earlier on (there was not a large quantity of it and some had appeared in journals), but Ferencz alludes conspiratorially to obstacles. The volume also contained some of the first Hungarian haikus and koans. Tarján 1994 traces some of the history of these oriental genres in Hungarian literature.

[24] Aczél 1974: 72.   [25] Tarján 1974: 466.   [26] Radnóti 1974: 124.

[27] The poem is entitled 'Zoltán Kocsis Plays a "Chromatic" Vidovszky Work According to the Instructions of the Composer'. While the pianist plays scales up and down the piano, the assistants insert objects between the strings that progressively alter the timbre and pitch of selected notes. By the end of the piece all the strings have been dampened: the last scale the pianist plays is silent. When Zoltán Kocsis programmed it alongside Ravel and Schubert in the Great Hall of the Academy in 1977, it was heard with disapproval and disappointment by several reviewers.

[28] Szitha 2004 discusses the connections between music and text in Jeney's compositions setting Tandori and e.e. cummings.

a poem dedicated to Jeney entitled 'Ajánlás' (*Dedication*); this Jeney would then set in his *Eight Tandori Songs* (1984–7) as 'Echoes of Orpheus' Garden'. In the same cycle he included a setting of Tandori's 'Zoltán Kocsis Plays a "Chromatic" Vidovszky Work According to the Instructions of the Composer'.

A further new development on the scene was a new choir founded by musicologists László Dobszay, Janka Szendrei and Benjamin Rajeczky in 1969. Rather like Dance House and the New Music Studio itself, the initial emphasis of Schola Hungarica was on education and outreach: few choir members were professional singers; rather, the choir provided a way for interested parties to learn about medieval music through singing it. Simultaneously offering a new way of engaging with that fetish of Hungarian music life, music's connection to language, it became one of the most important musical formations of the decade and published the first recording of Hungarian polyphony in 1973. Avoiding direct conflict with the Party, it argued for as wide an audience (and choir membership) as possible, and was not involved in music for religious ritual.[29]

Finally, the most provocative group was the Kassák House Studio, one of two theatre ensembles that had formed after the break-up of a university theatre ensemble in the previous decade.[30] Initially housed in a state-sponsored Kultúrház (House of Culture) and taking its name from those particular premises, it was influenced by the work of the Polish director Jerzy Grotowski, attempting to reinvent theatre through a focus on event rather than text, and process rather than product. *Labyrinth* (January 1971), for instance, was an exploration of dance-like movements and gestures drawn from the intonation of spoken language, also using music by Kurtág's son, György Kurtág junior. *Quick Changes* (July 1971) was a Dada impromptu for outdoor stage in which both Kurtág jnr. and Lászlo Sáry contributed music.[31]

The very nature of theatre as a partly improvised 'event' threw down the gauntlet to ongoing censorship practices, even though Kassák House Studio productions were not political in subject. When the script of one production was altered between the council's permission to perform and

---

[29] It evolved in tandem with, but independently of, the revival of music in churches discussed above. See Dobszay 1998. New Music Studio members sang in the choir, as did Kurtág.

[30] Kassák House was the name of the particular House of Culture where the theatre group worked. Lajos Kassák (1887–1967) was a poet, prose writer and visual artist who was involved in working-class movements and joined the Social Democrats in the early part of the century; he also founded two avant-garde journals, *A Tett* (Action) and *Ma* (Today). He suffered under the conservatism of inter-war Budapest, but was also unable to publish under Rákosi. As the naming of the culture house indicates, he was later rehabilitated.

[31] Detailed in supplement to *Színház* 14:10–11 (1991): 1. See also Buchmuller and Koós 1996: 2.

the première itself, for instance, the council had an excuse to ban its (further) performance in January 1972. According to the report prepared, the players had interpolated 'obscene scenes and texts' that were a threat to public morality.[32] The group was subsequently banned from the House of Culture, but simply relocated to the apartment of one of the founders, actor Péter Halász, in February that year.[33] Thereafter operating illegally under the new name of 'Lakásszínház' (Apartment Theatre) or merely under the postal address (20 Dohány Street), it was an ongoing 'event' that survived for three further years, balanced precariously between the government's tolerance and potential prohibition. The most adventurous exploits were probably those challenging received ideas about the human body. Gender metamorphoses of actors problematised human sexuality, the presentation of physical actions usually taken in private (urination, labour) challenged the boundary between public and private spheres, while other performances included activities not considered part of society at all, such as vein-cutting and blood-drinking.[34] Although Party officials and secret agents attended performances (and reports were prepared and archived), it nevertheless operated as a hub of samizdat culture. In other words, it functioned as a (monitored) channel for radical artists.[35]

All these new arrivals on the scene were understandably silent on political matters (all were, after all, dependent in some way on the state). The New Music Studio was no exception to the rule: it introduced its compositions as purely abstract laboratory research.[36] Their activities were indeed

---

[32] This report is reproduced in the supplement to *Színház* 14:10–11 (1991): 8. There were political groups as well, of course, including 'Orfeo', which explicitly attempted to challenge the regime. Archival documents reveal the way the secret police infiltrated radical circles and attempted to obtain copies of the samizdat text called *Szétfolyóirat*. According to one report prepared, five copies of this were produced by one person; half the pages were left blank but were filled up with more contributions by those receiving it; they then reproduced their copy five times – and so on. See 'Reports regarding the samizdat periodical entitled "Szét-folyóirat"'. (Listed under c3 web archive in Sources.)

[33] This would not have been possible in the previous decade. For two somewhat romanticised accounts of this situation see O'Quinn 1979 and Dasgupta 1986.

[34] Buchmuller and Koós 1996: 8. Also Eörsi 1991: 30.

[35] Extensive descriptions were prepared for the party. See 'Reports regarding the Lakásszínház'. (Listed under c3 web archive in Sources.) Whilst there was a major attack in *Népszabadság* in 1972, the group published a defensive response in the same party organ. See supplement to *Színház* 14:10–11 (1991): 14–15.

[36] Only through practice-based composition could composers interact dynamically with audiences and experience the performed reality of their works, composers explained. Interviews with Vidovszky (originally published in November 1976) and Jeney (originally published in June 1977). Feuer 1978: 91 and 112–15. Mária Feuer conducted short interviews with a range of composers (including Jeney and Vidovszky) between 1975 and 1978 that were published in *Élet és Irodalom*; these were then collected into a volume. See Feuer 1978. When the Studio's first recordings were released (1975), liner notes were written by the musicologist who worked within the group, András Wilheim. The most extended interviews with members appeared in *Mozgó Világ* (Moving World) in 1978, under the title 'Young Radicals'. See Kovács (András) 1978.

politically innocuous and could really provoke only nationalists or traditional concert audiences who were confounded by surprising constellations of composer, performer and musical work. Vidovszky's *405* (1972) 'exploded' the performer: while much of the piece was played by a pianist on the stage, a hidden ensemble contributed too, and a ring modulator transformed what they played and conveyed the result through loudspeakers into the corridors of the building.[37] More radically, his *Autoconcert* (1972) had no performer at all and the compositional process was purely conceptual: the nine-minute piece was composed of the gradual falling of instruments (suspended on a string) to the floor, and entropy brought about by two (hidden) technicians. Eötvös's *Elektrochronik* (1972) – prepared at the electronic studio in Cologne and presented by the Studio in Budapest in 1975 – was a further challenge to the paradigm, and was a more elaborate electronic work than had hitherto been heard in Hungary.

The fact that the New Music Studio was only musically – rather than politically – provocative is particularly clear once its development is set alongside that of the Kassák House Studio. While the latter was able to operate only illegally after 1972 (as the Apartment Theatre), in the same period the New Music Studio concerts entered the printed discourses of *Muzsika*, where the team of young reviewers was strongly supportive.[38] Whereas the Apartment Theatre was prevented from leaving the country to perform in international festivals between 1973 and 1975, the New Music Studio was able to travel to perform in Poland in 1973 and France in 1974.[39] In the autumn of 1974, moreover, one reviewer complained that the New Music Studio had been undeservedly sidelined by the first new-music festival 'Music of Our Time', but in the following year, the Studio's first concert at the Great Hall of the Liszt Academy was advertised within the festival brochure.[40] And although

---

[37] Vidovszky and Weber 1997: 18.
[38] The first review was Papp 1972, in which the Studio was presented as the means to bridge the gap between new music and the (uncomprehending) general public. Three New Music Studio concerts were reviewed in April, May and June 1973. There was proportionately less coverage in the ensuing year; the real breakthrough would happen only in 1976.
[39] Members of the Kassák House Studio had taken part in the Nancy Theatre Festival, performed at the Centre Américaine in Paris in 1971 and travelled to Poland in 1973, but their passports were withdrawn thereafter. Attempting to negotiate emigration, only in 1975, following the Helsinki Accords, were they able to travel abroad as 'tourists'. They then refused to return to Hungary – while the State attempted to command them home – and settled in New York, where they founded the Squat Theatre. For literature analysing or describing individual New York productions and generally assessing their work, see Shank and Shank 1978, Kőrösi 1981, O'Quinn 1980 and Shank 1992. See also the company's own documents and recollections in Buchmuller and Koós 1996: 48–205.
[40] Tallián 1974: 7. Ironically, it was postponed because of concerns about the propriety of the music programmed; but the concert did take place there in December. One reviewer alludes to the concert's postponement being due to 'technical reasons'. See Farkas 1976: 40. The real reason however, was that the title of Barnabás Dukay's piece, 'O', aroused suspicion. It was suggested that it might be linked with the sensational, erotic, art-house film *Histoire d'O*, based on Pauline

Breuer portrayed the whole concert as the very nadir of tedium, the New Music Studio was no longer operative only in the sphere of education, and at peripheral concert venues. It had graduated into a supported contributor to the official, mainstream establishment of Budapest music life.[41]

Kurtág's presence

Kurtág was often in attendance at samizdat theatre workshops, and was a close follower of the New Music Studio.[42] Observing this much, however, offers but a tantalising glimpse of his public visibility: all it suggests is that he was one of many people hungry for explorations beyond the legislated possible. In fact he was a somewhat private and elevated member of society, dignifying events by his presence. This elevation was registered by the New Music Studio when they composed an extended composition entitled *Hommage à György Kurtág*.[43]

In order to grasp how his eminence had developed, it is instructive to think back on the 1960s and view Kurtág's position sociologically. Three factors seem particularly significant, namely timing, networking, and use of language. And the first is relatively straightforward. Kurtág's change of compositional style and his symbolic gesture of writing an Opus 1 coincided with a moment in which people were eager for both musical and political change. He 'came of age' at an opportune moment: op. 1 was banned, but then rescued and performed, in an environment of exceptionally overheated political dissatisfaction.

The second factor is more complicated to establish, for the society was not one in which people developed documentary records of their activities – far from it. There is nonetheless ample evidence to argue that Kurtág had three types of influential contacts. One is symbolic: his association with

---

Réage's similarly scandalous 1954 novella, and made in 1975. Dukay's work was performed in the December concert, with the new title *Quadruplus*. Thanks to Zoltán Jeney, Tibor Tallián and László Vidovszky for this information. (Private conversations, June 2004.)

[41] Breuer 1976b. Kocsis published an apologia for the studio in the next issue of *Mozgó Világ* (Kocsis 1976); see also Kárpáti 1976: 23–4.

[42] A report prepared by the secret police lists those present as including 'Kurtág and his father'; (i.e. Kurtág's son György Kurtág along with the composer). See under 'Reports regarding the Lakásszínház', 'Jelentés', (10 March 1975), p. 183 housed at c3 web archive (see Bibliography). In a photo reproduced in Buchmuller and Koós 1996: 15, Kurtág's head can be seen poking out above a sheet stretched from wall to wall of a room. This performance was called 'Face to Face'. Documents, photos and recollections indicate that Kurtág (senior) was present at many Apartment Theatre productions, and on winning the Kossuth Prize in 1975 he distributed it between seven underground theatre groups. See Buchmuller and Koós 1996: 213.

[43] Reviewers were generally rather concerned to separate Kurtág out from the Studio's activities. Even when the Studio programmed his music, critics cordoned off the ostensibly irresponsible experiments of the young from the mature figure who was their mentor, arguing that nothing the Studio did had anything to do with Kurtág. Breuer 1976c. Farkas 1977.

figures of artistic importance such as poet János Pilinszky and painter Lili Ország endowed him with cultural respect in intellectual and artistic circles.[44] Another group of contacts was professional, of whom the most important was composer and cellist András Mihály. We have encountered Mihály in several guises already: illegal communist during the Second World War, defender of Bartók in 1949, apparatchik on trial in 1951 and founder and conductor of the Budapest Chamber Ensemble in 1968. But more importantly here, Mihály's Coaching of Kurtág's String Quartet op. 1, and his organisation of the Darmstadt and Budapest premières of *The Sayings of Péter Bornemisza*, resulted in concerts that provided the foundations for Kurtág's renown after 1956.

Finally, Kurtág's reputation was also spread through a network of performers and students, because after returning from Paris he worked as an accompanist at the Bartók Conservatory, and was subsequently employed as a pianist at the National Philharmonia where he accompanied a wide range of singers and instrumentalists. Already in touch with a large number of performers as a result, when he began teaching piano at the Liszt Academy in 1967 he encountered more of the younger generation. Clearly he developed thereby a wider reputation as pedagogue than would have been possible had he worked only in a composition faculty or with new-music enthusiasts. And when he left the piano faculty, taking up the post of Professor in the department of Chamber Music (where Mihály was Chair), he was in touch with a more diverse group of students.[45] And in the same year – as discussed at the end of Chapter 3 – the merits of his instrumental coaching were discussed in a newly published book.

This book did not merely promote his pedagogical strength, however. It also provided material testimony to a composer behaving rather differently from his peers, a composer behaving in a way that invited mythologisation. Indeed by 1975 a very specific reason was recorded for his apparent verbal reticence. Unlike other composers, explained a journalist, Kurtág could not introduce audiences to his music because of 'an ethical stance that makes it

---

[44] The nature of their contact is of less importance than the fact that they were understood as a group. Lili Ország's turn to a highly spiritual semi-abstract modernism and public recognition occurred in the early 1960s, parallel with Kurtág's own shift, and her work is referred to by art historian Katalin S. Nagy as 'lonely but not without companions . . . distant from the period's official, supported art, but close to the true representative creations of the 1960s spirit: Pilinszky, Kurtág, Béla Kondor'. Nagy 1993: 26.

[45] This move, moreover, was also significant in terms of how it coloured his reputation. Shifting from a sphere where the primary historical model was the virtuoso Liszt (whose reputation was always somewhat contested in Hungary), he entered one in which the associations with the repertory were spiritually and intellectually more elevated, and simultaneously, he came in line with a legendary professor of chamber music, Leó Weiner. See Beckles Willson 2004c for a discussion about pedagogical genealogies in Budapest.

imperative for [him] to communicate everything that can be said in music, and only that when he has found the appropriate form for it'.[46] In other words, unwillingness to speak publicly had been brought in line with Kurtág's earlier moral turn: refusing to build conceptual bridges between music and the outside world fitted the notion that he had rejected public success in favour of inner truth.

It would be simplistic to imagine that this idealist statement represents the only view held at the time or an unmediated representation of Kurtág's own reasoning.[47] Its explanatory grandeur might form an evocative background to the ways that the works themselves could contribute to emergent 'Kurtág myths', however. In the three sections that follow I trace paths through such possibilities.

Music and Passion

The most obvious starting-point is the poetry that Kurtág set, and his choice of the work of Pilinszky was highly significant. *Four Songs to Poems by János Pilinszky* op. 11 (1975) staged his alliance with a modernist poet who had been banned from publishing his work in the Stalinist years. Before we start to imagine Pilinszky as an obstreperous dissident, however, we do well to observe that the Kádár regime was not actually hostile towards him – despite his emphatically spiritual approach and lack of engagement with party rhetoric – and that he was celebrated in the press. The regime had, after all, allowed his explicitly religious *Harmadnapon* (*On the Third Day*) to be published back in 1959, a book that offers material testimony to a watchfully supportive attitude towards the Catholic Church. Pilinszky, in other words, was one more channel for exploring ideas that differed from the mainstream political policy, but that were nonetheless underwritten by the state.

The political provenance of the first poem, 'Alcohol', is nevertheless resolutely opaque: its text is inscrutable. In the song, moreover, the singer seems barely able to enunciate it. Rather than singing or even intoning the poem, he opens with an extended 'Ey' sound (the first syllable) that is to be

---

[46] According to a concert review of an event in the biannual series of 'composer–audience encounters', László Somfai made this announcement about Kurtág, and proceeded to introduce the composer's music himself. It is revealing to note that after the performance, Kurtág was available for informal discussion with those who wished, and was rapidly surrounded by people talking to him. Székely 1975: 15–16.

[47] Imre Földes, who conducted the interviews for the book, recalls that Kurtág's reason for not speaking publicly was that he did not merit it ('nem érdemli'). Phone conversation, October 2004. There is no particular reason to mistrust this: in 1967 Kurtág had twelve years behind him in which he had completed only five chamber works.

produced first on the palate, then with a 'pressed sound', and then *molto vibrato*. His unsettling contortions to vocal timbre finally give way to an intonation – on the same monotone D – of the first line of the poem. 'Ey' follows again, this time ushering in an intonation of line 2, broken only by an extended 'Ey' that passes through other vowels before settling on the last words of the line. The voice then takes on a quieter, 'guttural voice', then hums, before intoning the last, weird, lines. The whole poem is as follows:

Előhívom a lehetetlent,	I conjure up the impossible,
egy ház áll rajta s egy bokor,	a house stands on it, a bush,
egy néma, néma állat és	a silent, silent creature and
egy nadrágszár a szürkületben.	a trouser leg in falling darkness.[48]

The vocal cavity itself seems throughout to be painfully pinioned on a line, yet at precisely the moment of the poem's 'falling darkness' the voice sinks one semitone onto C♯; dropping one further to C natural, for a final, sustained thin vowel, 'üü'. A sustained bass zither D underpins the entire incantation.[49]

The last two songs of the collection also engage explicitly with corporeal struggle. In the third, 'Hölderlin', lurching rhythms created by the thick texture of strings are reminiscent of the *aksak* 'limping' dance patterns Bartók associated with Bulgaria. The explicitly mimetic sounds of the instruments seem to scratch and gnaw at themselves too, viola and cello playing partly *sul ponticello*, partly *col legno*, partly *battuto*, partly *tratto*. The voice rages above, until the moment at which it renounces life, when a 'resolution' surfaces in triple *piano* tremolo string playing (partly on harmonics); and a whispered last sentence.

December hőse, nyarak jégverése,	December heat, the hails of summers,
drótvégre csomózott madár,	a bird knotted to a piece of wire,
mi nem voltam én? Boldogan halok.	what was I not? Gladly I die.[50]

---

[48] Translation by L. T. András, as printed in the score, Editio Musica Budapest Z.7939. Original: Pilinszky 1997: 133. The collection sets two songs each from Pilinszky's *Denouement* (*Végkifejlet*, 1974) and *Crater* (*Kráter*, 1975). As was the case with all poems in these volumes, all four were previously published individually in literary journals, the first two in 1973, the second two in 1974.

[49] The score indicates bass 'citara' (presumably zither), viola da gamba or double bass *con sordino sul pont*. This accompaniment is optional.

[50] When he published it in 1974, Pilinszky dedicated this to Kurtág. (*Kortárs* 10 (September), 1349.) Translated here by Peter Jay. Pilinszky 1978: 32. Original: Pilinszky 1997: 146.

The title of the last song, 'Beating', implies blows, and the musical setting is correspondingly corporeal. In between groups of strikes and strike-like gestures in the instrumental group (two cimbaloms, string trio, zither, horn and clarinet), the voice gasps bits of the text, as if it is this singer, here on the stage, who is being beaten.

Most elviselhető.	Now it's endurable.
Most másra gondolok.	Now I think of something else.
Most semmi sincs.	Now there's nothing.
Most én vagyok.	Now I am myself.
Most minden van.	Now there's everything.
Most tűrhetetlen.	Now it's unbearable.
Most pedig, most és egyedül,	Now, though, now and alone,
itt és most, végképp egyedül	here and now, alone for good
csak te meg én.[51]	only you and me.[51]

Patently, then, and despite their reference to Hölderlin, these songs do not project the image of Kurtág's ethical elevation that one might expect from the way in which his public verbal reticence was discussed. They are earthy and visceral. But the second song, 'In memoriam F. M. Dostoevsky', provides a larger and very suggestive context for both their physical torments and Kurtág's discursively constructed moral loftiness. Its title invokes the revered and deeply religious novelist of nineteenth-century Russia; meanwhile, however, the poem itself alludes to Russia's arbitrary cruelty by presenting a humiliating unclothing:

Hajoljon le. (Földig hajol.)	Bend down. (Bends to the ground.)
Álljon föl. (Fölemelkedik.)	Stand erect. (Rises up slowly.)
Vegye le az ingét, gatyáját. (Mindkettőt leveszi.)	Take off your shirt and underpants. (Takes them off one by one.)
Nézzen szembe. (Elfordúl. Szembenéz.)	Turn and face me. (Turns away. Faces him.)
Öltözzön föl.	Put on your clothes.
(Fölöltözik.)	(Puts them back on.)[52]

[51] Translated by Peter Jay in Pilinszky 1978: 31. Original: Pilinszky 1997: 146.
[52] Translation by L. T. András, taken from the score (Editio Musica Budapest Z.7939). Original: Pilinszky 1997: 133.

Example 4.1. Kurtág, 'In memoriam F. M. Dostoevsky' (*Four Songs to Poems by János Pilinszky* Op. 11)

* ad lib: citara bassa (arco) o viola da gamba al fine

The performers articulate a confrontation between interrogator and interrogated: the bass-baritone speaks the text (to approximate pitches) in paired sections, and violin and double bass, *meno forte*, accompany each descriptive statement (see Ex. 4.1). This grows into a mini-narrative. Whilst the violin's dissonant double-stops and the plucked bass pizzicato initially follow the vocal line, they diverge increasingly from it, generating greater motion and variation, a process that reaches its climax on '(Turns away. Faces him.)'. The substantial pause that ensues invites reflection on the suggestion of the text: a naked man (powerless) stands in front of a clothed one (in command). Yet this pause is followed by sounds that transform the imaginary scenario. As if conjuring up the fairy-tale magic of a harp, a spread triple-stop on the violin introduces open fifths, *piano, quasi dolce*, and the double bass plays *arco*. The next command, 'Put on your clothes' is intoned *quasi falsetto*. The final bar provides consonant closure, in the form of the four open strings of the violin, partially supported by a natural harmonic C on the double bass. The condemned man was saved.

As a group of four, then, these songs present not only distorted vision and physical cruelty (with a specific political resonance), but also the hope of redemption (Dostoevsky's own death sentence was revoked at the last moment[53]). The music of 'In memoriam F. M. Dostoevsky', moreover, enacts a process of salvation through uninhibited corporeality: the moment of nakedness is a turning point of the intoned text. For if it seems initially that the power is in the hands of the one uttering the commands, then by the end it appears that the one stripped naked gains strength from his very nakedness, triggering a loss of voice in the commander, and a harmonic resolution to the entire episode. The song is thus metaphorical. It moves beyond the specifics of a prison interrogation (where an unclothing would not result in any such transformation in a real sense) to a level of intimating – while not describing – some of the powers of nudity.

The songs could, consequently, contribute to the idealised image of Kurtág that was emerging in the press. For writer Gábor Thurzó, lines 5 and 6 of 'Beating' touched on precisely the need to be searching – but never finding – Truth. 'Now there's everything' followed immediately by 'Now it's unbearable' encapsulated Thurzó's philosophy for life, according to which the point of his existence would be lost once everything was known and understood. He also found that the music *touched* him, physically: the sounds became more and more homely as he listened repeatedly so that finally he felt that they came from within him.[54]

We can, however, explore this physicalised idealism rather further by comparing the songs with Kurtág's *Szálkák* (*Splinters*) op. 6c. When the so-named four pieces for solo cimbalom were first performed in Budapest, not all writers were aware of the provenance of the title, which was a volume of Pilinszky's poetry published in 1973. János Breuer knew, however, and celebrated Kurtág himself as a 'true poet' when he heard it, a claim that is worth examining.[55] He quoted from 'Metronome', one of the poems published in Pilinszky's own *Splinters*, as an analogy for Kurtág's own mastery of silence and musical time:

---

[53] The volume in which this poem was published, *Denouement*, contains two other explicit references to Dostoevsky in the form of two poems about the character Stavrogin from *The Devils*, 'Stavrogin Takes His Leave' and 'Stavrogin Returns'. Stavrogin's name being Greek for 'cross', this unfortunate character was an entirely appropriate focus for Pilinszky's obsessions, as will become clearer below.

[54] Thurzó 1977.   [55] Breuer 1974a.

Mérd az időt,	Measure time
de ne a mi időnket,	but not our time,
a szálkák mozdulatlan jelenét,	the motionless present of splinters,
a fölvonóhíd fokait,	the angles of the drawbridge,
a téli vesztőhely havát,	the white winter of our execution,
ösvények és tisztások csöndjét	the silence of paths and clearings[56]

This claim for this poem's relevance to Kurtág was actually an amazing obfuscation, for Breuer had omitted its last two lines, precisely the lines that reveal the poet's primary source of inspiration:

a töredék foglalatában	in the setting of the fragmented jewel
az Atyaisten igéretét.	the promise of God the Father.

At one strike, in fact, Breuer had erased the single most significant element of Pilinszky's new volume (and, by extension, the title of Kurtág's new work). Although metaphysics had been a crucial part of Pilinszky's poetry from his very earliest work, *Splinters* was a particular milestone in the poet's development, not only because it broke with conventional forms, pared down poetic means and created an almost fragmentary texture, but because it also transformed death from being a source of terror and horror to something that might be welcome.[57]

Pilinszky's adherence to profoundly violent imagery remained unbroken, but now physical suffering was rediscovered as a vital force, and the poems drew repetitively on the ultimate Christian symbol for such suffering, the crucifix. Most importantly, one of the words he used for the crucifix was nothing other than 'splinter'. Thus the very title of his new volume bore the weight of the spiritual symbol, as indeed did Kurtág's own pieces. As the poem 'Before', for instance, suggests, the poet sees the day of judgement before him and:

... Az Atya, mint egy szálkát	... The Father, as if it were a splinter,
visszaveszi a keresztet ...	withdraws the cross ...[58]

---

[56] Translated by William Jay Smith. Vajda (ed.) 1977: 152. Original: 'Metronom', Pilinszky 1997: 99.
[57] Diószeghi 1973: 1676–7; Fülöp 1973: 78; Béládi 1973. This ability to face the future may have been a response to the new political situation as much as an internal shift within Pilinszky himself. At least one writer argued it was a response to general trends in Catholicism within the Eastern bloc, where there was an effort made to look beyond suffering and offering a vision for life (or afterlife) beyond it. (Diószeghi 1973: 1678–9.)
[58] 'Mielőtt' in Pilinszky 1997: 95. My translation.

Withdrawing the splinter of life leads here to salvation later on in the poem, represented by weeping at the Lord's Table with angels in attendance.

If we examine this transformative moment more fully, we gain a telling perspective for reading Kurtág. Pilinszky's splinter (crucifix) represents a universal human besmirchment: humanity, in its inherent evil, is as a whole deservedly and permanently nailed to a cross – we may even 'be' the nail in the flesh of humanity. Sheer physical mutilation thus shaped a number of poems, including 'Cattle Brand', in which:

A világ tenyerébe kalapált szeg, holtsápadt, csurom vér vagyok.	A nail driven into the world's palm, pale as death, I flow with blood.[59]

But the crucifix was also a representation of a cross-section of death with life. Its two physical dimensions were a constant reminder that human life was not a straight line from birth to death, thus it could remain a symbol of hope, evoking a repetitive encounter with Truth through which one could forget oneself (a sort of death), only to rediscover oneself.[60] The constant pain of being nailed to the cross was thus something to celebrate, just as was its echo, the piercing pain caused by splinters. As the second poem in the volume, 'To Jutta' concludes:

'Latrokként – Simone Weil gyönyörű szavával – tér és idő keresztjére vagyunk mi verve emberek.' Elalélok, és a szálkák fölriasztanak. Ilyenkor metsző élességgel látom a világot, és megpróbálom feléd fordítani a fejemet.	'As thieves – in the lovely words of Simone Weil – we are people beaten to the cross of time and space.' I faint, and the splinters arouse me. At such times I see the world with cutting clarity, and try to turn my head towards you.[61]

---

[59] Translated by William Jay Smith, adjusted by Peter Sherwood. Vajda (ed.) 1977: 154. Original: 'Marhabélyeg', in Pilinszky 1997: 110.

[60] Such 'deaths' or moments of revelation became for Pilinszky more consequential than physical death, which could never be truly experienced in itself. These sentiments are characteristic of Pilinszky's writings over the early 1970s, but are particularly clearly summarised in his 'Egy lírikus naplójából' [From the diary of a lyric poet], Új Ember 25 February 1973, reprinted in Pilinszky 1999: 694–5.

[61] 'Juttának', in Pilinszky 1997: 94. My translation.

Example 4.2. Kurtág, *Splinters* Op. 6c, movement 2

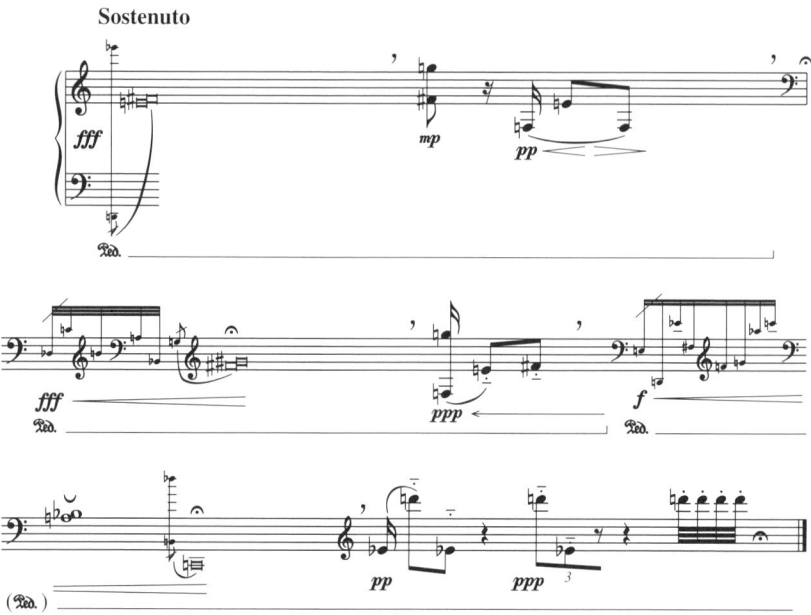

Here splinters are the fragments of a great crucifix borne by mankind as a whole, and they trigger a painful vision of truth. Thus physical suffering evolves into a means to superior understanding.[62]

Even on a superficial level, such an understanding of 'splinters' is a potent context for Kurtág's op. 6c. Movement 2, marked 'Sostenuto', is composed of three sweeping 'blows' to the strings, and their resonant aftermaths (see Ex. 4.2). During the dying resonances, lightly touched gestural fragments seem to make 'comments', the last one of which anticipates the lament motive of movement 4. We might imagine these three explicitly physical strikes as references to Pilinszky's crucifix, each percussive blow to the instrument a nail driven through flesh into the cross, and the fragments stirring after them are as if splinters under the skin.

Movement 4 labels itself as a reflection on death, not only subtitled *in memoriam Ştefan Romaşcanu*, but also drawing on musical weeping figures typical of folk laments and the *pianto* topic of the Baroque (see Ex. 4.3). And – as if an echo of Pilinszky's consoling and optimistic reflections on

---

[62] Reference to the nature of the splinters crops up throughout the literature. For example, in a 1973 interview with the poet (Török (ed.) 1983: 83), in commentary (Fülöp 1973; Béládi 1973) and in Ted Hughes' visionary essay on his work first published in 1976 (Hughes 1989).

Example 4.3. Kurtág, *Splinters* Op. 6c, movement 4, opening

mortality – while this first section evokes the sadness in death and loss, the second may evoke liberation from such pain. Above a 'tolling' bass note (D) in a continuous decrescendo from *fortissimo* to *quasi niente*, the widely displaced chromatic descent (from C♯ thirteen steps down to C natural) creates a broken melody of fragmentary musical shapes allowing the performer to create a sense of resolution and release.

Yet it is even more rewarding to bring this frame of reference to Four Songs op. 11. The nail through the palm hovers in the background there too ('a bird knotted to a piece of wire'); and a martyr's death is suggested immediately thereafter: '. . . (Gladly I die)'. Pilinszky's poems, as Ted Hughes argued, 'reveal a place where every cultural support has been torn away, where the ultimate brutality of total war has become natural law, and where man has been reduced to the mere mechanism of his mutilated body'.[63] Yet such anti-aesthetic, 'primal' moments in Four Songs are striking for the way that they stage extreme indignity and pain in order to transform it – such as in the moment of nakedness – into calm resolution. Degrading reduction, perversely, becomes a moment of transcendence in musical expression.

As already mentioned, not all critics were aware of the provenance of the title 'splinters', and none of the texts of Four Songs prompted them to mention the broader spiritual frame within which their poet existed.[64] Unsurprisingly they made no reference to the ways in which either work might be positioned within the current political reality either. Silence in that area does not remove the fact that references to Dostoevsky's near execution

[63] Hughes 1989 [1976]: 11.
[64] Reviewers were uniformly praising of the immediacy of op. 11: they focused on its exposure of the 'greatest secrets' of the composer's workshop, and the 'primal' connection it created between speech and song. Breuer 1975, Várnai 1975. Tallián 1974. For Wilheim (1975) *Splinters* was an 'unbroken whole' developing in an 'uninterrupted line', Gill (1982: 43) heard a single '*piece* in four *sections*', while Várnai (1974) openly puzzled about the strange title, for the music wasn't, he said, 'splintery' at all.

and being 'knotted to wire' could have been understood as an allusion to the suffering caused by the Soviet oppression, and perhaps human culpability more generally as well. The moments of resolution and salvation could even have been grasped as projections of martyrdom for a greater good.

Narratives of tragedy and redemption have a history in Hungarian mythology, as I mentioned in the Introduction, and recent events – those of 1956 in particular – fitted into the mould of Hungary's role as tragic 'witness'. The songs touched on precisely this set of ideas, even if only tangentially. Once presented on the musical stage, moreover, they publicly drew Kurtág into the sphere of Pilinszky's sacrificial religiosity, and they implicitly constructed the two artists in terms of a struggle to speak the truth through physical torment and anguish. And yet the government's convoluted polity led it to underwrite their presentation, and thus participate in an exploration of guilt, incarceration, and a celebration of revelation through suffering. The première of *Four Poems*, after all, took place in a particularly prominent and prestigious (state-supported) concert. To that event we can now turn.

Interlude: Games, *or passing the message on*

Kurtág's choice not to speak about his works was no obstacle to their canonisation (as we have seen), but until the middle of the decade there are no grounds at all for calling him a conscious strategist. His public manner would change, however, in two significant steps. The first was in 1975 when it was his turn for the honour that Durkó received in 1974, namely a portrait concert in the 'Music of our Time' festival. An entire evening was dedicated to his work and held at the Great Hall of the Liszt Academy, the most prestigious platform in the city. It was at this concert that *Four Songs* received its première, and Kurtág took an active role in his music's presentation at this point. It is tempting to see his involvement as a means of placing himself in a very specific and long-standing national tradition, for he had made one aspect of himself legible to everyone, and this was his devotion to teaching. The programme included the première of some of his (didactic) pieces for piano, *Játékok* (*Games*); these, furthermore, were performed by some of Kurtág's students, who thus placed his teaching right onto the public stage.[65] Yet more strikingly, however, the printed programme included a pithy autobiographical text that closed with a description of the composer's initiation into teaching in terms of professionally inherited responsibility, faith and passion:

---

[65] The most detailed study of *Játékok* available is Wischmann 1997. A number of shorter articles engage with one or more of the pieces. See, for instance, Hohmaier 2001 and Johnson 2002.

> When I was sixteen years old my piano teacher entrusted me with some of her pupils for coaching. Since then I have, almost without interruption, taught fervently.[66]

Pedagogical repertoire, student performers and candid personal dedication combined to offer a winning cocktail. The city was undergoing a renaissance in children's repertoire more broadly, and *Games* was an example of how the national pedagogic tradition was coming back to life.[67] In its anti-mechanistic, exploratory style it connected unmistakably with Veress's *Fingerlarks* of 1948 (discussed in Chapter 2), for each drew on the idea of an innocent child to harness children's playfulness, curiosity and bravura at the keyboard. But of course the primary model was obvious, and Kroó eloquently expressed what all critics said in one way or another: *Games* was a concentrated, purified version of Bartók's magnificent pedagogical series: it was the absolute 'quintessence' of *Mikrokosmos*.[68]

As the accolades flowed, then, they had a canonising and legitimating tone. Kurtág was now 'probably the most significant Hungarian composer', 'one of the most significant representatives of new Hungarian music'.[69] Little wonder that *Games*' influences that were less unequivocally celebrated went unmentioned. The New Music Studio is patently in the background: Volume I opens with an extensive table of 'Basic Elements', the palm strokes, elbow clusters and glissandi which parallel the Studio's process of 'starting from scratch'. The 'Key to Signs Used' also intersects with the Studio's interest in engaging with temporal relations more questioningly than would be the case with standard notation – in other words, *Games* encourage improvisation (see Ex. 4.4). The same tendency emerges in the pieces themselves, most of which lack barlines: durations unfold in a series that performers must construct relationally. Kurtág's work here can be understood as one of the Studio members constructed his own: 'composition equals research'.[70]

This workshop approach could also be understood as an echo of Schola Hungarica, as the Preface to the score of *Games* encourages performers to draw on all they know of Gregorian chant and free declamation. But pieces such as 'Walking' and 'Let's Be Silly', in which the body's relation with the keyboard is the theme, can become pieces of theatre, and if there is a Hungarian theatrical impulse they echo, it is surely the (by then banned)

---

[66] 'Korunk zenéje 1975': programme booklet p. 19.
[67] See, for instance, *Tarka-Barka* [Multi-Coloured], an anthology of piano music for children bringing together pieces by László Borsody, Attila Bozay, Lajos Huszár, Miklós Kocsár and József Soproni; Kurtág contributed nineteen pieces he called 'Pre-Ludes' (*Elő-Játékok*). Zeneműkiadó 7769.
[68] Kroó 1975 and Breuer 1975. See also the similarly ecstatic Farkas 1975 and Várnai 1975.
[69] Várnai 1975 and Breuer 1975.
[70] András Wilheim's introduction to the Studio's work cited in McLay 1982: 93.

Example 4.4. Kurtág, 'Key to Signs Used', from *Games*

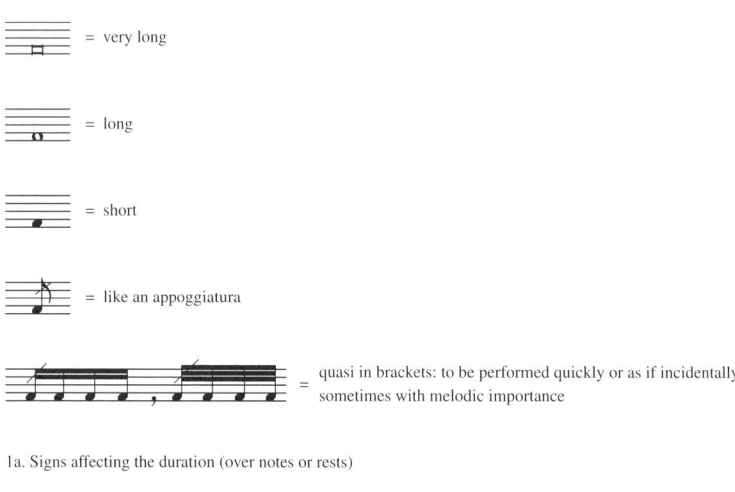

1a. Signs affecting the duration (over notes or rests)

⌢ = very long prolongation

⌢ = long prolongation

⌣ = shortened

1b. The range of sound values, in decreasing order:

Kassák House Studio and the Apartment Theatre (see Ex. 4.5). Embracing the body's connections with music in less than orthodox ways, such pieces lead the musical piece into unexpected fields of play. 'Quarrelling' has two versions in Volume I, only one of which has any sound. In the silent version, 'Dumb Show', the entire performance is a set of bodily gestures around the keyboard.

If Kurtág's first intervention in his public image was to construct himself as a teacher, his second was to remind the world that he was also a performer. Whereas in 1975 he had had his students playing *Games*, he was more assertive in 1979 and took the platform himself. By playing *Games* with his wife Márta, he transformed himself from a shadowy presence and a canonised text, straight into a live Event.

What could be the impact when the model of morality, the renowned pedagogue, possibly the leading voice of Hungarian music, stepped out of the modest shadows and offered his own music, with his very being, on the stage? How would a critic raise a pen to take account of the event? A predictable answer appeared in the pages of *Muzsika*, in which the critic

Example 4.5. Kurtág, 'Let's Be Silly', from *Games* Volume I

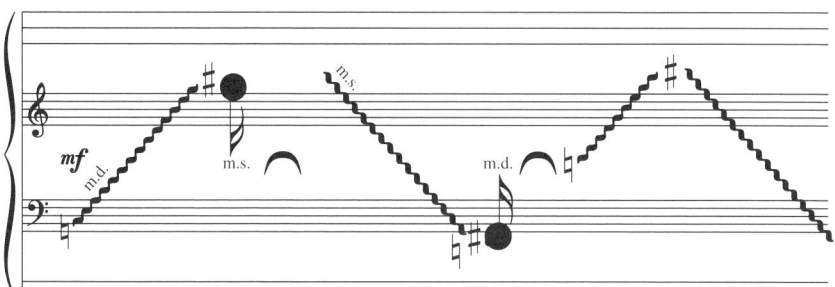

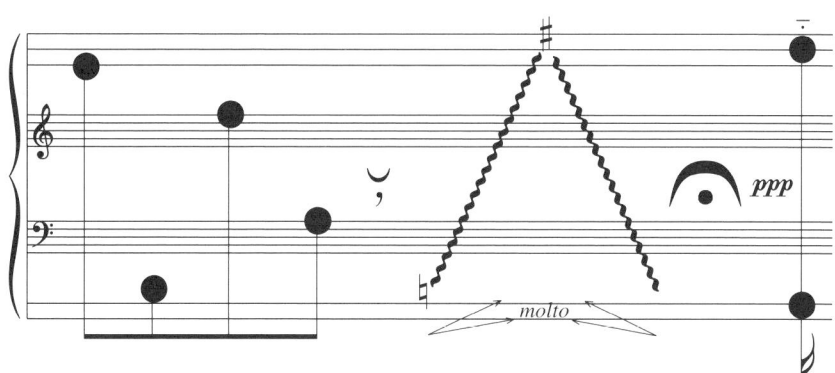

could barely bring himself to enunciate a view: 'I have no words', he wrote, 'with which to represent the experience that this concert provided. I have perhaps never before left a concert hall feeling the *significance* of the hour and a half so strongly.'[71] The ethical imperative of Kurtág's own reticence with words made it all but impossible for the critic to speak.

That is certainly the view that is suggested by sociology. And we can reinforce it with the fact that the authority of Kurtág's teaching was intimidatingly double-edged: it offered not only great rewards, but also tremendous personal cost, for his demands could be cruelly idealistic.[72] Of this, there will be more to discover in Chapter 6. But it would be impoverishing to stay with sociology alone at this point. If there was a powerful context for becoming speechless, that context could also be a powerful trigger for feeling genuinely overwhelmed. I would suggest, moreover, that it is worth

---

[71] Kovács 1979: 7. Italics original.
[72] The idealism inherent in the usual paradigm of classical music practice legitimates suffering in the interest of 'the music' – understood as above the performer, who is in its service. For more on this in the Budapest context see Beckles Willson 2004a: 147–59 (interviews with Erika Sziklay and Lóránt Szűcs, first performers of *The Sayings of Péter Bornemisza*) and Beckles Willson 2004c for an essay on the subject.

Example 4.6. Kurtág, 'Objet trouvé (2)', from *Games* Volume I

engaging with *Games* themselves to investigate ways in which these pieces may have *afforded* profoundly emotional responses, how they played into the emerging narratives.

It may at first seem very difficult to make the case. Many of the *Games*, after all, carry minimal compositional elaboration and bear strikingly modest titles, as if warning performers and listeners in advance that they are mere *objets trouvés*. In the first *Game* of Volume I, the pianist is to perform glissandi up and down the keyboard repetitively. In the second, repeated F♯s are presented in one hand against glissando passages played by the other (see Ex. 4.6). In other *objets trouvés*, however, namely genres from the past – Sarabandes, Waltzes, for example – there are rather specific references to other music. Such 'found' genres were part of precisely the European musical tradition to which Hungary wished to belong, and from which it felt barred by the Soviet Union. Additionally, although composers' earlier investigation of the western avant-garde had been understood and accepted, by the mid-1960s, as we have seen, many sought a return to more traditional roots.[73] Kurtág's 'playing' could contribute to an ongoing hope of recapturing something, especially when he placed himself on the platform *with his wife*, for that gesture could be experienced as a return to an intimate 'European' sphere of music practice – whether *Hausmusik* or salon culture.[74]

---

[73] This narrative is transparent in Kroó 1971, but had already emerged in reviews of Durkó and others during the mid-1960s.

[74] Conceivably it may have echoed with recollections of Bartók playing with *his* wife too.

After 1968: Budapest, Kurtág, and events

More subtly, though, the very brevity of Kurtág's *Games* maximises the ephemeral aspect of music. *Games* offer very elusive moments of 'presence' that evaporate almost as they are heard. Their minimal textual complexity, moreover, enforces a maximalisation of performative investment. If we turn for comparison to Tandori's poetry volume of 1973, *The Cleaning of an Objet Trouvé*, we can explore how this emphasis on performance quality can provide a more penetrating key to their impact.

Within the pages of Tandori's book we find several similarly minimal 'poems' consisting of the (almost) dispensable parts of language. A pair of parentheses, separated by a line, constitutes one that is entitled 'Two handles of a sepulchral urn from e.e. cummings' private collection'.[75] The visual image of the parenthesis is revealed to be just like an urn handle: this might well be an *objet trouvé* in the most concrete sense. We could compare this with Kurtág's 'Perpetuum mobile', the *Game* constructed from glissandi alone.

The 'found object' that is also a genre, however, is particularly interesting in this context and Tandori's 'The Sonnet' offers a striking parallel. It empties the content from the form, leaving only a formula, which the poet mocks with his parenthetical ruminations and creative hesitations:

A szonett	The Sonnet
a	a
b	b
b	b
a	a
a	a
b	b
(Ennél a sornál megakadt,)	(Got stuck on this line,)
b	b
a	a
c	c
d	d
d	d
c	c
d	d
d	d
(aztán mégis folytatta és befejezte.)	(then did finally continue and complete it.)[76]

---

[75] 'Halottas urna két füle e.e. cummings magángyűjteményből'. Tandori 1973: 28.
[76] 'A szonett'. My translation. Tandori 1973: 34.

Example 4.7. Kurtág, Prelude and Waltz in C, from *Games* Volume I

Music cannot have either 'form' or 'content' in the way that can a sonnet. The generic reductiveness of Kurtág's 'Prelude and Waltz' (*Games* Volume I) is instructive once set alongside 'The Sonnet', however, precisely because the two are so different from one another (see Ex. 4.7).

'Preludium and Waltz' shuns the development of melody, harmony and structure. It presents, instead, the basic metres and gestures that can suggest preludes and waltzes generally, and indicates further stylistic nuancing through specific markings of 'Libero' and 'Giusto', *forte* and *pianissimo*. It provides, then, instructions for bringing (any basic sort of) Prelude and (any basic sort of) Waltz into moving, dancing musical activity. Where Tandori takes an *objet trouvé* to toy with it and reflect ironically on the creative writing process, Kurtág's *objet trouvé* is something that a performer has to work with, and must focus specifically on the goal of making its most essential sonorous characteristics audibly present.

One might position this particular type of reduction in the context of the (ethically elevated) stripping and 'unmasking' of both instrumental harmonies and the human body in *Four Songs* discussed above. In this light it offers a moral imperative to focus on the armature of performance gesture as opposed to the complexities of (say) harmonic elaboration. Indeed a broader frame for its focus on performance can be developed in the context of Tandori's own *objet trouvé*, because this is no arbitrary concept. Rather, it is rooted in a poem by Attila József called 'Consciousness', an extract from which forms a motto for Tandori's book. József's *objet trouvé* shifts the whole idea into a new gear, and Tandori's motto is underlined in the quotation below:

Eszmélet	'Consciousness' (verse 10 of 12)
Az meglett ember, akinek szívében nincs se anyja, apja, ki tudja, hogy az életet halálra ráadásul kapja <u>s mint talált tárgyat visszaadja</u> bármikor – ezért őrzi meg, ki nem istene és nem papja se magának, sem senkinek.	An adult is someone bereft of father and mother beside his heart, who knows that life is a free gift, something extra thrown in on death's part, <u>and, like a found object, can be returned</u> any time – therefore, it's to be treasured. He is nobody's god or priest - his own self's least.[77]

In József's poem 'found object' is not merely a poem, but a metaphor for life itself, viewed as an extended moment to be cherished before death prevails in the moment of 'return'. The 'cleaning' in the title of Tandori's volume is only superficially an examination of a pair of parentheses, a poem, or language. It is also an attempt to comprehend humanity in general, such objects understood as fragments of the materiality of human life.

Despite the focus on authorial creativity in 'The Sonnet', moreover, Tandori himself reflected that his poems were worth no more than *objets trouvés* until they were read, understood and analysed. He described this interpretative process with the concept of *visszaadás* – as it appears in the motto as 'return' (see above). Indeed *visszaadás* means not only 'return', but also 'render' (as in meaning): in this light a poem is merely a thing that can potentially render meaning through its connection with a reader, through repetition and (re)interpretation. Until the connection is made, it is but an *objet trouvé*. And yet the significance of *visszaadás* in his motto is 'return' of

---

[77] 'Eszmélet', trans. John Bátki. Dávidházi et al (eds.) 1997: 297–303. (The original is also reproduced in this publication.) See 303 for this verse.

Example 4.8. Kurtág, 'Antiphony in f-sharp' from *Games* Volume II

life, i.e. death: the encounter with an *object trouvé* is but a moment analogous to death. This not merely a paradox. It is a rather subtle reflection on the transience of 'presence'.[78]

If we conceive Kurtág's performance of *Games* in this way, we can grasp how they may have been experienced very profoundly and elusively, namely as musical enactments of the process that Tandori's work, through József, describes. Repetition of simple elements, their rediscovery from new perspectives, their probing and setting into new contexts: these are musical manifestations of a fragile life placed under the microscope. After all, even a repeated F♯ may seem different when heard in a new context, as playing both Ex. 4.6 and Ex. 4.8 would invite us to remember. And as each new context, new sound and new sensation is discovered and understood, so it

[78] He made these remarks looking back on his earlier work with a fresh eye in 1978, Tandori 1978: 77.

is lost. Each is 'returned', instantaneously part of the past. Words reach out towards it impotently from the cage of the present. And pen-poised critics in 1979 are left simply gaping, as the elevated national icon steps down from the stage.

Music and teaching, music and seeking

I have used Kurtág's contribution to the reception of *Games* to illustrate his increasing participation in the role of the national composer-cum-pedagogue-cum-performer, and I have also attempted to listen to his awe-struck critics sympathetically, thus to elaborate on their sense of being overwhelmed. To close this chapter I present two more of his works in order to demonstrate the way that they too could contribute to his very particular public image.

The first, a group of songs for soprano and solo violin called *S. K. – Remembrance Noise. Seven Songs to Dezső Tandori's Poems* op. 12 (1975), contributes in two connected ways. Its music is engaged with the physical realities of learning to play the violin; meanwhile, its text provides a commentary on learning how to live. One becomes a metaphor for the other, rather in the way of Tandori's literary *objets trouvés* discussed above. In the first song the broader dimension is quite dramatically and biblically to the fore:

A damaszkuszi út	The road to Damascus
Most, mikor ugyanúgy, mint mindig,	Now, when just the same, as always,
legfőbb ideje, hogy	it is high time, that[79]

Kurtág's allusion to a Pauline conversion is clearly in tune with his partially masked reference to Pilinszky in *Splinters*.[80] It is particularly meaningful in the context of Kurtág as pedagogue, moreover, for Paul was not only one of the world's revolutionary mystics. He also considered himself a teacher. As the opening of a cycle, then, this verse hints at both revelation and instruction.

The music certainly effects conversion. Rather like the moment that the body was exposed naked in the Pilinszky song discussed above, as the words cease, the violin part abandons its chromatic line and presents perfect fifths.

---

[79] All these English and Hungarian song texts are taken from the published score, where translations are by László T. András.
[80] That of Tandori is less significant, insofar as his work repeatedly and disjointedly juxtaposed low with high, sacred and profane.

Example 4.9. Kurtág, 'So that We Never Get out of Practice', from *S. K. Remembrance Noise* Op. 12

It is as if they enact a moral imperative to abandon words, for music. But ensuing movements do not sustain the clarity or the religiosity of revelation. The musical themes – such as they are – are the violin itself, and the act of practising it. Songs 1, 4 and 6 begin with open fifths, teased with fragments of chromaticism; songs 3, 5 and 7 toy with other idiomatic violin patterns (arpeggios or scalic *moto perpetuos*) that are typical components of instrumental studies. These musical banalities are repeated constantly, and there is little sign of progression within them or beyond them.

The poems too tend to describe and then parallel this apparently fruitless practice, song 5 the most obviously. Its repeated, but inflected, words are analogous to the repeated, varied arpeggio practice of the violin (see Ex. 4.9):

Hogy ki ne jöjjünk a gyakolatból	So that We Never Get Out of Practice
Lesz vigasz	There's solace
Lösz vögösz	Thure's surlice
Lasz vagasz	Thare's salace
Lisz vigisz	Theere's silice
Lusz vugusz	Thoore's soolus

Song 3 uses repetition in an attempt to remember (see Ex. 4.10), but the project seems doubtful given that there is apparently no substance for the memory:

Example 4.10. Kurtág, 'Two Lines from "Tapes"', from *S. K. Remembrance Noise* Op. 12

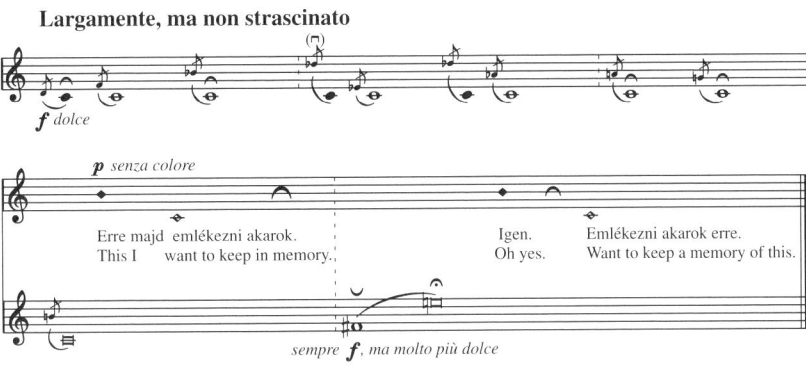

Tekercs (az utolsó két sor)	Two lines from "Tape"
Emlékezni akarok erre.	This I want to keep in memory.
Igen. Emlékezni akarok erre.	Oh yes. Want to keep a memory of this.

Song 6, more dramatically, reflects on the state of being itself. The text is as follows:

A puszta létige szomorúsága	The Sadness of the Bare Copula
Szerettem volna, ha úgy van.	I should have liked it to be so.
Nem volt úgy.	It was not.
Kértem: legyen úgy.	I said, let it be so.
Úgy lett.	So 'twas.

And while the violin seems to illustrate a state of 'how it was', it changes not at all when the voice requests 'let it be so'. After 'So 'twas', the violin simply repeats exactly what it played before (Ex. 4.11). The perception of change itself, it seems, is entirely unreliable.

How this explicit dissolution of certainty could feed directly into narrative constructions of Kurtág can emerge from a reading of *Twelve Microludes for String Quartet, Hommage à András Mihály* op. 13 (1977). This 'Hommage' gives pause for thought. We have already observed Mihály's shifting political positions and his increasing success in the new-music field, and by the time

Example 4.11. Kurtág, 'The Sadness of the Bare Copula', from *S. K. Remembrance Noise* Op. 12

Kurtág wrote *Twelve Microludes* Mihály was even Director of the State Opera. On one level Kurtág's reference to him seems simply a gesture of admiration to a prominent public musical figurehead who had supported his own career. But Mihály was also Head of the Chamber Music Department at the Liszt Academy, and was greatly admired for his teaching, thus *Twelve Microludes* is just as much a reference to Mihály's teaching as it is to his other activities. Perhaps it is *specifically* that, for Mihály was a model to Kurtág as teacher in the period in which he wrote the *Twelve Microludes*: Kurtág audited his teaching of Beethoven and Schubert String Quartets throughout the 1970s.[81] At the very least, the 'hommage' gesture displays Kurtág's involvement with teaching anew.

[81] Conversation with László Sáry, who also audited the classes. Budapest, January 2000. See also Kurtág's remark in 1993 that he learned much from auditing Mihály's classes: 'überhaupt habe ich sehr viel von ihm gelernt, hatte jahrelang bei ihm hospitiert'. Dibelius (ed.) 1993: 85.

Example 4.12. Kurtág, *Hommage à Mihály András. 12 Microludes for String Quartet* Op. 13, movement 1

If we regard the work as a projection of an interest in (string quartet) teaching, it yields some intriguing qualities. The opening movement can be approached not simply as the chromatic elaboration of a perfect cadence that it is, but also as a study in voicing and listening to the subtle elaboration of a cadence from within (see Ex. 4.12). Each player shifts at a different moment and is encouraged, by the carefully paced harmonic shifts, to listen with great attention to his or her position within the ensemble of four. But if understood as a perfect cadence, its metaphorical significance can expand further. The perfect cadence here is a fractionally expanded *objet trouvé* and – positioned alongside Tandori and József – is thus a means to elaborate on and discover facets of a very precarious life. In order to appreciate them fully, players might need to envisage how *momentous* could be the change in the second violin part from E to F♯ in bar 4, for instance, how *careful* the quasi-response of the cello would need to be immediately after it, and how *gingerly* the viola might then play the ensuing chord (after the 'breath') in bar 5. (Not to mention the last chord, the only moment at which all four players introduce a note at the same time.) Read in this way, the movement projects an elaborate test for the unity and coherence of a string quartet, a preparation, even, for drawing out the potential magic of a slow movement by Beethoven or Schubert.

The debt to such repertoire was apparent to critics, who quickly grasped *Twelve Microludes*' enigmatically brief exploratory moments in precisely these canonical terms. Breuer invoked late Beethoven, while Kroó passed through Frescobaldi, Baroque rhetoric, chorales, Beethoven, Schubert,

Schumann, Debussy and Webern in his expression of the work's living debt to musical tradition.[82] Commentators also used the quartet's lack of structural or dramatic teleology to suggest that it had a mysterious wholeness that could really only be understood in musical, rather than conceptual terms. Here, too, the quartet played into their romantic hands, for it closes with a rhetorical viola line that breaks off as if in an unresolved question. It ends as if illustrating Pilinszky's religious notion of the artwork as a 'Message *derived from* the Whole'.[83] Tallián's review thus argued that the opening 'romantic invocation' and concluding 'intense, lyrical epilogue' imparted a *longing* for a whole. As he expressed it, *Twelve Microludes* 'aroused the feeling of precisely the wholeness that is possible'.

Breuer, Kroó and Tallián, then, each articulated ways in which *Twelve Microludes* seemed not to make affirmations, but to seek revelation. Each of its movements communicated the searching *desire* for extraordinary presence moments. Tallián captured the miraculous impact of these when he wrote that characters emerged from the tiny forms in 'an *unbelievably* brilliant light', and just '*as they were born*'.[84]

We conclude this chapter with an image of Kurtág as teacher, but also, in his relationship to Mihály and in his exploratory 'moments', as seeker. The image is Pauline in intensity, and involves regarding *Twelve Microludes* as a product of passionate musical mysticism, and also seeing Kurtág as a quasi-spiritual leader (and follower): he comes into view, in other words, as a musical 'guru' in a 'guru system'.[85] We need only recall the political background of the recipient of his *hommage* to rehearse the apparent paradox between calculatedly invasive party politics and this mysticism. But actually, as these explorations have revealed, musical mysticism *thrived* in this particular regime. Kurtág was simply the one to benefit the most.

---

[82] Breuer 1978a; Kroó 1978. See also Tallián 1979: 7–8. References to these writers in this section will be from these sources.
[83] 'Egy lírikus naplójából' [From the diary of a lyric poet], *Új Ember* 11 June 1971. Reprinted in Pilinszky 1997: 647–8. My italics.
[84] My italics.
[85] I take the terms 'guru' and 'guru system' from Schiff 2003: 40. (See also Chapter 1 of this book, footnote 6.)

5 After 'The West': Ligeti looks back

1967, rather than 1968, was the big turning point for Ligeti because he became an Austrian citizen in that year. His public visibility would begin to grow in the wake of this change, when a profusion of his statements emerged in books and journals and he won secure employment as Professor of Composition at the Hochschule in Hamburg. By the mid-1970s he was not only professionally renowned, but legally and economically established in the West.

Such a strong framework reinforces recent arguments that the widespread notion of Ligeti as 'outsider' warrants challenging.[1] He was, in fact, anchored in the Western avant-garde music world: his music was not 'beyond' it at all, but grounded by it. On the other hand – and particularly with regard to the background I have offered in Chapters 2 and 3 – there is no doubt that he did present particular qualities from his past. Additionally, his new-found security actually facilitated public discussion of these, and their rootedness in Hungary. After all, he was no longer a political refugee.[2]

The most apt musical symbol for the new space that Hungary came to take in Ligeti's work is perhaps the tragicomic melting pot of *Le Grand Macabre* (1974–7), the theme of which could be read as a distant elaboration of the authoritarian/fear-driven regime from which he had fled. Indeed certain character names – chief of police as 'Gepopo' and Death as 'Nekrotzar' – make the connection explicit. Furthermore, although the opera presented new ideas, it also drew directly on music from Ligeti's earlier environment. Pentatonic tunes and *verbunkos* emerged within the surreal panoply of musical borrowings, and Ligeti even used an idea from his grotesque song 'A Merchant has Come with Giant Birds', discussed in Chapter 2, in order to characterise Gepopo.[3]

Of course the main point of *Le Grand Macabre* is not its reference to Hungary, but its response to the opera genre. For this reason the popular

---

[1] Wilson 2004.
[2] Although it seems unlikely that Ligeti was actually a target of the secret police, he may have retained a deep-seated anxiety about the possibility. In 1967 two Polish composers visited Hamburg and sought him out. They found it extremely difficult to locate him inside the Hochschule, but eventually found him hiding, and apparently terrified of them in case they were connected to the KGB. Informal conversation, Marta Ptaszynska, Chicago, 3 April 2006.
[3] Seherr-Thoss 1998: 90 and 301–2. This sets the 'merchant' of that song in a new light. Did Ligeti, in 1948, associate this merchant with an evil political power?

idea that Ligeti suddenly 'returned' to his past in the late 1970s needs treating with caution. There was certainly a major change in his attitude during the decade, but it is doubtful that it was really a 'return', or even that it brought him closer to his past. Human memory cannot work quite that efficiently. As Ligeti's 'Hungary' was essentially something that he elaborated for the purposes of his career in the West, a considerable part of it was tinged with fantasy.

Ligeti as émigré

Nowhere could this be more transparent than in the text Ligeti provided for a Festschrift in honour of publisher Ludwig Strecker. Whereas other contributors wrote a piece of scholarship, an account of their compositional activities, or a tribute to Strecker himself, Ligeti authored a chapter entitled 'Musical Memories of My Childhood and Youth'. His decision may seem baffling, for it is incongruous not only within the volume, but within discussions of new music in general. But it was typical of the nature of Ligeti's discursive character: communicative to the point of dazzling verbosity, and startlingly unconventional to boot.[4]

One crucial factor in the achievement of this impact was the inaccessibility of Ligeti's origins. When he began to speak of them in the late 1960s, Transylvania really was a long way from Germany, for it was of the 'East' in both contemporary political and in longer-standing exoticist terms. It is surely unsurprising, then, that the style of Ligeti's narrative here was almost that of a fairy tale (even if set in a small industrial town rather than a magic forest), for the fairy tale was the genre within which Transylvania could be made accessible. Ligeti's tone was whimsical, evoking his fear of crippled gypsies and his childlike wonderment about an apparently magical gramophone player: 'of course I looked for the tiny person who was inside . . . I imagined him with a large head that filled it, and with a tiny little body that had just enough space once squeezed up like a jack-in-the-box, but could produce a full singing sound only from a correspondingly fully grown head'.[5] And his description of how he regarded his first, rather pretty, piano teacher – as his ideal woman – was self-mocking, while at the same time surely calculated to endear. Who could fail to be amused by the description of his adolescent ambitions? Ligeti hoped to inspire girls to look beyond his

---

[4] His apparently overflowing humanity and humour, moreover, often left readers tantalised, and longing to know more. Lesle Lutz's much later justification for requesting that Ligeti speak about his youth and childhood is revealing of precisely this effect, for it was hardly the case in 1988 that 'one knows little about [it]'. Lutz 1988: 885.
[5] Ligeti 1973: 54–5.

pimply visage by writing a 'Great Symphony in A Minor with an eruptive explosion'.[6]

In a rather different way, the remoteness of his past was a resource for more serious self-defining statements too. Although he left the East in 1956, he explained in one interview, the move had not caused any rupture in his development: his plans in 1950 and his early *Visions* of 1956 contained the roots of his static compositions of the 1960s. Thus driving a neat wedge between himself and figures such as Stockhausen and Penderecki, he minimised his relation to the contemporary avant-garde.[7] His strength of separatist purpose is unmistakable, for he even published a (solipsistic) 'self-interview' in 1971, in which he stated that by the time he arrived in the West he was thirty-three years old and 'steeped in compositional assumptions and previous experiences of a *totally different kind*'.[8]

Those assumptions and experiences would only be really fleshed out in the 1980s, however. As the avant-garde discourse he inhabited became more accommodating to exotic and heterogeneous musical explorations, he could intimate that his Transylvanian childhood had a mythic proximity to living folk music. In interview with Pierre Michel he contextualised the places where he grew up with reference to Bartók and Kodály's collecting trips in the same area: Hungarian folk music, he explained, was still a part of daily life in the region. Having conjured up a soundscape in which folk music resounded everywhere, Michel succinctly summarised it for him: 'Folklore was your first approach to music.'[9] Indeed although initially Ligeti was careful to distinguish his own use of folk music from the methods of Bartók, stating clearly when discussing *Le Grand Macabre* in 1981 that '[m]y folklore ingredients are impossible, imaginary, unrelated to any nation', as years passed and his works evolved he became committed to attributing their debt to a unique past of his own.[10] The ostensibly cosmopolitan sound world of his childhood in the 1920s provided a fantastical explanation for his Piano Études of the 1980s.

---

[6] His word was 'Sprengkörperexplosion'. Ligeti 1973: 60.
[7] Stürzbecher 1971: 33 and 36. According to the preface, most of the interviews in this book were completed in 1968.
[8] Reprinted in *Ligeti in Conversation*: 128. My italics.
[9] Michel 1985: 129. This first long interview was made in December 1981 but by the time it came out, several others were already available. Oelschalgel 1989 is the most detailed account, but it is difficult to know how it should be treated as a historical source. Begun in 1978, it was completed in 1988, and finally edited by Ligeti in 1989. The delay in its publication is suggestive of Ligeti's reticence in publishing commentaries about the Stalinist period in Hungary.
[10] See interview with Claude Samuel, trans. Terence Kilmartin in *Ligeti in Conversation*: 111–23, at 119, and cf. Bouliane 1985 and 1989.

His personal history could move more distinctly into the realm of legend when he identified his wish to 'return to my origins, to Hungarian literature', for as he referred more often to the qualities of Hungarian literature and language, he moved closer to Hungarian nationalist mythology.[11] In 1984 he desired to write music that was organised like language, music with an emotional semantic as if it were a sort of language, and subsequently he focused on the importance of the Hungarian mother tongue specifically, profiting from a long tradition of Hungarian discourse to state that 'if Liszt had spoken Hungarian, he would have written music that was different'.[12] The implication was clear: Ligeti's own mother tongue was an ineradicable measure of his work's special character.

Just as these claims had historical roots, so too did Ligeti's remarks about the Soviet occupation of Hungary. The latter was a tragic, innocent victim, while the former had been the single, monolithic and oppressive obstacle against which he had struggled to become a progressive, Western composer. Thus he explained that although he entertained the idea of static music from 1950 onwards, the country was 'totally isolated' from the rest of Europe by then, and his experimental compositions were written exclusively for his drawer, as 'one could not perform that sort of thing'.[13] Asked in 1983 by Paul Griffiths whether he wrote 'serious' works during the occupation, he answered:

> Yes. There was a set of Arany ... songs which I wrote in 1952 and which were on the edge of what could be performed. Finally they were not performed ... If you wanted a performance or publication, you had to submit your work to a committee, and there might even be a private performance for that committee: that happened with my Arany songs ... My Arany songs were something between Bartók and Kodály, with some dissonances, and they were not acceptable.[14]

But here, memory had slipped straight into (tragic) myth. His Arany Songs were performed in the Second Hungarian Music Week in 1953, and were reviewed quite extensively – if critically – in one of the leading

---

[11] Bouliane 1985: 76.
[12] Hansen 1984: 474. Satory 1990: 114. It is worth observing that he made this comment while speaking Hungarian. Satory prefaced the published interview with the information that they began speaking in English, but switched to Hungarian – at which point Ligeti became a great deal more lively.
[13] Häusler 1983: 89. (Interview conducted in 1968.) This account of his turning-point in 1950 was also published in 1967, in his 'Anläβlich "Lontano"': see Kropfinger 1973: 135–7 for a critical reading of this text in the light of Benjamin's concept of 'aura'.
[14] Griffiths 1983: 12.

newspapers, by one of the most powerfully institutionalised Hungarian musicologists.[15]

His contemporary political perspective, too, was in the service of this myth. In 1988 he remarked that '[a]nyone who believes that a dictator will disarm is naïve... I am pro-America and pro-Thatcher above all.'[16] But this ultimately occluded his earlier despondency about Hungary's nationalist parochialism. Whereas when writing to Veress and Weissmann in 1956 and 1957 he had condemned Kodály's 'spinelessness' and Budapest's provincial self-satisfaction, now he simply demonised the Soviet Union. And it is uncertain how to read Ligeti's claim that compositional teaching had to conform to the doctrine of socialist realism (and that it had been advantageous for him to teach theory rather than composition as a result).[17] There is no evidence to suggest that teachers such as Farkas and Járdányi (both of whom taught Kurtág during the years that Ligeti taught theory) were actively promoting socialist realism. Would Ligeti have been forced to do so?

We could run through a great deal more creative acts of memory. He dramatically evoked the atmosphere of his entrance exam to the Liszt Academy with the black flag flying to announce the death of Bartók ('what a symbol for the beginning of my studies!'), but Bartók died only some weeks after the exam.[18] Repeating this tale five years later, he added some memories about the spontaneous friendship that evolved with the 'half-Jewish' Kurtág – and Kurtág corrected this peculiar sleight of hand as soon as he could.[19] But myths do have a function. Ligeti had a past, after all, of violence wildly estranged from his new, highly protected professional context. In what form could such a past appear? Self-promotional composer interviews allowed for self-exoticisation as a highly effective mask.

Just a very few moments offer us a glimpse beyond the mask. In 1981, for instance, when he was asked by Monika Lichtenfeld where he would

---

[15] Ujfalussy's review in the party organ, *Szabad Nép*, included the following: 'Setting "A legszebb virág" [The Most Beautiful Flower] is not an easy task, for the simple tone of folk song blossoms with the most unambiguous naturalness into the fiery pathos of patriotism. Ligeti captured the folk-song tone, but the natural blooming of patriotism rather less so. Perhaps that is why he did not even attempt to set the climax of the poem, the final verse that ignites in revolutionary fire... The talented young composer has a decided feeling for writing songs, but he should approach poetry more honestly, and with less complication [*okoskodás*]. He should dare to write lovely broad melodies with unperturbed joy.' Ujfalussy 1953.
[16] Lutz 1988: 887.   [17] Stürzbecher 1971: 35.
[18] Michel 1985: 129–30. But see Kurtág's 'Meine Begegnung mit György Ligeti' in Dibelius 1993: 70–1, at 70. Kurtág took the entrance exam with Ligeti, and then had to travel back to Romania. Bartók's death occurred some weeks later, once he was back there.
[19] Given Ligeti's interest in his own Jewishness (see Chapter 3 above), it is difficult to imagine that this was a true error on his part. Both Kurtág's parents were Jewish. 'Meine Begegnung mit György Ligeti' in Dibelius 1993: 70.

most like to live, Ligeti answered that he already had the ideal environment for composing in Hamburg, because of his students. He then speculated briefly about a dream life in California before abruptly scolding himself:

> Everything I'm just saying now sounds like the satisfied establishment, the complacency of a museum piece. But inside I'm not a *professor*, but a *clochard*. If you scratch my enamel surface a bit you'll find something else entirely underneath, namely anxiety and gloomy pessimism. I fled the Nazis, then fled Soviets to the West. What say I, established clown, about luxury and California? Phnom Penh was a flourishing city a few years ago, no different from Hamburg.[20]

This play on the notion of a bohemian 'clochard' was entirely in character, for it created an accessible persona while hinting at the dissonance of his early traumas. It was also neatly in tune with the musical monthly for which he spoke. After all, such a publication offered no frame for the ugliness of extermination camps.

But he had already related elements about his past some years earlier, in a context that was better suited to their utter brutality, namely a collection of essays entitled *Mein Judentum*, the contributors to which were almost exclusively Jewish writers living in Germany.[21] There is nothing humorous in Ligeti's own tale, but rather a dramatic, if sombre, account of his own maltreatment as a Hungarian Jew in Romania, his sheer luck in managing to stay alive in enforced labour during the war, and the extermination of some of his close family members. His grim narrative is made all the move intriguing by its occasional counterpoint with more troubling recent events, such as the recollection that the philo-semitism he encountered on moving to the West made him deeply uncomfortable, and that in his bewilderment and uncertainty he had considered converting to Catholicism.

For the purposes of *Mein Judentum*, then, he adopted no *clochard* position and had no fairy tale to tell: 'I have remained what I was, a Central European Jew, half assimilated and religiously unaffiliated . . . the inhibitions and resentments that we all – Jews and non-Jews – have borne since the time of Hitler are incurable: they are psychic facts with which we must live.'[22] In the light of these comments it seems particularly regrettable that he did not write his planned opera on Shakespeare's *The Tempest*, which would have provided us with a way of exploring Ligeti's identification with Prospero,

---

[20] Lichtenfeld 1981: 473. [21] Ligeti is the only composer; there is one painter. Ligeti 1978b.
[22] Ligeti 1978b: 246–7.

the character whose resigned detachment he linked with a Central European Jewish disposition. Prospero, *'c'est moi'*, he said.[23] In the absence of that it is surely revealing to note his sensitivity to the ongoing Cold War conflict, for it was surely an ever-present link to the most violent aspects of his past. How many other Western avant-garde composers would have remarked in 1983 that 'we live in permanent terror'?[24]

Hungary abroad?

It was not only Ligeti's textual statements that had increasingly obvious recourse to Hungary, of course, but also his works. Ligeti's new references, however, became apparent simultaneously with his re-engagement with tonality, musical representation, and very obvious reference to other musics. Thus, and because all these changes were part of a broad shift in the musical avant-garde, writers responded primarily with anxiety about regression. There was disquiet, for instance, that the consequently 'new' Ligeti was no longer progressive, but turning to 'neo-romanticism': although some heard the Horn Trio as a direct critique of the progress-laden bases for judging music, others heard it as 'suspiciously Romantic'.[25] Thus even where listeners recognised Ligeti's new recourse to Bartók, they understood it as part of a broader retrogressive phenomenon, rather than as a specifically Hungarian turn.

It was somewhat later that scholars engaged with the change in terms that linked it with Ligeti's national past. By the 1990s, and perhaps mainly thanks to Ligeti's own prompts, it was nonetheless clear that *aksak* rhythms and modally inflected harmonies and melodies were surfacing frequently to suggest East European folk music. These and other references amassed to form a considerable group: two pieces for harpsichord had 'Hungarian' in their titles, three choral pieces were set to Hungarian texts and several piano studies had titles in the Hungarian language. Bergande proposed that the re-emergence of the passacaglia, a compositional technique that became a staple in this period, was a sign of Ligeti's 'return' to Hungary.[26] Steinitz mentioned that Ligeti had 'gone back' to (a literary embodiment of) Hungary, and to his 'earlier Hungarian voice', while Dibelius positioned him as back in his 'musical home'.[27]

---

[23] Politi 1985: 125.
[24] Bouliane 1985: 89. (The interview was conducted in 1983.) See Seherr-Thoss 1998 for a sensitive examination of *Le Grand Macabre* from this perspective.
[25] Bossin 1984; see also *Classical Music* 7 April 1984 (no author specified).
[26] Bergande 1994.   [27] Steinitz 1996: 17; Dibelius 1994: 31–49.

In what follows I neither smooth these changes into the widespread transformation of the avant-garde, nor do I argue that we can explain them through Ligeti's unique past. Rather, I revisit some of the new music from the three perspectives already used in Chapter 3, and probe the ways in which Hungary became useful to Ligeti once again.

Language in music: home?

Die er mir wies, mit einer Schwermuth,	He showed to me, with such deep sadness,
Aber die Nahmen der seltnen Orte.	But all the names of those curious places
Und alles Schöne hatt' er behalten, das	And all the lovely things, he remembers still
An seeligen Gestaden, auch mir sehr werth,	Which, very dear to me also, are in bloom
Im heimatlichen Lande blühet	On blessèd shores, our native country,
Oder verborgen . . .	Or else concealed . . .[28]

In this extract from Hölderlin's 'Wenn aus der Ferne' an initial evocation of melancholic remembering reveals itself to be rooted in sheer physical displacement: the poetic 'I' and the man described share a cherished homeland from which they are distant. Ligeti's setting in *Drei Hölderlin Fantasien* is comparably suggestive of lost beauty, in which moments of great radiance are rent by violent interjections and harsh sonorities. Yet Ligeti's textual selection does not include these particular lines. Thus their limpid homesickness is but a shadow, and his omission renders the song (almost perversely) *not* a song about homesickness.

From whatever perspective the song's meaning is construed, it is one of the most musically violent that Ligeti composed in the decade. At the opening sixteen vocal parts generate a texture that blurrily slides from one sonority into the next, in a progression that passes from one unresolved chord to another, stretching ever further until abruptly 'broken' by a brisk interruption from voices introducing a new section. As Ex. 5.1 demonstrates through a vertical reduction of the polyphonic voices, these first twelve bars offer a chromatic progression of ever-straining desire that its microtonal vacillations can only intensify. The cloudy sonorities converge on an E major seventh, which seems to resolve on an A♭ major chord; this transforms itself

---

[28] Hölderlin 1994: 654–7, at 656–7. Trans. Michael Hamburger.

Example 5.1. Analysis of Ligeti, *Drei Hölderlin Fantasien* no. 1, bb. 1–13

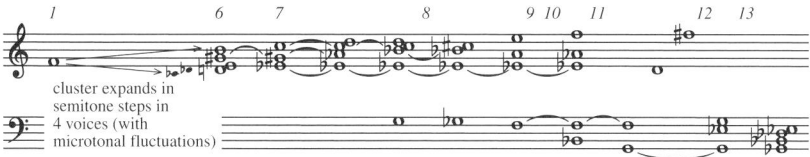

into an E♭ seventh and over a chromatic bass-line descent a series of almost – but not quite – diatonic chords shifts upwards step by step. As the bass sinks a perfect fifth to B♭, the chord above almost becomes a B♭ major seventh, but fails to do so before the bass moves (to G) and the uppermost voice to F♯. The quality of 'missed' consonance is replaced later in the song by violent cries of fear, and in contrast to the always slightly indistinct and nuanced micropolyphony, the large blocks of voices unite to cry 'Weh mir!', to almost shout out for 'sunshine', and to all but bellow 'the walls loom'. Such extremes of choral writing convey an emotion that is both hard-hitting and at the same time distinct from that transmitted by any other work by Ligeti. Whilst Monika Lichtenfeld justifiably describes the opening as mythical, music 'coming into being', its late romantic style separates it from Ligeti's distinctly corporeal 'presencing'.[29] It is the mysterious, 'primal', but rent quality of Mahler that is conjured up here: a fracturing beauty is evoked, and violently destroyed.

This dramatically painful setting – *not* about a lost homeland – offers a curious backdrop for Ligeti's emphatic glance 'home', his playful settings of Weöres in *Magyar Etűdök* (1983). Martin Bergande has argued that these require a thoroughly 'Hungarian' reading, reasoning that not only the poetry, but the illustrative dimension of the settings too, can be linked specifically to Ligeti's national past. Bergande also argues that the settings are radically different from Ligeti's more abstract use of text in the 1960s, setting his claim against the opposite view taken by Clytus Gottwald, according to which *Magyar Etűdök* is best contextualised precisely within the 1960s because its abstract musical construction can be neatly aligned with certain Boulez works.[30] The complexity of the musical processes is indeed staggering (it has already served two analytical studies very fully): multiple rhythmic and melodic canons interweave between and within the two choirs. Bergande nevertheless reinforces his 'Hungarian' view of the study with the proposal

---

[29] Lichtenfeld 1987. Monika Lichtenfeld has suggested that other textual omissions go to the heart of the music, in particular the reference to beauty recalled, from a distance where it has been lost: 'And all the lovely things, he remembers still . . .' Lichtenfeld 1987: 123.

[30] Bergande 1994: 38. See Gottwald 1983 and Englbrecht 1998: 125. Englbrecht agrees with Gottwald that the root is in the 1960s. For Ligeti's remarks, see Bouliane 1983: 77.

that such technical clarity was a sign of the systematic compositional thinking Ligeti perfected in his last years in Budapest: this, he argues, provided its 'content'.[31]

The idea is obviously quaint. Ligeti had no need to think back to Budapest to produce these techniques, because his thinking had developed in technical sophistication in the intervening years, and his compositions had become more virtuosically polyphonic. Indeed they explored a myriad of polyphonic possibilities, as the mirror canon of *Le Grand Macabre*, the *Passacaglia ungherese* (1978) and the micropolyphony of *Drei Hölderlin Fantasies* (1982) reveal. In fact, and as Bernd Englbrecht has identified, this first study fits neatly into a chronological position within Ligeti's ongoing polyphonic investigations. While related to *Lux aeterna* (1966) and *Le Grand Macabre* (1974–7), its complex construction, study-like compression and stylisation foreshadow the *Nonsense Madrigals* (1988–93), and in particular the dual metricity of 'Two Dreams and Little Bat'.[32] Once these musical techniques are understood as part of a historical continuum, then the only temporal 'rupture' in *Magyar Etűdök* – the only sign of any looking 'back' – is the recourse to Weöres.[33] But the first song is difficult to grasp as a retrospective, because Ligeti chose a poem that could be made to correspond precisely with one of his standard compositional 'types'. The poem's Hungarian language is incidental.

As I suggested in the Introduction to this book, Ligeti's pieces from *Lontano* through *Continuum* to the Piano Concerto frequently consist of musical sounds arriving softly and gradually accumulating and swelling, then dropping away until they can no longer be heard. 'Beginnings' and 'endings' are ungraspable: the effect is of a spontaneous emergence, and a dissolution. The first of the *Magyar Etűdök* follows this pattern: single short notes separated by silences accumulate as more voices enter, the short sounds are gradually replaced by increasingly sustained ones and the dynamic level increases; all parts then sink in register, thin out and lapse into silence. The poem maps out a parallel trajectory: something is dripping, but by the time we've learned that it is an icicle, the icicle has gone, melted clean away. The poem offers a narrative for Ligeti's 'arrival–dispersal' music: it is an elaboration of Nancy's

---

[31] Bergande 1994: 82. Bergande draws on Nordwall to claim this. See Nordwall 1971: 220. Although he seems to think he is drawing on Ligeti's own words, he is drawing on a curriculum vitae in the monograph, the provenance of which is unclear. The tone is that of an admiring and fascinated observer, presumably Nordwall.
[32] Englbrecht 1998: 130.
[33] All three poems date from the period in which Ligeti lived in Budapest, although he may not have known them then. We know from a letter he wrote to Weöres in 1972 that he had acquired the poet's (then) complete edition 'a couple of years ago'. Ligeti letter to Weöres 8 November 1972, see postscript. GLC, PSF.

momentary, always lost, 'birth to presence'. But the musical experience is prior, Weöres' poem merely provides a metaphor.

Csipp,	Drip,
csepp,	drop,
egy csepp,	one drop,
öt csepp,	five drops,
meg tíz:	then ten:
olvad a jégcsap,	the icicle drips away,
csepereg a víz.[34]	the water flows away.

The second of the studies is an entirely different matter, however, for its music does suggest a retrospective glance. At first sight it is a setting of two Weöres poems that presents one as a disruptive counterpoint to the other. There is nothing radically new in this technique: conflicting counterpoints were a feature of *Le Grand Macabre*. The style of the opening melodic line, however, is distinctly akin to Hungarian folk song, and the aura of echoes provided by counterpoint and upper-register sustained tones may seem conspicuously nostalgic. Dibelius even finds similarities in the choral style with Ligeti's earlier *Éjszaka – Reggel* (1955), in particular the way polyphonic voices slip over into calm, sustained closures.[35] But there are other references to the past too, for Englbrecht has shown manifest similarities to one of Kodály's folk-song settings, 'Evening Song'.[36] The periodic structure of the melody, its contour (see Exx. 5.2 and 5.3), the harmonic implications of its accompaniment, the ABA structure, the central 'fugato' section and the hummed ending – all these find a parallel in 'Evening Song'. Englbrecht concludes that the study is a homage to Kodály, a token of gratitude to the man who secured him a teaching position at the Liszt Academy, and a gesture of respect to the teacher of his own teacher Sándor Veress.[37]

Yet such a conclusion does justice neither to Ligeti's relationship with Kodály, nor to the relationship between 'Evening Song' and *Magyar Etűdök* no. 2. In fact, the closer one looks, the more it seems to be a 'response', rather than a 'homage'. Kodály's folk-song text is a prayer, in which the singer begs for an end to her wandering and hiding in foreign lands and asks God to send an angel to grant peace and to provide shelter. Weöres' first poem contains no such anguish, but evokes a rural scene in which an evening call to rest is made by church bells:

[34] Weöres 1975 (II): 69. My translation. [35] Dibelius 1994: 40.
[36] Englbrecht 1998: 136–9. [37] Englbrecht 1998: 146.

Example 5.2. Kodály, *Evening Song*, bb. 1–18

Example 5.3. Ligeti, *Hungarian Studies* no. 2, bb. 1–8

Example 5.3. (*cont.*)

After 'The West': Ligeti looks back

Árnyak sora ül a réten.	On the meadow lies a row of shadows.
Nyáj zsong be a faluvégen.	Flocks murmur at the village edge.
Zúg-dong sűrű raj a fákon.	Dense swarms buzz up in the trees.
Békák dala kel az árkon.	Frogs' songs rise in the ditches.
Bim-bam! torony üregében	Ding-dong! in the hollow tower,
Érc-hang pihen el az árkon.	clangs recline along the ditch.[38]

The second poem, however, 'Frogs' (Békák), subverts the gracious calm of the idyll, with a call not to rest, but to underwater coupling. The combination of poems offers no simple 'homage' to Kodály's plea for a rest from wandering, but a faintly lewd and humorous elaboration on it.

Brekekex	Ribbit
brekekex	Ribbit
brekekex!	Ribbit!
Gyere bújj	Come under the water if you love me!
víz alá	
ha szeretsz!	
Idelenn	Down here the weather is never rough!
soha sincs	
vad idő!	
Idelenn	Down here rain never falls![39]
sose hull	
az eső!	

The musical response is explicitly disorderly, so that the beautifully haunting opening is at first heightened by buzzing (swarms) and bells ringing, but becomes increasingly raucous as frog sounds impose themselves chaotically. The most intense moment of anarchic frogs and bells gives way suddenly to a sustained humming and a recall of the opening melody. We are back in the tear-flecked rural idyll: did we dream up the frog's anarchic intervention? The closing chord hummed by the entire choir is, as Englbrecht notes, what Lendvai called the 'acoustic' collection, a scale that for Bartók was a symbol of nature and purity.[40] But the central section suggests that Ligeti's 'nature' is rather different from that of Bartók – and that of Kodály too. The song is no reverent homage: it is an amiable prank.

---

[38] Weöres 1975 (II): 86. My translation.
[39] Weöres 1975 (II): 82. My translation.
[40] Englbrecht 1998: 144–5.

The final song, 'Market', is a contrapuntal vocal collage reminiscent of Stravinsky's market in *Petrushka*: a surfeit of vendors and a circus seems to congregate cacophonically. There are five poems and five choral groups, each of which has a leader to beat time, while the groups are coordinated by a flashing light or a beat track audible only to the leaders. Each poem setting is indebted in some way to folk song, and at the busiest moment, there are five different rhythmic patterns and seven melodies sounding (plus an eighth line imitating one of these). At the close, rather than becoming gradually inaudible in the manner of the previous two studies, they all come to a sudden stop. The fantasy (Transylvania again?) ends.

The tight control under which these apparently arbitrarily arranged singers operate, and the way they seem literally 'switched off' at the end, is an apt illustration of the control with which Ligeti 'returned' to his fairy-tale Transylvania. This place is conspicuously contained in music, in striking contrast with the pained, irresolvable searching of the Hölderlin setting discussed above. It is also markedly distinct from representations of 'return' in the work of exiles from the Soviet Union. As Svetlana Boym has demonstrated, Nabokov, for example, constructed his homeland 'through shudders and gasps, through labyrinths and gaps, through ironic epiphanies and the bullet holes of memory'.[41] Such pain-riven and realist explorations are not to be found in Ligeti's Hungarian settings at all. His mother tongue was not a channel to a painful past, but a resource for play.[42]

Language as music

The wordless choir of *Clocks and Clouds*, the onomatopoeia of *Magyar Etűdök*, and the percussive use of consonants in *Drei Hölderlin Fantasien* each continues the exploration of linguistic sonority and vocality that we encountered in Chapter 3. But Ligeti's work of the 1980s also feeds on language in a new way, using it at one remove, using language already pressed into music.

---

[41] Boym 2001: 340.
[42] We might observe that recent psychoanalytical research suggests that exiles may find it easier to speak about the more painful aspects of their lives in their second or third languages. A related case has been made regarding Beckett's initial 'finding himself' as a writer in his second language, French. 'Exiting' his mother tongue provided him with a displacement that made it possible to formulate pain. It is tempting to suggest that Ligeti reserved his more agonised expressions for settings of Latin and German texts, and, as we will see below, for instrumental music. See Szekacs-Weisz and Ward (eds.) 2005, in particular Pina Antinucci's 'I Need to Hide in My Foreignness. Will You Let Me?' and Julia Borossa's 'Languages of Loss, Languages of Connectedness'. Antinucci refers to Patrick Casement's analysis of Samuel Beckett (Casement 1982), in which Beckett's second language, French, 'represented and expressed the darkest aspects of Beckett's personality, which might have felt too threatening and dangerous in his analysis, and which a second language contained more safely inasmuch as it also functioned as a displacement.' Szekacs-Weisz and Ward (eds.) 2005: 67.

Example 5.4. Ligeti, 'Fém' (Metal), from *Piano Études*, extract

In the broadest terms, the rhetorical style of his music became much more pronounced: at specific moments complex and continuous musical processes cease and give way to discursive, periodic passages. The close of the Piano Concerto is one example, another is the close of 'Fém' (Metal) from the Piano Études, each of which recalls Bartók (see Ex. 5.4). A more specific example is his use of Beethoven's 'Lebewohl' (farewell) motive from his Piano Sonata op. 81a. Unmistakably 'Le-be-wohl', yet varied through Ligeti's chromatic variation, this formulates a new, dissonant, farewell in the first movement of the Horn Trio, and threads through the rest of the work. Another prime example, and a pervasive one, is the 'lamento motive', which also emerges for the first time in the Horn Trio, where it is a primary feature of the final, fourth movement.

Example 5.5. Bocet 'dupa soț' (Lament for husband)

The name of this motive originates with Ligeti himself, although its musical genesis is somewhat intractable.[43] Of course, and as has been much discussed, lament music is encountered throughout the world and has also been drawn on as an affective trope in art music, evoking a stylised weeping for which Dido's Lament is something of an archetype. In 1983 Ligeti said that he had had Hungarian mourners of the Székely region in mind when he wrote it; by 1989, he remembered it was Romanian ones.[44] The nature of peasant lament makes ethnographic collection notoriously difficult, but lament collections from both Hungary and Romania are large and diverse, and some Romanian laments do suggest possible models for Ligeti's chromatically descending motive.[45] Some are formed from repetitions of descending lines, although they are primarily modal rather than chromatic. (See Exx. 5.5a and b.[46])

The fourth movement of the Horn Trio, 'Lamento', is supported until its vast climax by a passacaglia, a sequence of five dyads that fall in pitch, the upper voice of which, analogously to a *passus duriusculus*, delineates

[43] Taylor 1994 was one of the earliest and most detailed studies; see also Steinitz 1996.
[44] Bouliane 1985: 83 (interview took place in 1983); and Bouliane 1989.
[45] They are sung on occasions of community or individual loss (when a researcher may have no access to them); singers do not regard them as aesthetic, but as mourning; consequently laments can rarely be sung to order, any more than they can be repeated; singers frequently break into weeping while singing. Indeed the laments are understood as cathartic, and healing. Kodály 1952: 38–42. See also Sperl and Suliteanu 1998: 78–9.
[46] The texts may be translated as: (a) 'My husband, my wife,/My husband, since you've been gone' and (b) 'My husband, my wife,/Tell me how you got on/Since leaving this place,/My wife! Don't leave me, my husband'. Trans. Alex Drace-Frances. According to Marin Marian-Balasa the confusion regarding who is being mourned indicates the artificial nature of the collecting process. The singers were demonstrating possible lament types, rather than lamenting. Reproduced from Sperl and Suliteanu 1998: 178–9. (a) was collected in Sebes in 1948; (b) was collected in Saliste in 1934.

a perfect fourth (while nevertheless recalling the 'Lebewohl' too). The five dyads and their inverted repetitions shift progressively downwards in register until bar 21, when they start again from where they began, this time to shift progressively upwards in register. Interwoven with this pattern is the lamento motive – initially a group of three distinct melodic descents, each one longer than the last – as well as pedal notes. As the movement develops, the three-section lamento motive breaks into less clearly defined lengths of descending lines and they become more rapid and overlap with one another. The climactic passage arrives as the passacaglia and various lament threads have climbed, stridently, into upper registers and the horn – having sounded only pedal tones hitherto – has stated the lamento motive very powerfully. A thundering bass, drum-like, explodes in the piano. Forceful, superimposed laments in all parts extend this explosion of sounds, giving way only gradually to quiet, almost static upper-register violin, and deep below, sustained horn. The piano enters briefly in between them for a final reflection upon the 'Lebewohl', before all the sounds die away.

Although the vocality of all these laments is their primary feature, the particular instrumental character of the horn plays an essential part. Given the link here with folk laments, and even though Ligeti has never mentioned it in ruminations on his childhood fear of death, one is tempted to speculate that he may have developed a subliminal association between the horn and death. In many parts of Romania a natural horn is used to announce mortalities in village communities: the intonation of single notes at sunrise, midday and sunset is as much a sound of death as is the weeping and lamenting.[47] From this perspective the horn's single pedal note accompanying the first bars of the Trio's Lamento can be heard as part of the sorrowful message. That the horn sounds like a natural horn (using 'natural' harmonics) ensures that an aura of the rural instrument's traditional proclamatory role is retained; and it also heightens the dissonance of the already chromatically placed lines, awakening and sustaining an intense desire that a consonant resolution be reached. Yet there is a constant 'failure' to resolve, for despite the perpetually descending lines, each one ends on a dissonance.

Another poignant failure can be traced from the close. Although Ligeti has described the last section as a 'photograph of a landscape that has dissipated into nothingness', it is actually a moment of supreme suspense and anticipation.[48] A vast space opens up between the upper-register violin, on

---

[47] Sperl and Suliteanu 1998: 72.
[48] Cited in Dibelius 1984: 57. (From the programme booklet of the première, 7 October 1982, Hamburger Bergedorf.)

prolonged harmonics, and the sustained low-register horn. What will fill it? The effect may recall Ligeti's discussion of Mahler's Symphony no. 1, in particular his fascination with that musical space between upper and lower registers at the opening, which gradually fills with fragmentary signals on oboe, bass clarinet and bassoon, before a full trumpet fanfare is finally introduced – not on the trumpet, however, but on the clarinet.[49] Here in the Horn Trio, in the space between the horn and the violin, a final horn call emerges, not on the horn, but on the piano. Never once are the horn calls heard on the horn: the 'presence' of the horn is at once its absence.

Ligeti's description of the movement's end points to links with the archetypal 'arrival–dispersal' movement type. Despite the relatively clear opening, there is indeed a shift from quietness, towards vast climax, towards gradual dissolution. It is far from certain, however, that Ligeti's photographed landscape provides a strong parallel, because the immediacy of this Lamento breaks into the listener with an elemental, embodied passion. Indeed the elemental quality of lament here is so evocative of weeping and wailing that no simple landscape could possibly engender the same impact. The sheer number of lamenting lines, the way they always fail to resolve, the way they are melodic but ever dysphoric and harshly dissonant, the way the bass of the piano thunders beneath their volcanic profusion: through all this, grief seems to become present. Although language fed to the 'Lebewohl' motive, and texts into the rhythms of folk laments, those are all dissolved here into sensations that words could not hope to contain. And yet we will return to this lamenting with new words in the next section.

Light and dark

The use of register in the Lamento indicates Ligeti's ongoing and dramatic recourse to musical extremes, and indeed the sudden plummeting from a high register to the lower depths had by this time become a persistent formal and dramatic feature of his work. Englbrecht went so far as to understand it as a Ligetian *topos*, a recurring musical event that reincarnated the plunge into hell that Kaufmann had identified in *Atmosphères*.[50] This apparent shifting from light into dark is also a feature of other, less dramatic moments in the Horn Trio, however. In the first movement, *Andantino con tenerezza*, the chromatically inflected 'Lebewohl' expands into a gently dissonant tapestry of threads among which occasional consonant chords shine out as if moments of light – to be cast into shadow again rapidly. The voice-leading does not generate a sense of motion towards such moments;

---

[49] Gottwald 1974: 8.   [50] Englbrecht 1998: 66 and 159.

rather, the various independently flowing lines coincide periodically, but sporadically, to bring them out unpredictably. In the second movement, *Vivacissimo, molto ritmico*, such a 'lightness' predominates, because the textures are transparent, and sonorities are so often consonant (thirds and sixths); yet once again there is no traditional tension between dissonance and consonance, one leading to the other. Rather, within the *moto perpetuo* the prevailing lightness is flecked with fleeting hints of darker shades. There is no obvious model for such a use of non-functional consonance, yet its proximity to tonality and modality hints distinctly at Bartók, especially in its repetitive, non-directional, yet dualistic mould.

Archaeological work in Ligeti's compositional process might yet suggest that a Bartókian basis – a 'musical mother tongue', even – may have haunted him more than is currently evident. His initial struggles with the Piano Concerto, for instance, suggest that his first attempts were distinctly Bartókian, and that he progressively transformed them into something else.[51] But it would patently be a mistake to identify such characteristics as part of a straightforward rerouting and re-rooting into Hungary. Although four out of the eight Piano Études written between 1985 and 1989 make obvious references to Hungary, others are more characterised by Scriabinesque harmony, jazz, Chopin, the gamelan or African rhythms. Whether or not Bartók lies behind this multi-faceted experimentation, and whether or not each virtuosic stylisation of something else was elaborated to *avoid* the pervasiveness of Bartók in Ligeti's thought, the final labyrinthine pieces cannot be penetrated to locate him at their centre.

The Piano Études that offer traces of a Bartókian play on consonant/dissonant harmonies are worth addressing carefully, however. 'Fém' (a Hungarian title meaning metal, the proximity of which to the word for light, 'fény', is suggestive) closes with a collection of chords that recalls the chorale-like opening of Bartók's Piano Concerto no. 3, in which, similarly, entirely unorthodox progressions 'resolve' repeatedly on unorthodox (non-triadic) consonances. 'Fanfares', analogously to the second movement of the Horn Trio, sets consonant dyads in counterpoint with a *perpetuo mobile* bass-line in an *aksak* rhythm. The 'fanfare' dyads are also related to the horn calls of the Trio, while additionally pointing back to the sixth of Bartók's Six Dances in Bulgarian Rhythm from *Mikrokosmos* Volume VI. If such similarities seem incidental, there is nevertheless one parallel that can be drawn quite profitably, that between Bartók's 'From the Diary of a Fly' (*Mikrokosmos* Volume VI) and Ligeti's Piano Étude no. 3, 'Touches bloquées'.

---

[51] See Steinitz 2001: 315–21, including four reproductions of early sketches.

Each of these pieces is very light in texture, predominantly consisting of one single line taken by each hand, and each line characterised by a great deal of staccato. Both pieces play with the tension between whole tones and semitones, and both are structured around expanding and contracting wedges: the Bartók study creeps up the keyboard in an elaborated chromatic line for its section of maximum tension, whereas Ligeti's simply leaps up seven and a half octaves for a climactic passage (in a reversal of his 'descent into hell'). Both pieces sweep down the keyboard thereafter in a chromatic line, that of Ligeti very much muffled. Each piece has a core sonority created by the repetition or sustaining of certain pitches, above and below which occasional 'rogue pitches' tantalise the listener with only partially suggested lines elsewhere. This also creates a sense of polyrhythm – Ligeti's major innovation in the decade. In short, within 'From the Diary of a Fly' we can trace a 'Ligetian' texture, hand disposition on the keyboard, harmonic shape and character, registral arc and polyrhythm: Bartók's piece may or may not have been an explicit model, but it surely helped at some point along the way.[52]

The shift in Ligeti's compositional style, from the very cloudy textures of the 1960s to more transparent ones such as these, made his sense of harmonic duality of consonance versus dissonance more obvious than it had been before. Responding to that, Floros attempted to interpret the tension between transparent sonorities and more opaque ones in the second movement of the Piano Concerto. Contrasting the shrieking dissonances – made yet more brutal by sirens and a guero – with the diatony and pentatony that follows, he observed, however, that despite these harmonies, the movement finally ends with chromaticism, which evokes melancholy and nostalgia.[53] Yet it is not clear that the diatony and pentatony could be understood here as an opposing pole to melancholy – unless that pole were taken to be a weeping and wailing. For the diatonic and pentatonic harmonies are there to support the Lamento motive, which pours down in cascades of glassy chords. Here the harmonies make the recognisable topoi complex, rather than participating in a dualistic play that generates emotions on one or other side of a balance.

This interpretive impasse reveals the extent to which the music of this period – and in particular that of the Études – is often rather less open to such hermeneutics than it seems. Puzzled commentators frequently cite fractal geometry and the 'impossible drawings' of Escher as metaphors for

---

[52] Given Ligeti's famous dream about being stuck in a cobweb (see Chapter 3), it is somewhat uncanny that Bartók conceived the fly in his 'From the Diary of a Fly' as being stuck in a cobweb. Suchoff 1993: 207.
[53] Floros 1991: 342–3.

Ligeti's bewilderingly complex music that toys with so many patterns, and refuses to give up its secret. But is this entrapping not the point, in fact? Are the pieces not masks?

A parallel for them might be found in apotropaic decorations, maze-like patterns and labyrinths, which in a wide range of cultures are created in order to provide protection. The belief is that evil spirits will be fascinated by the patterns, get lost in them, and forget to perform their demonic deeds.[54] The entangling obstacle of such labyrinths is akin to both the cognitive obstacle of Ligeti's studies and the wordiness of his verbal style that, as I suggested at the beginning of this chapter, enchants, yet leaves the listener tantalised. It keeps everyone at bay.[55]

One might reject the apotropaic parallel, but commentators remain captivated, and not only in intellectual terms. The shifting meters, overlapping melodies and polyrhythms ensure that there is a kinetic confusion too: a rhythm or a line can be sensed for a moment, and even absorbed in a physical sense. Yet it changes, and deceives, forcing renewed engagement. It is as if Ligeti has conjured in his listeners the same enthralment that Bartók had on encountering Bulgarian dancers. Amazed by the way they could keep pace with complex and rapidly changing *aksak* rhythms of five and seven, Bartók wrote with fascination about their capacity for movement.[56] His amazement can be simply enough explained: he could not make such movements his own. Precisely such a desire for corporeal engagement is kept tantalisingly out of reach in some of Ligeti's Études too. They trigger a Bartókian bafflement.

One further echo of Bartók is worth exposing in reference to this one, and it returns us to the Horn Trio. The third movement, *Alla marcia*, points directly to Bartók through its stylised use of the march topic. Moreover, the movement's central, gently flowing section offsetting the vigorous march distinctly recalls the way the *Marcia* of Bartók's Sixth String Quartet is interspersed with reflective and *sostenuto* sections. And the harder one looks, the more profitable the comparison becomes. The *mesto* theme of the quartet, which opens every movement, has a lament-like tone, a quality attributed

[54] Gell 1998: 83–90 discusses Celtic knotwork, South Indian threshold designs called *kolam* and the notorious labyrinth at Knossos (and its later representations).
[55] Such labyrinths have frequently been connected with the threshold between life and death. Legendarily, Daedelus' maze at Knossos was modelled on one that led to the Underworld; it has been reproduced at the entry to a vast twisting tunnel to a passage of graves at New Grange, in Ireland; and tattoos of intricate patterns have been understood in Southern India to protect a deceased person in the land of the dead. (Gell 1998: 86–90.) Conceiving the Piano Études as mazes, then, incorporates into them the preoccupation with death that is so evident in Ligeti's work elsewhere: the Études hover at the entry point.
[56] 'The So-called Bulgarian Rhythm', Suchoff (ed.) 1976: 40–9. See especially 48–9.

Example 5.6. Bartók, String Quartet no. 6, movement 4, bb. 1–6

to Bartók's sorrow about two things in 1939: the illness of his mother (she would die within a month of his completing the quartet), and the political imperative that he flee Hungary.[57] The stepwise descent of this theme is surely a forerunner to Ligeti's Lamento motive (see Ex. 5.6). The similarities may not be purely coincidence, for Ligeti's own mother died just as he was finishing the first movement of the Horn Trio.[58] His consequently composed *aksak* rhythms for the second movement, the March topos of the third and, above all, the Lamento of the fourth, then, can be regarded as yet more masked reflections on his current situation – here through the disguised filter of Bartók.

[57] See Walsh 1982c: 80–1.   [58] Steinitz 2003: 254.

Ligeti in Hungary

While these observations point to how Ligeti used his earlier connection with the East to reinvigorate his compositional work in the West, his private correspondence hints at a parallel project that made it possible. He wrote to Sándor Weöres, for instance, for advice about translating his poems for publication.[59] More importantly, he wrote in 1978 to someone in Baraolt, Romania, requesting a Romanian dictionary and encyclopaedia, Romanian literature (Arghezi poems, Caragiale theatre pieces and Creanga stories), Romanian folklore, Székely folk tales, ballads and poems, and recordings of folk music.[60] Presumably these were sources on which he hoped to draw in the next few years, in order to exoticise his style.

The question remains, however, as to what use Ligeti could be to musicians in Budapest. Writing in 1975, Kroó observed that he was an important figure for composers such as Maros and Szőllősy, and that the latter's work with sound masses could be attributed to Ligeti's influence (equally to the Polish school, however).[61] Maros and Szőllősy were certainly in touch with Ligeti during the 1960s and, in the case of Szőllősy, well beyond; meanwhile other composers travelling to the Warsaw Autumn festival, Darmstadt and Donaueschingen might have encountered him too.[62] But as we have seen, the prime currents shaping Budapest new music in the 1970s were the (American-influenced) experimentation and minimalism of the New Music Studio, a 'guru' figure whose status depended on romantic metaphysics, and a broad (often highly protective) concern about the future of the national music as such. It remains to be seen quite what contribution Ligeti could make.

Ironically, his first big splash came in none of these fields, and was an indirect consequence of another project entirely, namely the State Puppet Theatre. When in 1971 a recording of *Aventures* formed the basis for part of its programme of seven grotesques, 'Puppets and People', there was very wide coverage in the press, and critical responses were unanimously positive. All reviewers praised the production's pioneering approach to theatre and its profound intellectual content; and Ligeti's music was understood as being realised perfectly in the surrealistic dramatisation provided.[63] The

---

[59] Ligeti wrote to Weöres on 8 November 1972. GLC, PSF.
[60] Letter to Béla Lőrincz, 7 July 1978. GLC, PSF.   [61] Kroó 1980: 187–8.
[62] Conversations with Zoltán Jeney, István Láng, András Szőllősy and László Vidovszky have indicated that there was no difficulty in doing this. It seems from the Ligeti Collection at the Paul Sacher Foundation that Ligeti kept in touch with Szőllősy by letter throughout the 1980s, but not with any others.
[63] Reviews appeared in *Magyar Nemzet*, *Népszabadság*, *Színház*, *Film Színház Muzsika* and *Vigília*. The script was written by Dezső Szilágyi on the basis of the music. Letters from composer István

production was an adaptation of a similar group of pieces of the same title that had been partially suppressed earlier on. Vetted by the City Council, the Ministry of Culture and the Union of Theatrical Arts and then addressed at a political conference, the earlier version was performed in a restricted number of performances and for a discreet circle only. Similarly, the 1971 version with *Aventures* was initially allowed only a limited number of showings.[64] This censorship may have contributed to the excitement in the press, but subsequently it became a showpiece for the State Puppet Theatre's international tours, visiting France, Germany, England, Wales, Denmark, Yugoslavia and the Soviet Union in the 1970s alone.[65]

When Ligeti entered the 'Hungarian musical life' itself in 1970, however, there was no question of censorship, for he came by official invitation to judge a composition competition. Notwithstanding that accolade, in this very early stage of his reintegration into discussions – and it was only in December 1969 that his music was heard publicly – critics did not celebrate him with great warmth.[66] Indeed his initial return might be grasped as a collision between the notions of music as nation and passion, and an idea of music as transnational progressive historical development; there was certainly a wall of friction between the prevailing concerns of Budapest and the style of Ligeti's music. Critics acknowledged that he was a significant composer, but each time found fault either with the piece chosen for the programme, or the performance itself. There was no enthusiasm for the Chamber Concerto in 1971, for example, even though its contemporaneity and skilful use of effects was noted, and two writers were in agreement in 1973 that *Ramifications* was just 'buzzing'. Breuer found it meaningless.[67]

The collision can be adduced more precisely from the conversations Ligeti had with Hungarians, published after his visit. When Kroó asked competition jurors for their opinions about contemporary music's national

---

Láng (Music Director at the Puppet Theatre) to Ligeti kept him informed about the stagings, all of which were presented with a recording of *Aventures*. (GLC, PSF.) See Szilágyi 1978 for photographs of the production, in which pieces of clothing and clothes-holders moved, as if people.

[64] Selmeczi 1986: 113–18 and 139.
[65] Avignon (1973), Paris (1975), Belgrade, Moscow and Tallián (1978), Munich, London, Cardiff, Billancourt Boulogne, Dresden, Aarhus, Copenhagen, St Quentin and Le Havre (1979). See Selmeczi 1986. Between 1980 and 1989 it was performed in Atlanta, Charleville-Mézières, Reims, Vienna, Dresden, Berlin, Frankfurt and Weimar. Between 1976 and 1992 it was performed eighty-six times at the Puppet Theatre in Budapest. Private letter from Mrs Béla Götz, Artistic Administrator, Budapest Puppet Theatre, 21 June 2005.
[66] The first occasion I have traced was the Budapest Wind Quintet's performance of five of the Six Bagatelles (16 December). Why only five, again? A plausible explanation is that the score used in 1956 remained in the possession of someone in Budapest.
[67] Breuer 1971; Homolya 1971. Barna 1973: 36; Breuer 1973a.

character, Ferenc Farkas earnestly constructed the national musical myth. Hungarian music, he explained, was characterised by its cautious reception of novelty, a certain gesture and thought mode, a melodic style and structure indebted to the Hungarian folk song or language, and a marked distinction from the wide vocal leaps that had grown out of the German tradition (these, Farkas stated pointedly, did not need importing).[68] Ligeti urged a different view and evoked a Hungarian musical life on track for self-immolation: it was of 'existential importance', he said, that Hungarian composers were not crushed by the heritage of Bartók and Kodály.[69]

In another interview, although the question of 'the post-Bartók and Kodály generation' was put to all jury members, Ligeti's published response discussed the character of new music from the Western avant-garde turn of the 1950s instead, and recommended that Budapest should take a leaf out of Poland's book and join the new avant-garde world itself:

> The main value of the Warsaw Autumn has been that it secures a platform for the world's modern works, interpreters and critics. Were the 'Budapest Music Weeks' to set aside just three days for similar aims, and at least present the world's modern music with no more than six months' delay, the organisers could be sure of receiving colossal numbers of foreign visitors and huge international interest. Naturally the international publicity of today's Hungarian music would grow in leaps and bounds.[70]

Finally, he had an individual interview in which he discussed his own transformation, specifically in the light of the need he felt from 1950 onwards to move away from Bartók. Rather in the manner of Descartes, he said, he strove to forget everything and experiment with a single note. And even though some of the resulting pieces of *Musica ricercata* were Bartókian, the ones written with very few notes were 'totally individual'.[71]

Although these three examples reveal the extent to which Ligeti made his rejection of preservationist Hungarian music very clear, he nonetheless staked a claim, building himself a unique historical place right there in Hungary (this is usefully compared with his remarks of one year earlier discussed in Chapter 3 above). The germinal idea for *Atmosphères*, he recalled, came to him while taking a nocturnal walk in the Budapest castle district, and not only *Musica ricercata* but also the initial version of his 'first radically new piece', *Apparitions*, was actually written in Budapest. Hungarian and Romanian folk music, meanwhile, still had an indirect influence on him.[72] These statements marked him out from the category into which he had been placed, 'the avant-garde'. Nevertheless his desire to do this led to even

---

[68] Kroó (ed.) 1971a: 37, 52–3. [69] Kroó (ed.) 1971a: 40. [70] Kerényi 1971: 7.
[71] Varga 1972: 63–4. [72] Varga 1972: 59–60, 67.

more pointed claims about his rather particular position within Hungarian history. When he was closed off from music from outside Hungary between 1949 and 1956 there was actually a certain advantage, he said, because he learned to follow his own ideas: 'everything that I got to know [thereafter in Vienna and Cologne] was very interesting – Stockhausen, Boulez, electronic music, the Viennese School – but stylistically I'd say that they didn't influence me at all.'[73] In other words, Ligeti avoided classification as both Hungarian and 'avant-garde', because he was forced to become original while in Hungary and remained so on leaving.[74]

Notwithstanding the damning reproach to Hungary that was part of Ligeti's self-construction, the idea that he could have a special place within Hungarian music history and contemporary Hungarian musical life began to take off thereafter. (Perhaps – as in the case of Kurtág in 1968 – there was a sense that Ligeti might *redeem* the nation's musical life.) The state music publisher Editio Musica attempted to reissue his harmony book from the 1950s, and to publish his Romanian Concerto and his *Musica ricercata*, and at least two people approached him about a book of interviews.[75] Of these various plans, only one book of interviews was realised. But Kroó made a radio programme about him in 1971 and an extended interview was broadcast in 1973; several performers wrote to him requesting scores, asking his advice, or simply letting him know about their concerts, and many performed his music.[76] Thus solo works *Volumina* and *Continuum* were heard three and four times respectively; *Lux aeterna* was also heard four times (only once by the visiting Stuttgart Schola Cantorum), as was the Chamber Concerto (only once by Vienna's *die reihe*). *Atmosphères* found considerable praise in 1973 when performed by the Philharmonic Orchestra from the town of Győr. By the end of 1979, the only major acoustic works not to have been performed in concert in Hungary were *Apparitions*, *Aventures*, the Cello Concerto, *Lontano* and *Clocks and Clouds*.

The upshot of the renewed contact between Ligeti and Hungary ensured that by the end of the decade the attitudes both of Hungarians and of

---

[73] Varga 1972: 63–4.
[74] This offers a striking echo with Haydn's self-constructions of his life at Esterháza, and thus canonises Ligeti's claim to originality and the desert-like quality of Budapest with a neighbourly geographical and historical reference.
[75] See letters from László Sarlós; and László Eősze and László Kalmár (all Editio Musica), 8 February and 15 October 1973 respectively; Mrs László Somfai, 16 May 1974; and Péter Várnai, 9 November 1973. GLC, PSF. For Ligeti's harmony books see Ligeti 1954a and 1956.
[76] The interview book is Várnai 1979, translated by Gábor J. Schabert in *Ligeti in Conversation*. For the radio programmes see Kroó (ed.) 1971b (it is not clear from records at Hungarian Radio whether this was ever broadcast); and Lázár and Varga (eds.) 1973. See also letters from Gábor Lehotka, Endre Székely (on behalf of the Budapest Chamber Ensemble) and Zoltán Kocsis and László Vidovszky (on behalf of the New Music Studio). GLC, PSF.

Ligeti himself had changed considerably. There was no collision of views when he visited again in 1979 to hear a concert of his works, but rather, a rapprochement and celebration. On Ligeti's own side, he gave an extended and detailed interview in which he expanded considerably and more generously on his past in Hungary. He had benefited from the teaching of Lendvai, Farkas, Veress and Kadosa, he said; Bárdos remained an ideal for him, and 'Szabolcsi's Mozart analysis still holds good'.[77] He also identified a range of traces of his later work in the compositions he had written in Budapest, thus emphasising his historical link with Hungary.[78] Most symbolic of his new position was the way that he identified his String Quartet no. 2 as a much needed 'synthesis' of his Hungarian past with his later style.[79]

On the other side, writers embraced him as one of their own. One criticised his interviewer for not asking Ligeti the question that 'only a *Hungarian* could really ask', namely how he could work in a milieu so different from the Hungarian intellectual tradition in which he had grown up.[80] Kroó constructed him as a 'great composer' in the European tradition, identifying his 'greatness' in the way he entrusted his message to music alone, and claiming that 'like every other really important work in the European music tradition, Ligeti's *Requiem* comments with infinite honesty on fundamental matters and elemental human feelings'.[81] One critic struggled predictably with putting pen to paper, noting that it was difficult to write objectively about the long-awaited celebration of such an internationally renowned 'compatriot'.[82] The bluntest gesture of all came from Breuer, who argued that the tumultuous applause revealed that Ligeti, the cosmopolitan, had 'come home'.[83] In 1979, then, Ligeti was the long-lost (and found) great Hungarian.

And yet if there was a rapprochement between Ligeti and his Hungarian audiences, there was discord among the Hungarians themselves. Earlier in the same year the New Music Studio had presented his 'Musical Ceremonies', including the *Trois bagatelles* (silent but for one note) and *Poème symphonique* for one hundred metronomes. The sole reviewer of the concert made a point of 'defending' Ligeti from the Studio's antics, arguing that Ligeti, one of the most important composers of the West, had thought of the Ceremonies as just a 'grotesque joke', and had moved beyond such things.[84] Even the reception of the orchestral concert was fractured along the old lines of progress against passion. One writer was particularly explicit,

---

[77] Várnai 1983: 43, 71–3. (First published in Hungarian as Várnai 1979.)
[78] Várnai 1983: 47, 44.   [79] Várnai 1983: 16.   [80] Wilheim 1980: 42. My italics.
[81] Kroó 1979.   [82] Kovács 1980: 11.   [83] Kroó 1979; Breuer 1979.   [84] Homolya 1979.

critically proposing that whereas *San Francisco Polyphony* was 'intellectual', the Double Concerto somewhat superficially virtuosic, the *Requiem* was Ligeti's deepest and darkest music.[85]

The discord became more apparent in 1983, when Ligeti made a third official visit on the occasion of his sixtieth birthday. Despite the birthday concert and another interview (this time published in the English-language *The New Hungarian Quarterly*) there were no romantic claims about the great 'compatriot' published in the press.[86] One New Music Studio member and musicologist published an article in *Muzsika*, however, in which he revealed his revulsion for such claims. It was hypocritical of the Budapest 'musical life' to celebrate Ligeti's birthday, said András Wilheim. Only thirty people attended Ligeti's lecture, his scores were not fully available in Budapest libraries and performers did not care about his works, which had been presented in concerts in Budapest only sporadically. 'Let nobody delude themselves', he said in closing, that Ligeti has 'come home'.[87]

Wilheim's case was strong. In the 1980s there were far fewer performances of his works by Hungarians than there had been in the 1970s.[88] And although Hungarians performed the Ten Pieces for Wind Quintet and the Horn Trio, and the birthday concert presented the *Requiem*, *Clocks and Clouds* and the Cello Concerto, Wilheim's article and his radio programme on the Ten Pieces for Wind Quintet were the only published responses of any substance.[89] The sixtieth-birthday concert was reviewed in matter-of-fact tones in the national press, and not covered by *Muzsika*.[90]

And yet as we will realise in Chapter 5, Wilheim's tirade was not exclusively about Ligeti. Writers for *Muzsika* were increasingly disappointed in Budapest's new-music scene as a whole, and Wilheim's views were the most cutting of all. Ligeti simply provided a weapon in the new offensive for reclaiming support for and interest in new music, and in one sense was entirely inappropriate, for this particular one of the 'great masters of new

---

[85] Pándi 1979. Breuer also made clear that the *Requiem* was the most important work; Kroó's emphasis implicitly suggests the same.

[86] *The New Hungarian Quarterly* has traditionally provided non-Hungarians with a window on Hungarian culture. In this sense, its inclusion of an interview with Ligeti (Szigeti 1984) and an article on Ligeti (Wilheim 1984) was a clear appropriation of him for national display.

[87] Wilheim 1983a: 27. The article was also published in *The New Hungarian Quarterly*, but this final section, directed to musicians in Budapest, was excluded. See Wilheim 1984.

[88] The London Sinfonietta, the Kronos Quartet, the European Chamber Orchestra and the Arditti Quartet were among the many who came bringing Ligeti.

[89] See Wilheim 1983a and Wilheim 1981. Another article, by the horn player who premièred the work, gives an account of the struggles he had coming to terms with its novel syntax. Friedrich 1986.

[90] Although the tone of one writer on Ligeti in the early 1980s indicates some excitement, it seems to have been triggered primarily by her sense of outrage regarding the Paris production of *Le Grand Macabre*. It had completely misrepresented the work, she argued. Grabócz 1981b: 14.

music in the second half of the century . . . maker and shaker of universal culture' had far more exposure than did any of the others. But of course he was particularly appropriate in another sense, because he was understood as having a claim on Hungary: 'the string quartet he wrote *thirty* years ago has only *just* been premièred in Hungary by an *American* quartet', observed Wilheim accusingly.[91]

Perhaps most striking in Wilheim's position, however, is his pointed construction of Ligeti as a pioneer. In one respect this is symptomatic of his thesis (mentioned in Chapter 4 above) that 'composition equals research', in another, it is an elaboration of Ligeti's self-construction as an isolated individual; and it is also a putatively oppositional response to the nationalist and romantic discourse that enveloped Ligeti in Budapest. Wilheim constructed Ligeti's Horn Trio as a masterpiece that was not only 'the beginning of a new creative period' for Ligeti, but also a milestone in the history of music: 'musicology', he said, 'does not at the moment offer the methodological means which can describe [it] exactly'.[92] He regarded it as so novel that the whole constellation of musical possibilities for the future had changed.

Nevertheless his construction is not only interesting in this Budapest context, because – as I mentioned above – precisely this work was heard in the West as retrogressive or, indeed, as a challenge to the search for progress as such. There is, then, a distinct echo here of times gone by. Although the ethical ramifications are less explicit, Western responses recall the moment when Bartók was understood in the West as having 'compromised'; while Wilheim's response may remind us of Hungarian hopes of the same era, according to which Bartók's music could hold the path to the future. But 1983 was not 1947. Ligeti did not become the political football that did Bartók. 'Maker and shaker of universal culture' or not, his music was completely off the radar in the final strains of the Cold War.

[91] Wilheim 1983a: 27. Italics original. See also note 80 above.   [92] Wilheim 1984: 213.

6   After Budapest: out of Hungary?

There is no clear turning point between the 1970s and 1980s, although lurching shifts in détente were accelerated considerably by the Soviet Union's economic crisis. Its consequent problems were addressed productively only from 1985 with Mikhail Gorbachev's *perestroika* ('restructuring'), when a loosening up of economic policies, new arms agreements signed with the USA, and the military withdrawal from Afghanistan in 1989 all contributed to a reduction of hostility between East and West. Another major change was Gorbachev's parallel move towards *glasnost* ('openness'), which for the first time allowed the press to discuss aspects of past Soviet atrocities, current corruption, and the ongoing military activities.

Dissident activities in Poland also contributed to the Soviet regime's downfall, and also facilitated an eventual shift to multi-party politics. The underground activist Lech Walesa negotiated successfully with the Polish Communist Party on behalf of workers at the shipyard in Gdansk in 1980, an act that led to a national gathering of trade unions under the name Solidarity. Although Solidarity was suddenly outlawed in December 1981 and its leaders were imprisoned, the fickle and oppressive treatment it suffered turned it into a cause célèbre in both East and West. In the ensuing years other underground activities proliferated, some metamorphosing into independent, openly functioning parties, and governments in the satellite countries fell in 1989. Russia held open elections that year (the first since 1917), and the Soviet Union disintegrated in 1990.

Budapest, dissolution, and the end of the Cold War

Hungary's dissidents were neither so violent nor so unified as those of Poland, but they did organise a number of public events during the decade. Nationalists and leftists converged in the town of Monor in the summer of 1985, for example, the significance of which extended well beyond its day because the journal *Új Tükör* (New Mirror) recorded it in print. Some months after this meeting demonstrators gathered in Budapest, and the Writers' Union staged a revolt too. Meanwhile dissenting reformers published proposals for political and economic change, and formed three new political parties. Free elections took place in spring 1990, and the occupying Soviet forces had completely withdrawn by the middle of 1991.

The reforms that had been ongoing since the late 1960s, combined with new traffic between the opposing sides of Europe, contributed to the smoothness with which multi-party politics emerged. In the 1980s new contacts with the Western business world saw Hungary joining the International Monetary Fund and establishing its own private banks. A meeting of the European Cultural Forum for furthering discussions about the Helsinki Accords was held in Budapest, which in 1985 was the first such meeting to take place in the Eastern bloc. Moreover, in a different hotel in the same city the Helsinki Federation for Human Rights convened a simultaneous meeting for writers living in the West, addressing questions of censorship and European identity.[1] Such meetings not only sustained pressure on regimes in the East, but considerably shifted Western perceptions of that East.

Western perceptions were in any case already becoming richer. Novelist Milan Kundera had offered a new perspective two years earlier when he constructed the region of 'Central Europe' as a part of the occident that had been 'stolen' by Russia, but that retained a more essential dimension of life than the current (industrial, commercial) West.[2] His message was not a solitary plea, for a large number of dissidents were writing along similar, if not identical, lines: Václav Havel's 'Politics and Conscience' (1984) and György Konrád's *Antipolitics* (1982) provide notable examples. All these writers made arguments for an 'anti-political politics' that would overcome the violence and imperialism of both Soviet Russia and America by learning from the ethics of the oppressed liberals of Central Europe.[3]

Many sceptical questions emerged in the debates that followed. Could Russia really be blamed for the societies that had evolved in Eastern Europe? To what extent was Russia truly 'oriental' or separate from 'Europe proper'? Wasn't the whole Central European movement an uncritical nostalgia for the Habsburg days? Didn't it draw rather problematically on mythological narratives of victimhood and redemption? Yet however contentious Kundera's Central European intervention, it had an enchantment for many Western intellectuals. Austrian writer Egon Schwartz professed to seeing Central Europe as 'a symbol for what is not, but what should be, a spiritual attitude, and ethos'. And although Timothy Garton Ash could find little in common between its citizens other than their political powerlessness, he found the

---

[1] Timothy Garton Ash, 'A Hungarian Lesson', in Garton Ash 1989: 130–41, at 136–7. Writers attending included Hans Magnus Enzenberger, Amos Oz and Susan Sontag, as well as exiles from Eastern Europe such as Jiří Gruša and Danilo Kiš.

[2] Initially published in French in *Le Débat* 27 (November 1983): 3–22, then in English in *The New York Review of Books*. Kundera 1984.

[3] Havel 1986a: 249–81; Konrád 1984.

new Central Europe a fascinating and profoundly enticing 'kingdom of the spirit'.⁴

Several of the shifts in Budapest's musical life in the 1980s were the direct result of increased international traffic and the lifting of taboos about the past. The music of Swiss resident Sándor Veress, largely absent from concerts and printed discourses since his dissidence in 1949, began to re-emerge more prominently; the music of László Lajtha was taken up and promoted as an analogously neglected corpus.⁵ At the beginning of the decade these newly discovered repertories contributed to a musical life that remained lively, while three new composer ensembles founded in the latter part of the 1970s continued to provide audiences with new music from outside the country (American minimalists in particular, for some time).⁶ In 1984 yet another group emerged, the Amadinda percussion ensemble, and the summer Bartók Seminars at Szombathely became a further framework for contemporary music (see Chapter 4 for the origin of these Bartók Seminars).

There were two significant musical shifts in the decade. One was a diversification of approaches among composers of the New Music Studio. Jeney brought together a group of pieces in 1987 under the title of *Halotti szertartás* (*Funeral Rite*), laying the foundations of a choral work that would expand progressively for another eighteen years. Settings of Latin liturgical and para-liturgical texts and Hungarian poetry combined in a musical style reminiscent of Stravinsky's pared-down Latin settings, and they formed initial building blocks for a large, organically growing and individualised formal scheme.

The music of Vidovszky, meanwhile, continued to explore visual and electronic media, but also took a fresh approach to more conventional forces. His *Romantic Readings* (1985) was for ensemble (later arranged for orchestra) and its loosely bound tapestry of melodies was drawn from composers such as Dvorak, Grieg and Rimsky-Korsakov, in order that the gestures and comportment of traditional performers might be 'read' anew in a contemporary world.⁷ His so-called 'opera', *Narcissus and Echo* (1980–1), was conceived originally for a film. Although altered and extended substantially thereafter, its medley of musical styles from the early nineteenth century to the 1930s

---

⁴ Egon Schwarz, 'Central Europe – What It Is and What It Is Not', in Schöpflin and Wood (eds.) 1989: 143–56, at 154; Timothy Garton Ash, 'Does Central Europe Exist?' in Garton Ash 1989: 161–91, at 169.

⁵ Two books are representative of this change, one on Veress, one on Lajtha. See Berlász, Demény and Terényi (eds.) 1982 and Berlász 1984.

⁶ The Young Composers' Group (*Fiatal zeneszerzők csoportja*') and the New Music Workshop of Miskolc (*Miskolci Új Zenei Műhely*) were founded in 1976. The 180 Group (*180-as csoport*), founded in 1979 by composers László Melis (b. 1953) and Tibor Szemző (b. 1955) focused on group work and minimalist music and was clearly indebted to the New Music Studio.

⁷ Vidovszky and Weber 1997: 44–8.

is less of an opera than a zany tracing of light music of the Habsburg and post-Habsburg lands.[8]

Even though the Studio's part-member Péter Eötvös had lived abroad since the late 1960s and he only came to prominence in Hungary in the 1980s, his compositions can be grounded in Budapest through their engagement with time-honoured concerns of the country's musical thinkers, namely music's relationship with language and with human presence.[9] *Tale* (1968), for example, takes the narration of a Hungarian fairy story as the sound material for a contrapuntal electronic study, while *Insetti Galanti* (1970, rev. 1989) uses language in a way analogous to Ligeti's *Aventures*. As writers in Hungary noted, works such as *Cricket Music* (1970) and *Wind Sequences* (1970, rev. 1987 and 2000) use advanced techniques to elaborate remarkable sound effects without abandoning music's traditionally experiential nature.[10] Indeed from this perspective it is perhaps not surprising that in interviews of the 1980s Eötvös claimed that he experienced difficulties with living away from Hungary. The Hungarian language, he said, was crucial to him, for only in this mother tongue could he express himself properly: while living abroad he felt as if he was constantly in transit.[11] His influence in Hungary can be traced in the work of László Tihanyi (b. 1956), whose *A szelek csendje* (*The Silence of Winds*) (1984) uses complex abstract structural frameworks and transparent timbres that are clearly indebted to Eötvös.

The other (somewhat overlapping) shift was an emergence of neo-romanticism. György Orbán (b. 1947), who moved to Budapest from Transylvania in 1979, was one proponent, Sándor Szokolay was another. The latter's opera *Ecce homo* (1983) and his many choral pieces of the time construct a restorative Hungarian style through folk music, chant and tonality. János Vajda's (b. 1949) opera on Mann, *Mario and the Magician* (1980–5) draws on Hungarian styles not at all, but it is part of the same trend, clearly indebted to Puccini in its pacing and harmony.[12]

---

[8] The film was Gábor Bódy's *Narcissus and Echo*, inspired by Sándor Weöres' poem 'Psyché'. As Vidovszky observed, the libretto for his later work was a sort of 'revenge' for the nineteenth-century practice (that is part of the film) whereby Hungarian 'classics' were created by translating German pulp fiction. László Ungvárnémeti Tóth's Hungarian text, translated somewhat crassly into German, created a piece of German pulp fiction from a Hungarian classic. Vidovszky and Weber 1997: 38.

[9] He first attracted attention as a coach and conductor at the Bartók Seminars in Szombathely, and an LP was issued dedicated to his compositions in 1986. A tiny, but loyal, group of supporters wrote about him appreciatively, and he was also interviewed several times.

[10] Szitha and Peller 1986, drawing on liner notes by András Wilheim.

[11] Váczi 1987: 15. See also Váczi 1986a and 1986b.

[12] The fact that during *glasnost* a novella traditionally read as a statement about totalitarianism formed the basis for a dramatic, but by no means political opera is nothing if not striking. It may be a sign of post-communism before its time or, as Tallián suggests, a display of weariness in the impotence of both the supposed political power and a shallowly cynical society. The shooting with which the novella so shockingly closes is followed, in Vajda's opera, with a resumption of

Each of these shifts can be traced in the writings of *Muzsika* where by the beginning of the 1980s reviewers examined music exclusively in Westward-looking, modernist terms of 'progress'. Unsurprisingly, they commended the range of avant-garde music on the radio festival 'Music of our Century' in 1980, and recorded John Cage's visit to the Bartók Seminar with enthusiasm in 1986.[13] And predictably, they had concerns about neo-romanticism. One expressed alarm about young Hungarian composers' perspectives in 1980, which she regarded as both narrow and retrogressive.[14] Another attacked 'Music of Our Time' for its nostalgia in 1986, arguing that the festival had rigidified and that – just as in the 1950s Rudolf Maros's flat had rung with sounds of the future, and in the 1970s the New Music Studio had been at the cutting edge – one had to attend fringe events in Budapest to hear anything new.[15] Wilheim was the most damning, grumbling in 1984 that 'Music of Our Time' had become the single occasion in the year when new music was programmed in Budapest, and then describing the festival in 1985 as entirely lacking in quality.[16] When in the same year Budapest hosted the festival of the International Society for Contemporary Music, he complained that local performers were uninterested in new music, and he portrayed the administrators as inadequate to the task of organising the event.[17]

This anxiety about musical regression paralleled the disappointment of contemporary music criticism in the West, but is nevertheless usefully set in the context of Hungary's loosening political restrictions and the increased possibilities for travel outside the country. The vitality of the musical sphere had been dependent on the regime's physical and intellectual containment coupled with musicians' determination to compensate for it. When the borders of the country became more permeable, the need to create something at home became less pressing. As Tihanyi reflected in 1989, many people would actually prefer to get in their cars and drive over to Vienna to sample the Wien Modern festival than go to Budapest's 'Music of Our Time'.[18] But a consequence of increased freedom to travel was also a new perspective on conditions at home: it is likely, then, that freedom fed discontent.

---

bourgeois dance music with which the (by then deceased) hypnotist had so alarmingly entrapped his audience. Tallián 1999a: 75.

[13] The most steadfastly positive writer was Sándor Kovács.
[14] Grabócz 1980.   [15] Maróthy 1986a.
[16] Wilheim 1984. His comment was oddly inaccurate, for the New Music Studio (of which he was a member) continued to programme new music regularly until a certain thinning out following changes in 1986 (the Studio gave their rehearsal space to the new Amadinda percussion ensemble and Vidovszky moved to the town of Pécs); Jeney was living abroad for sizeable parts of 1986, 1988 and 1989. The word Wilheim used for Music of our Time was 'színvonaltalan' (Wilheim 1986: 5). See also his disappointed review of the festival in the previous year (Wilheim 1983b).
[17] Wilheim 1986.   [18] Tihanyi 1989a: 15–16.

In that by the end of the decade there was a broad sense that the Budapest musical life was unsatisfactory, it should cause no surprise that there was one more attempt to rehearse the narrative of its unity and national tradition. But this did not emerge from the small avant-gardist wing of Budapest, but from Zsolt Durkó. Explaining his plans to the press in 1988 he claimed tendentiously that the monolithic cultural model of the previous forty years had not provided opportunities for sixteen musicians who had now come together to form the 'Hungarian Musical Society'. These musicians, he argued, sought to create a more democratic music life by recalling and upholding Kodály's maxim that music should serve all.[19] The Society launched what would become an annual 'Mini-festival' in January 1989.

According to the first review, the Society did nothing to reinvigorate the Budapest musical life. *Muzsika* reported that it too had been swallowed up by the 'catastrophic' situation: its audiences were tiny.[20] On one level, then, the Society was yet another gesture towards a long-standing but ultimately thwarted desire for an idealised 'musical life' in Budapest. On another, however, it was one more exclusory construction, for although its Mini-festival represented a range of composers from both Hungary and abroad, one name was conspicuously and remarkably absent, namely Kurtág.[21] When Durkó described the Society in opposition to the 'monolith' in place since 1949, then, was the latter actually a euphemism for his wildly successful contemporary?

Kurtág's voices

Contemporary constructions of Kurtág bear this suggestion out. Indeed a eulogy from Breuer – once the voice of the monolith – had included the point that it would have been worth organising 'Music of Our Time' in 1983 purely in order to hear Kurtág's *Scenes from a Novel* op. 19.[22] One critic observed that even in the context of new music internationally, Kurtág's music simply provided more, and 'other' qualities; Kroó presented him in the English-language *New Hungarian Quarterly* as 'clearly ... the most important living Hungarian composer ... he has now been discovered also by Europe'. Even more expansively, the editor of *Muzsika* made an extended list of the foreign promoters of his music in 1987, arguing that Kurtág, the 'taciturn creator of our tiny homeland', was now regarded by a range of notable figures as one

---

[19] Feuer 1989: 3.   [20] Boronkay 1989: 8.
[21] I base this on 'Music of our Time' and 'Mini-festival' programmes from 1974 to 2002 and 1989 to 2001 respectively, each collated in the relevant programme booklets for 2002.
[22] Breuer 1983.

of '*the world's* best living composers'.²³ The new tone of reportage elevated Kurtág well beyond his compatriots – even above those such as Durkó who were also being recognised in the West – and presumably fuelled the sorts of resentment that had led to the formation of the Hungarian Musical Society.

Durkó's use of the word 'monolith' is a strong indication of the way that Kurtág was becoming a living legend, a process in which *Muzsika* had a major role. Soprano Adrienne Csengery appeared within its pages on a (literally) sacrificial mission: she had abandoned her mainstream operatic career for the new world of Kurtág, she said in interview, after deciding that 'I have to sing *Troussova* even if it kills me'.²⁴ Sándor Kovács, barely able to write in 1979, wrote similarly in 1983 that Kurtág's 'truth' simply knocked the pen out of his hand.²⁵ Another *Muzsika* critic wrote in 1984 that it would have been 'almost grotesque' to pronounce judgement over the piano playing of the composer's wife Márta, for her music-making was so direct, unmannered and homely.²⁶ Kurtág and his circle were beyond criticism.

By the mid-1980s, moreover, Kurtág had gained a new institutional framework, appearing regularly at the Bartók Seminar in Szombathely. As *Muzsika* reported it, pianist Zoltán Kocsis – in whose classes the atmosphere was 'incandescent' – instructed people to 'play as if [their lives] depended on it'; Péter Eötvös, appearing as conductor, rehearsed for 'twelve hours a day', while Kurtág taught 'for the entire day'.²⁷ Kurtág's celebrated position as 'guru' is unmistakable from the tone of a critic writing in 1986: his 'faltering word images and wonderfully sensualising metaphors', argued the critic, 'meant that for everyone [an] entire piece – *and in that moment that meant the whole of life itself* – turned on precisely this C♯, or that B♭'.²⁸

These quasi-cultic gatherings were surely of more resonance than the publication of individual reviews or interviews. Yet it seems nonetheless important to note that in this same decade, Kurtág changed policy towards public statement, making himself available in Paris and London for interview in 1981, and in the following year agreeing to contribute to a new book of interviews in Hungary.²⁹ Not that he had become more certain about what he wanted to say. The resultant publication appeared only in 1986 – nineteen years after the volume from which he had been absent – and as the interviewer Bálint András Varga would later reveal, between the conversations and their publication there were 'agonising months with revisions and re-revision and re-re-revision, words, sentence and their order changed . . . [which]

---

[23] Maróthy 1986b: 23; Kroó 1982a: 51; Feuer 1987: 5. My italics.
[24] Kerényi 1987.   [25] Kovács 1983: 22.   [26] Csengery 1984: 25.
[27] Boronkay 1985.   [28] Halász 1986: 4. My italics.
[29] Hungarian journalists covering the Paris and London concerts at which he spoke (premières of *The Messages of Miss R. V. Troussova* op. 17), expressed astonishment. Feuer 1981: 11; Grabócz 1981a: 34.

only stopped when I showed signs of a nervous breakdown'.[30] But Kurtág had finally made a public statement about himself, publicly exposing his childhood, training, and his struggles with composition.

The resultant text is a cipher for his position in Budapest life. Far from smoothing out traces of his reluctance to speak, it ensured that precisely this was out on display. Hesitant and somewhat meandering, it portrayed an uncertain composer who was unable to understand quite how he composed, and who was simply grateful when he managed to write at all (especially after escaping one of his regularly paralysing depressions). As we have seen, in Budapest there was a scenario in place within which the struggles described could be not merely appreciated, but even admired as part of his commitment to the most searching metaphysical questions. Even for those not persuaded by his candour it would have seemed 'grotesque' (perhaps even obscene) in this climate to attack. For Kurtág presented himself as weakness itself: 'the fact that I can write anything at all is, in itself, a great joy ... Sometimes, I manage to make something good out of nothing quite by accident. But more often than not I don't.'[31]

If Kurtág's text harnessed his very frailties to inscribe him into the idealist mythology in which he was enveloped, his compositions were nonetheless less readily anchored. Put simply, they were on the move.

Russian intimations

Most obviously, they shifted out of Hungarian and into Russian (later German, French and English too), a move at least partly motivated by Kurtág's encounter with Russian émigré Rimma Dalos, who translated the text of *The Sayings of Péter Bornemisza* for the record publication. Dalos's poems – unpublished as such until 1988 – provided the texts for all but one of the six songs in *Omaggio à Luigi Nono* for choir op. 16 (1979), *Messages of the Late Miss R. V. Troussova* op. 17 (1978–80) and *Scenes from a Novel* op. 19 (1981–2) for soprano and ensemble, as well as *Requiem for the Beloved* op. 26 (1986–7) for soprano and piano. During the same period Kurtág was also working on his *Songs of Despair and Sorrow* op. 18 for choir setting well-known Russian poets, but he completed that group of six only in 1994.

As the poets selected for *Songs of Despair and Sorrow* reveal – Lermontov, Blok, Esenin, Mandelstam, Tsvetayeva and Akhmatova – Kurtág's concern with Russian poetry was a great deal broader than the Dalos settings alone suggest. (In fact the scores of *Omaggio à Luigi Nono* (henceforth *Omaggio*) and *Messages of the Late Miss R. V. Troussova* (henceforth *Messages*) suggest

---

[30] Kurtág and Varga 2003: 126–7. For original, see Varga 1986.
[31] Kurtág and Varga 2003: 134. These are the last words.

this too, as they include printed mottos drawn from Lermontov and Blok.) The linguistic move is thus loaded with significance, for each of these poets suffered torment inflicted by Russia.[32]

Such a visible step – almost emblematic of *glasnost* – would have been out of line with Kurtág's hitherto opaque engagement with public political discourse, and it is perhaps unsurprising in this light that he did not complete *Songs of Despair and Sorrow* for some years. The Dalos poems, on the other hand, rooted in love relations and personal struggles (partly expressed through reflections on the Bible), were less transparently related to politics, and could readily be embraced as an enriched development of Kurtág's intensely spiritual world. 'Russia' – understood primarily as a Dostoevskian probing of religious, moral and philosophical questions – added a new depth to his metaphysics.

This line of reasoning shaped one of two types of response in Hungary. We might call it the 'loyal' one, for it sympathetically elaborated on Kurtág's own projected understanding of what he was doing. Most notably, musicologist György Kroó positioned Kurtág's new Russian works firmly within the European tradition by referring to the influence on *Messages* of both Schumann's *Frauenliebe und -leben* and Schoenberg's *Pierrot lunaire,* and drawing attention to the *Tristan* motto citation in *Omaggio.* He built beyond that and into the Russian language by explaining that it had a 'magic' and quality of 'soul' for Kurtág, and that in certain respects it was 'sacred' to him in the way that Latin had been for Stravinsky.[33] *Omaggio* was shaped not only by the acoustic and formal properties of the language, argued Kroó, but also by a quasi-universal questioning of the meaning – or meaninglessness – of life. Thus while its first movement set an apparently banal declension of the pronoun 'whose', the Lermontov motto above it, 'And life, when you carefully look at what lies all around, / Is empty and futile, a fatuous joke', elevated the song to philosophy.[34]

It would be a mistake to regard Kroó's arguments as lone attempts to veil what were transparent political statements for, as we have seen, Kurtág was understood as elevated beyond such things by a great many people. Kroó's writing is thus a good measure of the Budapest sphere in general, and is highly sensitive, moreover, to the metaphysical suggestiveness of a music

---

[32] Mikhail Lermontov (1814–41) was exiled twice to the Caucasus as a result of his poetry; Alexandr Blok (1880–1921) had faith – later painfully lost – in the revolution; Sergei Esenin (1895–1925) also lost his earlier faith in the revolution, was repressed as a 'hooligan' under the Soviet regime and committed suicide aged thirty. Osip Mandelstam (1881–1938), Marina Tsvetayeva (1892–1941) and Anna Akhmatova (1899–1966) were all persecuted under the Soviets.
[33] Kroó 1982a.
[34] This motto is part of the Lermontov poem 'So weary, so wretched' that Kurtág set in *Songs of Despair and Sorrow*. This translation is that of Anthony Philips, written for the première of *Songs* at the Edinburgh International Festival on 24 August 1996. (Programme booklet.)

Example 6.1. Kurtág, 'Rimma Dalos: O Love, the Edifier!', *Omaggio a Luigi Nono* op. 16, close

* mormorando, ben articolato

that is in itself evasively mysterious. Song 5 is exemplary in this respect. A reflection on 'love' as 'edifier' suddenly takes the form of ritualistic chanting: the main choir presents a complex rhythmic pattern of intersecting perfect fifths, above which a group of soloists enters with a haunting and ethereal monochord to point out that love is '*forgotten* by all'. And then it suddenly evaporates (see ex. 6.1). Thus, although the listener is presented with a realm of extraordinary intensity and colour, the place described or evoked is never specific and always slipping out of reach.

His reading of the final song is also highly evocative. The text is a reworking of one of Paul's Letters to the Corinthians, from Dalos's 'Writings of the Apostle Paul to Me'. Dalos transforms Paul (I Corinthians 16: 9), who refers to the 'adversaries' that prevent him from passing through a 'wide door' to

Example 6.1. (*cont.*)

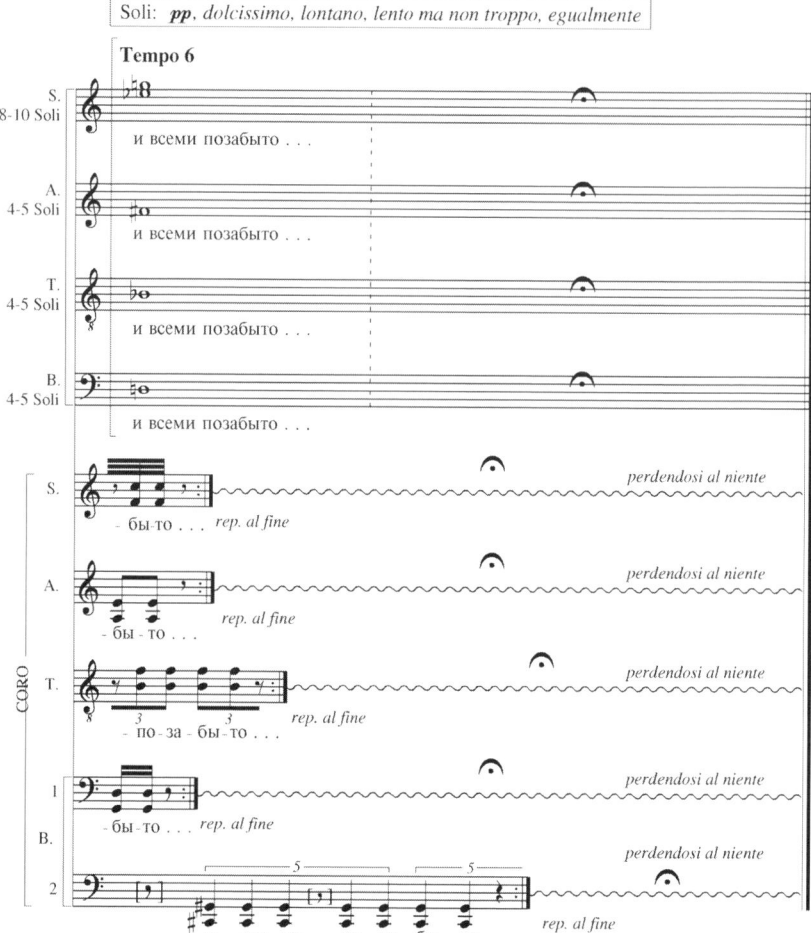

do 'effective work'. Her own poem is a reflection on inner struggles, fears of the poetic 'I':

... и отверста для меня	'... and the great, wide door
дверь великая и широкая.	is open for me.
да не смею пройти чрез иеё.	And I dare not pass through it.'[35]

But while Dalos had transformed Paul, Kurtág's song setting also transformed Dalos by dedicating his song to artist Lili Ország, whose many

[35] Translated by Geoffrey Norris. All extracts from works mentioned in this chapter are taken from the published scores unless otherwise indicated.

paintings of gates were understood as reflections on the final judgement. Consequently the Pauline desire to pass across a threshold to do work in life, and Dalos's suggestion of fearful hesitation, are overlaid with an anxiety about the approach to death. Hence Kroó, in a visionary explication:

> The male and the female quintets set before us the wings of the gate which – as if we were approaching them – seem to grow ever mightier . . . The threefold, fourfold piano dynamics and the sighing motif, for centuries part of European music, conveys (middle section) the anguished, panting, almost broken frame of mind, before the confession escapes: 'I do not dare'. The music, as a camera, records this moment for eternity, the gate, the gate of death opens onto infinity but the melody hesitates as if enchanted, there is no continuation: hope, as a receding, fading constellation (a prolonged E) gradually vanishes on the horizon. We feel the Russian-like choral sound, which imbues the music, to be authoritative, and when we do, Kurtág in actual fact has dared to step through the outer gate of his own style, and arrived at an even wider world.[36]

Kroó was not the only listener to invoke death: for one concert critic this final passing into mortality was the 'absolute' to counteract the meaningless relativity of the opening movement's reflection on life.[37] And notwithstanding their erasure of Paul and of Dalos, this interpretation can be neatly contextualised within Russian literature in which Death appears repeatedly, not only as a marker of the end of life, but as a threshold that leads to another dimension of existence.[38] This is an essentially imaginary, aesthetic sphere, protected from worldly life: in other words, one that Kurtág – in the eyes of his Budapest critics – already inhabited. Read through Russian literature, then, when critics invoked death, they were affirming their apprehension of an untouchable, unspeakable realm of existence to which Kurtág had privileged access. They affirmed his elevated position 'elsewhere'.

If this Kroó line of interpretation was 'loyal', that of aesthetician István Balázs was 'utopian', and also rather more adventurous, for it vacillated between poeticising and politicising. For Balázs, the 'wide door' was significant not for its evocation of death, but for its bridge between *Omaggio* and *Messages*. Aligning 'I dare not' with the Russian word 'trus', the stem of the name of *Messages*' protagonist Miss Troussova, Balázs found a prominent theme of the two works, namely cowardice. The significance of cowardice was that it described the degraded and broken position of the (once heroic) individual in society, whose attempts to bring change had

---

[36] Kroó 1982a: 210. [37] Feuer 1981: 13
[38] Engaged with, but not exclusively occupied by death, it is another more elevated sphere of reality, something intangible and beyond words. Catriona Kelly terms it 'the colours of "non-being", of death and spiritual life at one and the same time'. Kelly 2001: 144–5.

come to so little. And of course the individuals he had in mind were revolutionaries.

This reading had two subtly argued consequences. First, it meant that he regarded Russian as 'not merely the language of Dostoevsky, but also of Lenin and of October'.[39] Thus he recognised Akhmatova (one of whose love poems formed the second of the six songs in *Omaggio*) as an emblematically suppressed voice of the Soviet Union, and the Lermontov motto about the meaninglessness of life as a statement about the failed Soviet system.[40] Second, it meant that he reflected more penetratingly on the work's dedicatee (the reference to Nono was mentioned by others only as a consequence of Nono's suggestion that Kurtág should write for choir). As Balázs saw it, *Omaggio* was a response to Nono's use of resistance texts for his *Canti di vita e d'amore* and *Al gran sole carico d'amore*. *Omaggio*, he argued, staged a confrontation between the eruption of revolution (Nono) and the contradictions of state socialism (Kurtág): it was no mere gesture of respect, but 'the declaration of doubts, tough argument, intense sharing of thoughts'.[41]

Balázs's views on *Messages* were similarly shrewdly articulated. By contextualising the suffering of Miss Troussova within a history of tragic operatic heroines he constructed her as a cipher for an unloved (even betrayed) society. Troussova was not only Troussova, but also Ariadne, Pamina, Violetta and Judit. She was even comparable with the women of the liberation struggle projected by Nono's *Al gran sole carico d'amore*. She was the bearer of Eastern Europe's 'messages' to the rest of the world (and this was Balázs's utopia): her speaking Russian rendered the messages more eloquently than could any other.[42] In other words, Troussova was Eastern Europe, cowed by foreign occupation.

Balázs might have strengthened this view further had he known the actual provenance of the name 'Troussova', for it is the maiden name of the poet herself, Rimma Dalos. The death behind the 'Late' Miss R. V. Troussova is the marriage-cum-death of folk tradition, the mourned female deflowering and loss of carefree youth.[43] While apparently presenting the songs of a deceased woman, then, the cycle is (also) presenting the songs from a marriage. Viewed thus, Miss Troussova is not actually dead, but has simply crossed the threshold (another 'wide door'?) into marriage, a crossing

---

[39] Balázs 1984: 54. See also Maróthy 1982: 8, who made the same point when reviewing the Hungarian première.
[40] Balázs 1984: 54. [41] Balázs 1984: 60.
[42] Balázs 1984: 57, 53–4.
[43] See Kligman 1988: 76 for a discussion of this negative construction of a new step in the life-cycle of the woman, the entry into 'culturally sanctioned' sexual activity. Bartók's *Village Scenes* include examples of Slovakian wedding songs which are also mourning songs.

apparently as irreparable as death. Realising her incarceration within the domestic sphere would have strengthened Balázs's case, it might also have led him to draw further on Judit, or *Duke Bluebeard's Castle*, in order to do so. He could then have used the metaphor of marriage to reflect more on the relationship between Hungary and the Soviet Union. For the victim of *Messages* (Miss Troussova) is almost complicit. Certainly we cannot be sure quite 'which is which and who is who'.[44]

At the outset, for instance, Troussova finds herself in a chilly place (rather like Judit's shockingly cold and dark castle), where in 'a space of 6 by 4 metres / At a pressure of 6000 atmospheres of loneliness, / At a temperature of 400 000 degrees of unfulfilled desires, someone is freezing'. Just as Judit's scene is set by an orchestral introduction, so is Troussova's introduced by an instrumental preface. A high-register and explicitly out-of-tune violin line, obsessively vibrating viola and double bass wailing (this latter playing at an uncomfortably high pitch) are gradually joined by a range of similarly extreme instrumental timbres and tones above which the soprano voice sails in.

Whereas, however, Judit's passage towards her incarceration occurs apace with her step-by-step revelations about the space in which she finds herself, Troussova is much less innocent at the outset. Her voice is very much part of the writhing musical texture within which she reports: her long and sensuous setting of the word 'desires' echoes the richly complex textures and timbres of the accompaniment, and the focus throughout is on her self-dramatising voice, her near embodiment of the condition she describes. In fact, when she twice whispers 'freezes', then sings the word again in a mimetic, trembling stutter, then for a fourth time enunciates the word in a questioning tremble, she seems almost to relish the very extremes of her portrayal. In combination with similarly evocative, and similarly extreme, imitations in mandolin, cimbalom and other percussion instruments, there is a distinct suggestion of shuddering *titillation* on her part. This opening song conveys emotions from a marriage in which pain is insuperably entangled with pleasure.

Thus, where Judit's response to the chilly gloom she finds initially is to promise that she will 'open up the darkness' and make 'light shine' unendingly, Troussova's concerns are already different in song 2. For her, daylight has no association with happiness. The music offers a new perspective on the same set of unusual resonances: cimbalom and piano now suggest a shifting set of irregular chimes and are joined by the celesta, but the tickling and twanging effects re-emerge at intervals in a range of instruments.

---

[44] From the minstrel's Prologue to *Duke Bluebeard's Castle*. John (ed.) 1991: 46. Trans. John Lloyd Davies.

Troussova is now regretting the 'fall' of day, 'guillotine-like', that brought the death of trust between the pair. Light brought with it the death of intimacy and the revelation of deceit and loneliness, and it revealed, moreover, Troussova's namesake, 'cowardice'. The melismatic emphasis on this word parallels that of 'desires' in song 1, for each occurs at a climactic point in a gradual registral climb, and each features sustained presentations of C, B and B♭. Thus the recognition of cowardice overlays past desires. Daylight brings a 'Fall' in a new and ambiguous sense, on which Troussova reflects retrospectively.

Even as the cycle unfolds, Troussova's character remains comparable with that of Judit, simply drawing out its most violent potential. Bartók's character arguably has a self-immolating tendency, but that of Kurtág is overtly self-destructive. It is also more openly sexualised. In Part II Troussova describes her husband as unable to respond to her warmth, and thus recalls Judit's wish to warm Bluebeard's castle with her body, her vow to 'set it glowing' with her passion, with her flesh and blood. Miss Troussova also begins to sing very melismatically, something that might hint at Judit's florid vocal style. But her melismas are different: they are narrowly focused and obsessively repetitive, as she describes her incorrigible appetite. Buzzing with repetitions of the Russian 'ж' (zh), and gasping with a greedy lust, her need to envelop her husband is all-consuming:

жар, жар, жар ' – жар желания.	Heat, heat, heat – the heat of desire.
Я жажду тебя как живителъную,	I yearn for you as for life-giving moisture,
Прилъни ко мне	Cling to me
длиной своих ног,	with the whole length of your legs,
грудъю, впадиной живота,	with your chest, with the hollow of your stomach
. . .	. . .
Я хочу принятъ тебя всего без остатка.	I want to take in all of you, without anything left over.[45]

Moreover, where Judit yearns for Bluebeard's 'life-giving' qualities, Miss Troussova is fully aware of the danger she is in: 'your kiss will not save me – just poison me,' she shrieks. But it holds her back not one bit. Asking, 'Can't you see how I burn with desire for you?' her vocalising rises into an orgasmic climax of buzzing repetitions of 'heat'. As if physical pain is an object of her

---

[45] Translation from the score, by Stuart Campbell and Ksenia Norall.

desire, the initial musical accompaniment to the next song, 'Two interlaced bodies . . .', reinforces her description of their entangled bodies, 'red, white, black', with percussive explosions on cimbalom and xylophone that echo the torture chamber sound effects of Bluebeard's castle.

Would this not have furnished Balázs's reading rather fittingly?

Sadly, however, the utopian quality of his interpretation is now all too transparent. Kurtág's Russian works were – as he hoped – 'messages' from the East to the 'world', but they didn't say quite what he wanted them to. In England, Stephen Walsh was careful to find out what *Kurtág* wanted them to say, and this involved quite dramatically trivialising the impact of the Soviet Union:

> Though Russian is not necessarily a language regarded with equanimity by all Hungarians (for whom it is still a compulsory subject at school), Kurtág's interest in it is plainly apolitical. Indeed he has referred to it as a 'sacred' language. This may be a mistranslation, or only a partial translation, of his meaning; there is certainly some evidence that he regards it as a *secret* or esoteric language, and also that its sound intrigues him as such.[46]

What was really most striking for English audiences was the sensuality of the Russian-cum-Hungarian music. Possibly it fitted in with vague orientalist prejudices about the 'East'. As if feeling forced into a position of voyeurism, for instance, Walsh described the opening of *Troussova* as 'disturbingly erotic'.[47] Another writer suggested that a precedent for such music could be found in the *Erotica* of Tadeusz Baird, whom he referred to as Kurtág's 'compatriot'.[48] Baird was only a compatriot in the sense that he was in the East – for he was Polish.

But if orientalism was a vague backcloth to their interpretations, the press coverage may have honed them further. When interviewed, soprano Adrienne Csengery presented herself as a sort of medium, saying that 'Kurtág has chosen to sing in my voice.'[49] Her interview was published under the title of 'Beauty and the Monk', with her glamorous photo alongside, so there could be no mistaking the undertones of intimate excitements – especially in combination with her religious claim. Csengery's 'astonishing, almost Messianic commitment to Kurtág's vocal music' was observed by another writer, who had learned that 'Kurtág considers her the exclusive recipient of each new work for voice.'[50] One article labelled Kurtág a 'cult composer'.[51]

So much, then, for Balázs's sense that Kurtág 'nurtured no image': the package had transmogrified as it travelled West.[52] And what had seemed in

---

[46] Walsh 1982b: 14. [47] Walsh 1982b: 16. [48] Murray 1982.
[49] Larner 1986. [50] Walker 1986. [51] Potter 1986. [52] Balázs 1984: 51.

Hungary to be philosophical profundity, universal Truth, or a potent political plea, evolved in England into something merely exotically, or erotically, arousing.

Central European truths

In *Kafka Fragments* op. 24, however, the search for Truth is unmistakable, writ disconcertingly large. Not only do the texts posit its existence repetitively, but Kurtág's setting emphasises such moments. Thus the accompaniment of a text about an innocently slumbering child is diatonic, and perfect fifths underpin references to purity. Arnold Whittall observed that the search for purity and salvation is constant, and was prompted to puzzle whether Kurtág genuinely believed in such unsophisticated visions.[53]

The key to understanding these gestures is to remove the work from the German musical tradition and situate it in Budapest, something already suggested by the text itself.[54] Kafka, as Jewish Prague resident, was after all a child of Central Europe. For listeners in Budapest he followed logically after Kurtág's other poets Pilinszky, József and others, entirely in keeping with the composer's own world-view.[55] It is hardly by chance that when philosopher Péter Balassa attempted in 1989 to grasp what it meant for him to think about, and listen to, music 'here, in Central Europe, in Hungary, in Budapest', he came up with a constellation of ideas, events and musical works including precisely this one. 'Today, now, for me', he wrote, 'music is the music of György Kurtág. Most recently I heard *Kafka Fragments*... *Opus magnum*.... intellectual ecstasy and Central European irony: the meeting points of wise passions'.[56]

In the context of discussions above about the 'great wide door', it is worth spending a little time with Balassa's reading. Tellingly, his main argument was that *Kafka Fragments* had offered him a new understanding of Kafka's parable of the doorway 'Before the Law'. In this brief tale a man waits outside a guarded door all his life, repeatedly asking for entry, and repeatedly being denied it. Shortly before he dies, he asks why nobody else has approached the door in all the years he's been waiting. The guard tells him that the door

---

[53] Whittall 2001: 96–7.
[54] The German song tradition and German culture more broadly was a basis for Whittall to position Kurtág's German settings (including later ones of Hölderlin, Celan and Lichtenberg) as an understandably ambivalent, and thus critical, interrogation of a magnificent, yet oppressive, heritage. Whittall 2001: 89. Carola Nielinger-Vakil's reading took apparent allusions to Bach chorales as cornerstones of a tonal musical syntax that functioned primarily as something from which to strive for distance. Nielinger-Vakil 1998: 206–9.
[55] Csengery 1987: 27.   [56] Balassa 2004 (1989): 110.

had been meant for him alone, and that it is now to be closed. Listening to Kurtág's *Fragments*, Balassa suddenly sensed that the guard and the man waiting were one and the same person. In other words, he located the force preventing the man from passing through the door within the man himself. Failing to pass through a doorway was a function of one's own internal adversaries.

This play on the metaphor of the threshold, while never textually explicit in *Kafka Fragments* itself, is a powerful abstraction of one of the central tensions within it, namely between stasis and movement. This is evident not only in the many references to movement in the text, or the frequent allusions to a 'path'. Rather, the very constitution of *Kafka Fragments*, an hour-long cycle of forty fragments (grouped into Parts I–IV), embodies spasmodic but only very faltering advancement. Repetitive encounters with basic musical ideas do not develop: the three main types of violin material – double stops, arpeggios and stepwise melody – are endlessly tried out and cast away. On many occasions they are radically estranged from their conventional sounds, whether through percussive bowing techniques, pizzicato or harmonics. But although many are recurrent, in particular certain distinct sonorities such as open fifths, they fail to 'progress' in conventional terms.

This musically enacted struggle with movement is particularly significant in the way that it emerges in one fragment as a metaphor for the struggle to speak (Part IV, fragment 6):

Ich kann nicht eigentlich erzählen, ja fast nicht einmal reden; wenn ich erzähle, habe ich meistens ein Gefühl wie es kleine Kinder haben könnten, die die ersten Gehversuche machen.	I can't actually . . . tell a story, in fact I am almost unable even to speak; when I try to tell it I usually feel the way small children might when they try to take their first steps.[57]

We have already observed Kurtág's ambivalence towards language, an ambivalence manifesting itself in reluctance, and then a greatly hesitant willingness. But here it emerges rather differently from hitherto. Although Kafka's fragment presents impotence – and the toddling helplessness is carried through into the musical setting – the setting itself is dedicated to Pilinszky. And Pilinszky *celebrated* stuttering. He constructed it as a gift, something he himself had acquired from the aunt who nurtured

---

[57] Translation from the score, by Júlia and Peter Sherwood.

him as a child, and as a constant experience that helped him retain humility.[58]

On one level Pilinszky's embrace of powerlessness fits in with his vocation as a poet, touching again on the mystical line of his writing (and it also echoes Kurtág's discussions of his own work). But it can also be contextualised within the discourses of the new Central Europe discussed above, where part of the moral imperative in that 'kingdom of the spirit' was *never* to assume power by 'storming the Bastille' and taking the place of the ruling forces.[59] All positions of power were understood as inherently false, so refusal to take power was something to cherish in its own right.

This understanding of Truth as being inherently irreconcilable with power can be aligned with the longest fragment of all in *Kafka Fragments*, which occupies Part II all on its own. The 'true path' here is one of struggle:

Der wahre Weg geht über ein Seil, das nicht in der Höhe gespannt ist, sondern knapp über den Boden. Es scheint mehr bestimmt, stolpern zu machen, als begangen zu werden.	The true path goes by way of a rope that is suspended not high up, but rather just above the ground. Its purpose seems to be more to make one stumble than to be walked on.

Once again, the dedication – this time 'Hommage-message' to Pierre Boulez – suggests a great deal. In this long setting, the violin plays a gently and seemingly interminable pair of shifting lines that slide up and down in microtones (see Ex. 6.2). What is this, if not a celebration of the 'truthful' struggle of playing something imperfectly that a ring-modulator at IRCAM could produce to perfection without effort?[60] 'Truth', according to the text, can really only be a tripping over. If one does not stumble, but sails along successfully, one has relinquished individual thought for power.

The new Central Europe also provides an illuminating context for fragment 4 of Part II, taken from one of Kafka's letters to his (largely epistolary) lover Milena, in which a distorting glissando illustrates 'impurity' (see Ex. 6.3):

---

[58] He also used it as a means of explaining (and celebrating) his poetic brevity. See, for instance, an interview from 1969 reprinted in Török 1983: 145–6, and also a short discussion of the matter in Tüskés 1986: 17–18.

[59] Havel's 'Power of the Powerless' made this clear in 1978, and Konrád had argued for a 'counter-power that cannot take power and does not wish to', and decided that power and thought were incompatible. Havel 1985b and Konrád 1984: 231. See also Konrád 1984: 113: 'To have power, one must want power, and to think, one must want thought: you can't want both.' Garton Ash 1989: 170–1 discusses this attitude with reference to Konrád, Václav Havel and Adam Michnik.

[60] See also Whittall 2001: 94–5, for a slightly different reference to IRCAM and irony.

Example 6.2. Kurtág, 'Hommage-message to Pierre Boulez', *Kafka Fragments* op. 24, opening

Schmutzig bin ich, Milena, endlos schmutzig, darum mache ich ein solches Geschrei mit der Reinheit. Niemand singt so rein als die, welche in der tiefsten Hölle sind; was wir für den Gesang der Engel halten, ist ihr Gesang.

I am dirty, Milena, endlessly dirty, that is why I make such a fuss about cleanliness. None sing as purely as those in deepest Hell; it is their singing that we take for the singing of angels.

Example 6.3. Kurtág, 'I am dirty Milena', *Kafka Fragments* op. 24, close

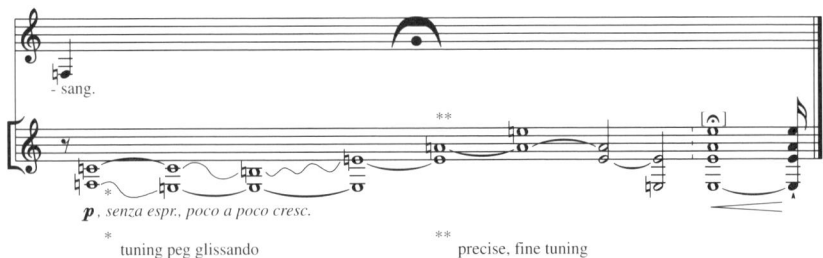

The self-scrutiny and distrust in the text is absolutely congruent with the writings of novelist and essayist Péter Nádas, which evince a profound sense of the corruptness and even infectiousness of society. For Nádas, only an obsessive examination of individual ethics could access a detachment from prevailing polity. As he explained in 1989, he practised constant vigilance, checking that he had not internalised any of the inhumane qualities of the society in which he lived. If he internalised them, they would modify his individual behaviour, and he would thus contribute to the regime.[61] Václav Havel had argued already in 1978 that the real problem with state socialism was the way that people lived a tissue of ideological 'lies' even while not believing them: in order to function as individuals they had to go through the motions of believing in what they were doing and saying, but consequently they 'confirm the system, fulfil the system, make the system, *are* the system'.[62] For Nádas, the only way forward was to violently reclaim the individual subject and to rebuild it from inside, even at the expense of more general social responsibilities or community action.

Many of the texts and musical symbols in *Kafka Fragments*, then, are voices that contribute – if in the explicitly aesthetic sphere of the 'kingdom of the spirit' – to those of these dissident individuals from 'Central Europe'. Thus while Whittall mused about Kurtág's apparent naïveté, Havel could have

[61] Nádas and Swartz 1992: 121–3 and 155–7.
[62] 'The Power of the Powerless', trans. Paul Wilson, in Havel 1985: 36–123, at 45. Italics original.

explained that 'truth' is inherently embedded within lies: 'Living the truth is . . . woven directly into the texture of living a lie. It is the repressed alternative, the authentic aim to which living a lie is an inauthentic response.'[63] If, in the West, it became necessary to question the idea of purity in – say – 'perfect' fifths, then here in the East it was imperative to hypothesise that it could still exist. And yet, of course, it was equally imperative to fail to reach it.

Hungarian ideals

As discussed in Chapter 2, Attila József had been appropriated by the communists in Hungary after 1945 and then used by Szervánszky in his first public statement of resistance in 1954. Kurtág's *Attila József Fragments* op. 20 (1981), focusing on some of the poet's more confessional, doubting fragments, revisits the more private world of József drawn on by Szervánszky. But it offers no sign of combative resistance. Rather, its tone is congruent with the private world of the individual discussed above, positing a personal 'Truth' distinct from the public political sphere. The very nature of the score itself amplifies this ethos: József's writings are reproduced in the poet's handwriting – along with his own corrections – and Kurtág's settings, in his.

A further 'truth' emerges in the basic polarity of the musical sonorities in which – analogously to *The Sayings of Bornemisza* discussed in Chapter 3 – consonance is associated with Godliness and chromaticism with sin. The penultimate fragment makes both musical and textual reference to *The Sayings* through quoting the melodic motive associated with 'sin' (compare Ex. 3.4 with Ex. 6.4). In the subsequent, closing fragment, the final line echoes *The Sayings*' celebration of faith in God's forgiveness of sin (compare Ex. 3.7 with Ex. 6.5) in its resonant chain of thirds. But whereas in the earlier work the textual sentiment was the all-embracing forgiveness of God, in *Attila József Fragments* it relates to a bowing down and becoming innocent. The musical link between them suggests that they may be synonymous, in other words that redemption may be attained by bowing down beneath knowledge, and allowing song to 'lean out' of one's lips.

19

Kásásodik a víz, kialakul a jég, és bűneim halállá állnak össze.	The water thickens, swelling into ice, and my sins gather into death.[64]

---

[63] Havel 1985: 57. (From 'The Power of the Powerless'.)
[64] Translations are taken from those by Peter Sherwood in the published score.

Example 6.4. Kurtág, 'The water thickens', *Attila József Fragments* op. 20

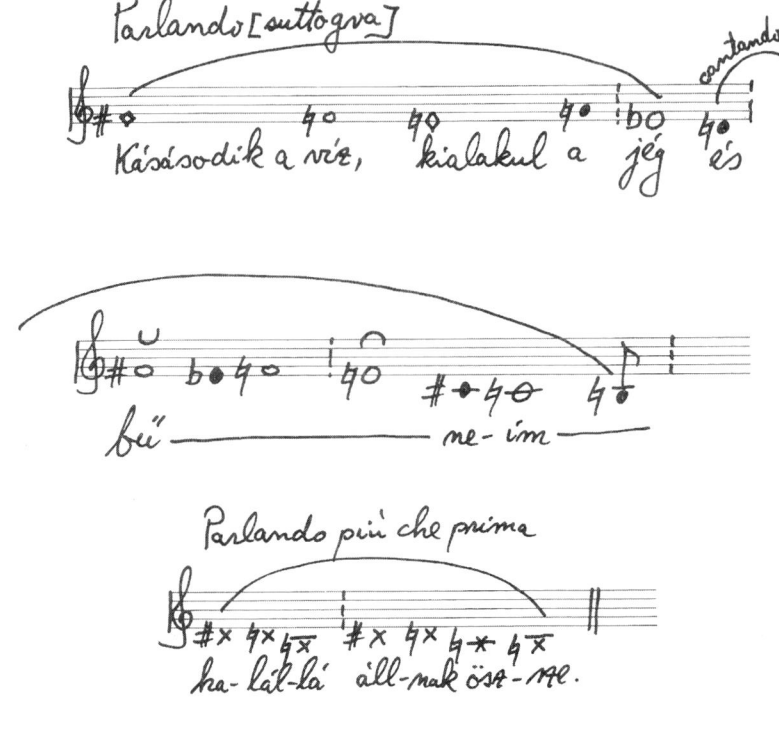

20

Ének, hajolj ki ajkamon,	Song, lean out of my lips
s te bánat, ne érj el, csak holnap.	and sorrow, don't reach me until tomorrow.
Mélyebbre kell még hajlanom,	I must bow down still further
hogy semmit nem tudón daloljak	to be able to sing without knowing anything.

Indeed the fragment preceding these two provides an explicit commentary on apparently innocent, spontaneous artistic creation:

18

Irgalom, édesanyám, mama, nézd, jaj kész ez a vers is!	Mercy, mother, mama, look, oh! this poem too is done![65]

[65] I have adjusted the translation from the score here, as the ensuing text will explain.

Example 6.5. Kurtág, 'Song, Lean Out of My Lips', *Attila József Fragments* op. 20

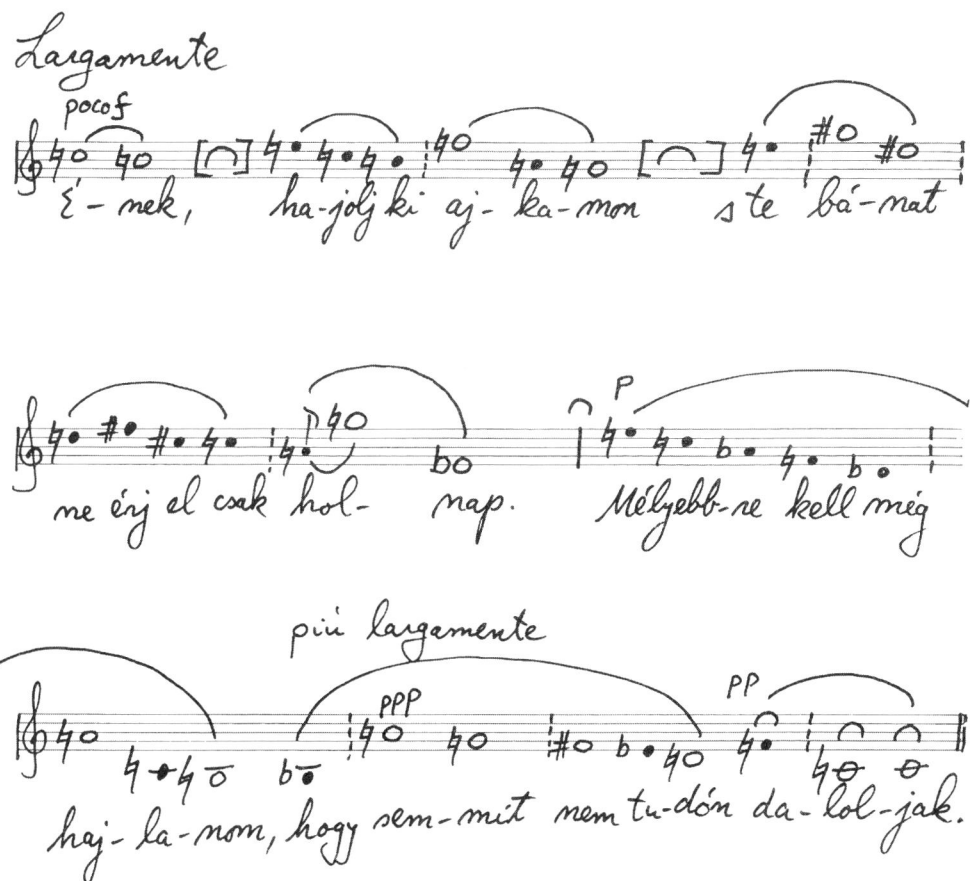

Once part of *Attila József Fragments*, however, this fragment is no longer a straightforward moment of rejoicing. In the English and German translations in the score, the exclamation 'jaj!' has been provided with a specifically painful tone ('oh woe!' and 'weh!').[66] Whereas the textual fragment includes a slick hexameter that symbolises a poetic achievement

[66] The translations were overseen by Kurtág. A psychoanalytic reading would recognise the event evoked as a child's arrival in the world of language, a traumatic happening indeed, for the entry into the conceptual sphere is at once the separation from the mother, it is the so-called 'Oedipal moment'. Also addressed directly to 'Mama', one of József's late poems portrays anger about the separation brought about by a mother's death: the poet begs her to speak to him again, but she remains silent. József committed suicide one year after writing this poem, but not before writing a verse in which he conceived his own death as a reunion with his mother. His Oedipal moment was unresolved: 'Mama' was ultimately his only object of desire. See János Bokay's 'Oedipal Poems of Sylvia Plath and Attila József' for an interesting analysis of József's 'Belated Lament' in comparison with Sylvia Plath's 'Daddy', which Plath wrote in the year preceding her suicide. Szekacs-Weisz & Ward (eds.) 2005: 153–67.

Example 6.6. Kurtág, 'Mercy, Mother', *Attila József Fragments* op. 20

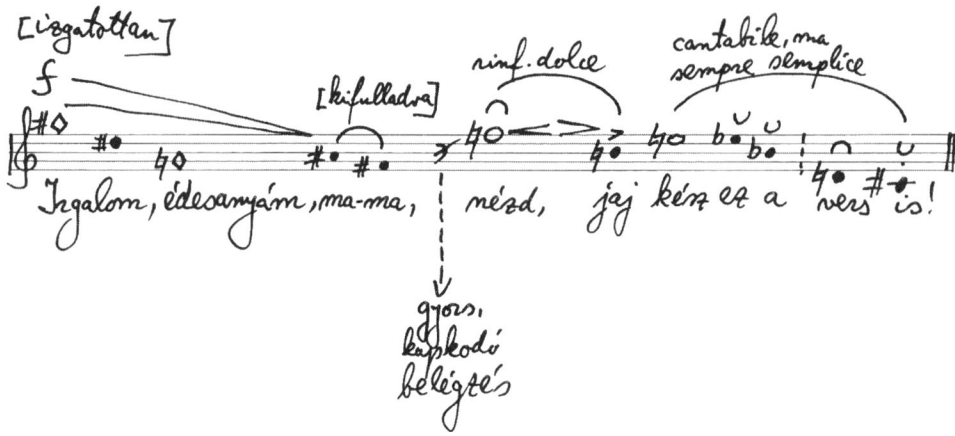

('kész ez a vers is'), the musical setting destroys its impact. The outcry to mother is so dramatic that it swallows up the rest of the song (see Ex. 6.6).

The three final fragments, then, provide a musical representation of the equivocality recognisable from Kurtág's own self-construction in interview. They sit between the celebration of linguistic stumbling, stuttering and naïveté on the one hand, and the (problematic) graduation to creative skill on the other. Rather akin to the conflict discussed above – the need to posit a Truth without ever reaching it – even the spontaneous creation of a poem is undercut instantly with self-chastisement and doubt. Indeed when discussing his compositional struggles Kurtág referred to this song in particular, commenting in a way that reinforced his helplessness (and thus innocence) rather than his skill in its composition:

> At . . . times, something is born within two minutes that never needs to be altered: 'Mercy, mother . . .', for instance. I wrote that down in pencil, and not a note has changed since then.[67]

If these last three songs project a highly personal realm of 'truth', other related 'truths' are suggested elsewhere, and the combination would be a powerful cocktail to shape the work's reception. Transparent references to both folk song and chant emerge in the context of explicitly pastoral texts, romantically conjoining folk song, religion, and nature. As Ex. 6.7 shows, fragment no. 8 is suggestive of a florid folk song and hints at pentatony, while the text evokes nature's luxuriant beauty:

---

[67] Kurtág and Varga 2003: 134.

Example 6.7. Kurtág, 'The Sweet Breeze Purls Along', *Attila József Fragments* op. 20

A nyárfák közt ezüst habokkal	The sweet breeze purls along
az édes szellő folydogál,	among the poplars, silver-foamed,
s csak fürdik benne aranyos tagokkal	and the gigantic summer
az óriási nyár.	just bathes in it, golden-limbed.

Fragment no. 15 is yet more obviously like a folk song in style, while biblical in textual reference: as Ex. 6.8 shows, the first line uses only the first four pitches of a D♭ major scale; the second line builds this one tone higher up to A♭, with added 'colouring' of D, F♭ and G not disturbing the firm sense of D♭. The final line resolves onto F♯ (the enharmonically notated tonic – G♭ – of a D♭ major sub-dominant).

Lesz lágy hús s mellé ifjú kalarábé,	There'll be tender meat with young kohlrabi,
ökör hízik és nő a csalamádé,	the ox grows fat and the green maize swell,
de az már a mi porunkból fakad.	but all this grows from our dust now.

Example 6.8. Kurtág, 'There'll Be Tender Meat', *Attila József Fragments* op. 20

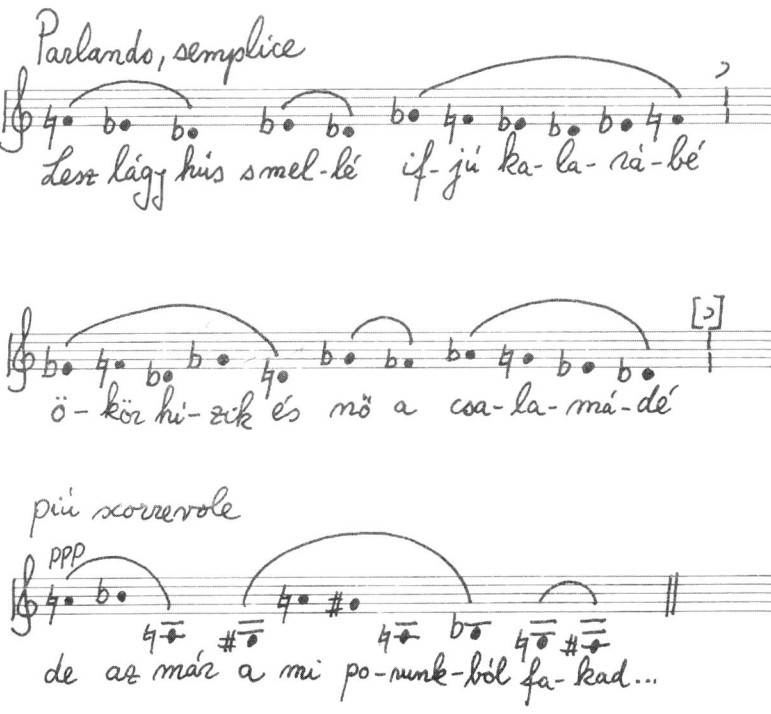

Not only do these songs respond to Schola Hungarica's chant workshops of the previous decade, but they also echo thirty-five years of Hungarian research into the connections between folk song and art music – research that retained widespread currency throughout that 1980s and even beyond.[68] The *Fragments* could tap into listeners' nostalgic idealism, their sense that folk song (including Hungarian folk song) was a foundational part of European art music, even a purer dimension of the same. Adrienne Csengery, moreover, seemed to reviewer György Kroó not to perform or interpret the *Fragments*, but to conjure them up as if she were herself their creator, as much as was Kurtág.[69] She embodied, surely, the idealised spontaneity of folk music.

When Kroó formulated his review, however, he was somewhat caught between Kurtág's presentation of an appealingly romanticised nature, and a need to understand *Fragments* as a contribution to progressive music. His

---

[68] Szabolcsi's work on tracing folk music in art music (noted above in Chapter 2) was, according to Dobszay, the first scholarly attempt to do this. László Dobszay provides an overview of such quests in Hungarian musicology, and a defence of their ongoing appropriateness in his 'Volksmusik und Musikgeschichte in Ungarn' in Fricke, Frobenius, Konrad and Schmitt (eds.) 1999: 9–27.
[69] Kroó 1982b.

solution was to praise the technical skill with which Kurtág could sustain twenty unaccompanied song fragments without any supporting textures, and then to argue that this quality made *Fragments* a part of the 'avant-garde'. To account for Kurtág's recourse to music from seven hundred years earlier, he simply fell back on mystification: Kurtág's move, he said, could only be the result of 'inner necessity'. But most significantly of all, Kroó actually gave a name to the hitherto unclassified phenomenon more precisely: it was 'melodic genius'.[70]

Voices from elsewhere

Kurtág's instrumental music provides us with neither extended texts nor extensive critical commentary from which to draw out interpretations such as those I have suggested above. Recognisable musical types nonetheless construct analogous constellations of association. The aesthetic of 'elsewhere', moreover, is patently in evidence in the form of death in *Grabstein für Stephan* op. 15c (1989) for solo guitar and ensemble, and *Officium breve in memoriam Andreæ Szervánszky* op. 28 (1988–9) for string quartet. These are explicit statements of remembrance. A third work, . . . *quasi una fantasia* . . . op. 27 no. 1 (1987–8), keeps this dimension somewhat hidden, but it is nonetheless concerned with the same matter: a citation from Hölderlin's famous poem of mourning, 'Remembrance' (Andenken), appears at the beginning of the final movement in the score.

The absence of further text is no obstacle to tracing other concerns of the decade in these works, for both musical symbolism, and the way the instruments are physically arranged, offer an equally, if not more, direct suggestion of them. In *Grabstein für Stephan* and . . . *quasi una fantasia* . . . the soloist in each work (guitar and piano respectively) begins with the simplest elements of music suggested by their instruments, and they are positioned centre stage, separately from the others. This not only makes plain our distance from the soloists and their simple ideas, but also makes their subsequent destruction alarmingly tangible. Concert listeners to *Grabstein* watch the solo guitarist playing minimally inflected open strings on the main stage while (possibly) cognisant of instrumentalists to the side of the hall, and (frequently) unaware of a further group at the rear. The guitarist's gently repetitive chords coax and lull the observer into a settled realm of harmony to the front. But presently, unpredictably explosive bursts of sound from behind – harshly dissonant and wildly gestural in nature – shatter the trusting bond that has evolved. The guitar continues, but faith in its

---

[70] The next reference to Kurtág as 'genius' was made by Tallián. See Tallián and Ujházy 1987: 47.

calm simplicity has been ruptured. The struggle of a by-now very familiar polarity of consonance and dissonance (purity and corruption?) envelops the audience, as if imprisoning it in a metaphorical engagement with life's vicissitudes.

It is not only the spatialisation of the instruments that encourages us to absorb the work on this kinetic and metaphorical level. Without the wager that one might gain from engaging with them in as full a sense as possible, the simple musical elements on offer would surely be dismissed as worthless. They are *objets trouvés* such as those already encountered in the 1970s and discussed in Chapter 4, or the symbols of purity and innocence encountered above. The open strings of the guitar provide one example and *. . . quasi una fantasia . . .* begins with another, a slowly descending C major scale. The first movement of this work offers little else. There are other descending scales and there is one ascending scale, while soft percussion beats and tremolos add timbres and punctuation to the shifting harmonic implications of the scales. Four harmonicas close the movement with briefly sliding triads: this harmonic closure hovers undecidedly among C major and D♭ major triads. The suspense, generated by the fact that barely anything happens, 'stages' the central movements 2 and 3, one of which is extremely quiet, yet tumultuously active (*Presto minaccioso e lamentoso*), and the next, violently abrasive and commanding, (*Recitativo*). The apparently suppressed lament and fear of movement 2 (subtitled with reference to Schumann's nightmare, 'Wie ein Traumeswirren') seems to be made shatteringly real in the marching, beating, menace of the *Recitativo*. Yet the final movement is apparently 'transcendent', at once recalling the simplicity and purity of movement 1's C major scales while also elaborating basic steps with sighs and chimes.

The 'transcendence', moreover, is of a particularly localised kind: this final movement is in itself an *objet trouvé* from Kurtág's own *oeuvre*, revisiting one of the chorale movements (no. 5) from *Hommage à András Mihály: 12 Microludes for String Quartet* op. 13, discussed in Chapter 4. And even the harmonicas of the first movement have a startling resonance: surely they are a reference to those of the lament-filled second movement of Ligeti's Piano Concerto (1980–8) (see Exx. 6.9 and 6.10). Ligeti himself recognised the main grounding of *. . . quasi una fantasia . . .*: he referred to it as Kurtág's 'self-portrait with music companions of Budapest'. The large-scale form and the apparently casual, yet precisely honed piano style, he suggested, captured the characters of Eötvös and Kocsis respectively; and the surrounding percussion ensemble, he proposed, might be the Amadinda ensemble.[71] He made no

---

[71] Ligeti 1996: 9.

Example 6.9. Kurtág, . . . *quasi una fantasia* . . . op. 27 no. 1, movement 1, close

mention of himself, though, as a companion. Did he position himself as alongside past masters Beethoven and Schumann, both of whom he sensed 'in the background'?

If such references suggest a complex drawing of Kurtág's past compositional companions and voices into his present one, then the last work he completed in 1989, the string quartet *Officium breve*, must offer the most suggestive of all. As Peter Hoffmann has demonstrated, Kurtág originally wrote eight out of its fifteen movements for other media, for they

Example 6.10. Ligeti, Piano Concerto, movement 2, close

are elaborations on pieces from *Games,* and from *Herdecker Eurythmie* op. 14 (1979).[72] The speech-rhythm of Kurtág's motto 'Virág az ember' (Flowers we are), which already emerged in chapter 3 when it was considered as part of *The Sayings of Péter Bornemisza*, shapes four of the short movements.

But *Officium breve* also incorporates the music of others. Movements 5, 7 and 10 refer explicitly to the canon in Webern's Second Cantata op. 31, which Webern himself referred to as a 'missa brevis'. Movement 5 is a 'Fantasy' on its harmonies, movements 7 and 10 are canonic extensions to Webern's own canons. Other movements in the quartet are closely connected: movement 4 uses the Webern row, for instance, and movement 6 is Webernesque in its canon of expressionistic sighs. Such dissonant movements resound as the polar opposites of other explicitly consonant ones: each of the opening two, for instance, contains a delicately soured perfect cadence in C major; movement 11 is resolutely in C major and, most startlingly, it is an extensive extract from Szervánszky's *Serenade*. In retrospect, the references

[72] Hoffmann 1992.

to C major, and the consonant 'sighs' that were in such contrast to those of the Webernesque movements, are revealed as having a very specific source.

According to the preface to the score, Kurtág included Webern within his memorial tribute to Szervánszky in order to acknowledge Szervánszky's 'conversion' to Webern in the latter part of his life. Did he, then, include the extract from the Hildegard Jone text that Webern himself set as a reference to some sort of redemptive power that Webern was to have for Szervánszky's work? The text describes the coming of the Messiah. If we make this connection, there is more than a touch of irony in the fact that the quartet closes with such a poignant breaking off of Szervánszky's *Serenade*, a work composed prior to his interest in Webern. It is incomplete, left explicitly unresolved.

Yet it is perhaps the temporal perspective that the juxtaposition of Szervánszky and Webern offers that is most intriguing (and symbolic). The consequent polarity (and even the harmonic tension between consonance and dissonance) in *Officium breve* conjures up the formalised East–West divide in Europe's music that prevailed in the late 1940s. In Budapest, Szervánszky and his *Serenade* represented an ideal for young composers such as Kurtág and Ligeti; in Darmstadt, Webern occupied a comparable position for others. This last work that Kurtág completed before the 'Iron Curtain' was lifted, then, resonated with the moment at which it had descended. And the (deceased) 'voices' of Webern and Szervánszky were made to sound again.

Epilogue: On 'Hungary', and (our) longing for Moscow

At the beginning of this book the intention was to construct three facets of Hungarian music, thereby nuance the Cold War polarity within which they could also be constructed and, additionally, investigate some ways of thinking how music's presence could productively complicate that project. The aim was never to construct a whole. And yet there is one lacuna that may seem distinctly odd, namely discussion about opera, the musical genre most frequently and obviously linked with nation. In a book dedicated to a nationally defined set of ideas, this may seem a peculiar neglect, thus I use this Epilogue to reflect a little on Hungary and opera.

The first observation to make is that one can trace a set of disjunctions in the relation between the country and the genre. During the Cold War period, Ligeti's *Le Grand Macabre* (1974–77, rev. 1996–7), composed in Germany, is the only opera by a composer of Hungarian origin to have become established in the international repertory; in Hungary, meanwhile, it was unperformed until 1998. The only opera to become popular in Hungary was Sándor Szokolay's *Blood Wedding* (1964), which, blatantly ignoring the official line on national opera according to which it should be modelled on 'revolutionary' historic opera by Ferenc Erkel, took Lorca as its source. Tallián would later remark that '[n]o historical analysis of the dramatic potency or impotence of musical nationalism and folksiness in Hungary speaks as loudly as the fact that this first Hungarian peasant tragedy had to be a Spanish one'.[1] If there was a desire for an opera that could be claimed as a product of the nation, the imperative that it should not address the nation as such was equally strong.

Responses to Petrovics' *C'est la guerre* bring this even more sharply into focus, because – as discussed in Chapter 3 – the opera engaged with a particularly shameful period in Hungarian history. It could be celebrated as a national event only in combination with a historical evasiveness. The evasiveness extended beyond Hungarian fascism in the Second World War and right into music: Pernye described it as the '*birthday* of modern Hungarian opera', with no mention whatsoever of *Duke Bluebeard's Castle*, composed precisely half a century earlier.[2] Pernye's view effectively erased Bartók's work (and also ignored the stage works of Kodály, Dohnányi and all other

[1] Tallián 1999b: 154. [2] Pernye 1961d: 22. My italics.

Hungarian composers to have written subsequently for the stage). At this moment, then, the birth of Hungarian opera was something hoped for, but its potential emergence on the basis of the past was unthinkable.[3]

One might contextualise Pernye's claim within the prevailing political rhetoric that condemned the (inter-war and wartime) Hungarian past in order to affirm the strength of the present. His anti-historical position is congruent with the post-'counter-revolutionary' era, in which the political line was that the new regime was utterly different from the Stalinist years. Operas of the ensuing twenty-five years also took subjects disengaged from the recent past, but they nonetheless, and rather suggestively, addressed the mythically destructive forces of humanity. Many of them projected personal self-annihilation. Durkó's *Moses* (1977) is an obvious example, and it also emblematises the redemptive utopia that is a crucial part of the sacrificial impulse; but Szokolay's *Ecce homo* (1984), drawing on Kazantsakis' *Christ Recrucified*, went even further. Faced with impossibly corrupt societies or complete chaos, central characters in these operas became self-denying to the point of suicide: self-immolation was apparently the only route to their utopias.

If we follow Tallián and understand these operas as ciphers for composers' frustrations at the ongoing occupation, they form a distorted mirror image of nationalist operas of the inter-war years. In Kodály's *Háry János* of 1926 the hero returns home after his wanderings to a Hungarian village that was actually, by then, part of Czechoslovakia. *The Spinning Room* of 1924–32 is set in the lost territory of mythically pure Hungarian origin, the Székely region of Transylvania – then part of Romania.[4] While the earlier period projected happy illusions, the later projected unhappy disillusion, but in both periods opera was a site of longing.

It is not my intention to close the book by re-entering Hungary from this perspective explicitly, but the theme will be useful to bear in mind in what

---

[3] That is not because a national opera history could not have been created. It could begin with nineteenth-century romantic historical dramas (Erkel), following these with Bartók's modernist *Duke Bluebeard's Castle* that reacted against them. The inter-war period would encompass Dohnányi's romantic *A vajda tornya* (The Vaivode's Tower), his comic *Der Tenor*, and Kodály's folksy sung pantomime *Háry János* and Singspiel *Székely fonó* (The Spinning Room). The 1950s could be grasped through polarised reponses to the new political situation: Kadosa's *Huszti Kaland* (Adventure at Huszt) with a libretto by Szabolcsi redefined historic national disasters as revolutionary triumphs, while György Ránki's *Pomádé király* (King Pomádé) drawing on Hans Andersen made a parody of the communist labour ethic (factory workers wove invisible clothes for the King). See Boros 1979 for an overview of operas between 1948 and 1978, including synopses and press reviews.

[4] The complexities of these mythical matters as they pertain to Hungary are discussed in Schöpflin 2000: 378–409 and 410–14. See also Overing's 'The Role of Myth: An Anthropological Perspective, or: "The Reality of the Really Made-Up"' in Hosking and Schöpflin (eds.) 1997: 1–18. See also Slavoj Žižek's 'Love Your Neighbor as Yourself! No Thanks!' in Žižek 1997: 45–85 and Žižek 2000: 3–11.

follows. In this Epilogue I step back and take a view in retreat, reflecting briefly on two operas that frame the 1920–89 period symmetrically. The first, *Duke Bluebeard's Castle* (1911), was partially stimulated by a striving for something purely Hungarian, yet could not be accommodated into the national longing that characterised the inter-war period in Hungary. Even in 1961, as we have seen, it was not used as a foundation stone of the nation's musical or operatic history. The second, Péter Eötvös's *Three Sisters* (1998), was written outside the country and after the Cold War was over, but seems to do precisely what could not be done in Hungary, namely draw on *Bluebeard*. It offers a new vantage point, opening up a new angle on the book's views on Hungary so far.

Bluebeard and *Three Sisters*

Although similarities between the two operas begin rather vaguely with their difference from anything written in Hungary in the meantime, on a simple structural level, *Three Sisters* seems quite clearly underpinned by *Bluebeard*. The fact that each opera has a 'prologue' is immediately striking, even if that of *Bluebeard* is spoken and that of *Three Sisters* sung. The way the prologues frame the operas with a set of dichotomies is a yet more profound commonality. *Bluebeard*'s prologue reflects on the 'inner' and 'outer' nature of the opera, presenting a riddle about the work's projection of body and soul. It also addresses the audience directly, inviting spectators to identify themselves with the characters on stage:

> Once upon an ancient time . . .
> A story introduced in rhyme:
> The tale is old, the moral new,
> Even the players could be you
> Yourselves, Ladies and Gentlemen
>
> You're watching me, I'm watching you,
> But which is which and who is who?
> Consider, safely in your beds
> Is the theatre here, or in your heads
> Ladies and Gentlemen?[5]

Three Sisters' dichotomy is primarily temporal, setting up a tension between 'now' and a time that is 'coming'; yet here too, the direct address to the audience is clear, and the audience members may well identify themselves

---

[5] John (ed.) 1991: 46. Trans. John Lloyd Davies.

with the people of the time that is 'coming', whom the sisters refer to as 'those who live after us':

> That music is so cheerful.
> I think we shall soon discover why we live, which we suffer.
> There will come the time when we shall know the reason for our suffering.
> But our suffering will turn to joy for those who live after us,
> and they will remember with kind words those who are living now.[6]

Moreover, each of the prologues invokes music. The minstrel of *Bluebeard* presents music as the instigator of the forthcoming narration, as an inseparable part of what follows, even as a sort of fabric entangling the characters and observers with one another. The invocation in *Three Sisters* is rather different, and this difference is germane to the entire opera: the three sisters associate music with a happiness entirely at odds with themselves, and also with loss. They cry out: 'Oh, how they're playing that music! They're leaving us, one's already gone, completely, completely and for ever.'

The two operas are also linked by their critical targeting of essentially nineteenth-century institutions, namely operatic singing styles, themes and roles. Where Bartók drew on folk music to create a vocal style distinct from that of German and Italian opera, Eötvös drew directly on particular acoustic properties of the Russian language and subverted traditional female roles by using an all-male cast. Bartók obstructed traditional dramatic progression by writing a ballade-inspired dialogue between two protagonists without a conventional plot or action. Eötvös selected a Chekhov text in which there are no heroic figures: the only sustained drama emerges through the frustrations of the everyday. Famously, the sisters feel bereft, bored and without purpose in their provincial setting; the tedium of their existence is underpinned by their endless pining for Moscow. Either Bartók or Eötvös could have heightened dramatic potential, but neither did. Bartók conceived a structure which turns on itself in an apparently immutable fashion: seven different facets of the same thing (Bluebeard's castle, or on another level, Bluebeard's inner character) emerge one after the other as a result of Judit's probing. In her quest to come to know him intimately she passes through a journey from darkness to light but, accompanied by ever proliferating appearances of blood, back into darkness. Eötvös rearranged Chekhov's four-act play into three 'Sequences', each presenting the same events but from the perspective of a different character. We gain a new version each time, but temporal progression is entirely confounded by ellipses, because

---

[6] Translated from the Russian by Anthony Philips. Libretto reproduced in CD booklet for DG 459 694–2 (1999). See page 71 for these opening lines.

no one Sequence contains the entire picture. Consequently the retelling resembles myth: just as the differences in the mythical relating of events bring us close to what really might have happened whilst keeping it far, far away, here we are painfully aware of the subjective quality of the events portrayed. Are they presentations of reality or projections of longing? (Or: what was Bluebeard really like?)

Longing and myth

The implicit longing of Judit, and the explicit longing of the three sisters, emerges in each of these operas in a mythologised abstraction. Yet that does not entirely mask their links with Hungarian historical mythology, something most obvious in the case of *Three Sisters*. What, if not a sort of territorial myth of origins lost, is the sisters' endless desire to return to Moscow? Their lives rotate around the loss of their father, who before being taken from them in death, had led them with him to the capital: if only they were in Moscow, they say, they would be reunited with the society in which they feel alive. If only their brother Andrey had taken a different career path, they cry, then he would go to Moscow and they could go with him. Their laments bespeak their sense of powerlessness, but in attempting to come to terms with their unhappiness, they draw on another myth, that of redemption. In Chekhov's epilogue, Eötvös's prologue, they explain their sadness in terms of the greater good: 'our suffering will turn to joy for those who live after us, and they will remember with kind words those who are living now.' Their lives are sacrifices for the good of others.

If such longings might be understood as metonymic of those discussed above in relation to Hungarian history and opera, they are nonetheless open to different readings entirely. A brief description of three productions may make this point quite clear. When *Three Sisters* was performed in Budapest in 2000, director István Szabó 'returned' the opera to Chekhov (albeit – irony of ironies! – in Hungarian translation), casting the sisters in female roles and clothing them in historical costume.[7] The move suggests a different sort of longing entirely, namely one for grand opera, for that mirror of bourgeois individualism and self-identification that the operatic medium used to represent. The same longing is explicit in a review applauding the decision to use female singers, according to which 'everyone should stay as they are – women as women'.[8] But precisely this realism rendered the production a disaster for another reviewer, according to whom Szabó 'squeezed

---

[7] Scenery: Attila Csikós; costumes: Györgyi Szakács.   [8] Tallián 2000: 27.

a weird piece into the conventional opera mould and the singers stood there following the practice of the Hungarian opera house'.[9]

A different facet of the opera's focus on longing was drawn out by a production by Inga Levant, which framed the desire of the sisters with that of Chekhov's more politically utopian characters.[10] Chekhov's Count Tuzenbach is a member of a revolutionary group: critical of society, he longingly foretells a time twenty-five years hence when everybody will work, after the 'great storm [that is] brewing' has cleansed the rotten world in which they currently live. *Three Sisters* was first staged in 1901, four years before the liberal revolution and sixteen years before the revolution that took communists into power in Russia. Eötvös responded to Tuzenbach's revolutionary dreams with his own irony, interweaving the Soviet National Anthem, as well as an imitation of the Moscow radio signal with which he grew up in Hungary, into the music of Andrey. Neither of these passing intertextual moments is obvious and neither has any major impact on the musical whole, but Levant, drawing on her personal anger and loathing for the workings of the Soviet Union, made it the theme of her production. By setting the opera in communist Russia, with an entirely red stage littered with debris, she superimposed the time of Chekhov with the time that was 'coming'. Her production made a specific critique of the hopes of the revolutionaries by situating them and the mournful sisters in the midst of the disaster that followed the political dreams.

It is, however, the original production by Ushio Amagatsu that is most intriguing from the perspective of longing. Its stage set comprised a stylised vision of Japan, with a large tatami mat, revolving panels, and rocks hinting at a Zen garden. Its colouring was of natural cane. The sisters, emerging from between the shifting panels, were decked in costumes and make-up reminiscent of Japanese Noh Theatre. Their faces painted white, they were thus masked by a uniform melancholy that barely shifted; their fixity was further emphasised by the full-length white robes in which they were each encased. Their countertenor voices added to their mystery.[11]

Ushio Amagatsu's stripping down Chekhov's characters of their gendered individuality led one of the original singers to claim that he and his colleagues represented not the living bodies, but the 'soul' of the three sisters.[12] Eötvös, too, emphasised his striving for universal expression. Rather

---

[9] Fáy 2000.
[10] Scenery: Johannes Schütz; costumes: Brigitte Reiffenstuel; lighting: Markus Miesch; video projection: Klaus vom Bruch. Düsseldorf, 1999.
[11] Scenery: Natsuyuki Nakanishi; costumes: Sayoko Yamaguchi; lighting: Ushio Amagatsu, Genta Iwamura. Opera National de Lyon, 1998.
[12] Alain Aubin, quoted in Moulinier 1999: 15.

than focusing on the specific events in the lives of the sisters, his interest was in the various constellations of the number 3; and 3, after all, is strongly associated with myth. As well as the obvious 'trio' of sisters, the three Sequences Eötvös created from the play and the proliferation of triangular relationships were his main concerns.[13] Put in another way, he identified with the plight of Chekhov's characters and aimed to present analogous dilemmas in human existence generally. He conceived them with gentle humour, looking at various types of longing and toying with its inescapability. There is that of Baron Tuzenbach's socialists for a new society, that of the sisters for Moscow and true love, that of Andrey for a new start, and that of the sisters' admirers, for the sisters themselves. In short, Eötvös attempted to present longing as a part of the human condition.

And yet this quasi-universal longing has a specific resonance for Hungary, as one further example reveals. While the opera is dominated by the human voice, the entries of Andrey's wife Natasha each coincide with some of its most extended instrumental episodes. Whereas much of the opera's music is lyrical, flowing and harmonious, these moments are mechanical and jerky; additionally, when Natasha sings, her line is grotesquely extreme in registral leap and dynamic shift. Her costume, coloured bright red in stark contrast to the set, built further on these musical characteristics. Even more strikingly, Natasha was cast as a black baritone. Her resonance as a disruptive outsider was thus manifold. Her appearances are red 'blots' on an otherwise white scene: just like the droplets of blood in *Bluebeard*, she is a stain, representing darkness and disruption beneath the luminosity of the surface, or a besmirching of the perfect yearned-for cleanliness. Analogously to the emergence of the dissonant blood motive in *Bluebeard*, her percussive presence makes itself increasingly felt, so that she seems to worm her way into the very fabric of the sisters' music and their crumbling emotional household. Additionally, however, her position as 'outsider' is so obvious as to be bizarre: her skin colour suggests a socio-political message writ large. Natasha is that anamorphotic blot on the landscape of the organic *Gemeinschaft* through which (and only through which) does the absent, and longed-for organic society come into view. The sense is that if only this black monster decked in red were not there, then everything would surely be better.[14]

---

[13] Beckles Willson 2002: 11.

[14] This sort of psychological dilemma is discussed in several places by Žižek, who draws on Lacan to identify the rogue fantasy element as *anamorphosis*. See, for instance, Žižek 1989: 87–100, and Žižek 1993: 219–26.

Coming home

By identifying echoes with *Bluebeard* and Hungarian mythology, I have constructed *Three Sisters* as a tangential, critical part of a narrative about Hungarian opera. Eötvös, it seems, has led us home with him, in a parallel with his own life that is also beginning to display a symmetry that none of his forerunners have managed. Bartók and Dohnányi, we recall, each left Hungary for political reasons and never returned, while Kodály never left. Ligeti left for political and professional reasons, never to return as a resident; Kurtág also left for professional reasons in 1993, and has never been a resident there again. Eötvös, however, left to study abroad, remained in touch with the country, and in 2004, moved back.

Our own odyssey, however, is not so neat. Let us recall the voice of the minstrel who opens *Duke Bluebeard's Castle*: 'which is which and who is who? . . . Is the theatre here, or in your heads, Ladies and Gentlemen?' If this is really another vision of Hungary that we have gained, then it is surely peculiar that it comes so evocatively into view when it elevates longing to myth, when it is sung in Russian, and when it draws on an image of the Orient. And what of our odyssey in time? Every day that passes enlarges the temporal distance between the reader and this period of history. It is not clear, then, in what respect these operas, poised on either side of it, could really have offered us a means to frame the period, grasp its essential historical features.

Through the three productions of *Three Sisters*, however, we do gain an appreciation of the national and temporal quicksand in which music history makes a place. Szabó reached directly for the Russian past at the expense of the temporal provocation of the libretto, while Levant overlaid the Russian past with one of its futures, a time that is itself now past. Each attempted to make these times and places present by staging an arrangement of objects (sets, costumes, props). Meanwhile, however, the music was also made present, and this had no connection with 'past' or 'elsewhere'. It was abstracted and cyclic. Precisely these abstract and cyclic qualities emerged in Amagatsu's production. But that simultaneously erased both historical time, and Russia.

As I argued in my Introduction, as historians we strive to construct a hermeneutics of the past, we argue our interpretations through documentary evidence. And yet as historians of music we are also under the spell of precisely the *musical* making present that these operatic productions make obvious. We cannot have 'come home', then, because there is no 'home' to come to. We have nonetheless listened, questioned, and listened again. And that is probably the best that we can do.

Personalia

Note:
The Liszt Academy was founded in 1875 but not named as such until 1925; I nonetheless refer consistently to it as the Liszt Academy below. The National Conservatory was known as such only from 1867 to 1949 (after which it became the Bartók Conservatory, a specialist music secondary school), although it opened in 1840 as a singing school.

Lajos Bárdos

1899–1986. Composer, choral conductor and music theorist.
Composition student of Kodály and Albert Siklós. 1928–68, Professor at Liszt Academy (church music, analysis, prosody, folk music); founder of several choirs and prominent choir conductor in Budapest, especially 1922–47; co-founder of publishing house Magyar Kórus (1931–50).

János Breuer

b. 1932. Music historian and critic.
Musicology student of Bence Szabolcsi. From 1958 academic employee of the Hungarian Musicians' Union; 1961–8, assistant editor of *Magyar Zene*, 1970–96 managing editor; from 1960 permanent critic of *Népszabadság*, the official daily newspaper. 1983–9, member and later secretary of directors' board of International Music Council's European Regional Group; 1990–7, member of the Hungarian Music Council.

László Dobszay

b. 1935. Musicologist and choral conductor.
Composition student of János Viski, also studied folk music with Kodály and music history with Bence Szabolcsi; also studied Hungarian literature at the Lóránd Eötvös University in Budapest. 1966–73, research fellow of Folk Music Research Group at the Hungarian Academy of Sciences' Institute of Musicology; taught at Liszt Academy from 1963 (Professor from 1992); founder and co-director of Schola Hungarica.

Zsolt Durkó

1934–97. Composer.
1961–3, composition student of Ferenc Farkas and then Goffredo Petrassi in Rome 1971–6, freelance composer, and Professor of Composition at Liszt Academy; 1982–97, chief advisor to Hungarian Radio. 1987, founded Hungarian Musical Society; 1988, established annual festival for contemporary music ('Mini-festival').

Péter Eötvös

b. 1944. Composer and conductor.
Composition student of János Viski and Ferenc Szabó; then studied conducting in Cologne 1966–7. 1968–76, performed in Stockhausen's ensemble; 1971–9, assistant at West German Radio's electronic studio. 1979–91, musical director of Ensemble InterContemporain in Paris; 1985–8, BBC Symphony Orchestra principal guest conductor; 1992–5, Budapest Festival Orchestra principal guest conductor.

Ferenc Farkas

1905–2000. Composer.
Composition student of Albert Siklós and Leó Weiner; then studied with Respighi in Rome, 1929–31. Lived in Vienna and Copenhagen composing for film before returning to teach in Budapest, 1935–41. 1941–6, taught in Cluj (Kolozsvár). 1949–75, Professor at Liszt Academy, where his students included Kurtág (c.1950 until 1955).

Ottó Gombosi

1902–55. Musicologist.
Composition student of Albert Siklós and Leó Weiner; then studied musicology in Berlin, 1921–5. From 1926, editor of *Crescendo*, Budapest's music journal (based on Vienna's *Anbruch*). 1929, left Hungary, living subsequently in Berlin, Rome and Basel. 1939, settled in USA: Professor at University of Washington (Seattle), University of Chicago and Harvard.

Pál Járdányi

1920–66. Composer and folklorist.
Began studies as violinist but became composition student of Bárdos and Kodály. 1941–8, worked as music critic; 1944–59, taught composition,

theory, solfège and folk music at Liszt Academy; from 1948, worked at Hungarian Academy of Sciences' Folk Music Research department, Director from 1960.

Sándor Jemnitz

1890–1963. Composer, music critic and conductor.
Composition student of János Koessler, then Max Reger in Leipzig 1908–11 (also studying conducting with Artur Nikisch). Worked in Germany as répétiteur and editor until 1916. 1924–50, music critic for *Népszava*, the newspaper of the Social Democrats, in whose workers' movements he was an active musician; 1945–7, president of the Workers' Cultural Union. After 1951 taught at the Bartók Conservatory, Budapest.

Zoltán Jeney

b. 1943. Composer.
Composition student of Zoltán Pongrácz and Ferenc Farkas, then Goffredo Petrassi in Rome, 1967–8. In 1970 co-founder of New Music Studio; since 1986, Professor of Composition at Liszt Academy, head of composition department from 1995.

Attila József

1905–37. Poet, essayist and translator.
First volume of poetry published in 1922. Studied at universities in Szeged (Hungary), Vienna and Paris. 1930, returned to Hungary and joined the illegal communist party. Represented the more experimental and urbane strand in Hungarian poetry; the journal he founded in 1936, *Szép Szó* (Beautiful Word), underlined that allegiance and his (urban radical) opposition to (ruralist) populism.

Pál Kadosa

1903–83. Pianist, composer and pedagogue.
Composition student of Kodály and piano student of Arnold Székely. 1927–43, taught at Fodor Music School; 1943 and 1944, taught at Goldmark Music School. 1927, founding member of Society of Modern Hungarian Musicians; 1932–8, coordinator of UMZE (New Hungarian Music Society). From 1945, Professor of Piano at Liszt Academy (Head of Department from 1948) where

his students included Kurtág, Zoltán Kocsis and András Schiff; 1945–9, vice-president of Hungarian Musicians' Free Association; from 1949, member of the Hungarian Musicians' Union.

György Kerényi

1902–86. Folklorist and music educationist.
Composition student of Kodály; also studied in Berlin (1930–1) and Rome (1932). 1933–50, edited choral music periodicals; 1934–40, researched folk music under Bartók's direction. 1946–8, superintendent of music education in Hungary. From 1949, Director of the Hungarian Academy of Sciences' Folk Music Research department.

Sándor Kovács

b. 1949. Musicologist and critic.
Studied piano, composition and musicology at the Liszt Academy (musicology under László Somfai and György Kroó). Research fellow at Hungarian Academy of Sciences' Bartók Archive, also taught at Liszt Academy from 1979.

György Kroó

1926–97. Musicologist and music critic.
Musicology student of Dénes Bartha and Bence Szabolcsi at the Liszt Academy. From 1957, Director of Music Education at Hungarian Radio; from 1961 taught musicology at Liszt Academy in Budapest (Professor and head of department from 1972).

László Lajtha

1892–1963. Composer and ethnomusicologist.
Composition student of Viktor Herzfeld, thereafter studying also in Leipzig, Geneva and Paris (with Vincent d'Indy). Also studied and graduated in law. 1910, began collecting folk song; from 1913 worked in instrument collection of the Hungarian National Museum, from 1924 in the Museum of Ethnography. From 1919, Professor at the National Conservatory, and from 1952 taught folk-song studies at the Liszt Academy.

Ernő Lendvai

1925–93. Musicologist.
Graduated in piano at Liszt Academy in 1949. 1949–57, taught at and served as director of music schools in Szombathely and Győr, 1960–5, worked as music producer at Hungarian Radio. 1954–6 and after 1973, taught theory at Liszt Academy.

Rudolf Maros

1917–82. Composer.
Composition student of Kodály. 1942–9, taught in Pécs; 1949, attended Alois Hába's classes in Prague; 1949–78, taught chamber music, theory and instrumentation at Liszt Academy. Attended Darmstadt several times from 1958; 1971–2, lived in Berlin. 1971–5, member of ISCM Presidium.

János Maróthy

1925–2001. Musicologist.
Philosophy student of György Lukács at the Lóránd Eötvös University in Budapest; musicology student of Bence Szabolcsi at the Liszt Academy. 1954–61, research fellow in the Music Sociology department of the Hungarian Academy of Sciences' Institute of Musicology; from 1974, taught at the Lóránd Eötvös University in Budapest (Professor from 1980).

András Mihály

1917–93. Composer, conductor and cellist.
Composition student of Pál Kadosa and István Strasser. 1946–8, principal cello, then 1948–50, Chief Secretary, then 1978–86, Director of Hungarian State Opera. From 1949 taught chamber music at Liszt Academy; worked for Hungarian Radio 1968–72; in 1968 founded Budapest Chamber Ensemble dedicated to contemporary music.

Antal Molnár

1890–1983. Writer on music, composer and violist.
Composition student of Viktor Herzfeld and (privately) Kodály. Member of Waldbauer String Quartet and Dohnányi-Hubay Piano Quartet. 1919–59, taught music history, aesthetics, chamber music and theory at the Liszt Academy.

Lili Ország

1926–78. Painter.
Graduated from Budapest Art College in 1950. Her figurative, somewhat surrealist work from the 1950s evolved into a more abstracted style that drew on religious icons and historical symbols to evoke a suggestive metaphysics.

András Pernye

1928–80. Musicologist and critic.
Musicology student of Bence Szabolcsi. 1959–74, music critic for daily paper *Magyar Nemzet*, 1960–3, lector at Zeneműkiadó (state publishing house for music); 1965–80, teacher at the Liszt Academy. 1962–9, producer of jazz series at Hungarian Radio.

Emil Petrovics

b. 1930. Composer.
Composition student of János Viski, Ferenc Szabó and Ferenc Farkas. 1960–4, music director, Petőfi Theatre Budapest; taught from 1964 at the College of Theatre and Film and from 1968 at the Liszt Academy (Professor from 1979). From 1986, music director of Hungarian State Opera.

János Pilinszky

1921–81. Poet, essayist, playwright, translator and novelist.
First poems published in 1940. 1946–8, editor of liberal journal *Újhold* (New Moon), after which he worked as a copy-editor and proofreader. From 1957 he wrote for the Catholic weekly *Új Ember* (New Man). All his poetry subsequent to his experience in military service in 1944 is marked by a fascination with human tragedy; it is frequently framed with religious imagery and at times epigrammatically concise.

László Sáry

b. 1940. Composer.
Composition student of Endre Szervánszky. Founding member of New Music Studio.

Albert Simon

1926–2000. Conductor.
Conducting student of János Ferencsik and László Somogyi, also studied in Bucharest with Constantin Silvestri and George Georgescu. During 1950s conducted Hungarian State Orchestra and Szeged Opera; from 1959, conducted National Philharmonic; from 1969, taught at the Liszt Academy. Conductor of the orchestra at the Communist Youth Alliance, and in 1970, founding member of New Music Studio.

Ferenc Szabó

1902–69. Composer.
Composition student of Leó Weiner, Albert Siklós and Kodály. 1927, founding member of briefly functioning inter-war Society of Modern Hungarian Musicians. 1932–45, lived in Moscow. 1949–51, President of Hungarian Musicians' Union; 1945–67, Professor of Composition at Liszt Academy; 1958–67, Principal of the Liszt Academy.

Bence Szabolcsi

1899–1973. Musicologist.
Studied law, history of literature and philosophy at the Lóránd Eötvös University in Budapest; and was composition student of Kodály and Albert Siklós. Also studied musicology (under Hermann Abert), and art history and history in Leipzig 1921–3 (where he also studied composition with Sigfrid Karg-Elert). Inter-war years, co-edited journals (with Aladár Tóth). From 1945, Professor of Music History at Liszt Academy, where in 1951 he founded musicology faculty. 1950–6, edited *Új Zenei Szemle*, 1960–73, edited *Magyar Zene* and *Studia musicologica*.

István Szelényi

1904–72. Composer and musicologist.
Composition student of Kodály, piano student of Arnold Székely. 1927, founding member of Society of Modern Hungarian Musicians. 1945–56, Professor at Bartók Conservatory, also becoming Director; 1956–72, taught theory at the Liszt Academy. 1951–6, edited *Új Zenei Szemle*.

Endre Szervánszky

1911–77. Composer.
After clarinet studies became composition student of Albert Siklós. 1941–8, taught composition and theory at the National Conservatory; 1945–9, music critic of the then Communist Party newspaper *Szabad Nép*. 1949–77, Professor of Composition at Liszt Academy.

Sándor Szokolay

b. 1931. Composer.
Composition student of Ferenc Szabó and Ferenc Farkas. 1955–9, worked for Hungarian Radio; 1959–94, taught composition at Liszt Academy (Professor from 1966).

András Szőllősy

b. 1921. Composer and musicologist.
Parallel studies in languages (Hungarian and French) and composition (with Kodály and János Viski; defended doctoral dissertation on the music of Kodály); also studied with Goffredo Petrassi in Rome, 1947–8. 1950–88, Professor of Musicology at Liszt Academy.

Tibor Tallián

b. 1946. Musicologist.
Student of Bence Szabolcsi, Dénes Bartha and György Kroó; also studied at Vienna University, 1971–2. 1972–91, research fellow at the Hungarian Academy of Sciences' Musicology Institute; from 1976, taught at Liszt Academy (Professor of Musicology from 1997; 1996–2002, head of department); from 1998, Director of the Institute for Musicology.

Dezső Tandori

b. 1938. Poet, novelist and translator.
Studied Hungarian and German at the Lóránd Eötvös University in Budapest; taught at schools and colleges until 1971, since when he has been a freelance writer. Uses pseudonyms Nat Roid, Tradoni, and Hc. G. S. Solenard when writing detective fiction. Particularly renowned for his concrete poetry, picture-poems and metaphorical poem-images.

László Tihanyi

b. 1956. Composer and conductor.
Composition student of Rezső Sugár and conducting student of András Kórodi at the Liszt Academy. Since 1979, has taught counterpoint at Liszt Academy. In 1985 founded new music ensemble Intermoduláció.

Aladár Tóth

1898–1968. Musicologist and critic.
Studied at Budapest University (doctoral dissertation on Mozart opera aesthetics). Inter-war years, music critic for dailies *Új Nemzedék*, *Pesti Napló*, as well as literary journal *Nyugat*, and co-edited music periodical *Zenei Szemle*. 1940–46, lived in Sweden. 1946–56, Director of the Hungarian State Opera House.

József Ujfalussy

b. 1920. Musicologist.
Studied classical philology, also composition (with Sándor Veress), music history (Bence Szabolcsi and Dénes Bartha) and folk music (Kodály). From 1948, member then director (1951–5) of music department at Ministry of Culture. From 1955, Professor of Theory and Aesthetics at Liszt Academy. 1969–80, research fellow at Hungarian Academy of Sciences' Bartók Archive; 1973, Director of the Musicological Institute; 1980–8, Principal of Liszt Academy; 1985–93, Vice President, Hungarian Academy of Sciences.

Sándor Veress

1907–92. Composer, folklorist and pedagogue.
Composition student of Emánuel Hegyi and Kodály; piano student of Bartók. Active in attempting to reform instrumental music teaching, published on pedagogy. 1927–43 and 1943–9, folk-music research at the Museum of Ethnography and the Hungarian Academy of Sciences respectively. 1943–8, taught composition at Liszt Academy. 1949, emigrated; from 1950, taught composition, pedagogy and theory at Conservatorium in Bern (1968–77, as Professor).

László Vidovszky

b. 1944. Composer.
Composition student of Ferenc Farkas, also Olivier Messiaen in Paris, 1979–71. Founding member of New Music Studio. 1973–83, taught music theory

at teacher-training college of Liszt Academy; since 1983 has taught at the Janus Pannonius University in Pécs.

Leó Weiner

1885–1960. Composer and chamber-music teacher.
Composition student of János Koessler. From 1908, taught theory at Liszt Academy; 1912–22, Professor of Composition; 1920–57, Professor of Chamber Music.

Sándor Weöres

1913–89. Poet, translator, playwright and essayist.
Studied *Geistesgeschichte* at the University of Pécs (Hungary), where he also obtained a doctorate in philosophy. First volumes of poetry (1934 and 1935) each won prizes; 1941–50, worked in libraries. Under Stalinism wrote mainly for children. Particular interests emerging from his large output are orality, Far Eastern mysticism, language games, music and myth.

András Wilheim

b. 1949. Musicologist.
1974–90, research fellow at Hungarian Academy of Sciences' Bartók Archive. 1973, joined New Music Studio; from 1982, taught music history at Liszt Academy.

Bibliography

Archives

Paul Sacher Foundation, Basel (PSF)

Documents from the György Kurtág Collection (GKC), György Ligeti Collection (GLC) and Sándor Veress Collection (SVC).

Hungarian National Archive (=MOL: Magyar Országos Levéltár)

The following documents are from the Hungarian Musicians' Union, held in dossier P2146, boxes 62–5, and appearing as 'MOL document' with a number corresponding to the list below in footnotes to Chapter 2.

1. 'Jegyzőkönyv a Magyar Zeneművészek Szövetsége hangverseny- és drámai zenei szakosztálya konzultációs csoportjának 1953. március 6.-i üléséről' [Minutes from the meeting of the subcommittee of the concert and drama music department of the Hungarian Musicians' Union, 6 March 1953]
   MOL: P2146/64. doboz.
2. 'Jegyzőkönyv az 1953. december 28.-i konzultációs üléséről' [Minutes from the subcommittee meeting, 28 December 1953]
   MOL: P2146/64. doboz.
3. 'Jegyzőkönyv az I. szakosztály 1955. junius 20.-i kozultációs üléséről' [Minutes from the meeting of department I, 20 June 1955]
   MOL: P2146/65. doboz.
4. 'A Magyar Zeneművészek Szövetsége és a DISZ Központi Vezetősége Ifjúsági Zenei Napjainak vitája 1952. október 26.-án' [Debate of the Hungarian Musicians' Union and the Central Committee of the Young Workers' Union, 26 October 1952]
   MOL P 2146/63. doboz.
5. 'Jegyzőkönyv a Zeneművészek Szövetsége 1953. VI. 30.-án megtartott plénum-válogató üléséről' [Minutes of the Musicians' Union meeting selecting (repertoire) for the Plenum, 30 June 1953]
   MOL P2146/64. doboz.
6. 'Jegyzőkönyv az I. szakosztály 1954. december 6.-i konzultációs üléséről' [Minutes from the meeting of department I, 6 December 1954]
   MOL: P2146/65. doboz.
7. 'Jegyzőkönyv a Magyar Zeneművészek Szövesége hangverseny és drámai zenei szakosztályának 1952. december 12.-i konzultációs üléséről' [Minutes from the

meeting of the subcommittee of the concert and drama music department of the Hungarian Musicians' Union, 12 December 1952]
MOL: P2146/63. doboz.
8. 'Jegyzőkönyv a Magyar Zeneművészek Szövetsége augusztus 28.-án tartott teljes üléséről' [Minutes of the Hungarian Musicians' Union full meeting, 28 August]
MOL P2146/62. doboz.

Hungarian Music Council (= MZT: Magyar Zenei Tanács)

The following documents are from the Hungarian Musicians' Union, in dated but unsorted files, and appearing as 'MZT document' with a number corresponding to the list below, in footnotes to Chapter 2.

1. 'Jegyzőkönyv a hangverseny és drámai zenei szakosztály 1951. szeptember 22-én délelőtt a Rádióban tartott plénumelőkészitő [sic] üléséről' [Minutes of the concert and drama music department meeting preparing the Plenum, held at the Radio, 22 September 1951]
2. 'Jegyzőkönyv az Elnökség 1951. október 5.-én tartott plénumelőkészitő [sic] üléséről' [Minutes of the Presidium meeting preparing the Plenum, 5 October 1951]

Artpool (VI Budapest, Liszt Ferenc tér 10. www.artpool.hu)

New Music Studio Archive

c3 Web Archive

In February 1998, Dániel Erdély and Miklós Peternák accessed documents from the Historical Archive (then *Történeti Hivatal* but now *Állambiztonsági Szolgálatok Történeti Levéltára*) relating to the Communist Party's attention to avant-garde groups between 1966 and 1988. At the time of writing these were accessible in a web archive at www.c3.hu/collection/tilos. Those referenced during Chapter 4 are as follows:

Reports regarding the samizdat periodical entitled 'Szét-folyóirat':
'Jelentés' [Report], 14 December 1973
'Jelentés' [Report], 3 January 1974
Extracted from dossier no. O-16268/2 ("Horgászok" ["Fishers"]), pp. 19–49
http://www.c3.hu/collection/tilos/21-3 and http://www.c3.hu/collection/tilos/28-29

Reports regarding the 'Lakásszínház'
'Javaslat' [Recommendation], 7 December 1973

Extracted from dossier no. O-16268/2 ("Horgászok"), pp. 15–16. http://www.c3.hu/collection/tilos/15-16

'Jelentés' [Report], 10 January 1974
Extracted from dossier no. O-16268/1 ("Horgászok"), pp. 238–52. http://www.c3.hu/collection/tilos/238-252

'Intézkedési terv' [Action plan], 24 January 1974
Extracted from dossier no. O-16268/2 ("Horgászok"), pp. 5–9. http://www.c3.hu/collection/tilos/5-9

'Jelentés' [Report], 10 March 1975
Extracted from dossier no. O-16268/2 ("Horgászok"), pp. 182–4 http://www.c3.hu/collection/tilos/182-184

Published, but unauthored programmes

I. Magyar Zenei Hét [Hungarian Music Week] (17–25 November 1951)
II. Magyar Zenei Hét (24 October to 1 November 1953)
III. Magyar Zenei Hét (7–14 April 1956)
Korunk zenéje [Music of Our Time] (1975, 1976, 2002)
Mini-fesztivál [Mini-festival] (2002)

Books and articles

Adorno, Theodore Wiesengrund 1948 (2003). *Philosophie der neuen Musik*. Frankfurt am Main: Suhrkamp.

Aczél, Géza 1974. 'Talált tárgy – elvesztett poézis' [Objet trouvé – lost poesis], *Alföld* 15:5 (May), 72–3.

Albèra, Philippe (ed.) 1995. *György Kurtág: Entretiens, textes, écrits sur son œuvre* (*Contrechamps* 12–13). Genève: Contrechamps.

Alföldi, Jenő 1973. 'Tér és idő keresztjén' [At the intersection of space and time], *Élet és Irodalom* 27 January, 11.

Anderson, Mark M. 1994. *Kafka's Clothes: Ornament and Aestheticism in the Habsburg Fin de Siècle*. New York and Oxford: Oxford University Press.

Balassa, Péter 2004 (1989). 'Molto moderato', in Péter Balassa, *Halálnapló* [Death Diary], Budapest: Palatinus, 95–125.

Balázs, Géza 1997. *The Story of Hungarian*. Trans. Thomas J. DeKornfeld. Budapest: Corvina.

Balázs, István 1984. 'A magánélet börtönében' [In the prison of private life], *Valóság* 17:5, 51–62; also published as 'Im Gefängnis des Privatlebens. Über zwei neue Werke von György Kurtág', *Schweizerische Musikzeitung* 123 (1983), 277–90; and as 'Dans la prison de la vie privée: A propos du lien interne entre deux oeuvres de György Kurtág', in Albèra et al. 1995: 145–58.

Balibar, Etienne 1992. 'Internationalisme ou barbarie?', *Lignes* 17 (October), 21–42.

Bálint, Sárosi 1973. *Zenei anyanyelvünk* [Our musical mother tongue]. Budapest: Gondolat.

Bibliography

Bárdos, Lajos 1949. 'A modális összhangtan alapjai' [The foundations of modal theory], *Magyar kórus* 19:2 (June), 1598–1604.

  1969. *Harminc írás 1929–1969* [Thirty essays 1929–1969]. Budapest: Zeneműkiadó.

Barna, István 1973. 'A győri Filharmonikus Zenekar koncertje (okt. 10.)' [The concert of the Győr Philharmonic, 10 October], *Filharmónia műsorfüzet* 1973/8, 36–38.

Beal, Amy 2000. 'Negotiating cultural allies: American music in Darmstadt, 1946–1956', *Journal of the American Musicological Society* 53:1 (Spring), 105–39.

  2003. 'The Army, the airwaves, and the avant-garde: American classical music in postwar West Germany', *American Music* 21:4 (Winter), 474–513.

Beckles Willson, Rachel 2001. '"Culture is a vast weapon, its artistic force is also strong." Finding a context for Kurtág's works: an interim report', in *Perspectives on Kurtág*, eds. Rachel Beckles Willson and Alan E. Williams, *Contemporary Music Review* 20:1–2 (Kurtág special issue), 3–37.

  2002. 'Péter Eötvös in conversation about *Three Sisters*', *Tempo* 220 (April), 11–13.

  2003. '"Behold! The long-awaited new Hungarian opera has been born!" Discourses of denial and Petrovics' *C'est la guerre*'. *Central Europe* 1:2 (November), 133–45.

  2004a. *György Kurtág's The Sayings of Péter Bornemisza op. 7*. Aldershot: Ashgate.

  2004b. 'Longing for a national rebirth: mythological tropes in Hungarian music criticism 1968–1974', *Slavonica* 10:2 (November), 139–56.

  2004c. 'A study in "tradition", geography and identity in concert practice', *Music and Letters* (November 2004), 602–13.

  2004d. 'Meeting points and national authenticity: Bartók from inside and out', in Masakata Kanazawa (ed.), *Musicology and Globalization: Proceedings of the International Congress in Shizuoka 2002* (Tokyo: Musicological Society of Japan, 2004), 384–8.

Beckles Willson, Rachel and Alan E. Williams (eds.) 2001. *Perspectives on Kurtág*. Harwood Academic. (*Contemporary Music Review* 20:1–2.)

Beddow, Michael 1994. *Thomas Mann: Doctor Faustus*. Cambridge: Cambridge University Press.

Béládi, Miklós 1973. 'P. J.: Szálkák' [P. J.: Splinters], *Kritika* 2, 22.

Bergande, Martin 1994. "*... halb experimentell, halb volkstümlich...*" *György Ligeti's Magyar Etűdök*. Saarbrucken: Pfau-Verlag.

Berger, Karol 2000. *The Theory of Art*. New York and Oxford: Oxford University Press.

Berlász, Melinda 1984. *Lajtha László*. Budapest: Akadémiai kiadó.

Berlász, Melinda (ed.) 2000. *Járdányi Pál összegyűjtött írásai* [The collected writings of Pál Járdányi]. Budapest: MTA Zenetudományi intézet.

Berlász, Melinda, János Demény and Ede Terényi (eds.) 1982. *Veress Sándor*. Budapest: Zeneműkiadó.

Bideleux, Robert and Ian Jeffries 1998. *A History of Eastern Europe*. London and New York: Routledge.

Blanning, Tim and Hagen Schulze (eds.) 2006. *Unity and Diversity in European Culture c.1800* (Proceedings of the British Academy 134). Oxford and New York: Oxford University Press.

Bónis, Ferenc 1987, 1988a and 1988b. 'Three days with Sándor Veress the composer', *The New Hungarian Quarterly*: Part I: 28:108 (Winter), 201–8; Part II: 29:109 (Spring), 217–25; Part III: 29:111 (Autumn), 208–14.

Bónis, Ferenc 1992a. 'Kodály Magyar Zsoltárának születése' [The birth of Kodály's Hungarian Psalm], in *Hódolat Bartóknak és Kodálynak* (ed. Ferenc Bónis), Budapest: Püski, 138–213.

Bónis, Ferenc (ed.) 1961. *Molnár Antal: Írások a zenéről* [Antal Molnár: writings on music]. Budapest: Zeneműkiadó.

(ed.) 1968. *Tóth Aladár válogatott kritikái* [The selected reviews of Aladár Tóth]. Budapest: Zeneműkiadó.

(ed.) 1974. *The Selected Writings of Zoltán Kodály*. Trans. Lili Halápy and Fred Macnicol. London: Boosey and Hawkes in cooperation with Corvina, Budapest.

(ed.) 1982. *Visszatekintés* [In Retrospect] I and II. Budapest: Zeneműkiadó.

Borio, Giannmario 1984. 'L'eridità Bartókiana nel Secondo Quartetto de G. Ligeti, Sul Concerto di Concetto di tradizione nella Musica Contemporanea', *Studi Musicali* 13, 289–307.

Borio, Giannmario and Hermann Danuser (eds.) 1997. *Im Zenit der Moderne: Die Internationalen Ferienkurse für Neue Musik Darmstadt 1946–1966*. Freiburg im Breisgau: Rombach Verlag, 1997.

Boronkay, Antal 1985. 'Bartók Szeminárium, 1985', *Muzsika* 28:10 (October), 8–9.

1989. 'Kortárs zene és kritika. Gondolatok a Magyar Zeneművészeti Társaság Minifesztiválja ürügyén' [Contemporary music and criticism. Thoughts apropos the Hungarian Musical Society's Mini-festival], *Muzsika* 32:4, 8–9.

Boros, Attila 1979. *30 év magyar operái* [30 years of Hungarian opera]. Budapest: Zeneműkiadó.

Bossin, Jeffery 1984. 'György Ligeti's new lyricism and the aesthetic of currentness: the Berlin Festival's retrospective of the composer's career', *Current Musicology* 37:8, 233–9.

Bouliane, Denys 1983. 'Entretien avec György Ligeti', *Sonances* 3:1 (October), 9–27.

1985. 'György Ligeti im Gespräch mit Denys Bouliane', translated from French by Herbert Henck and Denys Bouliane. *Neuland* 5, 72–90. (Originally published in *Sonances*.)

1989. 'Stilisierte Emotion', *MusikTexte* 28–9, 52–62.

Boym, Svetlana 2001. *The Future of Nostalgia*. New York: Basic Books.

Breuer, János, 1961a. 'Új művek, bemutatók' [New works, premières], *Muzsika* 3:5 (May), 37.

1961b. 'Két ünnepi hangverseny' [Two festive concerts], *Muzsika* 4:7 (July), 35–6.

1962. 'A korunk kamarazenéje' [Chamber music of our time], *Muzsika* 5:7 (July), 43–4.

1963. 'Modern kamarazene' [Modern chamber music], *Muzsika* 6:7 (July), 38.

Bibliography

1964. 'A Budapesti Fúvósötös bemutató estje' [The début of the Budapest Wind Quintet], *Muzsika* 7:1 (January), 40–1.

1965a. 'A magyar előadóművészet problémáiról' [On the problems of Hungarian performance]. *Magyar Zene* 6:4, 383–93.

1965b. 'Magyar bemutatók' [Hungarian premières], *Muzsika* 8:12, 6–7.

1969. 'Bécsi utazás magyar zenével' [Viennese excursion with Hungarian music], *Muzsika* 12:2, 9–11.

1971. 'Zenei krónika' (review including Ligeti's Chamber Concerto and *Volumina*), *Népszabadság* 19 October.

1973a. 'Zenei krónika' (review including Ligeti's *Ramifications*), *Népszabadság* 16 October.

1973b. 'Zenei krónika' (review including Jeney's *Hommage à Schoenberg*), *Népszabadság* 3 December.

1974a. 'Zenei krónika' (review including Kurtág's *Szálkák* op. 6c), *Népszabadság* 9 October.

1974b. 'Zenei krónika' (review including Ligeti's Chamber Concerto), *Népszabadság* 15 October.

1975. 'Zenei krónika' (review of Kurtág's composer portrait), *Népszabadság* 7 October.

1976a. 'Zenei krónika' (review of New Music Studio's first concert), *Népszabadság* 6 January.

1976b. 'Zenei krónika' (review including Ligeti's *Atmosphères*), *Népszabadság* 8 October.

1976c. 'Zenei krónika' (review including Új Zenei Stúdió), *Népszabadság* 20 October.

1978a. *Bartók és Kodály. Tanulmányok századunk magyar zenetörténetéhez* [Bartók and Kodály. Studies in Hungarian music of our century]. Budapest: Magvető.

1978b. 'Zenei krónika' (review including Kurtág's *Hommage à András Mihály: 12 Microludes for String Quartet* op. 13), *Népszabadság* 17 October.

1978c. *Tizenhárom óra Kadosa Pállal* [Thirteen hours with Pál Kadosa]. Budapest: Editio Musica.

1979. 'Zenei krónika' (review including Ligeti's composer portrait), *Népszabadság* 17 October.

1981. 'Zenei krónika' (review of Kurtág's opp. 16 and 17), *Népszabadság* 3 November.

1983. 'Zenei krónika' (review of Kurtág's op. 19), *Népszabadság* 2 November.

1984. 'Jemnitz Sándor és Arnold Schoenberg kapcsolatai' [Contacts between Sándor Jemnitz and Arnold Schoenberg]. *Magyar Zene* 25:1, 3–13.

1985a. 'Tóth Aladár két Berg-elemzése' [Two analyses of Berg by Aladár Tóth], *Muzsika* 27:2, 18–20.

1985b. 'Az első Webern-bemutató Magyarországon' [The first Webern première in Hungary]. *Muzsika* 28:7, 6–7.

1986. Emerich Balabán – Schönbergs erster Wegbereiter in Ungarn. Zur frühgeschichte der ungarischen Schönberg-Rezeption. In *Bericht über den 2.*

Kongreß der Internationalen Schönberg-Gesellschaft "Die Wiener Schule in der Musikgeschichte des 20. Jahrhunderts". Vienna: Verlag Elisabeth Lafite, 134–41.

1990. *A Guide to Kodály*. Budapest: Corvina.

1992a. *Fejezetek Lajtha Lászlóról* [Chapters about László Lajtha]. Budapest: Editio Musica.

1992b. 'Verfemte Musik in Ungarn', *Verfemte Musik: Komponisten in den Diktaturen unseres Jahrhunderts*, eds. Joachim Braun, Vladimir Karbusicky and Heidi Tamar Hoffmann. Frankfurt-am-Main: Peter Lang, 263–72.

1993. 'Az avantgardista Lajtha' [Lajtha the avant-gardist]. *Magyar Zene* 34:1 (March), 5–12.

2002 *Kodály és kora* [Kodály and his time]. Kecskemét: Kodály Intézet.

Breuer, János (ed.) 1978. *Zenei írások a Nyugatban* [Musical writings in *Nyugat*]. Budapest: Zeneműkiadó.

Buchmuller, Eva and Ann Koós 1996. *Squat Theatre*. New York: Artists Space.

Burde, Wolfgang 1993. *György Ligeti. Eine Monographie*. Zürich: Atlantis.

Carnegy, Patrick 1973. *Faust as Musician: a Study of Thomas Mann's Novel 'Doctor Faustus'*. London: Chatto and Windus.

Carroll, Mark 2003. *Music and Ideology in Cold War Europe*. Cambridge: Cambridge University Press.

Casement, Patrick 1982. 'Samuel Beckett's relationship to his mother-tongue', *International Review of Psycho-Analysis* 9, 35–44.

Chekhov, Anton. 1959. *Plays*, trans. Elizaveta Fen. London: Penguin Books.

Cioran, Émile M. 1998. *History and Utopia*. Trans. from French, Richard Howard. Chicago: University of Chicago Press.

Csengery, Kristóf 1984. 'Hangverseny' [Concert], *Muzsika* 27:5, 22–5.

1987. 'Lomtalanítás? Korunk Zenéje '87' [Clearout? Music of our Time '87], *Muzsika* 30:12 (December), 24–32.

Csizmadia, Ervin 1995. *A magyar demokratikus ellenzék 1968–88* [The Hungarian liberal opposition 1968–88] Volume I: Documents; Volume II: Interviews; Volume III: Monograph). Budapest: T-Twins.

Csobádi Péter 1953. 'Tömegzenénk tükre. A II. magyar zenei hét második kórus- és kantáta estje' [Images of our mass music. The second chorus and cantata concert of the Hungarian Music Week no. II]. *Népszava*, 1 November.

1956. 'A III. magyar zenei hét hangversenyei' [Concerts of the Hungarian Music Week no. III], *Magyar Nemzet* 17 April.

Czövek, Erna 1948. *Útmutatás a zongora Ábécé tanításához*. Budapest: Cserépfalvi.

1965. 'Új zene, új előadóművészet, új zenepedagógia' [New music, new performance, new music pedagogy], *Magyar Zene* 6:3, 227–36.

Dalos, Anna 2002a. '"Folklorisztikus nemzeti klasszicizmus" – egy fogalom elméleti forrásairól' ["Folkloric national classicism" – theoretical sources of a concept], *Magyar Zene* 40:2, 191–9.

2002b. '"Nem Kodály-iskola, de magyar". Gondolatok a Kodály-iskola eszméjének kialakulásáról' ["Not Kodály school, but Hungarian". Thoughts on the evolution of the Kodály school concept.] *Holmi* 14:9 (2002), 1175–91.

Dasgupta, Gautam 1986. 'Squat: Nature Theatre of New York', in *Before His Eyes: Essays in Honor of Stanley Kauffmann* ed. Bert Cardullo. Lanham: UPs of America, 93–102.

Dávidházi, Péter, Győző Ferencz, László Kúnos, Szabolcs Várady and György Szirtes (eds.) 1997. *The Lost Rider: A Bilingual Anthology*. Budapest: Corvina.

de Certeau, Michael 2000. *The Possession at Loudun*. Chicago: University of Chicago Press.

Demény, János (ed.) 1989. *Boëthius boldog fiatalsága* [The happy youth of Boethius. János Demény's selection of Antal Molnár's letters and writings]. Budapest: Magvető.

DeNora, Tia 1995. *Music and the Construction of Genius: Musical Politics in Vienna, 1792–1803*. Berkeley and Los Angeles: University of California Press.

2000. *Music in Everyday Life*. Cambridge, New York: Cambridge University Press.

Dibelius, Ulrich 1984. 'Ligetis Horn Trio', *Melos* 46, 44–61.

1989. 'Sprache-Gesten-Bilder: Von György Ligetis *Aventures* zu *Le grand macabre*', *MusikTexte* 28–9, 63–67.

1994. *György Ligeti. Eine Monographie in Essays*. Mainz: Schott.

Dibelius, Ulrich (ed.) 1993. *Ligeti und Kurtág in Salzburg: Programmbuch der Salzburger Festspiele*. Salzburg/Zürich: Residenz Verlag.

Diószeghi, András 1973. 'P. J.: Szálkák' [P. J.: Splinters], *Kortárs* 10, 1676–9.

Doboss, Gyula 1988. *Hérakleitosz Budán* [Heraclitus in Buda]. Budapest: Magvető.

Dobszay, László 1998. 'Thirty Years of the Gregorian Movement in Hungary', *Hungarian Musical Quarterly* 9:3–4.

2000. 'Chant themes in the contemporaneous composition in Hungary', *The past in the present: Papers read at the IMS Intercongressional Symposium and the 10th meeting of the Cantus Planus*. Budapest: Liszt Ferenc Zeneművészeti Egyetem, 445–81.

Domokos, Mátyás (ed.) 1990. *Magyar Orpheus. Weöres Sándor Emlékezete* [Hungarian Orpheus. In memory of Sándor Weöres]. Budapest: Szépirodalmi.

(ed.) 2003. *Weöres Sándor. Öröklét* [Sándor Weöres. Eternal life]. Budapest: Nap Kiadó.

Englbrecht, Bernd 1998. *Die späte Chormusik von György Ligeti: Analytische Betrachtungen im Hinblick auf Personalstil und Traditionsverhältnis*. Frankfurt-am-Main: Peter Lang.

Engelbrecht, Christiane, Wolfgang Marx and Britta Sweers 1997. *Lontano: "Aus weiter Ferne" – Zur Musiksprache und Assoziationsvielfalt György Ligetis*. Hamburg: von Bockel.

Eörsi, István 1991. 'Emlék és indítvány' [Memory and proposition], *Színház* 24:10–11, 30–1.

Eősze, László 1962. *Zoltán Kodály. His Life and Work*. Trans. István Farkas and Gyula Gulyás. London: Collet's, in collaboration with Corvina, Budapest.

Erdely, Stephen 2001. 'Bartók and folk music', in *The Cambridge Companion to Bartók*, ed. Amanda Bayley, Cambridge: Cambridge University Press, 24–44.

Evarts, J. 1968. 'Donaueschingen', *World Music* 10:2, 41–2.

F. L. (= László Flórián) 1930. [Concert review], *Muzsika* 2:1–2 (January–February), 51–2.

Fábián, Imre 1968. 'Új zenénk óriási sikere Darmstadtban' [Great acclaim for our new music in Darmstadt], *Muzsika* 11:11 (November), 11–12.

Fábián, Imre and Rezső Kókai 1961. *Századunk zenéje* [Music of our century]. Budapest: Zeneműkiadó.

Fáy, Miklós 2000. 'Ne fütyülj, Mása!' [Don't whistle, Masha!], *Népszabadság*, 5 April.

Farkas, Mária Sz. 1975. 'Zenei jegyzetek' (review of Kurtág's composer portrait), *Magyar Nemzet* 4 October.

1976. 'Az Új Zenei Stúdió hangversenye (dec. 27.)' [The New Music Studio concert], *Filharmónia műsorfüzet* 1976/3, 41–2.

1977. 'Kocsis Zoltán zongoraestje (márc. 2.)', *Filharmónia műsorfüzet* 1977/12, 57–8.

1978. 'Zenei jegyzetek' (review including Kurtág's *Hommage à Mihály András: 12 Microludes for String Quartet* op. 13), *Magyar Nemzet* 4 October.

Fasang, Árpád (jnr.) 1972. 'Rendhagyó sajtószemle' [Irregular press review], *Muzsika* 15:11 (November), 6–9.

Fenyő, Imre 1947. 'A Magyar Zeneművészek Szabadszervezetének beszámolója és hírei' [Report and news from the Hungarian Musicians' Free Association', *Zenei Szemle* 1:1, 62–64.

Ferencz, Győző 1993. 'The end of the word: the poetry of Dezső Tandori', *The Hungarian Quarterly* 34:131 (Autumn), 83–95.

Földes, Imre 1969. *Harmincasok. Beszélgetések magyar zeneszerzőkkel.* [Born in the 1930s. Conversations with Hungarian composers]. Budapest: Zeneműkiadó.

Feuer, Mária 1978. *Pillanatfelvétel* [Snapshot]. Budapest: Zeneműkiadó.

1987. 'Megint Kurtág' [Kurtág again], *Muzsika* 30:7 (July), 5–6.

1981. 'Szabálytalan beszámoló Londonból' [Irregular report from London], *Muzsika* 24:4 (April), 11–15.

1989. 'Kár lenne tévedni! Beszélgetés Durkó Zsolttal, a Magyar Zeneművészeti Társaság elnökével' ['It would be a shame to be mistaken! Conversation with Zsolt Durkó, President of the Hungarian Musical Society], *Muzsika* 32:4, 3–7.

Floros, Constantin 1991. 'Versuch uber Ligetis jüngste Werke', in *Für Gyorgy Ligeti: Die Referate des Ligeti-Kongresses, Hamburg 1988* (*Hamburger Jahrbuch fur Musikwissenschaft* 11). Laaber: Laaber Verlag, 335–48.

Forgács, Éva 2003. 'Enlightenment versus the national genius. Attempts at constructing both modernism and national identity through visual expression in Hungary 1910–1990'. Paper presented at 'Nation, Style, Modernism' conference held in Krakow in September 2003, organised under the auspices of Congrès Internationaux de l'Histoire d'Art by the Zentralinstitut für Kunstgeschichte in München and the International Cultural Centre in Krakow.

Fosler-Lussier, Daniele 1999. 'Béla Bartók and the transition to communism in Hungary, 1945–1955'. Ph.D. diss., Univ. of California at Berkeley.

2001. 'Bartók reception in cold war Europe' in *The Cambridge Companion to Bartók*, ed. Amanda Bayley, Cambridge: Cambridge University Press, 202–14.

2003. 'András Mihály and the legacy of Béla Bartók: the persistence of tradition', in *The Past in the Present: Proceedings of the International Musicological Society* (Budapest 2000). Budapest: Liszt Ferenc Academy of Music.

2004. '"Multiplication by minus one": musical values in East–West Engagement', *Slavonica* 10:2 (November), 125–38.

Fricke, Stefan, Konrad Frobenius, Sigrid Wolf and Theo Schmitt (eds.) 1999. *Zwischen Volks- und Kunstmusik. Aspekte der ungarischen Musik*. Saarbrücken: Pfau.

Friedrich, Ádám 1986. 'Egy kürtös gondolatai' [A horn player's thoughts], *Muzsika* 29:1 (January), 8–9.

Frigyesi, Judit 1996. 'The aesthetic of the Hungarian revival movement', in *Retuning Culture, Musical Changes in Central and Eastern Europe*, ed. Mark Slobin, Durham and London: Duke University Press, 54–75.

1999. *Béla Bartók and Turn-of-the-Century Budapest*. Berkeley and Los Angeles: University of California Press.

Fülöp, László 1973. 'Pilinszky János: Szálkák' [János Pilinszky: Splinters], *Alföld: Irodalmi és Művészeti Folyóirat* 24:3, 78–81.

1977. *Pilinszky János*. Budapest: Akadémiai kiadó.

Gárdonyi, Zoltán 1955. 'Distancia-elvű jelenségek Liszt zenéjében' [Appearances of the distance principle in Liszt's music], in *Zenetudományi tanulmányok Liszt Ferenc és Bartók Béla emlékére*, ed. Bence Szabolcsi and Dénes Bartha, Budapest: Akadémiai kiadó, 91–100.

Garton Ash, Timothy 1989. *The Uses of Adversity. Essays on the Fate of Central Europe*. London: Penguin Books.

Géfin, László K. 1997. 'Still beyond the pale: Hungarian emigré writing after the collapse of communism', *symploke* 5:1, 206–20.

Gell, Alfred 1998. *Art and Agency*. Oxford: Clarendon Press.

Geertz, Clifford 1973. 'Ideology as a cultural system', in *The Interpretation of Cultures*, New York: Basic Books, 193–233.

Gergely, Pál 1965. 'Papp Lajos Gordonkaversenye' [Lajos Papp's Cello Concerto], *Muzsika* 7:5 (May), 37–8.

Gerencsér, Rita 2000. *Zsolt Durkó*, trans. Peter Woodward. Budapest: Mágus.

Gerlich, Thomas 2000. 'Neuanfang in der "Wahlheimat"? Zu Sándor Veress' Hommage à Paul Klee', in *"Entre Denges et Denezy . . ." Dokumente zur Schweizer Musikgeschichte 1900–2000*, eds. Ulrich Mosch and Matthias Kassel, Mainz: Schott, 399–406.

Gerlóczy, Gedeon and Lajos Németh 1976. *Csontváry-emlékkönyv. Válogatás Csontváry Kosztka Tivadar írásaiból és a Csontváry-irodalomból* [Csontváry memorial volume. Selected writings of Tivadar Kosztka Csontváry and literature on Csontváry]. Budapest: Corvina.

Gill, Dominic 1982. 'Reviews – a collage' (From *Financial Times 1974–1981*). In Varga (ed.) 1982, 43–60.

Gombosi, Ottó 1927. 'A filharmónikusok műsora' [The programme of the Philharmonic], *Crescendo* 2:3 (October), 21–2.

1928. 'A Jonny-probléma' [The Jonny problem], *Crescendo* 2:8 (March).

Gooley, Dana 2004. *The Virtuoso Liszt*. New York and Cambridge: Cambridge University Press.

Gottwald, Clytus 1971. '*Lux aeterna*: zur Kompositionstechnik György Ligeti', *Musica* 25, 12–17.

    1974. 'Gustav Mahler und die musikalische Utopie. III: Die Achte. Epilog zu den Gesprächen mit Gyorgy Ligeti', *Neue Zeitschrift fur Musik* 135:5 (May), 292–5.

    1983. '*Ligetis Magyar Etűdök (1983)*' in Kolleritsch (ed.), 204–12.

Grabócz, Márta 1980. 'Bezártság, vagy elzárkózás? Gondolatok a főiskolai zeneszerzőkör hangversenysorozata ürügyén' [Secluded or isolated? Thoughts apropos the concert series of the Academy composer circle], *Muzsika* 23:6, 26–9.

    1981a. 'Kurtág-bemutató Párizsban' [Kurtág première in Paris], *Muzsika* 24:3 (March), 34–7.

    1981b. 'A kókler Halál. Ligeti operájának párizsi bemutatója' [Death as joker. The Paris première of Ligeti's opera], *Muzsika* 24:8 (August), 12–15.

Grant, M. J. 2001. *Serial Music, Serial Aesthetics. Compositional Theory in Post-War Europe*. Cambridge: Cambridge University Press.

Grassl, Markus and Reinhard Kapp (eds.) 1996. *Darmstadt-Gespräche. Die Internationalen Ferienkurse für neue Musik in Wien*. Vienna, Cologne and Weimar: Böhlau.

Griffiths, Paul 1983. *György Ligeti*. London: Robson Books.

Grünzweig, Werner and Gottfried Krieger (eds.) 1993. *Harald Kaufmann. Von innen und außen*. Hofheim: Wolke Verlag.

Gumbrecht, Hans Ulrich 2004. *Production of Presence. What Meaning Cannot Convey*. Stanford: Stanford University Press.

Hadas, Mikós 1987. 'A nemzet prófétája. Kísérlet Kodály pályájának szociológiai értelmezésére' [The prophet of the nation. A sociological interpretation of Kodály's career], *Szociológia* 4, 469–90.

Halász, Péter 1986. 'Bartók Szeminárium 1986', *Muzsika* 29:10 (October), 3–7.

    1995. 'Kurtág-töredékek' [Kurtág Fragments], *Holmi* 7:2 (February), 154–83.

    1998. 'Tradíció és kreativitás. Ligeti György Klasszikus összhangzattanáról' [Tradition and creativity. On György Ligeti's harmony tutor], *Muzsika* 41:5, 15–17.

    2002. 'Kurtág's dodecaphony', *Studia Musicologica Academiae Scientiarum Hungaricae* 43:3–4, 235–52.

Hansen, Mathias 1984. 'Musik zwischen Konstruktion und Emotion: Gespräch mit György Ligeti', *Musik und Gesellschaft* 34, 472–7.

Haraszti, Miklós 1977. *A Worker in a Workers' State: Piece-Rates in Hungary*. Trans. Michael Wright with a foreword by Heinrich Böll. London: Pelican Books.

Häusler, Josef 1983. 'Ligeti – Josef Häusler', in *Ligeti in Conversation*, trans. Sarah E. Soulsby, London: Eulenberg Books, 83–110.

Havel, Václav 1985a. *Open Letters: Selected Writing*. Selected, trans. and ed. Paul Wilson. New York: Random House.

    1985b. *The Power of the Powerless*. Trans. Paul Wilson, ed. John Keane. London: Hutchinson.

Helms, Hans G. 1999. 'Voraussetzungen eines neuen Musiktheaters' [1966]. In *Darmstadt-Dokumente I. (Musik-Konzepte Sonderband*, series editors Heinz-Klaus Metzger and Rainer Riehn). Münich: edition text + kritik, 330–44.

Hermann, Lula. 1941. 'Bartók Béla "Mikrokosmos"-áról', *Magyar Zenei Szemle* 1:3 (April), 52–5.

Hoffmann, Peter 1991. 'Die Kakerlake sucht den Weg zum Licht. Zum Streichquartett op. 1 von György Kurtág', *Musikforschung* 44, 32–48.

   1992. 'Post-Webernsche Musik? György Kurtágs Webern-Rezeption am Beispiel seines Streichquartetts op. 28', *Musiktheorie* 7, 129–48.

Hohmaier, Simone 2001. 'Analysis–play–composition. Remarks on the creative process of György Kurtág', in Beckles Willson and Williams (eds.), 39–50.

Hölderlin, Friedrich 1994. *Poems and Fragments*. Trans. Michael Hamburger. London: Anvil.

Homolya, István 1968. 'A Budapesti Kamaraegyüttes hangversenye (okt. 4)' [Concert by the Budapest Chamber Ensemble], *Filharmónia műsorfüzet* 40, 20–2.

   1971. 'A Budapesti Kamaraegyüttes hangversenye (okt. 13)' [Concert by the Budapest Chamber Ensemble], *Filharmónia műsorfüzet* 39, 21–2.

   1979. 'Ligeti Zenei ceremóniái (márc. 1)' [Ligeti's musical ceremonies], *Filharmónia műsorfüzet* 14, 35–6.

Hosking, Geoffrey and George Schöpflin (eds.) 1997. *Myths and Nationhood*. London: Hurst and Co. in association with the School of Slavonic and East European Studies, University of London.

Howat, Roy 1983. 'Review-Article: Bartók, Lendvai and the principles of proportional analysis', *Music Analysis* 2:1, 69–95

   1985. 'Letter to Lendvai', *Music Analysis* 4:3, 337.

Hughes, Ted 1989. 'Introduction', in Pilinszky 1989, 7–16.

Hutchings, Stephen C. 2000. *Russian Modernism: The Transfiguration of the Everyday*. Cambridge: Cambridge University Press.

Ignotus, Paul 1972. *Hungary*. London: Ernest Benn.

Ivasivka, Mátyás 1997. 'A cserkészet' [The scout movement]. In *Bárdos Lajos emlékkonferencia 1996.XI.16*, ed. Mária Póczonyi, Budapest: A Bárdos Lajos Társaság, 37–44.

Járdányi, Pál 1955. 'Bartók arca – két új könyv tükrében' [Bartók's face – in the light of two new books], *Csillag* 9:1, 2311–13.

Járdányi, Pál and Sándor Jemnitz 1948. 'Modern szerzők zenekari hangversenye' [Modern composers' orchestral concert]. *Zenei Szemle* 2:8 (December), 441–3.

Jemnitz, Sándor 1925. 'Musik 1924. Ungarn', *Musikblätter der Anbruch* 1, 33–5

   1927a. Review. *Crescendo* 1:10 (May), 16–17

   1927b. Review. *Crescendo* 1:10 (May), 7–8.

   1927c. A modern zene főbb áramlatai [The main currents of modern music], *Crescendo* 1:10 (May), 7–10.

   1928. Review. *Népszava*, 9 February.

1936. Review. *Népszava*, 13 March.

1960. 'Modern művek zenekari estje (január 14.)' [Modern orchestral works in concert], *Filharmónia műsorfüzet* 7, 34–5.

John, Nicholas (ed.) 1991. *The Stage Works of Béla Bartók*. London: John Calder.

Johnson, Tim 2002. 'Communication and experience: some observations on the relationship between composer and performer in Játékok', *Studia Musicologica Academiae Scientiarum Hungaricae* 43:3–4, 281–8.

Judt, Tony 2005. *Postwar*. London: Heinemann.

Kakavelakis, Konstantinos 2000. *Györy Ligetis Aventures and Nouvelles Aventures. Studien zur Sprachkomposition und Ästhetik der Avantgarde*. New York and Frankfurt: Peter Lang.

Kardos, Tibor 1972, 'Weöres Sándor pályaképe (1970)' [The career of Sándor Weöres (1970)], in *Élő humanizmus* [Living humanism], Budapest: Magvető, 564–96.

Kárpáti, János 1960. 'Bemutató hangversenyek' [Concert premières], *Muzsika* 3:7, 33–4.

1976. 'Bemutatók krónikája' [Chronicle of premières], *Muzsika* 19:3, 21–4.

1977. 'Bemutatók krónikája' [Chronicle of premières], *Muzsika* 20:3, 24–5.

Katanics, Mária 1997. '"Vedd észre, hol a fény"!' [Look where the light is!]. In *Bárdos Lajos emlékkonferencia 1996.XI.16*, ed. Mária Póczonyi, Budapest: A Bárdos Lajos Társaság, 123–30.

Kaufmann, Harald 1969. *Spurlinien. Analytische Aufsätze über Sprache und Musik*. Vienna: Verlag Elisabeth Lafite.

Kelly, Catriona 2001. *Russian Literature: A Very Short Introduction*. Oxford and New York: Oxford University Press.

Kenyeres, Zoltán 1983. *Tündérsíp. Weöres Sándorról* [Fairy pipes. On Sándor Weöres]. Budapest: Szépirodalmi.

Kerényi, György 1941. 'Bartók hangneme' [Bartók's key], *Énekszó*. 8:5 (March–April), 817–20.

Kerényi, Mária 1971. 'Világképünk és a kortárs zene' [Our world view and contemporary music], *Muzsika* 14:1 (January), 5–7.

1987. 'Csengery Adrienne portréfilmje' [Portrait film of Adrienne Csengery], *Muzsika* 30:3 (March), 44.

Keszi, Imre 1961. 'Kókai Rezső – Fábián Imre. Századunk zenéje' [Rezső Kókai – Imre Fábián. *Music of our Century*], *Magyar Zene* 2:4–5 (November), 197.

Kiš, Danilo 1996. *Homo Poeticus: Essays and Interviews*. Manchester: Carcanet.

Kiss, Béla 1946. *Bartók Béla művészete* [The art of Béla Bartók]. Kolozsvár: Ifjú Erdély Kiadása.

Kligman, Gail 1988. *The Wedding of the Dead: Ritual, Poetics, and Popular Culture in Transylvania*. Berkeley, Los Angeles and London: University of California Press.

Klobucka, Anna 1997. 'Theorizing the European Periphery', *symploke* 5:1, 119–35.

Klüppelholz, Werner. 1995 [1976]. 'Komposition von Sprachlauten: György Ligeti Aventures'. *Musik als Sprache*. Saarbrücken: Pfau-Verlag, 115–39.

Kocsis, Zoltán 1976. 'Néhány szó a legújabb magyar zenéről' [A few words about the most recent Hungarian music], *Mozgó Világ* 1976:3, 3–11.

Kodály, Zoltán 1952. *A magyar népzene* [Hungarian folk music]. Budapest: Zeneműkiadó.

Kolleritsch, Otto (ed.) 1983. *Personalstil – Avantgardismus – Popularität* (Studien für Wertungsforchung 19). Wien, Graz: Universal Edition.

Konrád, György 1984. *Antipolitics*. Trans. Richard E. Allen. San Diego, New York and London: Harcourt Brace Jovanovich.

Kontler, László 2003. *A History of Hungary: Millennium in Central Europe*. New York: Palgrave Macmillan.

Kontra, Miklós 1994. 'Szubjektív megjegyzések a magyar nyelvi tervezésről' [Subjective observations about Hungarian language planning], *Irodalmi Szemle* 12, 72–81.

Kőrösi, Suzanne 1981. 'Squat Theatre's "Mr Dead and Mrs Free"', *TDR/The Drama Review: A Journal of Performance Studies* 25:4, 75–81.

Kostakeva, Marija 1996. *Die imaginäre Gattung: Über das musiktheatralische Werk G. Ligetis*. New York: Peter Lang.

Kosztolányi, Dezső 1977. *Gondolatok a nyelvről* [Thoughts about language]. Bucharest: Kriterion.

Kovács, András 1978. 'Fiatal radikálisok' [Young radicals], *Mozgó Világ* 1978/5, 15–24.

Kovács, János 1955. 'Az V. Ifjúsági Találkozó zeneszerzői pályázatán kitüntetett magyar művek' [Prizewinning Hungarian works at the Fifth Youth Meeting composers' competition], *Új Zenei Szemle* 6:11 (November), 8–15.

  1960. 'Szervánszky hat zenekari darabjáról' [On Szervánszky's Six Orchestral Pieces], *Muzsika* 3:3 (March), 40–2.

Kovács, Sándor 1979. 'Korunk zenéje 1979 (1)' [Music of our Time 1979 (1)], *Muzsika* 22:12 (December), 1–9.

  1980. 'Korunk zenéje 1979 (2)' [Music of our Time 1979 (2)], *Muzsika* 23:1 (January), 8–13.

  1983. 'Korunk zenéje '82' [Music of our Time 1982], *Muzsika* 26:1 (January), 19–26.

Kroó, György 1958. 'Maros vonós-szimfóniája' [Maros' String Symphony], *Muzsika* 1:2 (February), 32.

  1971. *A magyar zeneszerzés 25 éve* [25 years of Hungarian composition]. Budapest: Zeneműkiadó.

  1975. 'Száz perc Kurtág' [One hundred minutes of Kurtág], *Élet és Irodalom*, 18 October.

  1978. 'Kurtág György kódjai' [György Kurtág's codes], *Élet és Irodalom*, 14 October.

  1979. 'Ligeti', *Élet és Irodalom*, 27 October.

  1980. *Ungarische Musik – gestern und heute*. Trans. Heribert Thierry. Budapest: Corvina.

1982a. 'Two major works from György Kurtág' [opp. 16 and 17], *The New Hungarian Quarterly* 13:85 (Spring), 208–12.

1982b. 'Egyetlen énekhangra' [For a single singing voice], *Élet és Irodalom*, 3 December.

1994. *Szabolcsi Bence* (vols. I and II). Budapest: Liszt Ferenc Zeneművészeti Főiskola.

Kroó, György (ed.) 1971a. *Kortárs zeneszerzők között* [Among contemporary composers]. Budapest: Zeneműkiadó.

(ed.) 1971b. 'Ligeti György'. Radio programme recorded 5 August; broadcast date unknown. Archive no. A – 134908/2, 55 minutes.

Kropfinger, Klaus 1973. 'Ligeti und die Tradition', in *Zwischen Tradition und Fortschritt* (Veröffentlichungen des Instituts fur neue Musik und Musikerziehung 13), ed. Rudolf Stephan, Mainz: Schott, 131–42.

Kundera, Milan 1984. 'The tragedy of Central Europe', in *The New York Review of Books*, 26 April, 33–8.

Kurtág, György and Bálint András Varga 2003. 'It's not my ears that do my hearing', *The New Hungarian Quarterly* 42:161 (Spring), 126–34.

Laki, Peter (ed.) 1995. *Bartók and his World*. Princeton: Princeton University Press.

Lampert, Vera 1973 (ed. and preface). *Jemnitz Sándor válogatott zenekritikái* [Selected music reviews of Sándor Jemnitz]. Budapest: Zeneműkiadó.

Larner, Gerald 1986. 'Beauty and the monk', *The Guardian*, 20 November.

László, Ferenc 2003. 'Ligeti a hídon. *A musica ricercata és a Hat bagatell: az exodus zenéi*' [Ligeti on the bridge. *Musica ricercata* and Six Bagatelles: musics of exodus], *Magyar Zene* 41:4, 361–76.

Lázár, Eszter and Bálint András Varga (eds.) 1973. 'Interjú kortárs zeneszerzőkkel' [Interview with contemporary composers]. Radio programme, recorded 12 February 1973, broadcast 19 April 1973. Archive no. A – 158719/2, 75 minutes 35 seconds.

Legány, Dezső (ed.) 1982. *Kodály Zoltán levelei* [Letters of Zoltán Kodály]. Budapest: Zeneműkiadó.

Leibowitz, René 1947. 'Béla Bartók, ou la possibilité du compromise dans la musique contemporaine', *Les temps modernes* 3:25 (October), 705–34.

Lendvai, Ernő 1947a. 'Bartók: "Improvisations" sorozatáról (1920)' [On Bartók's 'Improvisations' series], *Zenei Szemle* 3, 151–67.

Lendvai, Ernő 1947b. 'Bartók: Az éjszaka zenéje. (1926)' [Bartók: The music of the night (1926)]. *Zenei Szemle* 4, 216–18.

1948. 'Bartók: Szonáta két zongorára és ütőhangszerekre (az I. tétel analízise)' [Bartók: Sonata for two pianos and percussion (analysis of the 1st movement)], *Zenei Szemle* 12, 413–26.

1955a. *Bartók stílusa* [Bartók's style]. Budapest: Zeneműkiadó.

1955b. 'Bevezetés a Bartók-művek elemzésébe' [Introduction to the analysis of Bartók's music]. In *Zenetudományi tanulmányok Liszt Ferenc és Bartók Béla emlékére* [Musicological studies in memory of Ferenc Liszt and Béla Bartók], ed. Bence Szabolcsi and Dénes Bartha, Budapest: Akadémiai kiadó, 461–517.

1956. 'Válasz Sólyom K. és Újfalussy [sic] J. cikkére' [Response to K. Sólyom and J. Ujfalussy's articles], *Új Zenei Szemle* 7:1, 17–22.

1971. *Béla Bartók. An Analysis of his Music*. London: Kahn and Averill.

1984. 'Remarks on Roy Howat's "Principles of Proportional Analysis"', *Music Analysis* 3:3, 255–64.

1999. *Bartók's Style*. Trans. Paul Merrick and Judit Pokoly. Budapest: Akkord.

Lengyel, Balázs 1974. 'Rába, Tandori', *Élet és Irodalom* 16 February.

Lentsner, Dina 2001. 'The structure of what is beyond the words: musico-poetic analysis of the fragment from *Scenes from a Novel*, op. 19 by György Kurtág', *Studia Musicologica Academiae Scientiarum Hungaricae* 43:4, 323–32.

Lichtenfeld, Monika 1981. 'Musik mit schlecht gebundener Krawatte', *Neue Zeitschrift für Musik* 142, 471–3.

1987. '". . . und alles Schone hatt' er behalten . . .": Fragmente zu Ligetis Ästhetik', in *Gyorgy Ligeti: Personalstil – Avantgardismus – Popularität*, Vienna: Universal, 122–33.

Lichtenfeld, Monika (ed.) forthcoming. *György Ligeti: Gesammelte Schriften* (2 vols.). Mainz: Schott.

Ligeti, György 1948a. '*Veress Sándor*: Billegető muzsika' [Sándor Veress: Fingerlarks], *Zene-pedagógia* 2:3 (March), 43.

1948b. 'Bartók: Medvetánc (1908). Elemzés' [Bartók: Beardance (1908). Analysis], *Zenei Szemle* 5, 251–4.

1948c. 'Gát József: Kottaolvasás' [József Gát: Score-reading], *Zenei Szemle* 5, 277.

1948d. 'Österreichische Musikzeitschrift', *Zenei Szemle* 5, 284–5.

1948e. 'Kották' [Scores], *Zenei Szemle* 6, 337.

1949a. 'Neue Musik in Ungarn', *Melos* 16:1, 5–8.

1949b. 'Von Bartók bis Veress. Neues aus Budapest', *Melos* 16:2, 5–8.

1949c. 'Szervánszky Endre: Vonósnégyes. M. Művészeti Tanács kiadása', *Zenei Szemle* (August), 103.

1949d. 'Járdányi Pál: Szonáta két zongorára. (M. Művészeti Tanács kiadása)' [Pál Járdányi: Sonata for two pianos], *Zenei Szemle* (August), 103.

1949e. 'Sugár: Vonóstrió. (A. M. Művészeti Tanács kiadása)' [Sugár: String Trio], *Zenei Szemle* (August), 105–6.

1950a. 'Neues aus Budapest: Zwölftonmusik oder "Neue Tonalität"?', *Melos* 17:2, 45–8.

1950b. 'Népzenekutatás Romániában' [Folk-music research in Romania], *Új Zenei Szemle* 1:3 (August), 18–22.

1953. 'Egy aradmegyei román együttes' [A Romanian folk ensemble in the county of Arad]. In *Kodály Emlékkönyv. Zenetudományi Tanulmányok*, ed. Dénes Bartha and Bence Szabolcsi, Budapest: Akadémiai Kiadó, 399–404.

1954a. *Klasszikus összhangzattan* [Classical harmony], Budapest: Zeneműkiadó.

1954b. 'Járdányi Pál és Szervánszky Endre fuvolaszonatinái' [Pál Járdányi and Endre Szervánszky's Flute Sonatas], *Új Zenei Szemle* 5:12 (December), 26–8.

1955. 'Megjegyzések a bartóki kromatika kialakulásának egyes feltételeiről' [Observations on the conditions of Bartók's development of chromaticism], *Új Zenei Szemle* 6:9 (September), 41–4.

1956. *A klasszikus harmóniarend* [The system of classical harmony], (2 vols.). Budapest: Zeneműkiadó.

1957. 'Pierre Boulez: Entscheidung und Automatik in der Struktur 1a', *die reihe* 4 ('Junge Komponisten'), 38–63.

1973. 'Musikalische Erinnerungen aus Kindheit und Jugend', in *Festschrift für einen Verleger. Ludwig Strecker zum 90. Geburtstag*, ed. Carl Dahlhaus, Mainz: Schott, 54–60.

1978a. 'On music and politics', *Perspectives of New Music* 16:2 (Spring/Summer), 19–24.

1978b. 'György Ligeti', in *Mein Judentum*, ed. Hans Jürgen Schultz, Berlin: Kreuz Verlag, 234–47.

1993 (1960). 'States, events, transformations', trans. Jonathan Bernard. *Perspectives of New Music* 31:1 (Winter), 164–71.

1996. 'Önarckép pesti muzsikustársakkal: a ... *quasi una fantasia* ... op. 27 (1987–8) első tételének (Introduzione) rövid elemzése' [Self-portrait with musician companions from Pest: a short analysis of the first movement of ... *quasi una fantasia* ... op. 27 (1987–8)], *Muzsika* 39:2 (February), 9–11.

Ligeti in Conversation. 1983. [Discussions with Ligeti and Péter Várnai, Josef Häusler, Claude Samuel and himself.] London: Eulenberg.

Ligeti, Lajos (ed.) 1986 (1943). *A magyarság őstörténete* [The ancient history of the Hungarian people]. Budapest: Akadémiai kiadó.

Lobanova, Marina 2003. *György Ligeti. Style, Ideas, Poetics*. Berlin: Ernst Kuhn.

Lőrincze, Lajos 1953. *Nyelv és élet* [Language and life]. Budapest: Művelt nép.

1982. 'Lőrincze Lajos', in *Így láttuk Kodályt* [This is how we saw Kodály], ed. Ferenc Bónis, Budapest: Zeneműkiadó, 274–87.

Lukács, Georg 1964. *Essays on Thomas Mann*. Trans. Stanley Mitchell. London: Merlin Press.

Lutz, Lesle 1988. 'In meiner Musik gibt es kein Weltanschauung: Gespräch mit György Ligeti', *Das Orchester* 36, 885–90.

Mádl, Antal and Judit Győri (eds.) 1977. *Thomas Mann und Ungarn. Essays, Dokumente, Bibliographie*, Cologne and Vienna: Böhlau Verlag.

Mann, Thomas 1961. *Genesis of a Novel*. Trans. Richard and Clara Winston. London: Secker and Warburg.

Mann, Thomas 1968. *Doctor Faustus*. Trans. H. T. Lowe-Porter. London: Penguin Books.

Márai, Sándor 1996. *Memoir of Hungary 1944–1948*. Translated with an introduction and notes by Albert Tezla. Budapest: Corvina.

Maróti Gyula and László Révész [*c*. 1981?] Undated. *Öt évszázad a Magyar énekkari kultúra történetéből* [From five centuries of the history of Hungarian choral culture]. Budapest: Népművelődési Propaganda Iroda.

Maróthy, János 1950. 'Kadosa Pál három kantátája' [Pál Kadosa's three cantatas], *Új Zenei Szemle* 1:3 (August), 23–7.
    1974. *Music and the Bourgeois. Music and the Proletarian*, trans. Éva Róna. Budapest: Akadémia Kiadó.
    1975. *Zene, forradalom, szocializmus. Szabó Ferenc útja* [Music, revolution, socialism. The path of Ferenc Szabó]. Budapest: Magvető Könyvkiadó.
    1982. 'Korunk zenéje '81' [Music of our Time '81], *Muzsika* 25:1 (January), 6–14.
    1986a. 'A falakon kívül' avagy Korunk zenéje II' ['Outside the walls', or Music of our Time II], *Muzsika* 29:2 (February), 9–10.
    1986b. '22. Festival Pontino di Musica', *Muzsika* 29:10 (October), 22–3.
McLay, Margaret P. 1982. 'Experimental music in Hungary: the New Music Studio', in Varga (ed.) 1982, 92–106.
    1983. 'Twenty-five years of Hungarian music', *The New Hungarian Quarterly* 14:90 (Summer), 199–206.
    1984a. 'György Kurtág at the Bath International Festival', *The New Hungarian Quarterly* 25:96 (Winter), 207–12.
    1984b. 'György Kurtág's Microludes'. *Tempo* 151 (December), 17–23.
Meyer, Felix and Heidy Zimmerman (eds.) 2006. *Edgar Varèse: Composer, Sound Sculptor, Visionary*. Rochester: Boydell and Brewer, in cooperation with the Paul Sacher Foundation.
Michel, Pierre 1985. *György Ligeti. Compositeur d'aujourd'hui*. Paris: Minerve.
Mihály, András 1949. 'Bartók Béla és az utána következő nemzedék' [Béla Bartók and the generation following him], *Zenei Szemle* 3:1 (March), 2–15.
    1950. 'Válasz egy Bartók kritikára' [Response to a Bartók critique], *Új Zenei Szemle* 1:4 (September), 48–56.
Molnár, Antal 1925. *Az új zene.* [The new music]. Budapest: Révai Kiadó.
    1937a. *A ma zenéje* [Music of today]. Budapest: Somló Béla Könyvkiadó.
    1937b. 'Bartók Béla új kórusművei' [Béla Bartók's new choral works], in Bonis (ed.) 1961, 65–7.
    1947. *Az új muzsika szelleme* [The spirit of new music]. Budapest: Dante.
Moulinier, Pierre 1999. 'A contemporary grand opera', *Three Sisters* CD booklet (Deutsche Grammophon 459 694–2), 9–15.
Munkácsi, Bernát (collected) and Béla Kálmán (ed.) 1986. *Wogulisches Wörterbuch*, Budapest: Akadémiai kiadó.
Murray, David 1982. 'London Sinfonietta/Round House', *Financial Times* 3 August.
Nádas, Péter and Richard Swartz 1992. *Párbeszéd: Négy Nap Ezerkilencszáznyolcvankilencben* [Dialogue: four days in 1989]. Pécs: Jelenkor.
Nagy, Béla J. 1937. 'Dr. György Lajos: Anyanyelvünk védelme' [Dr. György Lajos: The protection of our mother tongue], *Magyar Nyelv* 33:3–4 (March–April), 120–1.
    1938. 'Szórend és hazaárulás' [Word order and national betrayal], *Magyar Nyelv* 34:9–10 (November–December), 331–5.
Nagy, Katalin S. 1993. *Ország Lili*. Budapest: Arthis.

Nagy, Olivér 1975. *A Magyar kórusművészet 30 éve* [Thirty years of Hungarian choral music]. Budapest: Zeneműkiadó.

Nagy, Olivér 1997. 'Portré-vázlat Bárdos Lajosról' [Portrait sketch of Lajos Bárdos]. In *Bárdos Lajos emlékkonferencia 1996.XI.16*, ed. Mária Póczonyi, Budapest: A Bárdos Lajos Társaság, 25–36.

Nancy, Jean-Luc 1993. *The Birth to Presence*. Trans. Brian Holmes and others. Stanford: Stanford University Press.

Németh, Lajos 1970. *Csontváry Kosztka Tivadar*. Budapest: Corvina.

Nielinger-Vakil, Carola 1998. 'K^2: on György Kurtág's *Kafka Fragments* op. 24', in 'Smallest possible wholes. Aphorism as a Recurring Problem in Musical Construction', Ph.D. dissertation, University of London, 198–225.

Nordwall, Ove 1966. 'Sweden' (introduction to and review of Ligeti's *Requiem*), *Musical Quarterly* 52:1 (January), 109–13.

  1971. *György Ligeti: Eine Monographie*. Trans. from Swedish (1968) by Hans Eppstein. Mainz: Schott.

O'Quinn, Jim 1979. 'Squat Theatre Underground', *TDR/The Drama Review: A Journal of Performance Studies* 23:4, 7–26.

  1980. 'Squat's "Three Sisters"', *TDR/The Drama Review: A Journal of Performance Studies* 24:4, 111–12.

Oeschlägel, Reinhard 1989. 'Ja, ich war ein utopischer Sozialist', *MusikTexte* 28–29, 85–102.

Op de Coul, Paul 1974. 'Sprachkomposition bei Ligeti: "Lux Aeterna". Nebst einigen Randbemerkungen zu den Begriffen Sprach- und Lautkomposition', in *Musik und der Sprache*, ed. Rudolf Stephan, Mainz: Schott, 59–69.

Ottó, Ferenc 1936. *Bartók Béla a Cantata profana tükrében* [Béla Bartók in the light of *Cantata profana*]. Budapest: Kéve Könyvkiadó.

Pándi, Marianne 1976. 'Zenei jegyzetek' (review including Ligeti's *Atmosphères*), *Népszabadság* 10 October.

Pándi, Marianne 1979. 'Zenei jegyzetek' (review including Ligeti's composer portrait), *Népszabadság* 6 October.

Papp, Géza 1997. 'A Magyar Kórus utolsó száma' [The last issue of *Magyar Kórus*]. In *Bárdos Lajos emlékkonferencia 1996.XI.16*, ed. Mária Póczonyi, Budapest: A Bárdos Lajos Társaság, 67–74.

Papp, Márta 1972. 'Új Zenei Stúdió', *Muzsika* 14:2, 26.

  2000. 'Composer at the border of Europe: György Kurtág and his Russian choruses', *Journal of the Asian Music Research Institute, Seoul National University* 22, 161–8.

Pernye, András 1959. 'Magyar szerzők' [Hungarian composers], *Muzsika* 2:8, 40–1.

  1960a. 'Szervánszky Fúvósötös' [Szervánszky's Wind Quintet], *Magyar Zene* 1:2, 200–2.

  1960b. 'Egy hét Budapest hangversenytermeiben' [One week in Budapest concert halls], *Magyar Nemzet*, 16 January.

  1960c. 'Mérleg' [Weighing up], *Muzsika* 3:8, 1–3.

1961a. 'Komponálási módszer avagy az anarchia ideológiája' [Compositional method or the ideology of anarchy], *Muzsika* 4:3, 30–2 (Part I); 4:4, 29–32 (Part II).

1961b. 'A dodekafónia formai problémái' [The formal problems of dodecaphony], *Muzsika* 4:5, 17–20 (Part I); 4:6, 32–4 (Part II).

1961c. 'A dodekafónia esztétikai problémái – összefoglalás' [The aesthetic problems of dodecaphony – summary], *Muzsika* 4:8, 21–3 (Part I); 4:9, 29–31 (Part II).

1961d. 'C'est la guerre. Petrovics Emil operájának rádióbemutatójáról' [On the radio première of Emil Petrovics's opera], *Muzsika* 4:11 (November), 19–22.

1962. 'Egy hét Budapest hangversenytermeiben' [One week in Budapest concert halls], *Magyar Nemzet*, 12 May.

1963a. 'Egy hét Budapest hangversenytermeiben' [One week in Budapest concert halls], *Magyar Nemzet*, 30 March.

1963b. 'Egy hét Budapest hangversenytermeiben' [One week in Budapest concert halls], *Magyar Nemzet*, 23 November.

Péteri, Lóránt 2000. 'Adalékok a hazai zenetudományi kutatás intézménytörténetéhez (1947–1969)' [Contributions to the history of national institutions for musicological research], *Magyar Zene* 38:2 (May), 161–91.

2002. '"Légy résen! Támad a burzsoá avantgardizmus". Magyar zenészek gyümölcsöző moszkvai tanulmányútja' ['Be alert! Bourgeois avant-gardism is on the rise.' Hungarian musicians' fruitful study trip to Moscow], *2000* 14:3 (March), 63–7.

2003 (I and II). 'Szabolcsi Bence és a magyar zeneélet diskurzusai (1948–1956)' [Bence Szabolcsi and the discourses of the Hungarian music life], *Magyar Zene* 41:1 (February), 3–48 (Part I) and 41:2 (March), 237–56 (Part II).

Petersen, Peter 1991. 'Bartók–Lutoslawski–Ligeti: Einige Bemerkungen zu ihrer Kompositionstechnik unter dem Aspekt der Tonhohe', *Hamburger Jahrbuch fur Musikwissenschaft* 11, 289–309.

Pilinszky, János 1978. *Crater*. Trans. Peter Jay. London: Anvil Press.

1989. *The Desert of Love*. Trans. János Csokits and Ted Hughes. London: Anvil. See also Hughes 1989.

1992. *Conversations with Sheryl Sutton. The Novel of a Dialogue*. Trans. Peter Jay and Eva Major. Manchester: Carcanet Press, in association with Corvina, Budapest.

1997. *Pilinszky János összes versei* [The complete poems of János Pilinszky]. Budapest: Osiris.

1999. *Publicisztikai írások* [Journalistic writings]. Budapest: Osiris.

Politi, Edna 1985. 'Entretiens avec György Ligeti', *Contrechamps* 4, 123–7.

Potter, Keith 1986. 'Cult Composer. Keith Potter profiles the Hungarian, György Kurtág', *International Music and Opera Guide*, 56–8.

Pusztay, János 1977. *Az 'ugor-török' háború után* [After the 'Ugrian-Turkic' war]. Budapest: Magvető.

Radnóti, Sándor 1974. 'Talált tárgy költészete' [The poetry of objets trouvés], *Új Írás* 14:4 (April), 123–7.
Raics, István 1966. 'Maros Rudolf: Eufónia 64', *Muzsika* 3:4, 6.
  1974. 'Bárdos Lajos zeneszerzői világa' [The compositional world of Lajos Bárdos], *Muzsika* 16:10 (October), 1–3.
Révész, Sándor 1997. *Aczél és Korunk* [Aczél and our time]. Budapest: Sík.
Romsics, Ignác 1999. *Hungary in the Twentieth Century*. Trans. Tim Wilkinson. Budapest: Corvina.
Sallis, Friedemann 1996. *An Introduction to the Early Works of György Ligeti* (Berliner Musik Studien 6). Cologne: Studio Verlag.
Salmenhaara, Erkki 1969. *Das musikalische Material und seine Behandlung in den Werken Apparitions, Atmosphères, Aventures und Requiem von György Ligeti*. Trans. from Finnish by Helke Sander in collaboration with the author (*Acta Musicologica Fennica* 2). Helsinki: Suomen Musikkitieteellinen Seura Musikvetenskapliga Sällskapet I Finland.
Samson, Jim 1985. '*The Music of Béla Bartók: A Study of Tonality and Progression in Twentieth-Century Music* by Elliott Antokoletz' (review), *Tempo* 155 (December), 54–5.
Sárközy István 1953. 'Tömegdalok, kórusok és kantáták a zenei hét hangversenyein' [Mass songs, choruses and cantatas in concerts at the Hungarian Music Week]. *Szabad Nép*, 31 October.
Sárosi, Bálint 1973. *Zenei anyanyelvünk* [Our musical mother tongue]. Budapest: Gondolat.
Satory, Stephen 1990. 'Colloquy: An Interview with György Ligeti in Hamburg', *Canadian University Music Review* 10:1, 101–17.
  1991. 'String quartet composition in Hungary, 1958–1981', Ph.D. dissertation, University of Toronto.
Schiff, András 2003. *Gondolatok a zenéről, zeneszerzőkről, önmagáról* [Thoughts about music, composers, and oneself]. Budapest: Vince.
Schmelz, Peter 2005. 'Andrey Volkonsky and the beginnings of unofficial music in the Soviet Union', *Journal of the American Musicological Association* 58:1, 139–208.
Schneider, David E. 1996. 'A context for Béla Bartók on the eve of World War II: The Violin Concerto (1938)', *Repercussions* 5:1–2, 21–68.
  2001. 'Hungarian nationalism and the reception of Bartók's music, 1904–1940', in *The Cambridge Companion to Bartók*, ed. Amanda Bayley, Cambridge: Cambridge University Press, 177–89.
  (forthcoming). *Bartók, Hungary, and the Renewal of Tradition: Case Studies in the Intersection of Modernity and Nationality*. Berkeley and Los Angeles: University of California Press.
Schneider, David E. trans. 1995. 'Béla Bartók: An Interview by Dezső Kosztolányi', in *Bartók and his World*, ed. Peter Laki, Princeton: Princeton University Press, 228–34.

Scholem, Gershom 1965. *On the Kabbalah and Its Symbolism*. Trans. Ralph Manheim. London: Routledge and Kegan Paul.

Schöpflin, George 2000. *Nation, Identity Power. The New Politics of Europe*, London: Hurst and Co.

Schöpflin, George and Nancy Wood (eds.) 1989. *In Search of Central Europe*. Cambridge: Polity in association with Basil Blackwell.

Seiber, Mátyás 1947. 'Kodály's *Missa brevis*', *Tempo* 4, 3–6.

Seherr-Thoss, Peter 1998. *György Ligeti's Oper* Le grand macabre, *erste Fassung. Entstehung und Deutung: von der Imagination bis zur Realisation einer musikdramatischen Idee*. Eisenach: Wagner.

Selmezci, Elek 1986. *Világhódító bábok: az Állami Bábszínház krónikája* [World-conquering puppets: chronicle of the State Puppet Theatre]. Budapest: Corvina.

Shank, Adele Edling and Shank, Theodore 1978. 'Squat Theatre's "Andy Warhol's Last Love"', *TDR/The Drama Review: A Journal of Performance Studies* 22:3, 11–22.

Shank, Theodore 1992. 'The shock of the actual: disrupting the theatrical illusion' in Patrick D. Murphy (ed.), *Staging the Impossible: The Fantastic Mode in Modern Drama*, Westport, CT: Greenwood, 169–81.

Sherwood, Peter 1996. '"A nation may be said to live in its language": some sociohistorical perspectives on attitudes to Hungarian', in *The Literature of Nationalism. Essays on East European Identity*, ed. Robert B. Pynsent, London: School of Slavonic and East European Studies, 27–39.

Smalley, Roger 1972. 'Colin Mason: a memoir', *Tempo* 100, 23–4.

Solymosi, Emőke 2000. *Lajtha László Vígoperája, A kék kalap (Le Chapeau bleu, op. 51)*. [László Lajtha's comedy opera, *The Blue Cap*], dissertation, Liszt Academy of Music, Budapest.

Sólyom, Károly 1955. 'Lendvai Ernő "tengelyrendszeréről"' [About Ernő Lendvai's 'axis system'], *Új Zenei Szemle* 6:1, 1–11.

Somfai, László 1974. 'Durkó Zsolt szerzői estje' [Zsolt Durkó concert], *Muzsika* 16:12 (December), 1–2.

   2000. 'Zenei köznyelv a 18. században. Kutatástörténeti visszatekintés Szabolcsi Bence gondolatának utóéletéről' [Musical vernacular in the eighteenth century. A retrospective of research on the thought of Bence Szabolcsi]. In *Zenetudományi dolgozatok 2000*. Budapest: Zenetudományi Intézet, 25–9.

Sperl, Ingo and Ghizela Suliteanu 1998. *Die Totenklage in Rumänien: musikethnologische und psychologische Studien (Bocetul în România: studii etnomuzicologice și psihologice)*. Studien zur interdisziplinären Thanatologie Volume 5. Münster: Lit Verlag.

Squat Theatre 1978. 'Answer: making a point', *TDR/The Drama Review: A Journal of Performance Studies* 22:3, 2–10.

Stalin, Joseph 1976. *Marxism and Problems of Linguistics*. Beijing: Foreign Languages Press.

Steiner, George 1975. *After Babel. Aspects of Language and Translation.* London, Oxford and New York: Oxford University Press.
  1996. *No Passion Spent. Essays 1978–1996.* London, Boston: Faber and Faber.
Steinitz, Richard 1996. 'Weeping and wailing', *Musical Times* 137 (August), 12–22.
  2003. *György Ligeti: Music of the Imagination.* London: Faber and Faber.
Stürzbecker, Ursula 1971. 'György Ligeti', in *Werkstattgespräche mit Komponisten*, Cologne: Gerig, 32–45.
Suchoff, Benjamin 1993. 'Synthesis of East and West: *Mikrokosmos*', in *The Bartók Companion*, ed. Malcolm Gillies, London: Faber and Faber, 189–211.
Suchoff, Benjamin (ed.) 1976. *Béla Bartók Essays.* Lincoln and London: University of Nebraska Press.
Suchoff, Benjamin (ed.) 1997. *Béla Bartók Studies in Ethnomusicology.* Lincoln and London: University of Nebraska Press.
Sz. B. (= Bence Szabolcsi) 1927. Concert review, *Pesti Napló*, 8 March.
Szabó, Attila T. 1970. *Anyanyelvünk életéből. Válogatott tanulmányok, cikkek* [From the life of our mother tongue. Selected studies, articles]. Bucharest: Kriterion.
Szabó, Helga 1983. 'Éneklő Ifjúság 1925–1944, I' [Singing youth, 1925–44, I], *Magyar Zene* 24:4, 376–415.
  1984a. 'Éneklő Ifjúság 1925–1944, II' [Singing youth, 1925–44, II], *Magyar Zene* 25:1, 92–112.
  1984b. 'Éneklő Ifjúság 1945–1975, I' [Singing youth, 1945–75, I], *Magyar Zene* 25:3, 306–32.
  1984c. 'Éneklő Ifjúság 1945–1975, II' [Singing youth, 1945–75, II], *Magyar Zene* 25:4, 418–35.
  1994. 'Lendvai Ernő emlékezete' [In memory of Ernő Lendvai], *Magyar Zene* IIIV/1, 23–4.
Szabó, László Cs. 1989. 'The knowledge of the evidence', *The New Hungarian Quarterly* 30:115 (Autumn), 42–51.
Szabolcsi, Bence 1948. 'Mai magyar szerzők művei' [Works of contemporary Hungarian composers], *Zenei Szemle* 2:8 (December), 444–5.
  1950. 'Bartók és a népzene' [Bartók and folk music], *Új Zenei Szemle* 1:4, 39–43.
  1951a. 'Sztálin nyelvtudományi cikkeinek tanulsága a zenetudomány szempontjából' [The lesson of Stalin's articles on linguistics from the perspective of musicology], *Új Zenei Szemle* 2:9 (September), 2–4.
  1951b. 'Intonáció, népzene és nemzeti hagyomány' [Intonation, folk music and national tradition], *Új Zenei Szemle* 2:12 (December), 1–5.
  1954. *Népzene és történelem: tanulmányok* [Folk music and history: essays]. Budapest: Akadémiai kiadó.
  1956. 'A III. Magyar Zenei Hét után' [After the Hungarian Music Week no. III] and 'Az előadás vitája' [The debate on the performances], *Új Zenei Szemle* 7:5 (May), 29–34 and 34–54.
Szabolcsi, Miklós (ed.) 1966. *A magyar irodalom története 1919-től napjainkig* [The history of Hungarian literature from 1919 to today], Volume VI of *A magyar irodalom története*, ed. István Sőtér.

Szekacs-Weisz, Judit and Ivan Ward (eds.) 2005. *Lost Childhood and the Language of Exile*. London: IMAGO MLPC and Freud Museum Publications.

Székely, András 1975. 'A zenei könyvtár és közönsége' [The music library and its audience], *Muzsika* 17:2 (February), 15–16.

Szelényi, István 1927. 'A reakció győzelméhez' [The triumph of the reactionary], *Crescendo* 1:12 (June–July), 2–6.

  1928. 'A modern zene főbb áramlatai' [The main currents of modern music], *Crescendo* 2:6–7 (January–February), 3–11.

  1941. 'Bartók "Mikrokozmosz"-a', *Énekszó* 9:9, 845–6.

  1942a. 'Bartók stíluskorszakai' [Bartók's stylistic periods], *Zenei Szemle* 2, 69–72.

  1942b. 'Újabb harmónia-rendszerek' [New harmonic systems], *Énekszó* 9:5 (April), 909–15.

  1944. 'Az egyházi hangnemek és a dúr-moll rendszer kapcsolatai' [Connections between church modalities and the major–minor system]. *Énekszó* 11:5, (April–May), 72–6.

  1956a. 'Tengelyrendszer, Tonalitás, Atonalitás' [Axis system, tonality, atonality]. *Új Zenei Szemle* 7:2, 2.

  1956b. 'Tengelyrendszer, funkció, Bartók zenéje' [Axis system, function, Bartók's music]. *Új Zenei Szemle* 7:3, 19–21.

Széll, Jenő (ed.) 1981. *Húzzad, húzzad muzsikásom . . . A hangszeres népzene feltámadása* [The rise of instrumental folk music]. Budapest: Múzsák Közművelődési kiadó.

Szigeti, József 1947. 'Magyar líra 1947-ben' [Hungarian poetry in 1947], *Fórum* 10 (October), 737–62.

Szigeti, István 1984. 'A Budapest interview with György Ligeti', *The New Hungarian Quarterly* 25:94 (Summer), 205–9.

Szilágyi, Dezső (ed.) 1978. *A mai magyar bábszínház* [Today's Hungarian Puppet Theatre]. Budapest: Corvina.

Szitha, Tünde 2000. 'Az amerikai minimálzene hatása az Új Zenei Stúdió zeneszerzőire az 1970-es és az 1980-as években' [The influence of American minimalist music on composers of the New Music Studio in the 1970s and 1980s], *Magyar Zene* 36:2, 127–40.

  2003. '"Talán az 'a' helyezése dönti el az eldöntetlen maradót . . .": Szöveg, dallam és hangrendszer összefüggései Jeney Zoltán műveiben' ['Perhaps the place of "the" decides the undecided remainder . . .' Connections between text, melody and pitch system in the works of Zoltán Jeney], *Muzsika* 46:8, 36–42.

Szitha, Tünde and Károly Peller 1986. 'Hanglemez. Eötvös Péter: Tücsökzene, A szél szekvenciái' [Recording. Péter Eötvös: Cricket music, Sequences of the Wind], *Muzsika* 20:7 (July), 46.

Tallián, Tibor 1974. 'Korunk zenéje a hangversenyeken' [Music of our Time in concert], *Muzsika* 16:12, 3–12.

  'Mózes – Durkó Zsolt operája' [*Moses* – Zsolt Durkó's opera], *Muzsika* 20:7 (July), 1–8.

  1979. 'Korunk zenéje (1)' [Music of our Time], *Muzsika* 22:1, 1–14.

1980. '"Termékeny közszellemet, szabad polifóniát, felszabadult tavaszi légkört . . ." Szabolcsi, a zenepolitikus' ['In favour of the productive public spirit, free polyphony, a liberated spring atmosphere'. Szabolcsi, the music politician], *Magyar Zene* 21:4 (December), 402–10.

1998. 'Magyar versenymű a 20. század első felében' [The Hungarian concerto in the first half of the twentieth century]. *Zenetudományi dolgozatok 1997–1998*. Budapest: Akadémiai kiadó, 151–62.

1999a. *Musik in Ungarn*. Frankfurt: Gemeinnützige Gesellschaft.

1999b. 'From Singspiel to post-modern. Two hundred years of Hungarian opera', *The Hungarian Quarterly* 43:169 (Spring), 144–156.

2000. '"És újrakezdjük az életünket": Eötvös Péter, Három nővér–Magyar Állami Operaház' ['And we start our lives all over again': Péter Eötvös: Three Sisters – Hungarian State Opera], *Muzsika* 43:6 (June), 22–7.

Tallián, Tibor, László Ujházy 1987. 'Hanglemez', *Muzsika* 30:8, 45–8.

Tandori, Dezső 1973. *Egy talált tárgy megtisztítása* [The cleaning of an objet trouvé]. Budapest: Magvető.

1978. 'Mi mondható róla, mondható róla' [What can be said about it, is sayable], *Híd* 42:1–2, 72–88 and 209–17.

1986. *Birds and Other Relations: Selected Poetry of Dezső Tandori*. Trans. Bruce Berlind. Princeton, New Jersey: Princeton University Press.

1989. *Vigyázz magadra, ne törődj velem. Válogatott versek (1959–1987)* [Take care of yourself, don't bother about me]. Budapest: Zrínyi Kiadó.

Tardy, László. 1997. 'Repertoár váltások a XX. századi magyar egyházzenében' [Repertoire changes in twentieth-century Hungarian church music], in *Bárdos Lajos emlékkonferencia 1996.XI.16*, ed. Mária Póczonyi, Budapest: A Bárdos Lajos Társaság, 139–48.

Tarján, Tamás 1974. 'Tandori Dezsőről' [On Dezső Tandori], *Kortárs* 14, 462–8.

1994. 'Két köntös: A szonett és a haiku' [Two guises: the sonnet and the haiku], *Holmi* 6:4, 524–35.

Taruskin, Richard 1997. *Defining Russia Musically. Historical and Hermeneutic Essays*. Princeton and Oxford: Princeton University Press.

2005. *The Oxford History of Western Music*. Volume V: 'The Late Twentieth Century'. New York and Oxford: Oxford University Press.

Taylor, Stephen Andrew 1994. 'The Lamento motif: metamorphosis in Ligeti's late style'. Doctoral dissertation, Cornell University.

Thurzó, Gábor 1977. 'Pilinszky és Kurtág' [Pilinszky and Kurtág], *Élet és Irodalom*, 22 October, 12.

Tihanyi, László 1989a. 'Napló, széljegyzetekkel. Beszámoló az idei Korunk Zenéje fesztiválról (a magyar szerzők közül Dubrovay, Székely, Orbán, Reményi, Ligeti, Kurtág, Sáry, Vidovszky, Durkó, Perényi, Bozay, Vajda, Kalmár művei' [Diary, notes. Report on this year's Music of our Time festival], *Muzsika* 32:12 (December), 13–18.

1989b. 'Távlatok, koncertek, arcok, tanulságok a szombathelyi Bartók Szemináriumés Fesztiválról' [Perspectives, concerts, faces, lessons learned from the Bartók Seminar and Festival in Szombathely], *Muzsika* 32:10 (October), 3–8.

Tokaji, András 1983. *Mozgalom és hivatal. Tömegdal Magyarországon 1945–56* [Movement and office. The mass song in Hungary 1945–56]. Budapest: Zeneműkiadó.

Toop, Richard 1999. *György Ligeti*. London: Phaidon.

Török, Endre (ed.) 1983. *Beszélgetések Pilinszky Jánossal* [Conversations with Pilinszky]. Budapest: Magvető.

Tóth, Aladár 1921a. 'A francia zene új iránya és Darius Milhaud' [The new direction of French music and Darius Milhaud], *Nyugat* (June). Reprinted in Breuer 1978: 163–5.

   1923b. 'Modern zene Budapesten' [Modern music in Budapest], *Nyugat* (December). Reprinted in Breuer 1978: 206–13.

   1923c. Review. *Pesti Napló*, 19 May.

Tóth, Dénes 1941. 'Bartók és az expresszionizmus' [Bartók and expressionism], *A Zene* 12:11, 178–9.

   1949. 'A VIT zenei eseményei II' [Musical events of the World Youth Meeting II], *Színház és Mozi* 2:35 (August 31), 20.

Traub, Andreas 1986. 'Sándor Veress, Lebensweg – Schaffensweg', in *Sándor Veress Festschrift zum 80. Geburtstag*, ed. Andreas Traub. Berlin: Verlag K. Haseloff, 22–97.

Traub, Andreas (ed.) 1998. *Sándor Veress. Vorträge Briefe*. Hofheim: Wolke Verlag.

Trencsényi-Waldapfel, Imre 1946. 'Az újabb magyar gyermekirodalom' [Recent Hungarian children's literature], *Magyarok* 2:9, 550–2.

Trumpener, Kate 2000. 'Béla Bartók and the rise of comparative ethnomusicology: nationalism, race purity, and the legacy of the Austro-Hungarian empire', in *Music and the Racial Imagination*, ed. Ronald M. Radano and Philip J. Bohlman, Chicago: Chicago University Press, 403–34.

Tüskés, Tibor 1986. 'Introitusz'. In *In memoriam Pilinszky János. Senkiföldjén* [In no man's land], ed. Zoltán Hafner. Budapest: Nap kiadó, 11–21.

Ujfalussy, József 1953. 'A zenei hét második kamarazeneestje' [The second chamber concert of the Music Week no. II], *Szabad Nép*, 2 November, 2.

   1958a. 'Magyar bemutató a Budapesti Fúvósötös estjén' [Hungarian première at a Budapest Wind Quintet concert], *Muzsika* 1:2 (February), 31.

   1958b. 'Modern és új. Megjegyzések egy zongorahangversenyhez' [Modern and new. Notes on a piano recital], *Muzsika* 1:7 (July), 27–8.

   1961. 'Farkas Ferenc szerzői estje' [Ferenc Farkas concert], *Magyar Zene* 1:9 (December), 82.

Ujfalussy, József 1967. 'Mit adhat a tradíció a világnak?' [What can tradition provide the world?], *Muzsika* 10:10, 1–2.

Uritskaya, B. 1951. 'Az intonálás nemzeti rendszere' [The national system of intonation], *Új Zenei Szemle* 2:9 (September), 5–9.

V. 1963. 'Ellesett beszélgetés' [Overheard conversation], *Muzsika* 6:11 (November), 16–19.

Váczi, Tamás 1986a. 'Újabb Ligeti-monográfia' [Recent Ligeti monograph], *Muzsika* 28:7 (July), 45.

    1986b. 'Beszélgetés Eötvös Péterrel – az elektronikus zenéről' [Conversation with Péter Eötvös about electronic music], *Muzsika* 29:12 (December), 29–33.

    1987. 'Beszélgetés Eötvös Péterrel (2)' [Conversation with Péter Eötvös], *Muzsika* 30:2 (February), 10–15.

Vajda, Endre 1947. 'Weöres Sándor új könyvei' [Sándor Weöres' new books], *Válasz* 1:3 (December), 278–9.

Vajda, Miklós (ed.) 1977. *Modern Hungarian Poetry*. Includes Introduction by Miklós Vajda and Foreword by William Jay Smith. Budapest: Corvina.

Varga, Bálint András 1972. *Zenészekkel-zenéről. Beszélgetések világhírű muzsikusokkal* [With musicians about music. Conversations with world-renowned musicians]. Budapest: Minerva.

    1986. *Három kérdés, nyolcvankét zeneszerző* [Three questions, eighty-two composers]. Budapest: Editio Musica.

Varga, Bálint András (ed.) 1982. *Contemporary Hungarian Music in the International Press*. Budapest: Editio Musica.

Vargyas, Lajos (ed.) 1989. *Kodály Zoltán: Közélet, vallomások, zeneélet* [Zoltán Kodály: Public life, confessions, music life]. Budapest: Szépirodalmi kiadó.

Várhegyi, György 1952. Untitled speech printed within 'Az Ifjúsági Zenei Napok vitája', *Új Zenei Szemle* 3:11 (November), 2–17, at 7–10.

Várnai, Péter 1968. 'Kurtág: Bornemisza Péter mondásai – concerto zongorára és szopránhangra, op. 7' [Kurtág: *The Sayings of Péter Bornemisza* – concerto for piano and soprano, op. 7], *Filharmónia műsorfüzet* 37, 20–1.

    1974. 'Zenei levél' (review of Kurtág's *Splinters* op. 6c) *Magyar Hírlap*, 5 October.

    1975. 'Zenei levél' (review of Kurtág's composer portrait), *Magyar Hírlap*, 4 October.

    1979. *Beszélgetések Ligeti Györggyel* [Conversations with György Ligeti]. Budapest: Zeneműkiadó.

Vasy, Géza 1998. *Az 1945 utáni magyar irodalom alkotói* [The creators of Hungarian literature after 1945]. Budapest: Korona Nova.

Vázsonyi, Bálint 1971. *Dohnányi Ernő*. Budapest: Zeneműkiadó.

Veress, Sándor 1944. 'Zeneszerszámok az óvodában' [Musical tools in the nursery], *Magyar gyermeknevelés* 10/11, 124–6.

Vidovszky, László and Kristóf Weber 1997. *Beszélgetések a zenéről* [Conversations about music]. Pécs: Jelenkor.

Vikárius, László 2004. 'Nationalism rejected or transformed? Béla Bartók's unconventional contribution to the chorus literature', in Primož Kuret (ed.), *Choral Music and Choral Societies, and Their Role in the Development of the National Musical Cultures. 18. slovenski glasbeni dnevi. 18th Slovenian Musical Days. April 22–25, 2003, Ljubljana, Piran, Slovenia*. Ljubljana: Festival Ljubljana: 180–98.

Viski, János 1950. 'Négy fiatal zeneszerző' [Four young composers], *Új Zenei Szemle* 1:7, 39–42.

Walker, Alan 2002. 'Ernst von Dohnányi: a tribute', *The Hungarian Quarterly* 43:165 (Spring), 119–40.

Walker, Lynne 1986. 'Composer of highly individual style', *The Scotsman*, 24 November.

Walsh, Stephen 1968. 'An introduction to the music of Zsolt Durkó', *Tempo* 85 (Summer), 19–24.

  1969. 'An outsider's view', *Tempo* 88, 38–47.

  1982a. 'György Kurtág: an outline study (I)'. *Tempo* 140, 11–21.

  1982b. 'György Kurtág: an outline study (II)'. *Tempo* 142, 10–19.

  1982c. *Bartók's Chamber Music*. London: British Broadcasting Corporation.

Weissmann, John S. 1957a. 'The Budapest Bartók Festival and after', *The Music Review* 18, 52–6.

  1957b. 'Guide to Hungarian composers: (I) the early decades of the twentieth century', *Tempo* 44 (Summer), 24–30; continued in *Tempo* 45 (Autumn), 27–31.

  1957c. 'Guide to Hungarian Composers: (II) the later decades and outlook', *Tempo* 46 (Winter), 21–4 and 27.

  1958. 'Guide to Hungarian Composers: (III) the later decades and outlook: conclusion', *Tempo* 47 (Spring), 25–31.

Weöres, Sándor 1975. *Weöres Sándor Egybegyűjtött írások* I–III [Sándor Weöres collected writings vols. I–III]. Budapest: Magvető.

Whittall, Arnold 2001. 'Plotting the path, prolonging the moment: Kurtág's settings of German', in Beckles Willson and Williams (eds.), 89–108.

Wilheim, András 1975. 'Kurtág György: *Szálkák*', *Filharmónia műsorfüzet* 15, 37.

  1978. 'Kurtág György: *Hommage à András Mihály: 12 Microludes for String Quartet*', Programme booklet, Korunk zenéje [Music of our Time] 1978, 13.

  1980. 'Várnai Péter: Beszélgetések Ligeti Györggyel (recenzió)', *Muzsika* 23:1, 41–2.

  1981. 'A hét zeneműve: Ligeti György: Tíz darab fúvósötösre' [Musical work of the week. György Ligeti: Ten Pieces for Wind Quintet], recorded for Magyar Rádió on 13 February 1981, broadcast 8 June 1981. Archive number A – 288687/1, 26 minutes 20 seconds.

  1983a. 'Egy új alkotói korszak kezdete. Ligeti György kürttriója', *Muzsika* 26:5, 23–7. (The main part of this was translated in English as Wilheim 1984.)

  1983b. 'Korunk zenéje, 1983. Krónika és utópia (1.)' [Music of our Time 1983. Chronicle and utopia], *Muzsika* 26:12 (December), 25–30.

  1984. 'Ligeti's Horn Trio', *The New Hungarian Quarterly* 25:94 (Summer), 210–12.

  1986. 'ISCM Budapest', *Muzsika* 29:6 (June), 3–7.

  1999a. 'Kadosa Pál szimfóniái: ambíciók és illúziók' [Pál Kadosa's symphonies: ambitions and illusions]. In *Zenetudományi dolgozatok 1997–98*. Budapest: Zenetudományi Intézet, 119–28.

  1999b. 'Prolegomena Szabolcsi újraolvasásához' [Prolegomena to a rereading of Szabolcsi] *Holmi* 21:9 (September), 1100–8.

  2001. 'Szabolcsi Bence huszadik százada' [Bence Szabolcsi's twentieth century], (MS).

Williams, Alan E. 2005. 'Budapest and NY: The New Music Studio 1971–1980', *Perspectives of New Music* 43:1 (Winter), 212–35.

Williams, Alastair 1997. 'Modernism inside out', in *New Music and the Claims of Modernity*, Aldershot: Ashgate Publishers, 73–94.

Williams, Bernard 2003. *Truth and Truthfulness. An Essay in Genealogy*. Princeton and Oxford: Princeton University Press.

Wilson, Charles 2004. 'György Ligeti and the rhetoric of autonomy', *twentieth-century music* 1:1, 5–28.

Wischmann, Claus 1997. 'Spaß am Experimentieren: Kurtágs Játékok für Klavier', *MusikTexte* 72, 51–61.

Woerner, Karl Heinrich 1973. *Stockhausen: Life and Work*. Introduced, translated and edited by Bill Hopkins. London: Faber.

Ziegler, Susanne. 1986. 'Zur Transylvanischen Kantate', in *Sándor Veress Festschrift zum 80. Geburtstag*, ed. Andreas Traub, Berlin: Verlag K. Haseloff, 225–57.

Zilcosky, John 2002. *Kafka's Travels: Exoticism, Colonialism, and the Traffic of Writing*. London: Palgrave Macmillan.

Žižek, Slavoj 1989. *The Sublime Object of Ideology*. London and New York: Verso.
 1993. *Tarrying with the Negative*, Durham: Duke University Press.
 1997. *The Plague of Fantasies*. London: Verso.
 2000. *The Fragile Absolute*. London and New York: Verso.

Zoltai, Dénes 1960. 'Diderot-tól napjainkig. Vázlatok a zeneesztétika történetéhez' [From Diderot to today. Towards an outline history of music aesthetics], *Muzsika* 3:12 (December), 26–9.
 1961. 'Bartók és az új zene filozófiája', *Muzsika* 4 (April), 1–3.

Index

180 Group (*180-as csoport*) 196

A Tett (Action) 134
acoustic scale 56
Aczél, György 78
Ádám, Jenő 16
Adorno, Theodor W. 34, 35, 71, 82, 84, 92–6, 105
African rhythms 183
Akhmatova, Anna 201, 202, 206
Amadinda percussion ensemble 196, 198, 222
Amagatsu, Ushio 231, 233
anti-Jewish laws and policies 22–3, 26
Apartment Theatre 135, 136, 137, 150
Appeal see Vörösmarty, Mihály
Auschwitz 105
avant-garde 18, 117, 131, 163, 165, 169, 189–90, 198, 199

Bach, Johann Sebastian 37, 56, 210
Baird, Tadeusz
   Erotica 209
Balassa, Péter 210–11
Balassa, Sándor 125
Balázs, Béla 64, 209–10
Balázs, István 205–7
Balibar, Etienne 22
Bárdos, Lajos 16, 19, 29, 44, 47, 53, 54, 55, 56, 58, 66, 67, 92, 191, 234
   'Modal harmonies in Liszt works' (*Modális harmóniák Liszt műveiben*) 57
   'The Foundations of Modal Harmony' 54
   The harsh winter has passed (*Elmúlt már a vad tél*) 48
   Shepherd's Pipe (*Tilinkó*) 44
   'Tonic or not?' (*Tonika, vagy nem?*) 58
Bartha, Dénes 63
Bartók, Béla 2–3, 14–18, 20–1, 23, 24, 25, 28, 30, 32–4, 36, 39, 40, 42, 49, 50, 52–3, 54, 55–9, 64, 67, 71, 72, 82, 84, 89, 92, 106, 107–8, 113–14, 119–20, 125, 130, 138, 140, 152, 165, 166, 167, 169, 177, 179, 183–4, 185–6, 189
   'Bear Dance' 57
   Cantata profana 18, 48, 53
   Concerto for Orchestra 33

Dance Suite 13, 33, 55
Divertimento 33
Duke Bluebeard's Castle 53, 207–9, 226, 227, 228–33
Four Hungarian Folksongs for mixed choir 18
From Olden Times 18
Improvisations on Hungarian Peasant Songs, Op. 20 17, 56
'The Marriage of the Cricket', from *For Children* 43
Mikrokosmos 43, 55, 109, 113, 149, 183
The Miraculous Mandarin 17, 33, 52
Music for Strings, Percussion and Celeste 57
night's music 53, 56
Out of Doors suite 56
Piano Concerto no. 3 183
Sonata for Two Pianos and Percussion 57
Sonatas for Violin and Piano, nos 1 and 2 57
String Quartet no. 6 108, 110, 185
string quartets 53
Székely Folksongs for male choir 18
Three Studies, Op. 18 17
Twenty-seven Choruses for women's and children's choir 18, 72
Village Scenes 73
'Bartók and Kodály school' 32
Bartók Conservatory 138, 234
Bartók Festival
   1948 28, 34
   1956 88, 90
Bartók Seminar (Budapest, 1946–49) 130, 198
Bartók Seminars in Szombathely 130, 196, 197, 200
Bayerische Radio 113
Beckett, Samuel 145, 178
Beethoven, Ludwig van 4, 56, 161, 223
   Ninth Symphony 105
   Piano Sonata, Op. 81a ('Lebewohl') 179
   string quartets 160
Béla Bartók Union (*Bartók Béla Szövetség*) 31
Berg, Alban 16, 17, 20, 61, 119, 132
   Chamber Concerto 80
   Four Pieces for clarinet and piano, Op. 5 17
   Violin Concerto 34
Bergande, Martin 169, 171–2

Berio, Luciano 81, 91
Berlin 188
Berlioz, Hector
    Symphonie fantastique 51
Bern Conservatorium 60
Bible, the 21, 202
Bliss, Arthur 59
Blok, Alexandr 201–2
Bódy, Gábor 197
Bornemisza, Péter 125
Borsodi, István 61–2
Borsody, László 149
Böszörményi-Nagy, Béla 61
Boulez, Pierre 59, 81, 91, 190, 212
    Le marteau sans maître 81, 91
    Sonata for Piano no. 3 87
    Structures Ia 91
Bozay, Attila 125, 128, 149
    Improvisations for zither 131
Brandt, Willy 127
Breuer, János 122, 124, 130, 132, 137, 143–4, 161–2, 188, 191, 192, 199, 234
Brezhnev, Leonid 127
Britten, Benjamin 90
    Albert Herring 80
    Sinfonia da Requiem 80
    String Quartet no. 2 80
Budapest Chamber Ensemble 125, 133, 138
Budapest Music Weeks 189
Budapest New Music Studio 131–4
Budapest Opera 48
Budapest Wind Quintet 188
Busoni, Ferruccio 43

Cage, John 132, 198
Calvinist Church of Budapest 20
cantata
    Soviet 45, 48–9
Carnegy, Patrick 104
Casella, Alfredo 20
Catholic church, Catholicism 28, 78, 128, 139, 144, 168
Celan, Paul 210
Central Committee of the Communist Party of the Soviet Union
    decree on modern music 35
Central Europe 195–6, 210–15
Chekhov, Anton 229–32
children's literature 64, 66
Chopin, Frederic 183
church 77, 128
    modes 55
    music 134
classicism 8, 17, 24, 33–4, 151
    Hungarian 16, 20

nationalist 15
Viennese 46
Cluj 120, 130
Cold War 1–2, 3, 30, 193, 226, 228
    cultural 1, 34
Cologne 86, 87, 90, 91, 132, 190
Communist Party 27, 92
Communist Youth Alliance 131–2
'Chamber Music of Our Time' (*Korunk Kamarazenéje*) 80, 123
Crescendo 16, 17, 60
Csengery, Adrienne 200, 209, 220
Cserépfalvi publishing house 28, 43
Csicsery-Rónay, István 61–2
Csontváry, Kosztka Tivadar 125–6
cummings, e. e. 133, 153
Curwen, John 24
Czechoslovakia 127, 227
Czövek, Erna 42–3, 63, 130

Dada 134
Dallapiccola, Luigi 20
Dalos, Rimma 201–2, 206
    'Writings of the Apostle Paul to Me' 203–5
Dance House movement (*Tánzház*) 129, 131, 134
Dann, Otto 2
Darmstadt 80, 87, 123, 125, 127, 129, 132, 138, 187, 225
Dávid, Gyula
    Viola Concerto 51
Debussy, Claude 16, 162
    Ondine 55
Decroupet, Pascal 113
Demény, János 91
Dénes, Vera 41
détente 194
diatony 114
Dibelius, Ulrich 169, 173
die reihe 86, 91, 190
divertimento 50
Dobszay, László 128, 134, 220, 234
dodecaphony 55, 56, 57, 58, 59, 60, 81, 82–5, 100, 113, 123
Dohnányi, Ernő 2, 14–17, 20, 23, 25, 226, 233
    Der Tenor 227
    Festival Overture 13, 15
    The Vaivode's Tower (*A vajda tornya*) 227
Donaueschingen 80, 187
Doráti, Antal 60
Dostoevsky, Fyodor 141, 143, 147, 202, 206
Dukay, Barnabás
    'O' 136
    'Quadruplus' 137
Dürer, Albrecht 104

Index

Durkó, Zsolt 124, 125, 131, 132, 148, 152, 199, 200, 235
   Fioriture ungherese 124
   Moses 131, 227
   Una rhapsodia ungherese 124
   Violin Concerto Organismi 124
Dürrenmatt, Friedrich 86
Dvořák, Antonin 196

East European Folk Music Institute 27–8, 29
Eastern Bloc 127–8, 144, 195
Editio Musica 190
electronic music 190
Élet és Irodalom (*Life and Literature*) 135
Éneklő Magyarok (Singing Hungarians) 31
Éneklő Munkás (Singing Worker) 27
Éneklő Nép (Singing People) 29, 31
Énekszó (Chorusing) 19
Englbrecht, Bernd 171, 172, 173, 182
Eötvös, Péter 132, 197, 200, 222, 235
   Cricket Music 197
   Elektrochronik 136
   Insetti galanti 197
   Nonsense Madrigals 172
   Tale 197
   Three Sisters 228–33
   Wind Sequences 197
Eötvös College of the Budapest University 22
Eötvös Lóránd University in Budapest 128
Erkel, Ferenc 15, 51, 226, 227
Esenin, Sergei 201, 202
Esterháza 190
European Chamber Orchestra 192
European Cultural Forum 195
expressionism 14

Farkas, Ferenc 32, 82, 83, 86, 123, 124, 167, 189, 191, 235
   Fruit Basket (*Gyümölcskosár*) 66
   Musica pentatonica 32
   Praeludium und Fuga 81
fascism 1, 22, 82, 226
Ferencsik, János 40
Fischer, Annie 23
Fodor Music School 23
folk instrument 131
folk laments 146, 181, 182
folk music 17, 30, 33, 35, 37, 53, 54–5, 63, 84, 92, 165, 169, 197, 220, 229
   Hungarian 16, 46, 50, 61, 130, 165, 189
   Romanian 24, 187, 189
   Russian 47
folklore 24, 39, 46, 61, 79, 129, 165, 187, 206
folksong 19, 20, 24, 31, 32, 39, 42, 43, 44, 45–8, 50, 53, 55, 56, 66, 167, 178, 218–20
   arrangements and transcriptions 40, 46
   German 46
   Hungarian 15, 19, 20, 27, 31, 43, 45–7, 48, 173, 189, 220
   Romanian 40, 54–5
   settings 44, 47
   Soviet-Russian 45
   suites 46–7
'formalism' 34, 36, 52, 54–9, 79, 82, 130
Frankfurt School 96
Frescobaldi, Girolamo 161
Frid, Géza 16, 23

Gadamer, Hans-Georg 7
Gallus, Joannes 54
Garton Ash, Timothy 195
Gát, József 43
genius 2, 3–4, 14, 15, 126, 221
Germanic music 32
Germany 13, 18, 19, 20, 23, 24, 91, 127, 164, 188, 226
Gilgames 119
Gill, Dominic 147
glasnost 194, 197, 202
Golden Section 56, 58, 72
Goldmark Music School 23
Gombosi, Ottó 16, 20, 23, 60, 61, 235
Gorbachev, Mikhail 194
Gottwald, Clytus 171
Gregorian chant 149, 197
Grieg, Edvard 196
Grősz, Archbishop József 29
Grotowski, Jerzy 134
Gumbrecht, Hans Ulrich 5
Győr Philharmonic Orchestra 190

Habsburgs 1, 195, 197
Hajdu, András 53, 72
   Gypsy Cantata (*Cigány kantáta*) 48
   'The rhythmic pattern of Bóbita' (*Bóbita ritmikája*) 72
Halász, Kálmán 8, 38, 46, 50, 53, 54, 87, 88, 89, 92, 100
Hamburg 163, 168
Hamvas, Béla 71
Haraszti, Miklós 128
Hausmusik 120, 152
Havel, Václav 195, 212, 214
Haydn, Joseph 190
Helms, Hans G. 96
Helsinki
   Accords 127, 128, 136, 195
   Federation for Human Rights 195
Hermann, Lula 55

Hindemith, Paul 17, 20, 57
  Des Todes Tod 80
  Septet 80
Histoire d'O 136
Hitler, Adolph 13, 168
Hoffmann, Peter 106, 223
Hölderlin, Friedrich 141, 170, 178, 210, 221
Holliger, Heinz 61
Homer 125
Hommage à György Kurtág 137
Honegger, Arthur 20
  Jeanne d'Arc 80
  Le roi David 80
  Symphony no. 2 (*Symphonie pour cordes*) 80
  Symphony no. 5 80
House of Culture (*Kultúrház*) 134–5
Howat, Roy 56
Huber, Klaus 61
Hughes, Ted 146, 147
Hungarian Academy of Sciences 18, 21, 28, 30, 59, 63, 78
Hungarian haiku 133
Hungarian koans 133
Hungarian literature 30
Hungarian music 31, 32
Hungarian Music Weeks 29
  first Hungarian Music Week (1951) 40, 49, 51
  second Hungarian Music Week (1953) 39, 49, 50, 51, 166
  third Hungarian Music Week (1956) 48, 52, 53
Hungarian Musical Society 199, 200
Hungarian Musicians' Free Association (*Magyar Zeneművészek Szabad Szervezete*) 28, 29, 30
Hungarian Musicians' Union 5, 29, 30, 37–9, 54, 78–81, 84
Hungarian mythology 148, 166, 233
Hungarian People's Republic 28–9
Hungarian Radio 31, 48, 80, 123, 129
  'Concert cycle of music from our century' (*Hangversenyciklus századunk zenéjéből*) 80
  'In Hungary for the first time' (*Magyarországon először*) 80
'Hungarian school' 33
  'new Hungarian school' 28
Hungarian Scouts' Song Book 19
Hungarian State Opera 48, 160
Hungarian State Puppet Theatre 187–8
Hungarian Workers' Party 27
Hungary's New Economic Mechanism (1968) 127
Huszár, Lajos 149

Independent New Artists 16
International Monetary Fund 195
International Society for Contemporary Music 198
IRCAM 212
Iron Curtain 225
Ives, Charles 20

Járdányi, Pál 29, 32, 34, 39, 40, 41, 47, 50, 52, 54, 58, 167, 235
  Divertimento concertante 50
  Vörösmarty Symphony 51
Jemnitz, Sándor 14, 16, 17, 20, 34, 81, 82, 236
Jeney, Zoltán 128, 131, 133, 135, 137, 187, 236
  Arthur Rimbaud a sivatagban (Arthur Rimbaud in the Desert) 133
  Complements (*Kiegészítések*) 133
  Eight Tandori Songs 134
  Funeral Rite (*Halotti szertartás*) 196
  Orpheus' Garden (*Orfeusz kertje*) 133
Jesus 133
Jewish origins 23, 120–2, 167, 168–9, 210
Jone, Hildegard 225
Journalists' Club 77
Joyce, James 30
József, Attila 51–2, 161, 210, 215, 217, 236
  'Consciousness' (*Eszmélet*) 155

Kabalevsky, Dmitri 51
Kádár, János 77–8
Kadosa, Pál 16, 18, 20, 23, 26, 38, 39, 40, 124, 191, 236–7
  Adventure at Huszt (*Huszti Kaland*) 227
  Lehrstück, Irren ist Staatlich 20
  Stalin's Pledge (*Sztálin esküje*) 48
  The Plan will Triumph (*Győz a terv*) 45
Kafka, Franz
  Metamorphosis 106
Kakania 122
Kakavelakis, Konstantinos 97
Kassák, Lajos 134
Kassák House Studio 134–7, 150
Kaufmann, Harald 96, 98, 103, 112–13, 119–22, 182
Kazantsakis, Nikos
  Christ Recrucified 227
Kelen, Hugó 38, 39, 41
Kerényi, György 16, 19, 55–6, 58, 63, 237
Kertész, Gyula 19, 63
KGB 163
Khachaturian, Aram 51, 79
Khrennikov, Tikhon 79
Kiš, Danilo 1, 195
Klee, Paul 91
Kocsár, Miklós 149

Kocsis, Zoltán 128, 133, 137, 200, 222
Kodály, Zoltán 2–3, 13–14, 15–16, 17, 18–21, 22, 23–5, 27, 28–9, 30–1, 32, 33, 34, 35, 36–7, 42, 45, 47, 50, 54, 55, 59, 63, 64–6, 67, 68, 77, 79, 83, 89, 90, 127, 130, 165, 166–7, 189, 199, 226, 233
  The Ballad of Panna Czinka (Czinka Panna balladája) 32
  Bicinia hungarica 24
  Buda Castle Te Deum 19
  Dances of Galánta 19
  'Evening Song' (Esti Dal) 173
  folksongs and dances of the interwar years 46
  Háry János 79, 227
  Hungarian Folk Music (Magyar népzene) 19
  Peacock Variations (Fölszállott a páva) 19
  Pioneers' March (Úttörő induló) 51
  Psalm 55 13
  Psalmus hungaricus (Hungarian Psalm) 14, 48
  Song Book for elementary schools 24, 44
  The Spinning Room (Székely fonó) 48, 227
  Hymn of Zrínyi (Zrínyi szózata) 51
Kolozsvár 86
Konrád, György 195, 212
Korunk (Our Time) 130
Kossuth Prize 44, 63, 79, 90, 128, 137
Kosztolányi, Dezső 21
Kovács, Sándor 198, 200, 237
Krenek, Ernst
  Jonny spielt auf! 16
Krohn, Ilmari 54
Kronos Quartet 192
Kroó, György 100, 102, 104, 149, 161–2, 187, 188, 190, 191, 192, 199, 202–5, 220–1, 237
Krúdy, Gyula 118
Kuczka, Péter 48
Kundera, Milan 195
Kurtág, György 2–5, 6, 7–8, 26, 41–2, 46, 47, 49, 50, 52–3, 66, 78, 85–7, 92–5, 104, 111–13, 115, 122–6, 129, 134, 137–62, 167, 190, 199–210, 217, 233
  Attila József Fragments, Op. 20 215–21
  Dance Song (Táncdal) 44
  early compositions for children 43
  Eight Duos for violin and cimbalom 107, 123
  Eight Piano Pieces, Op. 3 94–5, 123
  Four Songs to Poems by János Pilinszky, Op. 11 139–43, 147–8, 155
  Games (Játékok) 7–8, 148–57, 224
  Grabstein für Stephan, Op. 15c 221–2
  Greeting Song to Stalin (Üdvözlő ének Sztálinhoz) 47
  Herdecker Eurythmie, Op. 14 224
  Hommage à András Mihály: 12 Microludes for String Quartet, Op. 13 159–62, 222
  Kafka Fragments, Op. 24 210–15
  Korean Cantata 48–9, 124
  The Messages of Miss R. V. Troussova, Op. 17 200, 201, 202, 205–9
  Officium breve in memoriam Andreæ Szervánszky, Op. 28 221, 223–5
  Oh, If I were a Dove (Hej, ha galamb lennék) 43
  Omaggio à Luigi Nono, Op. 16 201–6
  Our New World is Evolving (Már új világunk épül) 47
  Pioneer Dance Song (Úttörő táncdal) 44
  'Pre-Ludes' (Elő-Játékok) 149
  . . . quasi una fantasia . . . , Op. 27 no. 1 221
  Requiem for the Beloved, Op. 26 201
  Scenes from a Novel, Op. 19 199, 201
  Signs (Jelek), Op. 5 94
  S. K. – Remembrance Noise (Sz. K. – Emlékzaj). Seven songs to Dezső Tandori's poems, Op. 12 157–9
  Songs of Despair and Sorrow, Op. 18 201–2
  Splinters (Szálkák), Op. 6c for solo cimbalom 143–7
  'Spring' (Tavasz) 50
  String Quartet, Op. 1 85, 93, 100, 106, 112, 114, 122–3, 137, 138
  Suite for piano duet 44
  The Sayings of Péter Bornemisza (Bornemisza Péter mondásai) 92, 98–103, 107–12, 125, 127, 138, 151, 201, 215, 224
  Viola Concerto 52, 122, 124
  Wind Quintet, Op. 2 100, 107, 123
Kurtág, György jnr 134, 137
Kurtág, Márta 125, 150–2, 200
Kurth, Ernst 57, 60

Lacan, Jacques 232
Lajtha, László 20, 27–8, 62, 63, 196, 237
  Missa in diebus tribulationis 1950 45
Láng, István 187
Láng, Paul 60, 125
language 3, 21–5, 32, 34, 36, 40, 49, 57, 64, 65, 66, 72, 130, 134, 137, 153, 155, 166, 182, 197, 202, 211, 217
  and music 134, 197
  Anglo-Saxon 22
  as music 92–8, 178–82
  Chinese 21
  common 36–7
  Greek, ancient 21
  Hebrew 21

language (*cont.*)
   Hungarian 1, 21–2, 64, 66, 69, 119, 129, 130, 133, 166, 169, 172, 178, 189, 197
   Indo-Germanic 66
   in music 96, 98–105, 170–8
   invented 65
   Japanese 22
   music as 105–14
   musical 43, 48, 53, 58, 92
   national 2, 37, 66
   Russian 202, 206, 209, 229
   Sumerian 21
   'tonal' 57
   Turkish 21
   Ugrian 21
Language Cultivation Council 22
Lassus, Orlando 57
Le Triton 20
Leibowitz, René 34
Lendvai, Ernő 52, 56, 59, 72, 107–9, 114, 191, 238
Lenin 206
Lermontov, Mikhail 201–2
   'So Weary, so Wretched' 202
Levant, Inga 231, 233
Lichtenberg, Georg Christoph 210
Lichtenfeld, Monika 120, 167, 171
Ligeti, György 2–6, 7, 8–9, 26, 28, 38–41, 42, 43–4, 46, 50, 52, 53, 54–5, 57, 58, 59, 64, 66–73, 78, 81, 85–92, 94, 105–6, 107, 111–22, 125–6, 163–93, 222, 225, 233
   'A Merchant Came with Giant Birds' 68–9
   Apparitions 117, 189, 190
   Arany songs 166–7
   Artikulation 85
   Atmosphères 98, 112–13, 114, 117, 182, 189, 190
   Aventures 96–8, 118, 187–8, 190, 197
   Cantata for a Youth Festival (*Ifjúsági kantáta*) 48
   Cello concerto 119, 190, 192
   Chamber Concerto 188, 190
   Clocks and Clouds 178, 190, 192
   Continuum 119, 172, 190
   Darkness and Light (*Sötét és világos*) 53
   Dawn (*Hajnal*) 67
   Dialogo and Capriccio 41
   Double Concerto 192
   Drei Hölderlin Fantasien 170–2, 178
   From the cradle to the grave (*A bölcsőtől a sírig*) 46
   Glissandi 117
   Gossiping women (*Pletykázó asszonyok*) 67
   harmony book from the 1950s 54, 190
   Hey, young people (*Haj, ifjúság*) 44
   Horn Trio 169, 179–83, 185–6, 192, 193
   Hortobágy for female choir 38
   Hungarian studies (*Magyar Etűdök*) 171, 178
   Le grand macabre 163, 165, 169, 172, 173, 192, 226
   Loneliness (*Magány*) 66, 67–8
   Lontano 7, 111–12, 114, 119, 172, 190
   Lux aeterna 96, 98, 114, 117, 172, 190
   Mein Judentum 168
   Morning (*Reggel*) 53, 67, 72–3, 173
   Musica ricercata 71, 189, 190
   Night (*Éjszaka*) 53, 67, 71–2, 73, 173
   Nouvelles Aventures 118
   Passacaglia ungherese 172
   Piano Concerto 172, 179, 183, 184, 222
   Piano Études 165, 179, 183–5
   Poème symphonique 118, 191
   Ramifications 188
   Requiem 98–9, 103–5, 114, 117, 118, 119, 191, 192
   Romanian Concerto 40, 41, 190
   San Francisco Polyphony 192
   Six Bagatelles for Wind Quintet 53, 71, 188
   String Quartet no. 1 (*Métamorphoses nocturnes*) 52, 64, 71, 92, 106
   String Quartet no. 2 92, 114, 119, 120, 122, 191
   Ten Pieces for Wind Quintet 192
   'The moon is dancing in a white robe' (*Táncol a hold fehér ingben*) 66
   Three Weöres Songs 66
   Trois bagatelles 191
   Tunes from Inaktelke (*Inaktelki nóták*) 38, 39, 44
   Visions 117, 165
   Volumina 7, 91, 117, 190
   Wind Quintet 119
   Winter (*Tél*) 67
Liszt, Franz 4, 15, 51, 138, 166
Liszt Academy 14, 23, 28, 29, 44, 59, 62, 66, 81, 129, 131, 133, 136, 138, 148, 160, 167, 173, 234
   Church Music Faculty 66
Liszt Society 24
'Little Drummers' 43
liturgical music
   Jeney 196
   Kodály 29
London Sinfonietta 192
Lorca, Federico García 226
Lőrincze, Lajos 36
Losonczy, Andor 123
Lukács, Georg 35–6, 83–4
Lutoslawski, Witold 113

Index

Ma (Today) 134
Machaut, Guillaume de 104
Maderna, Bruno 81, 91
Magyar Cantuale 19
Magyar Kórus 19, 29
Magyar Nyelv (Hungarian Language) 21
Magyar Zene (Hungarian Music) 4, 78–80
Magyarosan 21
Mahler, Gustav 119, 121
   Symphony no. 1 182
Mandelstam, Osip 201, 202
Mann, Thomas
   Doctor Faustus 35–6, 83–4, 100, 104–5
   Genesis of a Novel 84
Márai, Sándor 26, 27
Maros, Rudolf 46, 81, 86, 88, 187, 198, 238
   Bassoon Concerto 51
   Euphonia I–III 124
Maróthy, János 29, 30, 33, 83, 238
Marr, Nikolai Y. 36
Mason, Colin 62, 63
mass song 27, 31, 45, 47, 48
Mauriac, François 30
Melis, László 196
Melos 28, 46
Messiaen, Olivier 85
Mihály, András 23, 30, 33, 35–6, 39, 53, 123, 125, 127, 133, 138, 159–60, 162, 238
Milhaud, Darius 16, 17
mimesis 92–6
Mindszenty, Cardinal József 28, 128
Mini-festival 199
minimalism 187, 196
Ministry for People's Education 29
Modern Hungarian Musicians 16
Molnár, Antal 15–16, 17, 18, 20–1, 33–4, 54, 55, 83, 238
Mondrian, Piet 91
Monor 194
Monteverdi, Claudio 104
'Month of the Hungarian–Soviet Friendship' (1959) 79
Móricz, Zsigmond 64
Moscow 83, 127, 132, 188, 229–30
'mother tongue movement' 129
   musical 'mother tongue' 23–4, 31, 130, 183
Mozart, Wolfgang Amadeus 33, 122, 191
Mozgó Világ (Moving World) 135, 137
Müller-Widmann, Annie 59–60
Munich 60, 188
Municipal Orchestra 33
Municipal Theatre 48
Munkásdalos Szövetség (Union of Singing Workers) 23
music for children 19, 24–5, 42, 46, 149

Music for Strings, Percussion and Celeste 57
Music of our Century 198
'Music of our Time' (*Korunk zenéje*) 129, 131, 136, 148, 198, 199
Music Pedagogy 43
The Music Review 88
The Musical Quarterly 60, 121
Musikblätter des Anbruchs 16
musique concrète 82
Muzsika 4, 78–84, 130, 131, 136, 150, 192, 198, 199–200

Nabokov, Vladimir 178
Nádas, Péter 214
Nagy, Imre 77
Nagyvilág (Great world) 81
Nancy, Jean-Luc 6, 114, 172
Nancy Theatre Festival 136
National Hungarian Israeli Cultural Association 23
National Philharmonia (*Nemzeti filharmónia*) 80, 129, 138
nationalism 2, 14, 15–16, 17, 18–19, 21–3, 32, 42, 49, 51, 129–30, 132, 167, 193, 226
neo-romanticism 51, 169, 197–8
neoclassicism 14, 50, 60
Népszabadság (People's Freedom) 135
New Hungarian Music Society (UMZE) 20, 23
New Hungarian Musical Association 23
The New Hungarian Quarterly 192, 199
'New Land' 16, 17
New Music Studio 132, 134, 135–7, 149, 187, 191–2, 196, 197, 198
New Music Workshop of Miskolc (*Miskolci Új Zenei Műhely*) 196
Nietzsche, Friedrich 35
Nono, Luigi 91, 206
   Al gran sole carico d'amore 206
   Canti di vita e d'amore 206
   Il canto sospeso 91
Nordwall, Ove 87, 103, 104, 118, 120
nóta 47
numerus clausus 22
Nyelvőr (Language Guard) 21
Nyugat (West) 17, 30

objet trouvé 152–6, 222
Ockeghem, Johannes 104
opera
   German 229
   Hungarian 226–33
   Italian 229
Orbán, György 197
'Orfeo' 135

Orff, Carl 90
   Catulli Carmina 80
Ország, Lili 138, 204, 239
Ostpolitik 127, 129

Palestrina, Giovanni Pierluigi 57, 104
Paris 85, 86, 87, 125, 132, 136, 138, 188, 200
Pártos, Ödön 23
passus duriusculus 180
Patriotic Popular Front 129, 130
Penderecki, Krysztof 165
pentatony 24, 47, 49, 50–1, 55, 57, 73, 88, 113, 163, 184, 218
perestroika 194
Pécs 198
Pernye, András 82, 85, 95, 123, 226–7, 239
Pérotin 104
Petőfi, Sándor 49
Petrassi, Goffredo 20
Petrovics, Emil 62, 125, 239
   C'est la guerre 84–5, 125, 226
Philharmonic Orchestra 14, 17
Phnom Penh 168
Pilinszky, János 30, 129, 138, 139, 144, 145, 147–8, 157, 162, 210, 211–12, 239
   Crater (*Kráter*) 140
   Denouement (*Végkifejlet*) 140, 143
   'From the diary of a lyric poet' (*Egy lírikus naplójából*) 145
   On the Third Day (*Harmadnapon*) 81, 139
   Splinters (*Szálkák*) 143–6, 147
Pizzetti, Ildebrando 20
Poland 127, 136, 189, 194
Prague 210
Pravda 36
'presence' 2, 5–8, 9, 61, 73, 111–12, 114, 137, 150, 153, 156, 162, 173, 182, 197, 226, 232
Proust, Marcel 30
Puccini, Giacomo 197
Purcell, Henry
   Dido's Lament 180

Rajeczky, Benjamin 134
Rákosi, Mátyás 78, 134
Ránki, György 46, 124
   King Pomàde (*Pomádé király*) 227
Ravel, Maurice 17, 133
Red Army 26
'Reformed music' (*Megújhodott Muzsika*) 129
Reich, Terry
religious music 19, 45, 47
Renaissance models 19
Respighi, Ottorino 15
Révai, József 63

Revolutionary Council 77, 79, 83
Rimsky-Korsakov, Nikolai 196
Roma music 48
Romania 13, 22, 54, 120–1, 129, 130, 167, 168, 180, 181, 187, 227
Romanian music 54–5
romanticism 16, 24, 72, 130, 162, 169, 171, 193, 227
Royal Hungarian Pázmány Péter University 22
Russia 2, 194, 195, 202, 233
Russian poetry 201
Russian Revolution 79
Ruthenia 13
Rzewski, Frederic 132

Sacher, Paul 59, 60
   Paul Sacher Foundation 5, 61, 187
Saint Cecilia movement 29
Sallis, Friedemann 71, 72
Samuel, Claude 165
Sárai, Tibor 79
Sárközy, István 46
   Tanzspiel 46
Sárosi, Bálint 130
   Gypsy music (*Cigányzene*) 130
Sáry, László 131–2, 134, 160, 239
Scherchen, Hermann 20
Schoenberg, Arnold 16, 17–18, 20, 21, 33–4, 35, 55, 56, 57, 58, 59, 83, 113, 121
   A Survivor from Warsaw 80, 82
   Das Buch der hängenden Garten, Op. 15 17
   Pierrot lunaire 202
   Three Piano Pieces, Op. 11 18
Schola Hungarica 134, 149, 220
Schreker, Franz 16
Schubert, Franz 133, 161, 162
   String Quartets 160
Schumann, Robert 162, 223
   Frauenliebe und Leben 202
   'Wie ein Traumeswirren' 222
Schütz, Heinrich 125
Schwartz, Egon 195
Scriabin, Alexander 183
Seiber, Mátyás 16, 88, 112
   Besardo Suite no. 2 80
   Clarinet Concertino 80
   String Quartet no. 3 80
serenade 33, 39, 50
Serly, Tibor 16, 23
Shakespeare, William
   The Tempest 168
Shostakovich, Dmitri 79
Simon, Albert 132, 240
Singing Youth (*Éneklő Ifjúság*) 19

Index

Singspiel 46
Slovakia 13
Social Democratic Party 27, 134
socialist realism 34, 78, 79, 81, 90, 167
Soldiers' Orchestra 40, 47
solfège 24, 43, 44–5, 60
Solidarity 194
Sólyom, Károly 58
Somfai, László 130
Somogyi, László 62
Soproni, József 149
Soviet
    Communist Party 34
    composers 34
    doctrines 51
    expansionism 127
    occupation 3, 65, 166, 194
    thaw following Stalin's death 52–3
    Union 1, 13, 28, 31, 34, 35, 36, 42, 45, 77, 79, 83, 85, 127, 152, 167, 178, 188, 194, 195, 206, 207
Squat Theatre 136
Stalin, Josef 13, 36, 38, 66, 77
    City (*Sztálinváros*) 50
Stalinism in Hungary 44, 81, 165
Star (*Csillag*) 72
Stein, Marianne 85
Stockhausen, Karlheinz 91, 132, 165, 190
    Gruppen 85
    Piano Pieces I–IV 86
Strauss, Richard 17
Stravinsky, Igor 16–17, 20, 60, 196, 202
    A Soldier's Tale 80
    Le sacre du printemps 55
    Octet 80
    Oedipus Rex 80
    Petrushka 178
Studia Musicologica Academiae Scientiarum Hungaricae 78
Stuttgart Schola Cantorum 190
Sugár, Rezső
    Heroic Song (*Hősi Ének*) 48
Sulyok, Ferenc 86, 87, 88, 92
Sweers, Britta 7, 8
Switzerland 60–1, 91
Szabad Nép (Free Folk) 167
Szabó, Ferenc 16, 17, 20, 26, 30, 32, 50–1, 52, 53, 56, 88–9, 127, 240
    In Fury Rose the Ocean (*Föltámadott a tenger*) 49
    Liberated melodies (*Felszabadult melódiák*) 49
    Song about Lenin (*Dal Leninről*) 45
    Song Singing (*Notaszó*) 46–7
Szabó, Istán 230–1, 233

Szabolcsi, Bence 15, 17, 26, 27, 28, 29–31, 33, 35, 37, 52, 63, 66, 130, 191, 220, 227, 240
    Bartók Seminars 28, 33
Székely, Endre 30
    Wind Quintet 50
Székely region 180, 227
Szelényi, István 16, 17, 33, 58
    'New Harmonic Systems' 55, 240
    Symphony of a Factory (*Egy gyár szimfóniája*) 45, 63
Szemző, Tibor 196
Szervánszky, Endre 20, 23, 32, 33, 39, 40, 47, 62–3, 215, 241
    Clarinet Concerto 51
    Concerto in Memory of Attila József 51–2, 53, 88
    Serenade 32, 50, 63, 224–5
    Six Orchestral Pieces 81–2
    Soldiers' Cantata (*Honvéd kantáta*) 47
Szétfolyóirat 135
Szigeti, József 65, 192
Szigeti, Pál 132
Sziklay, Erika 151
Szociológia (Sociology) 128
Szokolay, Sándor 132, 241
    Blood Wedding (*Vérnász*) 226
    Ecce homo 197, 227
Szőllősy, András 29–30, 50, 53, 63, 81, 187, 241
Szűcs, Lóránt 151

Tallián, Tibor 131, 137, 162, 197, 226, 227, 241
Tandori, Dezső 133–4, 157, 161
    Fragment for Hamlet (*Töredék Hamletnek*) 133
    'Dedication' (*Ajánlás*) 134
    The Cleaning of an Objet Trouvé (*Egy talált tárgy megtisztítása*) 133, 153–6
Tardos, Béla 88
Tarka-Barka (Multi-coloured) 149
Taruskin, Richard 1, 6
Tempo 88, 89, 124
Thurzó, Gábor 143
Tihanyi, László 198, 242
    The Silence of Winds (*A szelek csendje*) 197
Tóth, Aladár 13, 14, 16, 17, 23, 242
Transylvania 13, 22, 164, 165, 178, 197, 227
Traub, Andreas 61
Tsvetayeva, Marina 201, 202
twelve-tone music *see* dodecaphony

Új Ember (New Man) 129, 162
Új Tükör (New Mirror) 194

Új Zenei Szemle (New Music Review) 4, 37, 44, 48
Ujfalussy, József 58, 81, 82, 83, 130, 167, 242
Újhold (New Moon) 30
USA 91, 127, 167, 194, 195

Vajda, János
   Mario and the Magician 197
Varèse, Edgard 20, 91, 132
Varga, Bálint András 200
Vatican 77, 78, 128
Végh Quartet 60
verbunkos 33, 47, 163
Veress, Sándor 20, 32, 43, 59–63, 88, 91, 167, 173, 191, 196, 242
   Fifteen Children's Choral Pieces 20
   Fingerlarks (*Billegető muzsika*) 43, 149
   Hommage à Paul Klee (1951) 60, 91
   Piano Concerto (1952) 61
   Second String Quartet 60
   Sinfonia Minneapolitana (1952-53) 61
   String Trio (1954) 61
   Térszili Katicza 59
   Transylvanian Cantata 20
   Transylvanian Dances 60
Vidovszky, László 131–2, 133, 135, 137, 187, 197, 198, 242–3
   405 136
   Autoconcert 136
   Narcissus and Echo 196
   Romantic Readings (*Romantikus olvasmányok*) 196
   The Death of Schroeder (*Schroeder halála*) 133
Vienna 4, 17, 90, 120, 121, 188, 190, 198
Viennese School 190
Vietnamese Solidarity Committee (1965) 128
Vikár, Béla 20
Vincze, Imre 49
Viski, János 88
   Piano Concerto 88
Vogul poetry 69
Vörösmarty, Mihály 13, 51
   Appeal (*Szózat*) 13, 14, 15, 51

Wagner, Richard 56, 57
   Tristan und Isolde 55
Waldbauer-Kerpely String Quartet 15
Walesa, Lech 194
Warsaw 129
   Autumn Festival 187, 189
Webern, Anton 17–18, 34, 86, 91, 102, 107, 123, 132, 162
   Cantata, Op. 31 224–5
   Five Pieces for Orchestra, Op. 10 86
   Five Pieces for String Quartet, Op. 5 86
   Four Pieces for Violin and Piano, Op. 7 17
   Quartet, Op. 22 86
   Six Pieces for Orchestra, Op. 6 86
   String Quartet, Op. 28 86
   Symphony, Op. 21 86
   Three Short Pieces for Cello and Piano, Op. 11 17
   Variations for Orchestra 86
   Variations for Piano, Op. 27 86
Weill, Kurt 20
Weiner, Leó 54, 138, 243
Weissmann, János *see* Weissmann, John S.
Weissmann, John S. 23, 63, 88, 89, 90–2, 167
Weöres, Sándor 30, 48, 64–71, 72, 171–8, 187, 243
   Éjszaka (Night) 71
   Hideg van (It's cold) 64
   'Hungarian Studies' 65
   'Istar's Journey to Hell' (*Istar pokoljárása*) 119
   'Loneliness' (*Magány*) 67, 71
   Lunar boatsman (*Holdbeli csónakos*) 68
   'Psyche' 197
   'Rag-carpet' (*Rongyszőnyeg*) 65, 69
   'The Harsh Winter Has Passed' (*Elmúlt már a vad tél*) 48
   'Wells of Fire' (*Tűzkút*) 81
West Berlin 129
West German Radio 132
Whittall, Arnold 210, 214
Wien Modern festival 198
Wilheim, András 135, 149, 192–3, 197, 198, 243
Williams, Bernard 9
Wilson, Robert 129, 130
Woerner, Karl 87
Wolff, Christian 132
Working Youth Alliance 44
World Youth Meeting 48
Writers' Association 77
Writers' Union 194

The Young Composers' Group (*Fiatal zeneszerzők csoportja*) 196
Youth Music Days (1952) 44
Yugoslavia 127, 188

Zathureczky, Ede 86
Zene-pedagógia (Music Pedagogy) 42
Zenei Szemle (Musical Review) 28, 120
Zeneműkiadó 40
Zhdanov, Andrei 34–5
Žižek, Slavoj 232
Zoltai, Dénes 83–4